“My Greatest Quarrel with Fortune”

CIVIL WAR SOLDIERS AND STRATEGIES
Brian S. Wills, Series Editor

Richmond Must Fall: The Richmond-Petersburg Campaign, October 1864
HAMPTON NEWSOME

Work for Giants: The Campaign and Battle of Tupelo/Harrisburg, Mississippi, June–July 1864
THOMAS E. PARSON

"My Greatest Quarrel with Fortune": Major General Lew Wallace in the West, 1861–1862
CHARLES G. BEEMER

“My Greatest Quarrel with Fortune”

Major General Lew Wallace in the West, 1861–1862

Charles G. Beemer

The Kent State University Press KENT, OHIO

Library of Congress Catalog Card Number 2014049003
ISBN 978-1-60635-236-6
Manufactured in the United States of America

Library of Congress Cataloging-in-Publication Data
Beemer, Charles G., 1940–
"My greatest quarrel with fortune" : Major General Lew Wallace in the West, 1861–1862 / Charles G. Beemer.
pages cm — (Civil War soldiers and strategies)
Includes bibliographical references and index.
ISBN 978-1-60635-236-6 (hardcover : alkaline paper) ∞
1. Wallace, Lew, 1827–1905. 2. Wallace, Lew, 1827–1905—Adversaries. 3. Generals—United States—Biography. 4. United States. Army—Biography. 5. Command of troops—History—19th century. 6. Tennessee—History—Civil War, 1861–1865—Campaigns. 7. Fort Henry, Battle of, Tenn., 1862. 8. Fort Donelson, Battle of, Tenn., 1862. 9. Shiloh, Battle of, Tenn., 1862. 10. United States—History—Civil War, 1861–1865—Campaigns. I. Title.
E467.1.W2B44 2015
355.0092—dc23
[B]
2014049003

19 18 17 16 15 5 4 3 2 1

CONTENTS

ACKNOWLEDGMENTS

I had the rare privilege of studying and learning the basics of the historian's craft under two of the very best, Dr. William R. Hochman and Dr. William B. Hesseltine.

A student of Allan Nevins, Bill Hochman formally introduced me to the world of history, particularly the American Civil War era, and patiently helped me to begin to understand the many intricacies of that world. He contributed significantly to my love of history and to making my undergraduate years at The Colorado College an educational and pleasurable adventure of the highest order.

In my years of graduate work, Bill Hesseltine at the University of Wisconsin proved to be the opposite type of scholar and teacher. There always seemed to be a "right" interpretation for this extraordinarily gifted, acerbic, yet never irascible man. As synthesized in his *The Historian's Ten Commandments* that right interpretation was an ideal to be pursued vigorously, with painstaking, though never slavish, attention to detail and form. His untimely death in 1963 abruptly terminated what had been a difficult yet beneficial apprenticeship.

It was not until years had passed that I truly got to know both men and appreciate what each had meant to me. I intuitively sense that they are entitled to most of the credit for what the reader discovers herein.

I owe a tremendous debt to Dr. Brian Steel Wills, Professor of History and Director of the Center for the Study of the Civil War Era at Kennesaw State University, and to Dr. Stephen D. Engle, Professor of History at Florida Atlantic University. Both of these men reviewed and analyzed the manuscript. They offered brutally honest suggestions along with numerous words of encouragement. Through their efforts, each allowed me to reach a point in the telling of Wallace's story that I never could have attained on my own.

A heartfelt note of thanks goes to Dr. Frank Cassell, a Wabash College alumnus and good personal friend. Frank generously gave of his time on several occasions to read and review parts of the manuscript, offering many valuable insights, all the while protesting that he was not a Civil War historian.

Various others have been extremely helpful and patient as this project moved toward conclusion. Joyce Harrison, Acquiring Editor, The Kent State University Press, did a fantastic job of shepherding me through the initial phases of the publishing process, responding quickly and on point to numerous questions and making many helpful suggestions. Grace Morsberger, my talented Copy Editor, was likewise more than just helpful. She tirelessly took me through the world of punctuation and citations with many pertinent and thoughtful suggestions. Mary Young, Managing Editor, The Kent State University Press, was the perfect person to finalize the process of transforming my manuscript into this book. With a firm awareness of deadlines tempered by an empathy for the ill-informed, she patiently brought order out of my personal chaos. I am extremely grateful to all three ladies for their hard work and professionalism.

The entire staff of the General Lew Wallace Study and Museum in Crawfordsville, Indiana, and in particular Larry Paarlberg, its dynamic director, was always ready to answer a question or suggest alternate and additional points to consider. John Lanborn, Librarian and Director of the Lilly Library, and Beth Swift, Head Archivist at the Robert T. Ramsay, Jr., Archival Center, both at Wabash College, also located in Crawfordsville, were with me from the very beginning with invaluable help and suggestions. Suzanne Hahn, Director of Reference Services, Indiana State Historical Society Library, in Indianapolis, promptly sent me whatever information I requested or quickly and expertly told me where I might find items the library did not have in its collections. I could never have finished the project on a timely basis without the internet expertise and professional insights of my good friend George Ferguson of gfgraphics in Waynesville, North Carolina. To all these, and to any I may have inadvertently overlooked, I am deeply grateful.

Finally, I would like to thank my wife Nancy for her endless hours of concern and support. She always knew just the right words of encouragement to say. She never failed to pick up my spirits. I could never have written word one without her. More importantly, literally every night for so many years, she lovingly prayed that the Good Lord would bless and guide me in my efforts the next day. She alone knows what her presence in my life and all those prayers have meant to me.

Statue of Major General Lew Wallace. National Statuary Hall, Washington, D.C. Renaissance man and novelist of international acclaim, fittingly shown as an American Civil War soldier. (Architect of the Capitol)

INTRODUCTION

During the four years of the American Civil War, Lew Wallace seldom spoke of fortune. When he achieved success in a military adventure, he knew he alone was responsible. If others said he failed, he characteristically found fault with them. When subjected to criticism, he directed his anger toward one of two targets. If he were discussing a specific military incident, he focused upon the failures of a superior officer. If he were disparaging the Union war effort, which he frequently did both publicly and privately, he concentrated upon the spiteful influence of "the West Point clique," a group of professional soldiers seldom identified by name. He rarely looked inward to take responsibility for his own shortcomings.

His march to the Shiloh battlefield on April 6, 1862, significantly affected his subsequent military career. He was not embarrassed by his actions that day. He never apologized or sought forgiveness for his role in what transpired on the banks of the Tennessee River. Frankly, he was angered and offended that others saw and interpreted his movements and his motives in a different light than he.

As he spent nearly half a lifetime debating and revisiting those events, it is not surprising that he increasingly illuminated them in the context of the role fortune might have played in determining his destiny. In an 1884 letter to Ulysses S. Grant, he twice mentioned the word "fortune" with respect to his experiences at Shiloh. He told Grant he regretted having explicitly followed the orders Grant had issued to him. In so doing, Wallace stated, he had rendered himself and his men unable to "share the fortunes of the day with you, whether they were good or bad." He told Grant his personal conclusion was "For your sake and my own, general, and for the cause generally, it was unfortunate that Rowley [Grant aide, Captain

William R. Rowley] had not lost his way, as it was said I had mine."[1] More than a decade later, Wallace complained to another Union veteran that Shiloh was for him "that awful mystery."[2] For the last forty-three years of his life, Wallace committed himself to the proposition that he must never surrender to what he termed his "Greatest Quarrel with Fortune."[3]

In the 1850s, seeing his state become increasingly involved in a sectional conflict, Wallace educated himself for war. When the South fired upon Fort Sumter, he was prepared. He was a volunteer, civilian, amateur soldier possessed of a goodly amount of self-taught knowledge. On more than one battlefield, he demonstrated a significant talent for waging war. At Romney, he exploited audacity and surprise to procure a minor but significant victory over the Rebels. At Fort Donelson, as a desperate measure and in direct disobedience to orders, he made and executed a superb battlefield command decision. Based upon the efficacy of his judgment and actions, he accurately claimed he had preserved the integrity of the Union right flank and saved Grant's military career. At Shiloh, he led the 3rd Division, Army of the Tennessee. During the second day of the battle, he fought the Confederates as competently and respectably as any of Grant's other division commanders.

In six months, he had risen from the rank of colonel, commanding the 11th Indiana Volunteer Regiment, to that of major general, leading the 3rd Division of the Army of the Tennessee. His rapid rise to the top exposed just as quickly the fatal flaw in his military character. He never was a team player. He never thought it necessary to think about how to co-exist with those in the military with whom he disagreed. The events of the first day at Shiloh brought that flaw to the forefront of his relationships within the military. It would be a major factor in the untimely and unwarranted collapse of his career as a battlefield commander. To Wallace's perceived regret, it would be a career ending without glory or honor.

Throughout his life, Lew Wallace pursued adventure relentlessly, always emphasizing the highly personal component of his pursuit. A successfully completed adventure carried with it the opportunity to achieve personal honor and glory. While he often undertook his quests in the name of his state or his country, he never lost sight of the fact that he always stood at the center of his endeavors. "I joined the army," he wrote to his wife's brother-in-law in early 1862, "because I thought possibly I could be of service to the government . . . and [to] win an honorable place in history."[4] He expressed similar sentiments years later in his *Autobiog-*

raphy. As he had witnessed the pending sectional conflict unfold, he had seen that it promised to be "long and great . . . crowded with opportunities for distinction not in the least inconsistent with patriotism."[5]

Wallace believed passionately in the Federal Union. In his opinion, from the days of the Mexican War, sectional competition and conflict among four principles, "Freedom, Slavery, Individual Rights, [and] Popular Government" had dominated politics. As "Mr. Douglas's Compromise," the Compromise of 1850, failed "the great quarrel had been aggravated far beyond peaceable settlement." Wallace had resolved "to hold myself in readiness to go with the side proposing to uphold the integrity of the Union—this without regard for section or party."[6]

When the war broke out, Wallace embraced it not only in defense of Federalism but also as the vehicle for the adventure of a lifetime filled with prospects for personal honor and glory. In a late July 1862 recruiting speech in Cincinnati, Wallace spoke to his first goal, denouncing "the fiendish spirit of the leaders of the unholy rebellion" and condemning "the bitter and undying hatred with which the rebels regarded the Federal Government." A year earlier, anticipating his first major battle in the eastern theater, he enlightened his wife Susan concerning his other objective in going to war, "Such a fight, you know, will realize my life-long wish. I would not miss it on any account."[7]

Wallace embarked on many continuing quests during his life but two in particular dominated his story. The first was his love of knowledge; the second was his military career. He pursued both with uncommon zeal and commitment. The two adventures were united by a third shared characteristic. As Wallace pursued both knowledge and success in the military, he demonstrated repeatedly he could not function effectively within a structured environment with anyone with whom he disagreed, whatever the reason, whatever the forum. He never took kindly to anyone exercising control over him.[8] Neither the structured formality of the academic classroom nor the rigid, unquestioning obedience all soldiers owed to the military chain of command suited him. The systems within which others pursued their dreams were simply too rigid and dogmatic to accommodate and inspire him. Because of his ingrained values, he learned early in life that if he were to succeed in either quest, he must educate himself. He did so amazingly well.

Wallace never enjoyed the near universal personal fame and acclaim in his military endeavors that he attained with the publication of his novel,

Ben-Hur: A Tale of the Christ. Benson J. Lossing, the American historian and a close personal friend, once observed that Wallace was equally at home with the Muses as with the military. He intimated that Wallace had only to assert himself in either or both disciplines to secure the fame he so fervently sought.[9] Lasting military laurels were never to be his; Wallace was incapable of sustaining a working relationship with most of the military figures he interacted with during the war. In addition, four long years of war demonstrated conclusively that the day of the amateur soldier was rapidly disappearing. Professionalism, based upon training at and graduation from West Point, was fast becoming the prerequisite for a long and productive career in the military.[10] Even had Wallace desired and then secured an appointment to West Point, it is doubtful he could have sustained the demands of the system it represented and thus been graduated and awarded a commission.

For Wallace, the realism of battle was simply irresistible. In 1846, he explored this realization in a letter to his father in which he proclaimed "the wonders of war are gradually revealing themselves to my sight." In that same letter, the soon-to-be nineteen-year-old 2nd lieutenant addressed the other, darker side of war and thus identified the dichotomy of human responses to it. "There is nothing else on earth in which splendor is mingled to a greater degree with misery," he continued, "it is strange also how soon it blunts the finer feelings of our nature and absolutely murders all sympathy or pity." Nevertheless, he truly enjoyed the experience of war. After Fort Donelson he wrote to his wife Susan, "I find myself just as anxious to go forward as ever. I find my interest in battles rather increased than otherwise—in fact, I like the excitement and in very truth, I have never heard music as fascinating and grand as that of battle." Wallace was nevertheless painfully aware that the waging of war represented man's greatest inhumanity to man. After Shiloh, he told Susan "this soldering business sadly deadens that very good thing so carefully cultivated by Christians—humanity."[11] There is no evidence that Wallace was a warmonger. He found in war a cause to represent and an exciting opportunity to pursue honor and glory. Yet, simultaneously, he was intensely sensitive to the human costs, death, disability, and disease, as well as the other sacrifices attendant thereto. Having lived from an early age with the harsh reality of his mother's untimely death, Wallace was able to internalize and balance these disparate human responses. After Shiloh, among other things, Wallace genuinely missed the exciting drama of waging war.

Clockwise from above left: Major General Henry W. Halleck. (Library of Congress); Major General Lew Wallace in Command at Memphis, Tennessee (*Harper's Weekly* [July 12, 1862]); Major General Ulysses S. Grant. (Library of Congress)

In the first year of the war in the west, Wallace came into contact with Maj. Gen. Henry Wager Halleck and Brig. (later Maj.) Gen. Ulysses S. Grant. Each was a professionally trained soldier; each a graduate of West Point. Grant looked upon West Point as vehicle for advancement within a chosen career. Halleck believed a West Point experience was indispensable for personal and professional success in the army as well as for the ultimate protection of the country's vital interests. Both were Wallace's superior officers. Each, for distinctly dissimilar reasons, dominated and ultimately determined the outcome of Wallace's military career.

Long before he ever met or knew anything about Wallace, Halleck was bent at the very least on limiting the military influence and career of anyone who was not a professional soldier. Halleck saw himself as the consummate West Point trained professional soldier. It was not Wallace himself that so agitated Halleck, but what he represented. Wallace was a civilian, amateur soldier dressed up in a uniform attempting to be a part of Halleck's professional world. Halleck knew that a person like Wallace could be trouble. The presence of a civilian amateur in the command structure of the military would sooner or later incite a clash of wills to the detriment of the army. A civilian amateur, more so than a professionally trained soldier, was destined to make a horrid mistake in battle at the cost of many lives. The professional army would win this war without the civilian amateur. In Halleck's mind, Wallace, because he was so out of his element, was the kind of person who created more problems than he solved. A Wallace type merely stood in the way of the ultimate success of Halleck's army. Halleck would do his best from the beginning of the war to get rid of as many "Wallaces" as he could.

Grant was more taciturn, more prosaic in demeanor and style than Wallace. An officer who served under Grant once described him as a man of "plain manners," a person of "unostentatious ways." Grant possessed "none of the gold and glitter, none of that pomp and circumstance about him" that other Union general officers seemed to exude; he was "plain and unobtrusive . . . remarkable for decision, reticence, and determination. There was no pretension about Grant."[12] Wallace was more flamboyant, vocal, imaginative, and passionate than Grant. More likely than not, Wallace was too independent, self-centered, and unrestrained to suit Grant's temperament. Both had a keen belief that warfare should be waged offensively, with boldness and audacity. Neither suffered indecision or inactivity gladly. In the first year of the war in the west, both often received orders from superiors that suggested hesitancy, thus mandating the status quo. Upon such occasions, Grant generally remained silent and executed his orders. Wallace often did neither.

It is doubtful Grant and Wallace could have sustained a long-term working relationship. Wallace had reason to wonder if Grant valued him for his military talent. He knew Grant really did not get along personally with him. The latter feeling was undoubtedly mutual. Wallace suspected Grant did not value the military contributions he knew he had made on several occasions. Wallace was more than aware that Grant had never officially or personally acknowledged his deeds and accomplishments at Fort Donelson. Wallace had difficulty accepting this perceived slight. During his appearance before the Congressional Joint Committee on the

Conduct of the War and in the aftermath of Shiloh, Wallace cast aside any and all possibilities he might have had for a continuing relationship with Grant. Ultimately, whatever faith and confidence Grant reposed in Wallace as a military commander and comrade faded away. True, Halleck first put Wallace on the shelf, dismissing him from active battlefield command, but Grant kept him there.

"The fact is," Wallace once wrote in explanation of his Shiloh legacy, "I was the victim of a mistake."[13] By late 1862, Wallace began to suspect that his prospects for once again commanding troops in battle were growing dim. Wallace determined to rectify this. He set himself firmly on the path to believing that whatever his problems within the framework of the military were, he was not at fault. He did not plan to seek accommodation, but rather to take the offensive to regain that which had been taken so indiscriminately from him. Wallace never realized that for him, Shiloh was the darkest of alleys from which no escape was possible. He could not see how, through his ill-advised appearance before the Congressional Joint Committee, he had offended the professional military establishment. Other than his comrades-in-arms, most of whom were, like him, civilian amateurs, he never realized how few friends he actually had. Despite his successes on the field of battle, he never grasped that off the field he was his own worst enemy.

About this time, early December 1862, Wallace reflected this close-mindedness and naiveté in a sarcasm-laced letter to Susan. Wallace noted that the Union army remained at risk "until, plenty of iron is infused into our discipline—until, in fact, we have discipline." Concluding with a severe and unwarranted criticism of Lincoln, Wallace pronounced, "It is mistaken humanity in President Lincoln not to allow shooting in our army." Perhaps, however, with this letter, Wallace was demonstrating that he was beginning to learn a lesson from all his travails. He had offered his thoughts for a change in the privacy of a letter to his wife rather than in a public forum.[14]

Wallace feared that inactivity dulled his military senses.[15] Many of his most serious problems within the rigid structure of the chain of command came about when a superior officer ordered caution in a situation Wallace believed begged for decisive action. More than that, however, he sensed that others were conspiring to remove him permanently from battlefield command. It was time to act, boldly and decisively. This, then, was the mindset of the man who delivered a letter to the highest-ranking officer in the U.S. army in March 1863, thus firmly setting in motion his Shiloh controversy, the cover-up of that controversy, and Wallace's never-ending personal odyssey to rectify and restore his reputation.

Reflecting upon "Shiloh, Bloody Shiloh," many of those who participated that day as well as those who subsequently wrote about it suggested that Wallace misunderstood or misread Grant's orders. The Wallace detractors, then and now, believe that Wallace "took the wrong road" and that as a result at Shiloh he was "lost." His critics claim furthermore that even after Grant's aides found him, Wallace "continued with a slow and leisurely pace" toward the battle. This meant he and his 3rd Division did not participate in the fighting on April 6, arriving on the field of battle as night was falling.

The contrary view is decidedly closer to the truth. Wallace was a victim at Shiloh: a victim of mistakes and errors committed by Grant and his aides, a victim of his own arrogance and inflated sense of self-importance, a victim of a decided prejudice against the civilian, amateur soldier, and, lastly, a victim of an intentional cover-up. In command of the 3rd Division of the Army of the Tennessee, Wallace made few mistakes at Shiloh. Unquestionably, he did not make any of the mistakes his critics so generously claimed he did. He had an excellent idea at all times what he was doing, where he was going, and why he was going there. Wallace was one of very few general officers in Union blue able to make that statement on April 6.[16]

At a very crucial juncture midway through his march to the Shiloh battlefield, Wallace made a fatal decision. For the first and perhaps only time in his military career, he decided not to act boldly and audaciously. He denied the very maxims and personal beliefs about waging war that had heretofore characterized his military adventures and brought him success. At a crucial juncture, Wallace rejected "l'audace" as a military maxim, sensing that the new orders he had just received from Grant through Capt. William R. Rowley were correct for the time and place in which he found himself. He would gradually thereafter develop a deeply felt and profound regret that he had reached that conclusion and thus obeyed those orders. For one thing, in turning his back on his instincts and following orders given in the most bizarre manner and circumstance, he denied both himself and his country the possibility of having a genuine hero that day.

To the end of his life, Lew Wallace was well aware that many allegations of error and misconduct at Shiloh had been heaped upon him. Yet, despite his written request, no court of inquiry or court martial was ever convened to hear and render judgment on the evidence against him. He retained the rank of Major General of Volunteers until his death in 1905. As his life came to a close, Wallace seemed to believe that in his Shiloh odyssey he had failed his state, his country, his men, and himself in his adventurous pursuit of honor and glory. In fact, he had not.

CHAPTER ONE

The Adventure Begins

Lew Wallace began his life's journey in Brookville, a thriving agrarian and commercial community located in southeastern Indiana at the fork of the Whitewater River. The Indiana General Assembly had located a land purchasing and registration office there in 1820, which contributed significantly to the growth and prosperity of the community.[1] His Scotch-Irish grandfather, Andrew, was a successful businessman who at various times had been a surveyor, as well as the owner and operator of a general store, a book and newspaper publishing concern in Cincinnati, and most recently a tavern. His father, David, had served nearly six years in the army, including four years as a cadet at the U.S. Military Academy. He was graduated ninth of twenty-four in the class of 1821. As a newly commissioned 2nd Lieutenant, he stayed at West Point for more than a year, instructing future officers in mathematics. Resigning his commission, David returned to Brookville. He read the law and gained admission to the state bar in late 1823. In 1824, he married Esther French Test, the daughter of John Test, a leading local attorney and a member of the U.S. House of Representatives. Lew, the second of four children, was born on April 10, 1827.[2] Shortly thereafter, David embarked upon a political career under the political banner of the Whig party. After three terms in the Indiana General Assembly, Hoosiers elected him lieutenant governor in 1834 and governor in 1837.[3] At birth, Lew joined a solidly respectable, educated, professional, middle-class family.

In 1825, the Indiana Legislature closed the Brookville land office and moved its lucrative activities to the capital at Indianapolis. With its departure, Brookville's prosperity soon disappeared. So, too, did the David Wallace family. In early 1832, David moved Esther and their four sons to

Covington in the western part of Indiana on the banks of the Wabash River.[4] Little more than five years old when he arrived, Lew's independent, searching, and self-reliant spirit flourished in Covington.[5] In a moment of solitary reflection, Wallace distilled the essence of his spirit into a description of his first encounter with the mighty Wabash River. "It looked so wide, so deep, so like the passing of a flood going down in its majestic way to what would be a deluge when it was at last arrived. Yet it had a coaxing power. My fears were soothed, and I went, and, as it were, laid my hand on its mane; and thence we were friends. No one better than [Charles] Dickens knew what conjurers such things are to imaginative children. I became its playmate the summers through." Whether it was the Wabash or the Kankakee, Wallace readily adopted the river as his symbol for independence and self-reliance.[6]

Wallace roamed the hills and dales, woodlands and streams surrounding the Wabash for only a few short years until David, the newly elected governor of Indiana, moved his family to Indianapolis in 1837. During his Covington years, ages five to ten, Lew experienced two highly personal encounters with death. Both, arguably, left him more independent and self-reliant than he might otherwise have been. On the journey to their new home in 1832, Lew and his younger brother John fell ill with scarlet fever. "He, poor boy, died," was the stark epitaph Wallace entered in his *Autobiography.* Lew survived, perhaps only because his mother continually administered "horrible draughts of saffron tea, hot almost to [*sic*] scalding" to the ailing child. The one indelible memory for the five-year-old from this encounter was "the large, brown eyes of my mother swimming in tears." Then, two years later, several months after Lew's seventh birthday, "galloping consumption" claimed Esther, "leaving me so young that her sweet motherliness is a clearer impression on my mind than either her qualities or her appearance." His mother's death, significantly accented by his father's frequent absences from the home for political reasons, created a void in parental authority for Lew. In December 1836, almost three years after Esther's death, David presented Lew and his two brothers with a stepmother, Zerelda Gray Sanders, the daughter of Dr. John Sanders of Indianapolis. During his early years, Lew never quite provided as large a place in his heart for Zerelda as he reserved for his departed mother.[7] For an impressionable youth, these two events and the consequences which flowed from them, broadened and deepened the mold of his unquenchable spirit of independence and self-reliance.[8]

Two adventures he embarked upon relatively early illustrate the hold this spirit of independence and self-reliance had on him. He wanted nothing to do with what most would call conventional restraints. Hence, barely thirteen, he decided on his own to take his absent father's place "as a delegate to the great convention held at Tippecanoe battle-ground in the interest of General William Henry Harrison. That my delegacy was by self-appointment did not, as I saw it then, interfere with its attractiveness. In plainer terms, I ran away." A few miles from Indianapolis, his companion deserted him and went home. Wallace continued by himself on the Michigan Road to LaFayette "in mortal fear lest I should be turned back by some one of the Indianapolis delegates who knew me." He was gone for over two weeks without permission. The apparent highlight of his trip was his act of swiping a red flannel petticoat, a Democratic symbol of an alleged Harrison scandal, from atop a tavern where it flew in derision of the 1840 Whig presidential candidate. He then paraded his newly acquired trophy down the street to the "hurrahs" of the wildly enthusiastic Whigs as well as to "a storm of threats and curses" from those favoring the re-election of Martin Van Buren. Two years later, in 1842, Wallace learned that men were fighting and dying for honor and glory in the struggle for Texas independence from Mexico. He and a companion secured a flatboat and began paddling down the White River bound for New Orleans to join up. Zerelda's father, accompanied by a local constable, apprehended the young adventurers ten miles south of Indianapolis and took them home for punishment.[9]

The master of the Wallace house neither "spared" nor "spoiled" his son when it came to discipline. "It would be unjust to my parents," Wallace reflected in his *Autobiography*, "to suppose they made no effort to control me. The rod in my father's hand was terrible for the moment." His father's efforts lacked that essential ingredient that made punishment both tolerable and worthwhile in the long run. Painful as it was, punishment was simply a momentary penalty, completely lacking an implied promise of better things yet to come. Wallace thought even less of the method of reprimand administered by his mother. "The punishments resorted to by my mother were annoying. . . . More potent were her entreaties and tears. The contrition they brought about lasted until the vitality which was the unconquerable part of my nature drove me to going again. It seemed that I must go. The Wandering Jew was not more possessed in that way; only his possession was a curse, and mine, the completest [*sic*] happiness. Going was life."[10]

From the beginning, it was virtually impossible to reconcile Wallace's inordinate desire to "go," his zealous quest for "life," and his unrestrained and independent "spirit" with a structured educational environment. Such formalities were not for him. Wallace never permitted the school house, the classroom, or the often incompetent schoolmaster to exercise dominion over him. Like many a youngster in his time and place, he reveled in the freedom of the woods and the streams. When forced to sit silently before his teacher, Wallace often refused to use his "bluestone" pencil to calculate his sums or to decline his verbs. As many hours as possible were "divided between making pictures of and fighting battles on my paper slate." Handsome lines of heroic soldiers faced hordes of hostile Indians as imaginary battles ensued. Years later, Wallace drew a humorous picture of the restraining influence that his formal educational experiences exercised upon him. He recalled that on his very first day in school "a little girl ate my pencil, and I took my first flogging because I could not produce it."[11] At the age of nine, on his own initiative, he finagled admission into the preparatory school at the newly founded Wabash College in Crawfordsville. Here he fell subject to the heavy hand of a tutor who "was one of the army of indiscriminates [*sic*] who think they are doing their duty in giving impossible tasks to helpless incapables, and, if they are small, punishing them." "Discipline," Wallace acknowledged, "had to be maintained," just not at his expense. His tenure and formal education at Wabash lasted a little more than a month before he succumbed as "the woods and little river invited me, and I accepted and took to them." Wallace fondly remembered that "the river was the siren with a song everlasting in my ears. I could hear it the day long. It seemed specially addressed to me, and was at no time so sweet and irresistible as when I was struggling with the multiplication tables or some abstruse rule of grammar."[12]

In 1840, Lew and his brother William spent an academic year at Professor Samuel K. Hoshour's Academy in Centreville, Indiana. For Wallace, even though this was yet another formalized, structured educational experience, the time spent at Hoshour's Academy represented "the turning point of my life." Hoshour was in one respect a typical schoolmaster. He "wielded the rod and vigorously." Yet, he did so with "with discrimination and undeniable justice." Wallace credited Hoshour with immediately perceiving that he had little aptitude for and even less interest in mathematics. So, "instead of beating me for it," according to Wallace, Hoshour "humanely applied himself to cultivating a faculty he thought within my power," reading and writing. This Hoosier schoolmaster became Wallace's ideal since he "taught me how to educate myself up to every practical need." Wallace's formal education came to an end when he left Hoshour's tutelage. All in all, he had spent less than three full academic years in any kind of a formal schoolhouse. He had not been graduated from any school at any level.[13]

While the schoolroom would never suit nor hold him, Wallace nevertheless spent a lifetime of adventure garnering knowledge. Possession of knowledge was a prerequisite to success. Upon his return from Centreville to Indianapolis, he participated in one or two literary societies. Encouraged by his own youthful zeal, he wrote his first "epic," a short story with the curious title of "Travels of a Bed-Bug." He soon followed with his first historical novel, written in the style and tradition of Sir Walter Scott. Later in life, Wallace described his *The Man-at-Arms: a Tale of the Tenth Century,* as "sophomoric" and full of "fervid sentimentalism." On the other hand, he obviously deplored the inexplicable loss of this manuscript, calling that event "one of my standing regrets." As if to underscore the point, he spent ten pages discussing and analyzing his "sophomoric" effort in his *Autobiography.*[14]

Lew became passionate about the fireside readings his father began to orchestrate in 1842. David designed these sessions for both Lew and William. The young men read aloud or recited Shakespearean sonnets and plays from memory. Both boys made Lord Macaulay's *Essays* a family favorite. David, like Hoshour before him, required readings in Oliver Goldsmith. John Milton's poetry was a staple. The eclectic *Edinburgh Review* came from abroad monthly and stimulated their minds. The three of them would sit around a winter's fire for hours reading aloud James Fenimore Cooper and Washington Irving for pure adventure or Thucydides and George Bancroft for history. David also sharpened his sons' ability to think and speak clearly, frequently requiring them to engage in impromptu "declamations." These sessions served Lew as the foundation for a lifetime of learning. From that point forward, Wallace taught himself what he really wanted to know about those subjects that interested him the most—history, all things military, comedy, tragedy, poetry, adventure, the human spirit, politics, religion, writing, even horticulture, but never mathematics.[15]

Wallace could never spend enough hours devouring William H. Prescott's histories of the conquests of Cortés and Pizarro. Reading and vicariously living the chivalric ideals Sir Walter Scott put to paper was a must for him. A copy of Plutarch's *Lives of the Noble Greeks* and Romans, reciting the heroic accomplishments of the ancients, could always be found in Wallace's possession during the war. Wallace's travels through the world of knowledge reached their zenith in 1880 with the publication of his highly regarded novel *Ben-Hur: A Tale of the Christ.*

Sometime in 1843, David abruptly sent Lew out into the world on his own. "Were I to die tonight," David allegedly told his son, "your portion of my estate would not keep you for a month. I am sorry, disappointed, mortified; so, without shutting the door upon you, I am resolved that from to-day you must go out and earn your own livelihood. I shall watch your course hopefully. That is all I have to say." Wallace claimed his father's course of action was neither unexpected nor unjust. "There was no argument," he wrote, "no reproach, no entreaty. The affair was merely as if one party were making the other a present; and such in fact it was—he had given me my freedom." One might wonder whether Wallace's immediate reaction to his father's expulsion was as benign as it was sixty years later. Lew said he suffered little and felt no pain as his father summarily dispatched him into the world at the age of sixteen.[16] Custom and tradition had not restrained him so far. These conventions would not hold him back as he became a man, a thinker, a doer, a dreamer of sorts, a restless seeker of adventure, absurdly self-confident, and highly ambitious.

In 1848, Mary Clemmer, a long-time friend of Lew's soon-to-be wife Susan, described Wallace as being thin and tall, "nearly six feet high." Possessed of "profuse black hair, a dark, beautiful face, correct in every line, keen black eyes deeply set," even in a crowd, Wallace appeared as "a king of men." More to the point, Ms. Clemmer characterized the young Wallace as "a man of conviction, earnest in every nerve of his being, intensely earnest."[17] Meredith Nicholson, a fellow author and adventurer, knew the elder Wallace quite well as a man "of medium height, erect, dark to swarthiness, with finely chiseled features and keen black eyes, with manners the most courtly, and a voice unusually musical and haunting." Nicholson conceded his "youthful hero worship" of Wallace, dubbing him one of "many of our Hoosier Olympians." Nevertheless, Nicholson took full measure of both the youthful and elder Wallace, noting "his life was filled with drama—with melodrama, even." He was inordinately curious by nature, "both a dreamer and a man of action" and "his curiosity led him into the study of many subjects, most of them remote from the affairs of his day." Always "busy about something," Wallace was "an aristocrat and a democrat; he was wise and temperate, whimsical and injudicious in a breath." Yet, Nicholson concluded, "with all this rich experience of the larger world, he remained the simplest of natures."[18]

During his formative years, Wallace had roamed the woodlands of western frontier Indiana, fishing its streams, hunting its small game, thriving and developing his lifetime values with every adventure he encountered. He had drawn strength from the reality and symbolism of the mighty river. The untimely death of his beloved mother combined with his father's frequent absences for political reasons largely destroyed any possibility he would grow to maturity in a structured and disciplined family environment. All his life, he continually exhibited an independent, self-reliant, and self-absorbed spirit. He believed that so long as he provided the right amount of effort and gumption, nothing could possibly get the better of him. He exhibited this unquenchable spirit when in 1849 he opened a law practice in Covington without any visible signs of support. In a letter to his brother, Wallace rhetorically asked—"How am I getting along? Ah, passingly well!" Wallace's pride and self-assured spirit would have allowed him to admit to nothing less. "If I haven't made money," he expounded enthusiastically, "I've at least paid expenses and maintained myself." He knew tomorrow inevitably promised better than today. "I came here with a vow to succeed or starve," he proudly proclaimed, "the future, too, looks cloudless in its promise." He was bold, brash, and splendidly confident. "Activity of trade must revive—indeed is already reviving: the year's successful crop will 'open up' hundreds of law suits which have slept merely for want of the 'breathe of life'—money! Win? I'll make it win! I'm sworn—determined."[19]

At the age of twenty-two, Wallace was just beginning to establish himself in the practice of law. He had decidedly more prospects than resources. Nevertheless, it was time to marry. He set his sights quite high. In that same letter to his brother, Wallace told William that he was near to completing his conquest of the Elston stronghold in Crawfordsville. Susan, "the greatest girl living," was the object of his desires. She was also the daughter of Issac C. Elston, the man with the honorific title of "Major," reputed at one time to be the richest man in the state. "With the family," Lew informed William, "I stand fairly admitted and recognized. The last time I was there, they showed me to the public in their family carriage, the old Maj. himself driving. Still the old gent. don't like me, and you know, I'm not famous for strict adherence to the gold rule 'return good etc.'" He had allies in his attempted conquest. Joanna, Susan's sister and the Elston's second eldest daughter and her husband, Henry Smith Lane, a prominent attorney and politician, "are *muy amigo.*" Doggedly confident, Wallace expected to "make 'a good egg' out of an infamous world after all."[20]

Wallace married Susan on May 6, 1852. For the next fifty-three years, she was the directing and perhaps commanding influence in his life. In

Clockwise from top left: Lew Wallace, c. 1852. (Collection of Mrs. Blair Miller); Susan Arnold Elston Wallace. (Lew Wallace Study); Henry S. Lane, Lew's brother-in-law, Governor of Indiana, 1860–1860, and U.S. Senator from Indiana, 1860–1866. (Library of Congress); David Wallace, Lew's father and Governor of Indiana, 1836–1840. (Lew Wallace Study)

announcing the birth of their only child in February 1853, the proud father wrote to William that he had given much thought to his child's name. "The fellow's name shant be David,—that's too plebeian—nor William,—that's very pretty for a child but unfit for a man,—nor Edward, that's too pretty for either man or baby. I have determined that the most aristocratic and democratic, the most romantic and unpedantic [*sic*], the most noble, manly, appropriate and significant of all that 'best becomes a man' is 'Lew'. I have high hopes of whacking the opposition into satisfaction with that 'clipeding'."[21]

Subsequent events revealed another fact about Wallace's new life. The boy was ultimately christened Henry in honor of Susan's brother-in-law, Henry Smith Lane. Wallace had succumbed to a truth which would dominate the remainder of his life—the man who one day would lead a division in battle did not give the orders on the home front. Not long after Henry's birth, the Wallace family moved to Crawfordsville. Lew continued to practice law and began to participate in state politics. From then on, Wallace called this community home.

Three episodes during the 1850s depict how Wallace continued to follow the unrestrained, independent flow of the mighty river. In each, he proved just how eclectic and dynamic in thought and action he had become. In 1852, while politicking for a friend in a state election, Wallace demonstrated ingenuity, spontaneity, and more than a dash of audacity. He had just finished speaking on his candidate's behalf in a small county village. As his opponent began to ply his political charms, Wallace crossed the street and went into a tavern where he had heard "the notes of a violin wretchedly played." Convincing the "fiddler" to loan him the violin, Wallace struck up a rendition of the "Arkansas Traveller." "The effect was instantaneous," he concluded in his *Autobiography*. "The silver tongue of my antagonist lost its cunning. His hearers, partisans and enemies alike, were smitten with restlessness." Later evaluating his ability to destroy, even momentarily, the effectiveness of his opponent, Wallace concluded that "the 'Arkansas Traveller' in the right key and time, and with the right expression, could have silenced Pericles, or Mirabeau, or any of those accounted of the divine in oratory."[22]

The second descriptive event for Wallace occurred in 1853. Exhibiting the breadth of historical interests that dominated his life, he completed the initial draft of his first serious novel, *The Fair God or, The Last of the 'Tzins: A Tale of the Conquest of Mexico*. It was ultimately published in 1873.

Lew Wallace, c. 1855. (Lew Wallace Study)

Finally, in 1856, sensing what lay upon the horizon, Wallace organized a group of civilians in Crawfordsville and Montgomery County into a militia company known as the Montgomery Guards.[23] Just as he had earlier displayed prowess with a violin, Wallace demonstrated once more that he was a man of action. For more than four years, the Montgomery Guards participated in formal military drills and encampments throughout Indiana and the Midwest, garnering a regional reputation for self-taught military ability as well as professionalism. In December 1860, Wallace wrote to John G. Davis, a Democratic member of the U.S. House of Representatives from Indiana, seeking Davis's help in obtaining for personal use a number of the military textbooks then required in the classrooms at West Point. These military treatises were generally unavailable to civilians unless the Secretary of War consented. In a second letter to Davis, dated January 3, 1861, Wallace bemoaned the fact that such books "were printed for the exclusive use of the Army officers." He suggested that Davis make it one of his personal objectives while in Congress to seek the "reversal of the confounded system of West Point exclusiveness." Rhetorically, he asked the congressman, "what can a miserable little army of seventeen thousand men do toward defending this country?" Wallace condemned the current situation wherein "the government encourages the idea of centralizing all military knowledge in the one Academy: the effect of which is not only to create a military snobbism but to place the bravest and most aspiring of the volunteer millions at the feet of a little club of *sou-lieutenants*." Reflecting upon his military service in Mexico in 1846, Wallace concluded, "I have a right to complain of this. I have seen it and felt it keenly."[24] In his last letter to Davis, Wallace requested copies of treatises written by Dennis Hart Mahan, then one of West Point's greatest military philosophers.

Wallace went to war on April 14, 1861. His name was not particularly well-known beyond the borders of his state. The day before, Wallace was living and practicing law in Crawfordsville. His schedule for that day included arguing a legal matter in circuit court in the nearby community of Frankfort. Indiana governor Oliver P. Morton sent a telegraph to the court summoning him to accept his offer to be the Adjutant General of the State of Indiana. "Fort Sumter has been fired on. Come Immediately," Morton demanded.[25] So anxious was Wallace to heed the summons that he reportedly raced to the bench, showed the telegram to the judge, and received permission to leave the courtroom. He entrusted the further management of the case to an associate and simply walked out of the trial on his way to war. He concocted a political trade with Morton, agreeing to take the proffered post as adjutant general, provided the governor give him command of one of the newly formed regiments when he had finished his administrative duties on behalf of the state. On April 25, Wallace resigned, having successfully initiated and placed in motion in a brief ten-day period many of the programs that rapidly moved Indiana from a peacetime to a wartime entity. He took command of the 11th Indiana Volunteers as its colonel. Within the year, his name, though not necessarily a household word, would be known far beyond the boundaries of his beloved home state of Indiana.

CHAPTER TWO

A Meteoric Rise

During his military career, and indeed throughout his life, Wallace valued and pursued personal honor as intensely as he did personal glory. He first manifested this trait during the Mexican War. In 1846, Wallace recruited a company of men and went to war. He and his men were assigned to the 1st Indiana Volunteer Regiment. To his dismay, the 1st Indiana never engaged in any fighting in Mexico greater than a skirmish or two of little significance. Neither Wallace nor the 1st Indiana fought at the battle of Buena Vista. Nevertheless, this battle had a profound and lasting impact upon him. In time he would use Buena Vista as a symbol to demonstrate that he knew not only how to lead men in battle, but also how to appeal to their innate sense of honor to inspire them to achieve greatness.

Wallace had grown up in the Age of Jackson, when, politically speaking, men generally professed more allegiance and loyalty to their state than to the federal government. This was certainly true for Wallace. At Buena Vista, in late February, 1847, Gen. Zachary Taylor, a professional Regular Army officer, commanded various state contingents of volunteer soldiers combined with several units of the Regular Army against Santa Anna's Mexican forces. Hoosier William A. Bowles commanded the 2nd Indiana Volunteers, a part of Brig. Gen. Joseph Lane's brigade. Neither Bowles nor Lane was a professional soldier. Both were civilian amateurs who had been appointed to command primarily because of their political influence and connections within the state. When Santa Anna initiated the offensive at Buena Vista, neither Taylor nor his second-in-command, Brig. Gen. John E. Wool, each of whom were professionally trained, was anywhere near the point of Mexican attack. To counter the advancing Mexicans, Lane ordered the 2nd Indiana, along with a battery of three artillery pieces, to a location at least thirteen hundred yards in advance of his main body of troops. The men of the 2nd Indiana, though outnumbered approximately ten to one, initially performed competently in their advanced position. Slowly but surely, enemy numbers alone began to overwhelm the regiment. The inexperienced Bowles collapsed under the stress of the situation, finally crying out "cease firing, and retreat" three times. With this, the right wing and then the left wing of the 2nd Indiana turned inward toward the rear and began to unravel as a fighting unit. Once men saw their friends and neighbors to their right and left hurriedly leaving the field, the retreat on the American left, which Bowles's panic and cowardice had precipitated, became general. Col. Jefferson Davis, a West Point trained professional soldier, advanced his 2nd Mississippi Rifles. Taylor, arriving on the battlefield, coordinated this maneuver, pushing the 2nd Illinois and the 3rd Indiana forward from the American reserve. Davis and Taylor's efforts gradually stabilized the line. Shortly thereafter, Taylor's army checked the advancing Mexicans and went forward to victory at Buena Vista.

In his official report of the battle, Taylor concluded that the 2nd Indiana and Bowles in particular acted in a reprehensible and cowardly manner. He discounted as immaterial any reason why Bowles and the regiment panicked. A subsequent court of inquiry confirmed the charges against Bowles, finding that he lacked the capacity to serve as a colonel in the army and further that he had instigated the near calamity of the day by issuing the infamous order "cease firing, and retreat."

Justified or not, Taylor had stained the honor of an individual Hoosier. However, in his official report of the battle written weeks before a court of inquiry convened, he inexplicably went one step further. He labeled all the men of the 2nd Indiana "fugitives," stating that as a whole "the 2nd Indiana could not be rallied and that except for a handful of men, the 2nd Indiana took no further part in the action." Taylor actually praised Bowles, noting that the disgraced colonel had found a rifle, joined the rear ranks of the 2nd Mississippi regiment, and fought gallantly the remainder of the day. The court of inquiry contradicted Taylor's conclusion damning the men of the 2nd Indiana. The members of the court found that nearly two hundred men of the 2nd Indiana, or three-quarters of the regiment who answered regimental roll call that morning, halted their retreat and returned to the field as an unofficial unit to fight until the Mexican Army left the field.

For some inexplicable reason, Taylor stubbornly refused to modify his official report. All subsequent investigations demonstrated that Taylor had erred in the allegations of cowardly behavior he cast against the 2nd Indiana. Even Wool contradicted his superior officer. Old Rough and

The Eleventh Indiana Volunteers Swearing to Remember Buena Vista at Indianapolis, May, 1861. Sketched by Mr. James F. Gookins. (*Harper's Weekly* [June 22, 1861])

Ready held firm. Hoosiers were outraged.[1] Wallace believed Taylor was guilty of an indefensible lie. In 1848, when the Whig Party nominated Taylor for the presidency, Wallace openly voted with the Democrats, notwithstanding the fact that his father had once been the Whig governor of the state. His pen was particularly venomous as he campaigned against Taylor in the presidential election of 1848. Taylor had viciously slurred the name and the honor of Indiana. Wallace would not forget.

In early May 1861, Wallace took the first step on this mission of redemption. As the 11th Indiana prepared to depart the state capitol for patrol duty at Evansville along the Ohio River, Wallace marched his regiment to the state house lawn to receive its regimental colors from the women of Indianapolis. The time to assume the offense in defense of his state and country had arrived. The time to create an enduring symbol for this moment was at hand. It was time to redeem the reputation of his native state. Taylor could no longer redress the wrong. He had died over a decade earlier. His ex-son-in-law, the commander of the 2nd Mississippi at Buena Vista, was still very much alive. He would do quite nicely as the villain. It took but a moment for Wallace to tell his men that it was the son-in-law who "assisted in proclaiming the Second Indiana cowards, if, indeed, he did not originate the accusation." The ignominy heaped upon the 2nd Indiana had been that man's responsibility for "he induced that officer [Taylor] to repeat the slander in his official report." Hoosiers had the richly ironic opportunity to redeem the state's honor for now the ex-son-in-law, Jefferson Davis, was the president of the Confederacy. *Harper's Weekly* published an artistic rendition of this event in its June 22, 1861, edition. With the majestic Indiana state house framing the background, the *Harper's* artist pictured the men of the 11th Indiana surrounding a standing, bareheaded Wallace with sword drawn. Thousands of Hoosier spectators were seen intently observing the proceedings. The correspondent for *Harper's* reported that Wallace gave a brief speech. He then ordered his men to remove their caps, kneel, and extend their right arms. The entire regiment then "took an oath before God that, with His help, they would not only avenge themselves of the insults cast at the flag of the nation, but furthermore of the contumely and wrong received by the Indiana troops at the hands of Jeff Davis during the war with Mexico. To keep this oath more continually before them they have adopted the motto 'Remember Buena Vista' as their war-cry."[2] With that, the 11th Indiana, accompanied by its inspired and inspiring leader, went to war.

Leaving Indianapolis, Wallace and the 11th Indiana marched to Evansville, Indiana, with orders to monitor and interdict Southern trade and smuggling on the Ohio River. Men, many oblivious to the political events swirling round them and some outright sympathetic to the Southern cause, were currently engaged in this illicit trade mostly to the benefit of the South. Wallace viewed this task as one far beneath his ability and dignity. He had come to fight, to defend his country, to win glory and honor, not to board water-bound vessels in search of contraband.

Wallace knew his purpose was to engage and defeat the enemies of the Hoosier state and of the Federal Union. He arrived in Evansville totally prepared to execute that mission. "No man entered the war more earnestly and with greater enthusiasm than I did. It was impossible for anyone to have done so," he wrote on August 16, 1863, to his good friend Benson J. Lossing. "I do not mean by this," he explained, "that I was more ambitious or that I loved my country better than other men. In addition to those motives, however, I had others: among these were a natural love of arms and above all a yearning to lift the reputation of my native State. The superciliousness and egotism of the South had also stung my pride of action. I longed to assist in punishing them for their arrogance as well as their crimes."[3]

In addition to being primed for war both mentally and emotionally, Wallace was well equipped to wage it, notwithstanding his lack of West Point credentials. In the late 1850s, he began assembling a personal library of military treatises. In 1856, he organized and led the Montgomery Guards in regular drills all the while expanding his own knowledge of the art and science of war. He boasted to Lossing that he became "perfectly conversant with company tactics." He voluntarily substituted these for the "infantry evolutions" favored by the U.S. Army, finding such procedures to be "so prescribed." Instead, he "taught the Zouave drill which I introduced in the West about the same time Ellsworth did [in New York and then in Chicago]. This same drill I carried into my old regiment and to it many a brave soldier is indebted for his life." "Nor did I stop there," Wallace told Lossing. "I sent for and procured all the military text books of West Point and studied them closely. You can thus understand how the breaking out of this war found me a fair theoretical soldier, that is, with a theoretical knowledge of Engineering, Artillery and organization of Cavalry." Never one to let a solid statement of fact stand on its own merit, Wallace characteristically concluded that "[f]ew graduates of the Academy knew more about an infantry command than I did. There was not a regiment of infantry in the field that excelled my 11th Ind. Regiment in drill and discipline."[4]

Wallace had presented solid evidence that he had thought extensively about the pending conflict. A few days before the firing on Fort Sumter, he demonstrated that he was prepared to seize the initiative and to gain a march upon the suspected treachery of the recently seceded Southern states. In a letter to Susan's brother-in-law, Henry S. Lane, now a U.S. senator from Indiana, Wallace advocated that Lane encourage Secretary of War Simon Cameron and the Lincoln administration to loan Indiana 1,000 to 1,200 rifles from a federal arsenal. Governor Morton of Indiana would administer the program once Washington had given the aid necessary to implement it.[5]

Wallace proposed to handpick a regiment of men committed to serving their country for five years or "during the war." Wallace's men would have both the privilege and the responsibility of electing company officers. The governor would order these newly elected officers to come to Indianapolis at the state's expense. Once assembled, Wallace would take command and school these men for two or three months in "tactics, outpost duty, field fortifications, &c," the expertise of Mahan at West Point. Having completed their days in the classroom and on the drill field, these newly commissioned officers would "go home and instruct their commands, who could then in a short time be ready to render efficient service when called out." "Without some such preparation," Wallace informed Lane, "our people, though ever so willing, cannot aid the Government as they ought." Wallace was suggesting that with the assistance of the federal government, Indiana would look to the future and create a homegrown cadre of "ninety-day wonders." The language of the subject matter Wallace proposed to teach to these men was without question the language of West Point.

As soon as the 11th Indiana arrived in Evansville, Wallace began a personal campaign to prove that it was the best regiment in the Union army. In a letter to Susan dated May 6, 1861, he expressed great pride in the 11th Indiana, observing that without firing a shot, his regiment had "behaved admirably. The city [Evansville] hardly realizes its presence and with the citizens, it is fast growing popular. When we came, there was but one flag flying, now there are many. The truth is, before our arrival, the Union people were afraid to show their true colors." The mere presence of the 11th Indiana changed that for the better, Wallace believed, and "now they [those with Union sentiments] develop boldly and rapidly." The 11th Indiana was a well-trained unit capable of inspiring confidence and patriotism among the citizenry. Wallace understood his duty in this regard and subjected his men to "incessant drilling. Every day, rain or shine, I put my regiment through ten hours. In addition to being taught knowledge of arms, the men had to be seasoned."[6] At Evansville, Wallace confirmed the validity of what he had studied and learned—for the sake of a well-prepared army, there was no substitute for the rigors of daily drill.

Wallace also grew impatient in Evansville. He began to exhibit his belief that orders that did not mandate movement against the enemy at all times were inconsequential and obeying them was subject to interpretation. He was simply in a hurry to get to the battlefield. He vented his frustration with seemingly do-nothing-accomplish-nothing orders. Rather than seek out and fight the enemy with bullet and bayonet, Wallace's superior officer had directed him to take "a detachment of my men to intercept a couple of steamboats." A week later, with his military fervor cooled sufficiently for the moment, he told Susan that his new encampment at Evansville was "rather pleasantly situated."[7] He quickly reverted to an observation more consistent with his reason for being in the army in the first place. He explained that his new campsite was not particularly well suited "for the object of sending me here, the defense of Evansville." In fact, to that end, "it is miserable, as the principle exposure is from the river, which I do not command and cannot see." If his orders promised dull duty and made little sense, he was already demonstrating a ready and seemingly uninhibited will to question them. He vowed to seek and find "opportunity." To date, he concluded, his stay on the banks of the Ohio River had been a "disappointment;" he planned to "improvise."[8]

On June 5, Wallace and the 11th Indiana suddenly departed Evansville with orders to march to Cumberland, Maryland. The trivialities and boredom of patrol duty along the Ohio River were over. The march to adventure, glory, and honor had begun. The regiment passed through Cincinnati the next night and arrived in Cumberland on June 10. Wallace was ready for action. Two days later, he found his opportunity.

On Wednesday, June 12 around 10:00 P.M., with approximately 800 men of the 11th Indiana, Wallace boarded a train. Twenty-one miles later, he arrived at New Creek Station on the north branch of the Potomac River. In the early morning hours of June 13, he and his men began a twenty-three mile march south to Romney, Virginia [now West Virginia], over a road "leading along high bluffs and narrow passes." Arriving at Romney around 8:00 A.M., the Hoosiers sprinted across a bridge spanning the south branch of the Potomac River about seventy-five yards away from a brick structure housing a Rebel patrol. Wallace "led a second company across the bridge and by following up the ravine got them into a position that soon drove the enemy from the house and into a mountain to its rear." Rather than march in line down the road that led to the bluff upon which Romney was located "as the rebels expected," Wallace advanced "five companies in skirmishing order and at double-quick time up a hill to the right, intending to get around the left flank of the enemy, and cut off their retreat." This Zouave-inspired maneuver, unorthodox for most military minds of the day, proved to be successful as whatever Confederate forces were then occupying Romney retreated immediately before Wallace and his men got into position to cut them off. Without cavalry to pursue them, the affair was concluded. Utilizing complete surprise, Wallace captured one Confederate major, killed two Rebel soldiers, and wounded one. The 11th Indiana took possession of a number of Confederate tents as well as "an excellent assortment of surgical stores." In the process, Wallace destroyed "quite a number of rifles" and accomplished all his intended activities before nightfall. He returned to Cumberland late on June 13 by the same route. According to

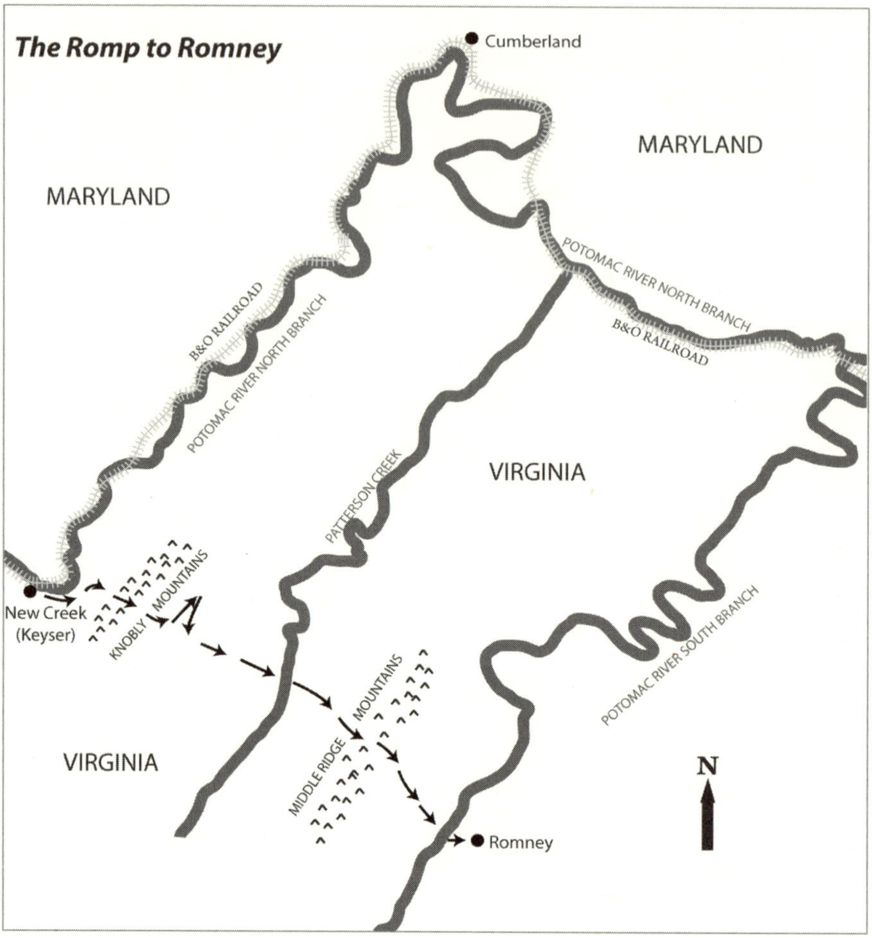

The Romp to Romney. (Map by George Ferguson, gfgraphics, Waynesville, N.C.)

Wallace, he and his men had negotiated a round trip of eighty-seven miles, at least forty-six of them on foot, over several low-lying mountain ranges, one such march being in the dead of night, and fought a skirmish, all in less than thirty-two hours. Wallace concluded his first battle action report with a characteristic boast that he had accomplished his mission "without leaving a man behind, and what is more, my men are ready to repeat it to-morrow."[9]

Wallace had subjected his men and the Zouave tactics by which he had trained them to the test of battle. On that level, Romney had been a complete and highly satisfying victory. Men under him would fight as Zouaves at Fort Donelson in the famous countercharge on the right on Saturday afternoon, February 15, 1862. Until such time as Wallace's 3rd

Division simply outran its supply lines and reserves that day and thus found itself resolutely checked by a murderous enfilading artillery and rifle fire from Confederate trenches on a hill south of the town of Dover, the Zouave method of fighting a battle had boded well for complete success that afternoon. Wallace once again employed such tactical maneuvers on the second day at Shiloh. According to the correspondent of *Frank Leslie's Illustrated Newspaper*, his men "fought harder and advanced further than the others," all of which "proves a superiority in his [Wallace's] mode of fighting." The correspondent described this manner of fighting to his readers, noting that by "taking advantage of the ridges," Wallace provided excellent shelter from enemy fire for his main force "while his skirmishers advance, crawling close up to the enemy and picking off his artillerists while [Wallace's] batteries from some vantage ground in the rear, keep up a heavy fire." Once having attained a commanding position on the field with comparatively few casualties, Wallace's men opened fire on the Confederates. As soon as the Rebel line began to waver, "a charge is made and a new position gained." The *Frank Leslie* correspondent concluded, "Gen. Wallace's division is working splendidly. The fame of the 11th Indiana and 8th Missouri regiments awakens a similar *esprit de corps* in the newer regiments constituting the division, and their superiority is gaining them renown and confidence throughout the whole army."[10] Wallace would fight his battles throughout the war in the tactical style of the Zouaves. The skills necessary to accomplish this were daily honed on the drill field and then demonstrated with great success at Romney.[11]

On the other hand, in initiating and carrying through the Romp to Romney, Wallace may have been able to glean a vague pretense for his actions from his orders but little else. On June 6, his commanding officer, Maj. Gen. Robert Patterson, a veteran of the War of 1812 and the Mexican War, instructed his new subordinate to halt "your forces at Cumberland . . . and there to await further orders." Apparently, Patterson was not quite sure when such orders would be forthcoming. Thus he instructed Wallace to spend the time "securing the bridges over the Potomac and Green Spring Run. . . . Gather as much reliable information as possible of the disposition of the people of Maryland and Virginia in that vicinity and extend your inquiries by secret agents south into Virginia and east along the lines of the Baltimore and Ohio Railroad." Patterson encouraged Wallace to "Let the inhabitants feel you are in their midst as friends and protectors." The last part of Patterson's order gave Wallace all the pretense he wanted to justify his surprise march on Romney. "Should you gain information of the gathering, for offensive movements, of armed bodies of men not too powerful to be overcome by a force you can safely detach," Patterson ordered, "capture or rout them by surprise, if possible, and seize and hold as prisoners of war all parties injuring the lines of communication, or arrayed or plotting against the peace of the United States."[12]

When he issued this order, Patterson had yet to meet personally with his young subordinate. He surely was not suggesting that Wallace take his presumably green and untested regiment on a midnight mountain excursion deep into enemy territory to confront a Rebel force of unknown strength and size. Patterson certainly did not envision that his order authorized Wallace to lead his men some forty or so miles from their base camp at Cumberland in the dead of night, cutting themselves off from the railroad, their only line of communication, march them further into the interior of enemy territory, surprise and defeat the enemy, and return, all within less than two days. It is not recorded just exactly how Patterson responded when he received news that Wallace had done just that.

Wallace was one step ahead of the veteran Patterson. The same day he returned to Cumberland, he submitted his report, blatantly reminding Patterson that "I have already received your approval of my enterprise, for which I am very much obliged."[13] The correspondent for the *Philadelphia Inquirer* helped to defuse the potential destructive force of such a statement, noting in his June 14 dispatch that in the "lightning dash" to Romney, "Gen. Patterson directed Col. Wallace." The *Inquirer* repeated this assertion in its June 17 issue. Two weeks later, Wallace set the record straight in a letter to Lane: "The Romney fight was my own. I can say nothing about that, except that the Southern accounts of it have given me great amusement, hardly less than the frequent assertions which have fallen under my eye that it was ordered by Gen. Patterson, then by Gen. [Thomas A.] Morris. The whole thing was of my own planning and ordering."[14] Wallace had taken an extraordinary gamble and it had paid off magnificently. Both before and after the midnight romp, Wallace probably gave little thought to the consequences should that gamble have failed.

Romney had been a brilliant tactical maneuver. The fact that it netted significantly fewer prisoners and supplies than anticipated can be attributed to its one glaring weakness. It was based upon faulty, almost nonexistent intelligence. Nevertheless, Wallace had acted. After all, it was the Rebels who had unceremoniously run away as soon as the Hoosiers broke across the bridge at the base of the town. As the correspondent for the *Wisconsin Patriot* explained, "Upon reaching Romney, the Zouaves advanced at 'double-quick' time and the Secessionists never stopped for anything, but whiled [*sic*] 'faced about,' and by their actions invited the Indianians [*sic*] to a foot-race, and were sufficiently careful to take a long start."[15] Without question, Wallace would have followed them. But Wallace also knew the teachings of Dennis Hart Mahan. Without cavalry, pursuit was impossible. Had Wallace possessed solid intelligence about the inconsequential number of Confederate soldiers and the paucity of Rebel materials and supplies at Romney, arguably he might have hesitated to risk so much for so little. On the other hand, he might not. The element of surprise so valued by Mahan was entirely his to control. Patterson's orders in his mind at least gave him authority to maneuver. Patently, Romney, on the south branch of the Potomac River was "in the vicinity" of the Baltimore and Ohio Railroad. The prize beckoned and without too much thought, the colonel of the 11th Indiana seized it.

Romney was Wallace's first action toward the attainment of glory and honor for his men, for his state, for his country, and most assuredly for himself. On June 17, the correspondent for the *Philadelphia Inquirer* praised the men of the 11th Indiana, noting that Romney had been achieved "in the most effective manner," consistent with "the way thorough-bred soldiers do their work." On June 21, the *New York Herald* correspondent opined, "without exception, he [Wallace] has the finest looking regiment of men I ever saw; they are evidently what is claimed for them—a regiment of picked men; they are completely uniformed and equipped, and under the most perfect drill and discipline. The influence of the Colonel over them is almost unbounded—where he leads they will follow." Calling Romney "one of the most extraordinary feats of our campaign," the *New York Tribune* attributed its significance to "the crack Western regiment, 11th Indiana (Zouaves), Col. Lewis Wallace commanding." Last, on June 17, the *Philadelphia Inquirer* maintained that though directed to Romney by Patterson, Wallace demonstrated "discretionary power in a manner that stamps him as a field officer of marked ability."[16] Before Romney, relatively few people, particularly in the East, had ever heard the name Lew Wallace. After Romney, the Northern press was doing more than its fair share to alter and increase their level of awareness.

With its element of surprise, the Romp to Romney produced a significant unintended consequence. Gen. Joseph E. Johnston reported to the

Confederate War Department that upon first hearing of activity at Romney, he believed "two thousand Federal troops supposed to be the vanguard of McClellan's army" had occupied the town. Johnston informed Adj. Gen. Samuel Cooper that he had immediately dispatched two regiments under Col. A. P. Hill by train from Harpers Ferry to Winchester to "take the best position and best measures to check the advance of the enemy." Then, on June 15 with Romney still in the forefront of his tactical plans, Johnston ordered his entire army, wagons, ordinance, and supplies evacuated from Harpers Ferry and concentrated at Winchester. For Johnston and the Confederacy, it was an unequal exchange of real estate.[17]

The war correspondent for the *New York Herald* had praised Wallace for training his men well, commending in particular their "drill and discipline." On June 27, Wallace dispatched a squad of thirteen men from the 11th Indiana toward Frankfort, Virginia, to gather information on Rebel strength and intentions. This venture would put those skills to the test. Unexpectedly, Wallace's scouts happened upon a contingent of forty-one Confederate cavalry. A running skirmish ensued. Wallace's men killed eight Rebels and captured seventeen enemy horses. The Confederates managed to wound only one Indiana trooper. The fighting broke off and this seemingly innocuous affair appeared at an end. As the Hoosiers approached their camp at Cumberland, however, the Rebels, now reinforced to seventy-five in number, drove them onto a small island near the mouth of Patterson Creek. By the time this round of the conflict was over, an additional twenty-three Rebels lay dead while a number had been captured. The Confederates succeeded in killing only the Union soldier they had wounded earlier in the day.

Serving as his own publicist and propagandist, Wallace filed his official report with General Patterson on the action at Kelly's Island. He described the skirmish as "one of the boldest, most desperate, and fortunate on record, abounding with instances on the part of my scouts of the rarest coolness, skill and courage." Recognizing the value of propaganda in wartime, Wallace did not hesitate to suggest that the Union soldier who was killed that day had been "brutally murdered by his captors." Several war correspondents seized upon the substance and tone of Wallace's report, embellishing it according to their tastes. Within a week, the correspondent for the *New York Herald* reproduced Wallace's dispatch to Patterson nearly verbatim, labeling the skirmish at Kelly's Island "a very brilliant affair." The *Herald* concluded that "the indignation of the

Zouaves at the probable brutal murder of their comrade was almost unbounded, and it was with difficulty that Colonel Wallace could restrain some of the company to which the deceased man belonged from wreaking their vengeance on the prisoners."[18]

On July 8, the *Philadelphia Inquirer* intensified the rhetoric characterizing the Kelly's Island affair as "one of the most bloody and desperate fights we have ever heard of. The men of the 11th Indiana who fought that day entered into the deadly strife with the heroism of the Spartans of old." The *Inquirer* went on to note that the action "was a daring achievement of Col. Wallace's men, and reflects undying honor upon all those immediately engaged. No man doubts the valor of the Eleventh Indiana." Publishing a slightly less dramatic account on the front page of its June 29 edition, the *New York Times* duplicated the major portions of Wallace's Kelly Island report while identifying it as a "sanguinary skirmish" that produced a "brilliant victory." Wallace and his 11th Indiana Zouaves were rapidly gaining a national reputation.[19]

On June 29, the *Wisconsin Patriot* attributed a quote to Wallace concerning the actions of his men at Kelly's Island, noting "Colonel Wallace says: 'My boys are entitled to all the honor; they won it bravely; let them have it. They have not forgotten Buena Vista'." Soon thereafter, Wallace wrote again to Lane, proudly pronouncing that "my report of the skirmish on Kelly's Island, near Patterson's Creek, is not only true, but, in fact, too lightly colored." Wallace obviously relished all the moments of glory he was fast accumulating.[20]

Wallace was not finished with Kelly's Island. On June 27, the same day he described the incident to Patterson, he ventured outside the military chain of command. On his own initiative, he sent a slightly more sanitized version of the report to Maj. Gen. George B. McClellan, commander of the Department of the Ohio. As with Patterson, Wallace included a rhetorical flourish at the end, suggesting to McClellan "the report of the skirmish sounds like fiction, but it is not exaggerated. The fight was really one of the most desperate on record, and abounds with instances of wonderful daring and coolness." Regardless of his motives for his correspondence directly with McClellan, Wallace had engaged in a course of conduct that to a professional soldier was unthinkable. He had demonstrated that the chain of command meant little to him, particularly in those instances where the mere act of observing the customs, traditions, and dictates of the chain limited his personal ambition.[21]

Wallace's officious attempt at self-adulation did not seem to bother McClellan. As the commander of all Union forces in Maryland and western Virginia, McClellan could have censured Wallace for insubordination. On this occasion, Wallace was fortunate as McClellan chose to ignore Wallace's breach of military etiquette. In fact, later that same day, McClellan sent a dispatch to Lt. Gen. Winfield Scott in which he noted "Wallace had a very handsome skirmish near there [Cumberland] yesterday, killing seventeen." The next day, continuing to be impressed with his newfound Hoosier colonel, McClellan sent another telegram to Scott, stating "the following dispatch [June 27] from Colonel Wallace is so gratifying, that I send it to you entire."[22] Wallace, the civilian, amateur soldier, had gambled once more. He had ignored the professional bias the military had for its procedures. This time he reaped extraordinary dividends. He had successfully brought the name of the 11th Indiana Zouaves and its colonel to the immediate attention of the two most influential and powerful men in the Union army at that time. Both Scott and McClellan had endorsed Wallace's actions.

At Romney, for a supposedly untried amateur, Wallace demonstrated an advanced degree of military thinking and skills. At Kelly's Island, his men proved that Wallace had drilled and trained them well. One of the West Point textbooks that Wallace had asked Davis to obtain was Dennis Hart Mahan's *An Elementary Treatise on Advanced-Guard, Out-Post, and Detachment Service of Troops and the Manner of Posting and Handling Them in the Presence of an Enemy*, more commonly referred to simply as *Outpost*. Based upon a decade and a half of research and instruction at West Point, Mahan had written this treatise in 1847. Until his forced retirement from West Point and premature death in 1871, Mahan continued to lecture on its axioms almost religiously.

Mahan was one of America's foremost interpreters of Baron Antoine Henri Jomini and his treatises on Napoleon and other continental European wars of the eighteenth and early nineteenth centuries. "In looking back on military history," Mahan wrote, "it may with truth be said that nothing is impossible to a determined will." Wallace had little difficulty identifying personally with that particular statement. Mahan believed that "a determined will" consistently recognized and applied certain immutable principles of war. All winning strategic campaigns and the tactical maneuvers incident thereto were based upon the successful application of concepts such as "speed," "mobility," "surprise," "pursuit," "initiative," "activity," "audacity," and "vigor." Having no cavalry at Romney, Wallace could not implement "pursuit." Otherwise, in western Virginia, Wallace had successfully invoked all these concepts. Furthermore, Mahan persistently advocated an earlier commander's dictum that "military success resided in the legs of the soldiers." He labeled this concept "celerity of movement." Mahan preached that "no great success can be hoped for in war in which rapid movements do not enter as an element." Celerity and pursuit made for complete victory in battle. "If Fortune is on the side of the heavy battalions," Mahan concluded, "she also frequently grants her favors to superior activity and audacity."[23]

Molding his Romney experience around the principles of celerity, surprise, and audacity, Wallace demonstrated that he had a clear understanding of Mahan's teachings. It was equally obvious that Wallace had been incredibly lucky at Romney. Mahan accepted this as well. "In war," he wrote, "as in every other art based upon settled principles, there are exceptions to all general rules. It is in discerning these cases that the talent of the general is shown."[24] Even though he had made his literary acquaintance only months before the war broke out, Wallace was rapidly exhibiting a kinship with Mahan.

Interestingly, many Union military leaders, trained professionally at West Point before the war and thus direct beneficiaries of Mahan's classroom observations, often demonstrated how quickly they forgot the teachings of one of the masters. During the first years of the war, officers like McClellan, Buell, and Halleck, all West Point graduates, frequently displayed a pronounced failure to implement what Mahan had taught them about "a determined will" and "celerity of movement." Inertia was often their watchword and response. A fog of apprehension and innate conservatism frequently stifled their initiative.[25]

In the immediate aftermath of Romney, Wallace again demonstrated that fatal character flaw that in time drastically shortened his military career. Although on this occasion he did not specifically disobey any orders, he certainly let others know what he thought about those orders and the men who issued them. The day after returning to Cumberland, Wallace learned that the Rebels, about three thousand strong, had regrouped at Romney with the intention of advancing on Cumberland. Though not true, the information appeared credible and thus portended a genuine threat. On June 15, Patterson telegraphed Brev. Maj. Gen. George Cadwalader to send reinforcements only "in the direction of Cumberland," ostensibly in support of Wallace, although "no risk, however, must be run to endanger your own force lest you be cut up in detail."[26] Knowing the contents of this order to Cadwalader, Wallace informed Patterson that he was prepared to evacuate Cumberland but only pursuant to a direct order to do so. Wallace wanted to fight.

In a dispatch to Patterson's adjutant, Maj. Fitz-John Porter, Wallace stated that his men were dangerously low on ammunition. Unless resupplied very soon, the 11th Indiana could not hope to stand against the Rebels. As he would do to his detriment so often in the future, Wallace then ventured well beyond the pale of military respectability. He declared to Porter that this increasingly desperate situation was not his fault. He explained that he had contacted his immediate commanding officer, Brigadier General Morris, requesting sword-bayonets and rifle cartridges. Morris had not responded. Wallace made no attempt to ascertain if Morris had made his decision because he was low on ammunition also or because he had concluded that resupplying Wallace was contrary to Patterson's orders. It really made no difference to Wallace which of these reasons was true. Regardless of the fact he was a superior officer, Morris deserved to be criticized. Wallace would oblige. "General Morris has acted very strangely towards me," Wallace protested, "I would fight them in some of the mountain passes on the other side of the river if he had done the fair thing. It is useless to depend for help on him or General McClellan." Wallace had some remarkable talents. Remaining silent when it was in his best interests to do so was not one of them. At a totally inopportune moment with one field dispatch, Wallace had verbally assaulted three members of the professional West Point establishment [Morris, class of 1834; Porter, class of 1845; and McClellan, class of 1846] and in a rather bizarre manner questioned the competence of two of them.[27]

During his three months in the Eastern Theater, Wallace had played upon the "Remember Buena Vista" theme regularly. The day after arriving in Cumberland, the same being the day before the Romp to Romney, Wallace wrote to Patterson "I hope you will excuse it, but I cannot help concluding with an earnest expression of the hope that you will not forget me when you advance upon Harpers Ferry and Richmond, if such be your aim. . . . I hail from a State which, since Buena Vista, has been under a cloud of slander. Do not, I beg you, withhold from us the only chance we may ever have to show the people of the East that Indiana has as much courage as loyalty, and can and will fight to the last man to crush out treason and vindicate her lost honor." A week later, still at Cumberland but with Romney safely behind him, Wallace telegraphed Porter imploring him to "Beg the general [Patterson] for God's sake not to leave me behind when he marches. I want to show him how we can fight." On July 10, Wallace wrote to Susan that a major battle was looming, involving perhaps as many as 35,000 men on each side. To participate in such an event was a lifetime dream. "The whole thing," Wallace told Susan, "is very exciting, as you can doubtless imagine." It would be the ultimate opportunity to "remember" as well.

Exciting indeed, but Wallace missed the First Battle of Bull Run through no fault of his own. During early July 1861, both Union and Confederate forces were maneuvering toward a confrontation that ultimately took place on Bull Run Creek in northern Virginia. On July 5, Wallace and the 11th Indiana left Cumberland to join Patterson at Martinsburg, Virginia [now West Virginia]. Patterson was doing his best to coordinate his troop movements with those of McClellan and Brig. Gen. Irvin McDowell. On July 12, Patterson reiterated his July 9 request to Lt. Gen. Scott that he be permitted to base his line of operations anchored on Charlestown and extended toward Harpers Ferry. Scott ordered Patterson to establish such a line. Then, the next day, Scott backtracked, ordering Patterson to focus on keeping the enemy at Winchester. Thus, on July 14, Patterson advanced on Bunker Hill, shifting further away from Bull Run.

Amid the confusion born of inexperience in the tactical maneuvering of large numbers of troops and being compelled to fathom when, and if, McClellan might move and where, Patterson had another problem, uniquely his own. His army of 18,000 Union soldiers was filled with Lincoln's original three-month state volunteers. Patterson reported that these soldiers were fast becoming "very restless at the prospect of being retained over their time." Most of the volunteers had been mustered into service between April 15 and April 30 and their muster-out dates, though staggered over a two-week period, were fast approaching. Neither Patterson nor the War Department had a solution for this problem. As Patterson informed Scott on July 18, "some regiments have been given warning not to serve an hour over time. To attack under such circumstances against the greatly superior force at Winchester is most hazardous." In the end, Johnston evaded and eluded Patterson, transferring his army on July 19–20 from Winchester over the Manassas Gap Railroad to Bull Run where it joined Confederate forces under Gen. P. G. T. Beauregard.[28] Excessively worried about the expiration of service time for the original three-month

Portrait of Wallace as a Zouave Colonel. (*Frank Leslie's Illustrated Newspaper* [August 10, 1861])

volunteers, Patterson allowed himself to believe Johnston was still at Winchester. Under prevailing conditions, Patterson believed he was incapable of attacking Johnston, but, by proper maneuvering, he might just keep Johnston where he was. To his very great displeasure, Wallace was scouting a nearly empty Winchester when Union and Confederate forces clashed at First Bull Run. Wallace had been left behind for the first big battle.

On the other hand, this time greatly to his pleasure, Wallace and his men once again became national celebrities. On August 10, 1861, a sketched portrait of Wallace appeared in national syndication in *Frank Leslie's Illustrated Newspaper*. The "Special Artist accompanying Major-General McClellan's command" pictured Wallace astride a magnificent charger decked out in all his Zouave military finery, including pantaloons, blouse, and kepi, surrounded by members of his staff, most of whom were similarly attired. In the same issue, an unnamed correspondent for *Frank Leslie* wrote three paragraphs of unstinted praise for Wallace and his Zouaves.

To date, Wallace had demonstrated "gallant, daring, yet prudent leadership." Under his command, the Eleventh Indiana had advanced, "acting offensively with gallantry and success and maintaining itself against all the efforts of the enemy in a difficult and dangerous country." The correspondent then enunciated a theme that would be repeated often about Wallace. "Colonel Lewis Wallace is loved by his officers—a fine body of brave gentlemen—and by his men to a point of devotion; and it is little to say that they would follow wherever he led, no matter what lay before them. He is the personification of the bold and enterprising soldier, perfectly fitted in the position he occupies." Wallace, the correspondent noted, had a "frank, earnest manner," combined with a "warm-hearted impulsiveness," all designed to "endear" him to his men and simultaneously "win their perfect obedience and respect."[29]

Just three weeks earlier, following Romney and Kelly's Island, the 11th Indiana had received another round of national publicity through a series of photographs in *Harper's Weekly.* These showed the men of the 11th Indiana in various scenes of camp life, drill, gymnastics, and skirmishing, likewise dressed in their Zouave uniforms. Not wishing to overlook their handsome and energetic leader, the caption accompanying these pictures identified the men as "the Eleventh Indiana Zouaves Colonel Lewis Wallace, a regiment which is likely to make a name for itself in the present war." The national press had served the public with two examples of a fledgling military hero. Wallace was on the ascent. On September 3, 1861, the U.S. Senate confirmed his first general's star and his meteoric rise.[30]

On July 23, two days after First Bull Run, Patterson published Special Orders No. 124. By this order, he dispatched the 11th Indiana to Hagerstown, Maryland, to board trains bound for Indianapolis and their mustering out as three-month volunteers. The remaining text of the order was music to the ears of the young Hoosier colonel. "The commanding general," Patterson stated, "parts with this gallant regiment with regret. It has earned a good name in action and sustained it in a patriotic manner by voluntarily tendering its services to remain in this command if in danger." Patterson had rendered to the army and his superiors both a professional evaluation of talent as well as a heartfelt expression of appreciation. Patterson was going nowhere. Already on July 19, two days before First Bull Run, the War Department had notified him that he was to be discharged from active duty and that the army no longer required the services of this sixty-nine-year-old veteran warrior.[31]

THE ELEVENTH INDIANA REGIMENT OF ZOUAVES, COLONEL L. WALLACE.

CAMP RECREATIONS.—FROM TATTOO TILL TAPS.

CAMP RECREATIONS.—JUST AFTER DRESS PARADE.

DEPLOYED AS SKIRMISHERS.—[FROM A PHOTOGRAPH.]

RALLYING BY FOURS.—[FROM A PHOTOGRAPH.]

FORMED IN HOLLOW SQUARE.—[FROM A PHOTOGRAPH.]

11th Indiana Volunteers (Zouaves), camp life and training. (*Harper's Weekly* [July 20, 1861])

Special Orders No. 124 was also an implicit recognition that Patterson had erred in the handling of his command before Winchester and perhaps, thereby, denied Wallace a golden opportunity for honor. Unlike the day several weeks earlier when he had complained bitterly that two superior officers had thwarted an opportunity for him because neither would supply him with the ammunition required to confront the enemy, this time Wallace said nothing. In this light, perhaps Special Orders No. 124 did nothing more than save Patterson from having to bear the brunt of a Wallace-style verbal onslaught. In the year ahead, however, Wallace did not hesitate to question the competency and sometimes the character of those he believed had personally let him down, thereby leaving him behind.

The 11th Indiana arrived in Indianapolis on July 29 to a "most enthuseastic [*sic*] reception—mothers wifes [*sic*] friends lovers all fell into the arms of the Soldiers. All order was given up to these indiscriminate salutations."[32] The men were mustered out as three-month volunteers on August 2. During the re-recruitment process, Wallace had an opportunity to combine his considerable skills as an orator with an emotional appeal based upon the one thing that set his men apart from the vast majority of Union soldiers at the time. They had proven their skill and worth as trained Zouave fighters. On August 14, Wallace wrote to the Evansville *Journal* that Union general Nathaniel Lyons had been killed at a battle "fought near Springfield, Missouri," at Wilson's Creek. Wallace announced that Union forces were then in "full retreat." General Frémont had called upon Governor Morton to send "all the available forces of Indiana." It was time for his Zouaves to act. "Return to camp," Wallace proclaimed in his letter to the *Journal.* "I will give you back your old rifles, your old officers, and the ever glorious flags. The Eleventh awaits you—your country calls you louder than ever." He concluded, "let us make a new renown on the banks of the Mississippi. Fill up the camp, Zouaves, and I will march you to-morrow." The plea was printed by the *Journal* on August 15. It was reprinted verbatim by the *Philadelphia Inquirer* four days later. Wallace and his Zouaves continued to be a national phenomenon. The *Inquirer* said Wallace's "bulletin to the Indiana Zouaves" had "the Napoleonic ring."[33]

Nearly to the man, the ninety-day volunteers were mustered back into service as three-year volunteers on August 31, 1861. Colonel Wallace retained command of the regiment.[34] Originally, Wallace had anticipated receiving orders to join McClellan's command in western Virginia. Union defeat at Wilson's Creek and the death of Lyons changed everything. As late as September 6, the situation remained in doubt. Calvin Fletcher, a leading Indianapolis merchant, wrote in his diary that day that Wallace's original orders were countermanded at the train depot and "it is a matter of doubt whether they go East or West."[35]

Wallace and the Zouaves of the 11th Indiana went to St. Louis. He still yearned for his first big fight, but he had succeeded in gaining a great deal of honor and glory for his regiment, his state, his country, and himself. Furthermore, and of great importance to Wallace, he and his men had vindicated the honor of Indiana. Despite not having been at Bull Run, Wallace had fought and led in the East in such a way that Buena Vista had been remembered.

CHAPTER THREE

Paducah

Once in St. Louis, Wallace attempted to announce the 11th Indiana's arrival to Maj. Gen. John Charles Frémont, Union commander of the Department of the Missouri. At Frémont's headquarters, "politicians, not soldiers" kept him waiting. Told twice in one day that the famous Pathfinder was "too busy" to see him, an irritated Wallace quickly found the nearest telegraph office. He "begged Governor Morton to have [him], if possible, ordered to Cairo or Paducah."[1] On September 10, 1861, with new orders in hand, Wallace led his regiment to Paducah, Kentucky, on the south bank of the Ohio River at the mouth of the Tennessee River. Three days later, he learned that President Lincoln had submitted his name for promotion to Brigadier General of Volunteers. The U.S. Senate had confirmed. So far, Wallace had done quite well for his men, his state, his country and himself. He believed this was just the beginning. He would not and could not rest. Forced inactivity remained his greatest enemy.

Brig. Gen. Ulysses S. Grant and the Union army first entered Paducah on September 6, 1861. With this uncontested act, Grant obliterated the myth of Kentucky's neutrality just as Confederate generals Leonidas Polk and Gideon Pillow had done four days earlier at Columbus in northwest Kentucky on the east bank of the Mississippi River. Grant immediately issued a proclamation, informing the citizens of Paducah that he had come neither to "injure" nor "annoy" them, but to "protect" them "as your friend and fellow-citizen." As the military representative of the Lincoln administration, Grant pledged that each individual citizen could follow his "usual avocations without fear or hindrance. The strong arm of the Government is here to protect its friends, and to punish only its enemies." When the loyal people of Paducah were once more able to defend themselves and "to maintain the authority of your Government and protect the rights of all its loyal citizens," Grant vowed to withdraw federal troops.[2]

Before returning to headquarters at Cairo, Illinois, Grant instructed Brig. Gen. Eleazer A. Paine, his newly appointed commander at Paducah, "to take special care and precaution that no harm is done to inoffensive citizens. That the soldiers shall not enter any private dwellings nor make any searches unless by your orders. . . . Exercise the strictest discipline against any soldier who shall insult citizens or engage in plundering private property."[3] In his proclamation and his orders to Paine, Grant clearly delineated Lincoln's initial policies for occupation of a Southern city and for dealing with Southern white civilians and their property. Wallace started for the West the same day Grant issued his proclamation. Upon his arrival, he discovered he already had ample grounds to disagree with one of the major wartime policies of the Lincoln administration and the military arm of that administration upon which enforcement of the policy fell. He would find himself at odds with any superior officer whose task it was to enforce that policy.

On August 16, while awaiting the formal mustering-in of the 11th Indiana as three-year volunteers, Wallace had written an open letter to the "Democrats of Johnson County, Indiana." lending his considerable talents to recruiting Hoosiers to embrace the Union war effort. He was intent upon destroying both the idea and the reality of Southern secession. He had little sympathy and even less love for the wayward Southerner. "I was for compromise," he insisted, "but the guns of Sumter awoke me from that folly. Compromise is impossible while the blood of Manassas cries from the ground, and two hundred thousand armed traitors sleep behind those gory intrenchments in Virginia."[4]

"The business of Democrats," Wallace proudly proclaimed, "is to put down this rebellion, not by compromise, for that is impossible, but by arms, which demands every man's aid." To advocate peace or even leniency at this moment led only to "a divided Union, a broken Government, a powerless people, submission to JEFF. DAVIS, a long farewell to popular government and ages of mocking at our fathers for having been such impracticable dreamers." Make no mistake, Wallace exhorted those who heard or read his words, "this contest is not for negro liberty, but for our liberty, inseparable from our Constitution and Union, not for the subjugation of the South, but for its liberties and the enforcement of the laws of the fathers; it is for peace under circumstances that will make peace desirable—the rebellion expiated, the Government vindicated, and the quiet of the future guaranteed by example of what awaits treason." Wallace urged the Democrats of Johnson County to lay aside petty party politics and to unite under the banner of Union against Disunion, passionately concluding, "Let us never surrender. Let us fight sooner, giving all we have of life and treasure to the holy war, thanking God that our days were given us for purposes so glorious. . . . Never say peace while treason flies a flag or marshals an army."[5]

Wallace's feelings toward the Southern secessionist were clearly more intense and vindictive than those expressed by Grant in his proclamation. The Lincoln administration believed a policy of "conciliation" with its enemies offered the best opportunity for the restoration of peace and the Union.[6] Wallace's approach to resolving the same problem came closer to "humiliation." A confrontation between the Hoosier general and any member of the military establishment acting to enforce Lincoln's policies seemed quite likely. This clash of ideas and personalities came about less than three months after his arrival in Paducah during the so-called Woolfolk affair. For Wallace, in particular, this incident also occurred because of the boredom and anxiety created by forced inactivity.

At Paducah, Wallace quickly settled into the routine of camp life. On October 27, he described what he called a "normal day" in a letter to Susan. "I get up about 6:30 in the morning," he wrote. "Breakfast at 7, attend guard mounting at 8. Look over the morning reports, and sign my Brigade return and forward it at 10. Till 12 I am occupied issuing orders for the day. Dine at 1. Have officers school till three. At 3:30 mount old John, the best horse in the service and drill the 23rd Ind. Reg't. until 5. After that, bed time, a very uncertain hour, sometimes 9, sometimes 2 o'clock—nothing except Plutarch, always good company, and officers visiting me." Lengthy drill time, regular officers' meetings, schooling, and quiet time for reading, usually military history, characterized each day in camp. On November 9, he told Susan more about his new brigade, consisting of the 11th Indiana and a new regiment fast becoming a second favorite, Col. Morgan L. Smith's Zouave-trained 8th Missouri Volunteers. "Today," Lew wrote, the11th Indiana and 8th Missouri "looked and maneuvered magnificently. If ever they have the luck to be set before the enemy, the butters [Butternuts] will be swept out of the way like chaff." He concluded with a sharp criticism of one prevailing practice, noting "that one of the incomprehensibilities of the management of this war is, that the best regiments are held back and the greenest ones put forward."[7]

In a very short time, Union occupation of Paducah became filled with routine, too much excess time, too much gossip, and way too much boredom. Seeking to offset all this, Wallace found comfort in re-reading Plutarch's *Lives,* which he characterized for Susan as "legitimate military reading, taking on fresh color and warmth read in the face of the enemy we long to meet." He wrote that he attempted to keep busy drilling his men and leading his brigade. He was keenly aware that he and his men could engage in such activities only up to a point. He feared his life in the army was going nowhere. There was no room to romp to anywhere. There were no sufficient outlets for pent-up energy and anxiety. Even Plutarch had its limits. [8]

"Another week gone," a restless Wallace complained to Susan on September 22, "two that I have been here—two more of war, and no glimmer of peace ahead. Nothing to do but grin and bear it. Let us be patient. It is very hard to be so, tho'. Defeat follows defeat—mismanagement after mismanagement."[9] Two months later, a combination of inactivity, boredom, patriotism, and intense frustration born of a perception that no one seemed in a hurry to do anything to defeat the enemy drove Wallace to participate in an act of questionable military propriety. It fell to Wallace's commanding officer at Paducah, Brig. Gen. Charles F. Smith, to interpret Wallace's act in terms of Grant's proclamation and his orders to Paine. It became Smith's responsibility to determine just how improper Wallace's conduct was that day.

On November 25, elements of the 11th Indiana marched past the Paducah home of Robert Owens Woolfolk, a Southern sympathizer. As he had apparently done on several prior occasions, Woolfolk chose that moment to unfurl a Confederate flag from a second story window of his home and loudly celebrate the name of Jefferson Davis. On this day, however, Woolfolk made his display in the presence of men who had not experienced much excitement since their arrival in camp over two months earlier. Moreover, these men were not only fighting for the Union against the Confederacy but they had also knelt in the Capital Square in Indianapolis, raised their right hands, and vowed to Remember Buena Vista. The men of the 11th believed the man Woolfolk so vociferously praised had been responsible for creating the unjustifiable stain upon the character and integrity of the Hoosier state.

According to most accounts from the war correspondents, Wallace's men, without Wallace's presence or knowledge, immediately reported the Confederate flag insult to General Smith. The offended men of the 11th Indiana urged Smith to order Woolfolk to take down the Rebel Stars and

Bars. Smith, declining to become involved, rejected the request. He chose rather to uphold the spirit of Grant's proclamation embodied in Grant's orders to Paine to avoid harming "inoffensive citizens" and to respect their private property. Grant had been clear that Union soldiers were not to enter private homes "unless by your [Paine's] orders" and that "the strictest discipline" was to be enforced against any Union soldier who was found to be "engaged in plundering private property."

After Smith made his decision, the same soldiers of the 11th appealed to Wallace, now their brigade commander, to correct the insult. It is unclear whether these men first told Wallace of their impromptu meeting with Smith and what, to them, was its unfortunate outcome. Either way, it was still Wallace's responsibility to consult with Smith. After receiving their appeal and without further discussion with Smith, Wallace personally led his men back to Woolfolk's home. He demanded the Confederate flag be removed. Woolfolk refused. Wallace immediately ordered a squad of the 11th to enter the private home of the Confederate sympathizer, proceed directly to the second floor window, remove the Confederate Stars and Bars and hoist the Stars and Stripes. This was done with no further damage to Woolfolk's person or property.

Capt. Thomas J. Newsham, Smith's assistant adjutant general, arriving on the scene, loudly criticized the Hoosiers' actions. A fistfight between Newsham and Capt. Fred Knefler, Wallace's assistant adjutant general, ensued. Wallace took no part in the fray, which did not last long and apparently did little physical harm or damage to either participant. At the same time, Wallace made no effort to stop the fisticuffs.[10] Most reports gave Knefler the victory. No charges were filed by either man and at least for that night, the flag of the United States flew proudly over the Rebel abode. Upon being advised of what had transpired at Woolfolk's private home, Smith was horrified.

Smith issued General Orders No. 36 two days later. He labeled the matter "a proceeding of a mutinous character," an act by which its participants "have subjected themselves to prosecution under the Articles of War." Smith deplored this "mortifying" occurrence, the first that had happened under his command in his thirty-seven years of military service. Smith was certain the entire affair constituted a serious breach of military discipline. "Unarmed citizens" in wartime were due a certain degree of "moderation" and "forebearance [*sic*]." Encouraging the men under his command to guard against excessive "enthusiasm for the flag," Smith warned that "property, liberty, government—every thing [*sic*] precious—has been committed to the army. When the army supplants the commander, or turns from the path of order, or bursts the bands of discipline, it makes itself a thing of terror and ruin." Smith announced that he intended to let the matter lie without further investigation if only for the sake of those who had been engaged in it. Those men must acknowledge at least to themselves and exhibit through their future conduct a genuine recognition that their actions against Woolfolk had threatened "the observance of law." Smith was aware his actions might subject him to criticism from those above him. He believed he could withstand such personal censure so long as the participants learned from their mistakes.[11]

The Northern press was reluctant to let the matter die. To that end, the correspondent for the Evansville (Indiana) *Journal* cast Wallace in the role of agitator, if not the instigator, of the Woolfolk incident, reporting, "After dress parade, General Wallace went, with the Eleventh Indiana, to carry into execution the designs of the soldiers." At the same time, however, the *Journal* applauded Wallace for strong leadership. At what may well have been a crucial moment, Wallace promptly acted to restrain his men's enthusiasm once Woolfolk and the Rebel flag had been put in their proper place. "The boys were in a frenzy of excitement," the *Journal* reported, "[a]fter the ceremony was performed, General Wallace elevated himself upon the fence and said:—'Boys, the flag is floating now; go to your quarters, boys; you have done your duty, now go back'." On the other hand, there were minority reports. The correspondent for the *Missouri Democrat* maintained that Wallace was in camp, in his tent, attending to his official duties, when three or four of his junior officers made the initial demand upon Woolfolk and then sought General Smith's assistance. The *Democrat* confirmed that Smith had refused the men's request. "The matter having been reported to General Wallace," the correspondent for the *Democrat* concluded, "he sent his aide-de-camp with a squad of men to order the traitorous flag to be taken in, and if Woolfolk refused, then to take it in, and erect the Stars and Stripes over the house." Thus, while Wallace ordered his men into Woolfolk's house to remove the flag if Woolfolk refused to take it down, it is doubtful, according to this report, that Wallace was personally present when this series of events occurred.[12]

For Wallace, the spirited patriotism of the moment transcended all else. Similarly, that emotion unduly excited and overly stimulated the imagination of many of the war correspondents. The men of the 8th Missouri, allegedly "headed by its officers," commandeered a fire engine and raced uptown toward Smith's quarters, which they would have "washed out" had Wallace not intervened. Pvt. Thomas Wise Durham, 11th Indiana, recalled almost fifty years later in his *Memoirs* that Smith ordered his "bodyguard" to arrest all offending members of the 11th Indiana.[13] According to Durham, upon hearing this order, "Wallace formed his regiment inline of battle and told the guards to tell General Smith that he would not allow any of his men to be arrested for tearing down a rebel flag and that he [Smith] would have to whip his [Wallace's] regiment before he could arrest them." Fortunately, such strong emotions quickly waned.

The daily routine and the boredom of camp life soon dissipated what the *Democrat* correspondent had labeled "the intense excitement." Undoubtedly, routine and boredom had been major causes of the incident in the first place. Even so, the *Democrat* concluded, "Wallace's insubordination is enthusiastically approved," by perhaps everyone save Smith.[14]

Smith had issued General Orders No. 36. The command structure of the army had reaffirmed Grant's proclamation to the people of Paducah. If Smith considered Wallace to have been insubordinate and to have breached military protocol, he had disposed of those issues in No. 36 without naming names. The incident had occurred; the press had enjoyed having its say; calm had been restored in Paducah; and Smith had done his young brigadier an immense favor. For reasons that he never made known, Smith chose neither to court-martial nor to censure Wallace publicly over the Woolfolk affair. Yet, two months earlier, Smith had addressed Wallace with words that made such a lasting impression upon Wallace that he quoted them from memory in his *Autobiography*[15]: "Obedience," Smith stressed, "being the soul of military organization, I hold it the beginning and the end of duty. It is the rein in hand by which the superior does his driving. . . . Genius is determinable by the manner of obedience." Even though Wallace may have demonstrated leadership in acting to end the near-riotous conduct of some members of the 11th Indiana, he had failed to obey Grant's duly-issued order and Smith's decision to enforce it. Ordinarily, that act would have cost the offending officer dearly. Smith chose to say and do nothing beyond issuing General Orders No. 36.

Wallace's participation in the Woolfolk incident demonstrated once again that he could and would have problems with those who exercised authority over him or were critical of his actions, particularly when he disagreed with them.[16] He never refrained from saying exactly what was on his mind, often blaming others for troubles he had helped to create.[17] As he ordered his men to remove the offending Stars and Bars from Woolfolk's window, he demonstrated that he could lead men in battle, but he could not follow. Most damning of all, he also confirmed he had no desire to change any of that. With General Orders No. 36, Smith gave Wallace ample opportunity to prove he could be a "team player." Wallace refused.[18] Not for the first time and certainly not for the last, Wallace chose a different path.

Ironically, the man who potentially had the most to lose from the Woolfolk affair was Smith. The writer for the *Chicago Tribune* accused him of "making an ass of himself." In support of his reporter's story, Joseph Medill, abolitionist, editor, and co-owner of the *Tribune*, wrote to Secretary of War Cameron on December 6 that "this man Smith is doubtlessly a secession sympathizer—if not worse." In addition, a correspondent, summarizing the Woolfolk affair to his readers of the Richmond, Virginia, *Dispatch* was certain that "Gen. Smith, right or wrong, has lost the confidence and respect of the troops under his direction." Seeking to bolster Confederate wartime morale, the *Dispatch* writer concluded that while Smith settled the Woolfolk affair with General Orders No. 36, the aftermath would "breed difficulties in that division of the army, which will completely impair its efficiency and usefulness, unless a new commanding general is assigned to it."[19]

The Indianapolis *Daily Journal* echoed the sentiments to replace Smith. The *Journal* writer began by characterizing General Orders No. 36 as "sensible" and exactly what "the good of the service demands." He believed "the Indiana boys were insubordinate, and by strict military law obnoxious [subject] to severe censure or punishment." On the other hand, "the provocation they received was so great that they may be fairly exonerated from blame." Smith's decision to let the matter die a natural death following the issuance of General Orders No. 36 was fashioned from his "good sense" and "moderation." The initial blame for the incident, however, rested squarely on his shoulders. He should have "prohibited Mr. Woolfolk from defying the loyal sentiments of his men." The consequences that flowed from that failure, according to the *Journal*, were "in no slight degree attributable to himself [Smith.]" "We are confident," the writer concluded, "that his transfer to some other command is a necessity."[20]

The hope, as expressed by the *Tribune*, Medill, the Richmond *Dispatch*, the Indianapolis *Journal*, and undoubtedly others, that the Woolfolk affair would lead to Smith's downfall was not fulfilled. Neither Grant, Halleck, nor Cameron spoke officially on the Woolfolk affair. From their respective points of view, it was as if Woolfolk had never happened. Inasmuch as Smith had been Commandant of Cadets during two of Grant's four years at West Point, it is doubtful Grant would have turned against his mentor over something like Woolfolk. Despite his proclamation to the citizens of Paducah he did not have strong views about or fully endorse Lincoln's policy of conciliation. Grant was not a political man and therefore he undoubtedly felt that General Orders No. 36 had resolved the matter. On the other hand, Grant was very fond of Smith. Thus, it is quite possible that Wallace's participation in the Woolfolk incident was one of the first, if not the first, in a series of black marks Grant came increasingly to recognize and chalk up against Wallace. For his part, having finalized the Woolfolk episode with the issuance of General Orders No. 36, Smith appeared to have forgotten altogether about this somewhat comic, albeit quite serious, affair.

Wallace had begun his stay at Paducah pleasantly surprised by his promotion to brigadier general. Acceptance of this new rank, however, meant he would no longer be directly in command of his beloved 11th Indiana. He turned to Smith for advice. He was grateful that Smith accommodated him. Smith, he wrote, treated him honestly and fairly and "I went back to camp from the lecture a much wiser man, and a very grateful one; and when the commission came it was accepted." With days of dull and repetitive camp life turning into weeks and months of forced inactivity leading up to and beyond the Woolfolk incident, Wallace forgot that Smith had based all his advice that night upon the rules indelibly printed in a book entitled *United States Army Regulations.*[21]

Whatever else Smith might have said or done, he believed in and lived those rules. Wallace never learned to play by army rules, neither that night in Smith's presence nor that day with Woolfolk nor seemingly ever. The concept of the chain of command was sacrosanct. Wallace rigorously observed the dictates of the chain, but only as he applied it to those beneath him. He never grasped that the essence of the chain of command was that it ran both ways. The Woolfolk incident turned Wallace in the one direction he never should have gone—against Smith. Prior to Paducah, and probably from the very beginning of his military experiences, Wallace had started a journey down a road to self-isolation, cutting himself off from the very people in the power structure he would need if he wanted to remain firmly near the top. At Paducah, Wallace had had the opportunity to reverse this course. He elected not to do so.

There was one pragmatic reason why Wallace should have regarded Smith as an ally as well as his commanding officer. Smith's 2nd Division consisted of two brigades. When Wallace became a brigadier general, he took command of the 2nd Brigade. Brig. Gen. Eleazer A. Paine, senior to Wallace in both date of commission and tenure of command, led the 1st Brigade. Although Paine was a West Point graduate, he had resigned from the service in 1840 just fifteen months after receiving his commission. He returned to service in 1861 as a civilian volunteer, recruiting the 9th Illinois regiment following Fort Sumter in response to Governor Richard Yates's call for volunteers. From the outset, Smith and Paine did not get along.

In early November 1861, Grant informed Smith he intended to take Belmont on the Missouri side of the Mississippi River. Grant ordered Smith to maneuver on the Kentucky side of the Mississippi in a feint to relieve pressure on Grant's attacking forces. On November 6, Smith directed Paine "to make a demonstration on Columbus, but not to attack it without special orders." The 1st Brigade was not to engage the enemy "unless pressed thereto from necessity." Although Paine's troops marched from and returned to Paducah without a skirmish, Smith was angry. He was convinced that "from the start," Paine intended to disobey his orders in an "attempt to gain notoriety without reference to the public interest or his plain duty as a soldier." On November 11, five days after Belmont and two weeks before the Woolfolk incident, Smith requested a court-martial for Paine. He charged that, seeking personal gain, Paine had disobeyed orders duly issued to him by his superior officer. Furthermore, Smith claimed that as Paine's troops returned to Paducah "several regiments straggled home in parties without the semblance of military array—a mere armed mob; and that the property of citizens was wantonly destroyed, and in some instances robbery by violence committed." Smith set these charges out in detail in General Orders No. 32. Although Wallace had not participated in any of this, he certainly was aware of the particulars as Smith announced that "this order [would] be read at the head of every company in the camp."[22]

Two weeks later when the Stars and Bars were being forcibly removed from Woolfolk's home, Paine gave Wallace "assurance of his co-operation."[23] Wallace knew Paine had just incurred Smith's wrath. Simple prudence dictated that Wallace should avoid Paine at all costs even if this meant agreeing with Smith on Woolfolk. There was no matter of honor or principle involved in disregarding Paine's overture. If Wallace did so, then Smith would see him as a team player. As a practical man, Wallace had no reason to join Paine as an object of Smith's anger. Grant was responsible for issuing the controversial proclamation and order in the first place. Smith was only attempting to enforce both. To stand in opposition to a fellow officer who might not have committed any wrongful act whatsoever would be disgraceful. Furthermore, if he had been at all attentive to what was going on around him, Wallace ought to have some notion of Grant's loyalty to and fondness for Smith. On the other hand, to join actively with Smith meant sacrificing personal honor. Wallace saw only dishonor in allowing the Rebel Woolfolk to trample so haughtily on the Stars and Stripes. In the final analysis, Wallace permitted patriotism to prevail over prudence and practicality. Wallace did not align himself with Smith in either the Paine or the Woolfolk matter. He was oblivious to any compelling reason to do so. He never comprehended how such situations as these might be turned to his benefit without sacrificing his principles. He was simply too candid and forthright for his own good. He had his standards, beliefs, and perhaps his altogether too romantic notions of things. These he would uphold to the very end. No one should dare to contradict him.

In a similar vein, Wallace never acknowledged, not even to Susan, that a senior officer had given him a prime assignment even when that assignment suggested that the officer regarded Wallace as a trustworthy and capable subordinate. For instance, Wallace never expressed appreciation for the fact that at the end of December 1861, Smith selected him, not Paine, to lead a reconnaissance toward Viola, Kentucky. Even though Paine was currently out of favor, he was still the senior brigadier and by right of military protocol should have been assigned this command. Wallace likewise appeared indifferent on January 28, 1862, when Grant chose him, not Paine, to take command of all troops then being assembled at Smithland, Kentucky. He manifested the same nonchalance on February 3, when both Grant and Smith designated him, not Paine, to participate in a journey up the Tennessee River into the heartland of the Confederacy. Paine, not Wallace, was left behind at Cairo to construct and improve existing fortifications.[24] In fact, Wallace took no unusual notice of Smith and Grant's participation in any of these three decisions. Virtually as a matter of course, Wallace deemed himself entitled to such compliments and commands. Thus, on such matters, he kept his own counsel with nary a nod of gratitude or appreciation to anyone. After all, he had earned them.

CHAPTER FOUR

The Twin Rivers Campaign and Fort Henry

The day after Wallace arrived in Paducah, Smith invited him to his headquarters. While poring over maps together, Smith told Wallace he thought the Union army's position at Paducah was "precarious" and that he was very concerned that Maj. Gen. Leonidas Polk might suddenly swoop down on Paducah from his fortress on the Mississippi River at Columbus. Then, Smith pointed to the Tennessee and Cumberland rivers and identified them as the "lines leading into the heart of the seceding states." Using the two rivers as a means of access northward, Polk could possibly catch Paducah in a pincer movement and prevail against the smaller force that Smith then commanded. After a time, Smith terminated any further discussion of the matter by "smoking silently, half bent over the map." Wallace reminisced in his *Autobiography* that he was "impressed by his [Smith's] remark about the Tennessee and Cumberland rivers, [I] followed them in their tortuous courses, vaguely suspecting the use to which they would be put."[1]

The Twin Rivers campaign, the great invasion into the Confederate heartland, allegedly had many authors. One was Colonel Charles Whittlesey, a West Point graduate serving as an engineer under Brig. Gen. Don Carlos Buell in the Department of the Ohio and who, within months, would command a brigade under Wallace. On November 20, 1861, Whittlesey posed a series of written questions to Halleck, now in command of the Department of the Missouri. "Will you allow me to suggest," Whittlesey wrote, "the consideration of a great movement by land and water up the Cumberland and Tennessee Rivers?" Stating that Nashville was the ultimate goal, Whittlesey suggested such a move would force "the evacuation of Columbus by threatening their [Confederate] railroad communications." In addition, such an advance would compel Confederate Brig. Gen. Simon Bolivar Buckner to retreat from Bowling Green, Kentucky, "by threatening his railway lines." For all that such a plan promised, Whittlesey asked, "is it not the most passable route into Tennessee?" A week later from Louisville, Buell

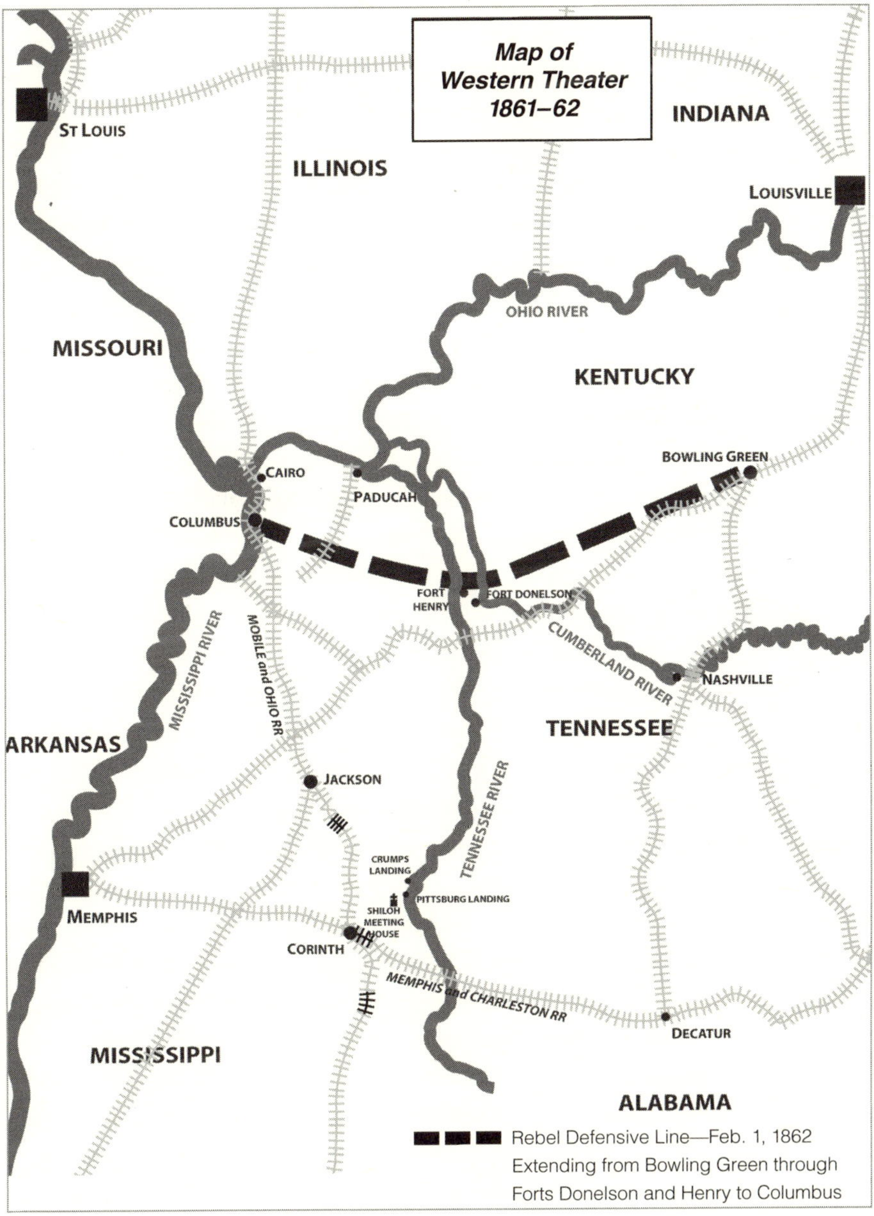

The Western Theater. (Map by George Ferguson, gfgraphics, Waynesville, N.C.)

told McClellan he thought it would be "plausible" to strike toward Nashville by sending "two flotilla columns upon the Tennessee and Cumberland so at least to land and unite near the State [Kentucky/Tennessee] line." In mid-December 1861, Halleck entertained brigadier generals George W. Cullum and William T. Sherman at his headquarters in St. Louis. Responding to an inquiry from Halleck, Cullum mapped out the existing Confederate defensive line, stretching from Bowling Green, Kentucky, on the Green River on the Confederate right, southwest into Tennessee to Fort Donelson on the Cumberland River, then west to Fort Henry on the Tennessee River, still in Tennessee, and on to Columbus, Kentucky, anchoring the Confederate left on the Mississippi River. Sherman then identified "the very center" as the "optimum point" at which to strike that line. Halleck penciled in a line running north to south roughly along the Tennessee River pointed directly at Fort Henry, noting "That's the true line of operations."[2]

Wallace had little, if anything, to do with the planning of the campaign. He certainly would be a full-fledged participant. The Twin Rivers campaign ushered in his first great adventure in pursuit of honor and glory in the West. The initial tactical objectives of the Twin Rivers campaign were Fort Henry on the Tennessee River and Fort Donelson on the Cumberland River.

The Tennessee River and the Cumberland River, both flowing south to north, provided Americans in 1860 with wide and uninterrupted avenues of ingress and egress into west-central and west Tennessee. A traveler could start at Paducah, where the Tennessee River joined the Ohio River, and journey uninterrupted all the way to Decatur, Alabama. On the Cumberland River, merchants could ship grain, cotton, and leather goods all the way from Nashville to Smithland, Kentucky, at the confluence of the Cumberland and Ohio rivers. An ever-increasing number of miles of railroad track completed in the two decades before 1860 knitted this vast area together, making it more integrated and more essential to the economic welfare of the South. People and goods now traveled inland from Louisville on the Ohio River cross-country to Memphis on the Mississippi River by means of the Memphis and Ohio Railroad. Personal travel and commercial shipments now passed from Chicago to Mobile on the Mobile and Ohio Railroad. With the possible coming of war, many prominent Southerners began to appreciate that both rivers likewise presented ominous avenues for Northern invasion into their vast heartland. Protection of that heartland, its rivers and railroads, its abundant raw materials, foodstuffs production capabilities, and burgeoning manufacturing facilities, became an overnight imperative. The Confederacy must build forts on both the Tennessee and the Cumberland rivers to close off both as avenues of possible Northern aggression.[3]

Tennessee Governor Isham G. Harris spearheaded the Confederate effort to construct these forts. The "Birmingham Narrows" in Kentucky was the ideal location as the two rivers flowed within three miles of each other. Then, in April 1861, the Kentucky legislature proclaimed its neutrality. Neutrality theoretically made Kentucky off-limits to fort construction or any other type of military activity by either side. Harris therefore found locations in Tennessee a few miles south of the Kentucky–Tennessee state line where a distance of only about twelve land miles separated the two forts. The two sites, Fort Henry on the Tennessee River and Fort Donelson on the Cumberland River, were far from perfect.[4] Both would do, however, given the compelling need to complete construction quickly combined with the perceived desire to respect the myth of Kentucky neutrality.

Topography and nature conspired to make Fort Henry the worst by far of the two locations chosen. Writing in 1864, Robert R. Howison observed that the glaring weakness of Fort Henry was its physical location. "It was on a flat—low and sunken—with higher ground around it." The fort "was subject to enfilading fire from at least three points on the opposite side [of the river] and the same number of points commanded it on the eastern bank, all at easy cannon range." Howison failed to consider the fact that the Confederates were hastening to complete construction of Fort Heiman on the west bank of the Tennessee on a bluff overlooking the river and overshadowing Fort Henry. Nevertheless, his observations were accurate. Fort Henry's chief liability as a defensive structure was simply that "it was not only liable to point blank fire from gunboats when the river rose, but was subject to overflow from the very floods which brought the enemy upon it."[5]

In much the same manner, Confederate Brig. Gen. Lloyd Tilghman, who commanded at Fort Henry, acidly summarized its fate. "The history of military engineering records no parallel to this case," he concluded, "An enemy had but to use their most common sense in obtaining the advantage of high water, as was the case, to have complete and entire control of the position." Confederate Naval artillerist Capt. Jesse Taylor also served at Fort Henry. Immediately upon being posted there, he assessed the situation and reported the fort's gross deficiencies to the political authorities in

Nashville as well as to Confederate generals Polk and Albert Sydney Johnston plus the chief army engineer, Maj. Jeremy F. Gilmer. No one paid any attention. "Knowing that the crude ideas of a sailor in the navy concerning fortifications would receive but little consideration when conflicting with those entertained by a 'West Pointer' [Gilmer, class of 1839; Brig. Gen. Bushrod R. Johnson, class of 1840]," Taylor concluded, "I resolved quietly to acquiesce. My investigation convinced me that we had a more dangerous force to contend with than the Federals—namely, the river itself."[6]

According to Howison, the site chosen for Fort Donelson on the Cumberland River was "much more judicious. It had the advantage of a considerable elevation, commanding a sweep of the river, and enabling its guns to deliver a plunging fire." The engineers had built Fort Donelson on top of a bluff 120 feet above the Cumberland. Commodore Henry Walke, the commander of the Union gunboat *Carondelet,* upon first seeing Donelson noted that the fort had three batteries with a total of fifteen mounted guns. The lower river battery was approximately twenty feet above the level of the river, the upper river battery around fifty feet above, while the third battery was on the crest of the bluff. Walke understood that the Confederates at Fort Donelson need not be concerned with the flooding of the fort's guns and magazines. He further realized that the Confederate gunners could direct a withering downward fire on any approaching Union gunboats. Later he wrote that Fort Donelson "occupied one of the best defensive positions on the river . . . the hills and woods on the west side of the river hid part of the enemy's formidable defenses, but the black rows of heavy guns, pointing down on us, reminded me of the dismal-looking sepulchers cut in the rocky cliffs near Jerusalem, but far more repulsive."[7]

Donelson was an earthworks fort constructed immediately behind those river batteries approximately half a mile north of the town of Dover. West of Donelson, nature amply protected the entire area with a patchwork of ridges, hollows, creeks, marshes, and steep ravines. Just north of the fort, Hickman Creek, a brackish stream and marshy swamp, ran west to east through a small ravine before emptying into the Cumberland. The area on the north side of Hickman Creek was heavily wooded and thick with underbrush. Describing all this, the war correspondent of the *Missouri Democrat* looked east from a point on the Union left toward the river. He saw these natural and man-made fortifications "beginning on the Cumberland, at the southerly side of Dover, and extending toward the main fort" to the north "around the top of the high ridges before us to the head of the backwater on the north [Hickman Creek], here and there with bastion-works of a formidable character and at all points with formidable batteries sweeping the more available approaches." "To get to the Confederate rifle pits," the *Democrat* correspondent observed, Union forces would have to scale those ridges that "vary from one hundred and fifty to three hundred feet in height, and are covered with the most dense timber and undergrowth, concealing in great measure, the character of the enemy's defenses."[8] Wallace, describing the fort's land defenses, observed, "Taking in the ravine of the creek, a system of hollows, almost wide and deep enough to be called valleys, inclosed [*sic*] the town and the two hills, their bluffest [*sic*] ascent being on the townward [*sic*] side. Westward of the hollows; there were woods apparently interminable as well as impenetrable."[9]

Throughout January 1862, Grant peppered Halleck with requests to advance up the Tennessee River with at least the minimum intent of capturing Fort Henry.[10] In St. Louis, Halleck procrastinated. He feared that Grant was too impetuous and reckless and too likely to create rather than resolve a situation. He did not trust Grant to follow orders. Finally, on January 29, in an attempt to force Halleck to take action, Grant extended a formal invitation to him. "In view of the large force now concentrating in this district and the present feasibility of the plan, I would respectfully suggest the propriety of subduing Fort Henry, near the Kentucky and Tennessee line, and holding the position."[11] Stating the obvious, Grant suggested that any further delay would give the Confederates additional time to strengthen their defenses and that the capture of Fort Henry would give the Union a valuable base of operations on the Tennessee River. The capture of Fort Henry, Grant predicted, "will, besides, have a moral effect upon our troops to advance them toward the rebel States." Grant concluded with a diplomatic challenge: "The advantages of this move are as perceptible to the general commanding as to myself, therefore further statements are unnecessary."[12]

Notwithstanding the nature and frequency of Grant's communications, it is probable that Halleck would have continued to dig in, drag his heels, and do nothing had he not received an emergency dispatch on January 30 from McClellan. That same day, Halleck hurriedly telegraphed Grant that McClellan had just informed him "that Beauregard left Manassas four days ago with fifteen regiments for the line of Columbus and Bowling Green. It is therefore of the greatest importance that we cut that line before he arrives. You will move with the least possible delay."[13] True,

Davis had ordered Beauregard to join Confederate forces in the West. He arrived, however, not with fifteen regiments but only with his personal staff. Had McClellan not fallen prey to a rumor concerning Beauregard's troop strength and forwarded that rumor to Halleck, Union troops might well have remained on the banks of the Ohio River for many more weeks. Once armed with this news and without further hesitation or consideration, Halleck dispatched an order to Grant instructing him to "immediately prepare to send forward to Fort Henry . . . all your available forces. . . . Fort Henry should be taken and held at all hazards."[14]

Years later, Wallace pondered anew the question of who had designed the strategy that propelled Union forces up the Tennessee River in early February of 1862. As he did so, he looked once more at the Tennessee and "its offer of a highway to the rear of the Confederate hosts in Kentucky and the State of Tennessee; its silent suggestion of a secure passage into the heart of the belligerent land from which the direction of movement could be changed" either west toward Memphis or east toward Richmond, and "its many advantages as a line of supply and general communication." These strategic considerations were readily apparent to "every military student who, in the summer of 1861, gave himself to the most cursory examination of the map."[15]

Notwithstanding this cogent postwar analysis, Grant in fact had already had the last word on the authorship of the Twin Rivers campaign strategy. In late March 1862, Grant wrote to his patron, Illinois Congressman Elihu B. Washburne, that the credit for the Twin Rivers campaign strategy "is variously attributed." Noting that Union gunboats had been up and down the two rivers many times during the fall and winter of 1861, Grant offered, "Gen. Halleck no doubt thought of this route long ago and I am shure [*sic*] I did." The critical part of the plan was the selection of the proper officer to lead the attack. "As to how the battles should be fought," Grant concluded, "both McClellan and Halleck are too much of soldiers to suppose that they can plan how that should be done at a distance. . . . The job being an important one neither of the above Generals would have entrusted it to an officer who they had not confidence in. So far I was highly complimented by both."[16]

The tactical plan for the capture of Fort Henry was relatively straightforward.[17] Grant ordered the 1st Division under Brig. Gen. John A. McClernand to march in a southeasterly direction from its overnight camp on the east bank of the Tennessee River a few miles north of Fort Henry.

Grant instructed McClernand to cut the road leading from Henry to Donelson, thus preventing "all reinforcements to Fort Henry, or escape from it." Astride the road, McClernand would then hold his position "in readiness to storm" the fort. At the same hour, Smith, with the major portion of his 2nd Division, including Wallace's 2nd Brigade, would depart its temporary camp on the west bank of the Tennessee below the fort. Grant charged Smith with the objective of surrounding and then capturing Fort Heiman, located high on the bluffs on the west bank of the Tennessee overlooking Fort Henry. Simultaneously, Flag Officer Andrew H. Foote would attack the fort from the river with his iron- and timber-clad gunboats. In a coordinated effort, the navy and Foote combined with the 15,000 soldiers of the Army of the Tennessee would capture Fort Henry. The battle was to begin at 11:00 A.M., February 6.

McClernand marched toward the Henry–Donelson Road precisely at 11:00 A.M. Unusually heavy rains over the preceding several days thwarted the timeliness of the march. McClernand reported to Grant that "[t]he roads had become heavy and the streams swollen, rendering the march difficult." Having accompanied the 1st Division on this march, the war correspondent for the *Cincinnati Gazette* wrote, "the storm of the previous night had soaked the soft alluvial soil of the bottoms; until under the tread of the troops, it speedily became reduced to the consistency of soft porridge of almost immeasurable depth, rendering marching very difficult for infantry and for the artillery almost impassable." Meanwhile, Smith, on the opposite bank of the Tennessee, encountered the same conditions, resulting in the same unexpected delays. The *Boston Journal* war correspondent accompanying the 2nd Division noted, "At starting [the march], the bands enlivened the movement, till the horrible condition of the roads compelled them to cease." By the time McClernand and Smith reached their designated objectives, Foote and his gunboats on the swollen Tennessee River had already accepted the surrender of Fort Henry and its depleted garrison.[18]

Four Union ironclads, the *Essex*, the *Carondelet*, the *Cincinnati*, and the *St. Louis*, followed by three timberclads, the *Conestoga*, the *Tyler*, and the *Lexington*, had steamed upriver toward Fort Henry at precisely 11:00 A.M. Reaching a point 1,700 yards north of the fort, the navy had commenced its bombardment. The flotilla ultimately closed to within near point-blank range. Union naval guns did great damage at Fort Henry that day. The artillery fire from the fort was somewhat effective, but nowhere near as telling. Confederate projectiles were able to strike all the boats in Foote's flotilla, but only once, when a shell struck the *Essex*, exploding inside her boiler, was a Union vessel put out of commission. At approximately 12:35 P.M., a Union naval shell scored a direct hit disabling a Confederate 24-pounder rifled gun inside the fort. Shortly thereafter, a primer fuse got stuck in the vent of the fort's 10-inch Columbiad, rendering it inoperable. When a Union shell exploded, causing "the death of 2 men and disabling several others," only four of the original eleven artillery pieces inside Fort Henry remained in action. Tilghman struck the colors and surrendered the fort to Foote less than two hours after the battle began. Delayed by ankle-deep mud, Grant had not yet arrived.[19]

The incessant winter rains draining down the Tennessee River valley flooded the river around Fort Henry, raising its normal level significantly. Union gunboats had the advantage of firing on the fort from a level and even a slightly downward trajectory. Confederate Lt. Col. Randal W. McGavock of the 10th Tennessee recorded in his journal that "The River was very high and the Ft. surrounded entirely by water. The guns of the boats and those of the Ft. were nearly on a level, giving them every advantage."[20] To make matters worse, large portions of the fort were actually underwater even before the battle began. Confederate Lt. Col. Milton A. Haynes, Chief of Tennessee Artillery, reported that on the night of February 5, he rode from Fort Donelson to Fort Henry. "Not being able to cross the backwaters in the night,"[21] Haynes did not enter the fort until the next morning when he was able to commandeer a small boat and row through the front gate. Confederate artillerist Taylor, one of the first to be concerned about the impact that the swollen waters of the Tennessee would have upon Confederate ability to defend Fort Henry, recalled after the war that "when the action began, the lower part of the fort was already flooded, and when the colors were hauled down, the water was waist deep there; and when the cutter came with the officers to receive the formal surrender, she pulled into the 'sally-port'." Taylor concluded that "[i]f the attack had been delayed forty-eight hours, there would hardly have been a hostile shot fired; the Tennessee would have accomplished the work by drowning the magazine."[22]

For Union forces in the West, Fort Henry had been a significant beginning. The correspondent for the *Missouri Democrat* enthusiastically proclaimed on February 7 that "[t]he spinal column of the rebellion is undoubtedly broken just in the small of the back, at the railroad bridge over the Tennessee." The *Cincinnati Gazette* reported that with the fall

The Capture of Fort Henry, Tennessee. Sketched by Mr. Alexander Simplot (*Harper's Weekly* [March 1, 1862])

of Fort Henry "an entrance has been effected into the Confederacy at a point where they least expected it, and the backbone of the rebellion is broken."[23] No-nonsense Grant had little time for rhetoric or revelry. He was ready to proceed without delay. On the evening of February 6, he telegraphed Halleck: "Fort Henry is ours. . . . I shall take and destroy Fort Donelson on the 8th and return to Fort Henry." To his wife, Julia, he wrote, "Fort Henry is taken and I am not hurt. This is news enough for to-night. . . . Kiss the children for me."[24]

In fact, the army had played a very limited role in the battle for Fort Henry. It had not fared well in the mud caused by the rains and the flooding Tennessee River. For the same reason, Wallace had had little opportunity for honor and glory at Fort Henry. The steamers had brought Grant's 1st and 2nd Brigades from Paducah to both banks of the river in the early evening hours of February 5. That night, Wallace wrote Susan that Union forces had the "advantage in every sense of the word, in numbers, character of troops, and last, but not least, Cause." He believed Union gunboats would prevail at Fort Henry but acknowledged that the navy had yet to be tested. As most soldiers do on the eve of battle, he concluded this letter with a solemn reflection. "I only pray," he wrote, "that I may do my duty tomorrow, so that, if I come back to you, as I hope and believe I will, it will be in honor."[25] The next morning, starting at 11:00, he and his men trudged through the muddy byways and rain-swollen creeks and tributaries of the Tennessee, up a tree-covered hill some two hundred feet high to a bluff and on toward Fort Heiman.

Private Thomas Wise Durham of the 11th Indiana described the approach to Fort Heiman. "We had to wade across a bay where the icy water came up to our armpits," he wrote. "We put the bayonets on our guns, hung the cartridge boxes on the bayonets and held our guns above our heads to keep the powder dry." Durham remembered that as the 11th Indiana approached the fort, the Rebel defenders, too few in number to resist the advances of a brigade, "'skiddaddled' with very little show of resistance" and Wallace's troops stopped "to eat their dinner for them before it got cold."[26] Upon entering the fort, Wallace recalled in his *Autobiography*, he found "dinner was ready. I looked into a kettle yet boiling and discovered a block of fresh pork 'done to a turn'. By the kettle, a pot simmered, spraying the air with the aroma of coffee. A pone of corn-bread adorned a bench near by, and under the lid of a mess-box rudely constructed a little rummaging disclosed salt, pepper, vinegar, and white sugar in lump. General Smith, upon invitation, came and shared my good-fortune."[27]

There could have been a battle at Fort Heiman. Seeing the Union army and navy moving upriver toward Fort Henry and realizing that the heavy guns at Fort Heiman had yet to be permanently mounted, on the evening of February 5, Tilghman ordered Heiman abandoned except for a small rear guard of two companies. Wallace was frustrated. Later, he would spend a moment reflecting on just how curious it was that "downright hard fighting was always escaping me, or I it."[28] By the time Wallace and Smith finished their impromptu midday meal, Tilghman's sacrificial and forlorn band of artillerists, totaling less than one hundred men when the battle began, had surrendered the fort to the Union navy.

Wallace had marched to Fort Henry as the commander of Smith's 2nd Brigade. Once there, his exploits evidenced a certain color and attractiveness but he did virtually no fighting. To his considerable frustration, he extracted little honor and glory from his Fort Henry experience. Nine days later at Fort Donelson, Wallace confronted a drastically different set of circumstances. As was his usual course of action, he met them head-on. In so doing, he achieved glory and honor. At least, he thought he did. It was in his future, moreover, to savor yet another meal provided by his enemy. Only this time, it would be breakfast.

CHAPTER FIVE

Fort Donelson, February 13–14, 1862

The rapidly rising floodwaters of the Tennessee River had made Fort Henry's capture unexpectedly swift and easy. In the same manner, nature stymied Grant's plans to move immediately against Fort Donelson. No matter Grant's intentions, he was compelled on February 8 to lament that "at present we are perfectly locked in by high water and bad roads and prevented from acting offensively as I should like to do. . . . I contemplated taking Donelson to-day, with Infantry and Cavalry alone, but all my troops will be kept busily engaged saving what we now have from the rapidly rising waters."[1] Finally, on February 12, under fairer skies and receding waters, Grant began the twelve-mile march to Fort Donelson on the west bank of the Cumberland River. To his consternation, Wallace was left behind at Fort Henry in command of a 2,500 man reserve. Grant's 15,000-man army marched to Fort Donelson in half a day.

Meanwhile, on February 8, Confederate Brig. Gen. Bushrod Johnson had no more than 3,500 Rebel soldiers under his command at Fort Donelson. On February 10, Brig. Gen. Gideon Pillow, with regiments from Tennessee and Virginia numbering 2,800 men, arrived to take command of the fort. Lt. Col. Nathan Bedford Forest and the 3rd Tennessee cavalry rode in later that same day. Brig. Gen. Simon Bolivar Buckner, with a division of Kentucky infantry and cavalry, reached the fort on February 11, and Brig. Gen. John B. Floyd, with a brigade of Virginians, took command from Pillow early on the morning of the 13th. The total Confederate force defending Fort Donelson now numbered a few hundred more than 15,000 men. Had Grant been able to attack the fort on February 8 as he had intended, Union forces that day would have outnumbered Confederates by more than four to one. By the time the Union army completed the march from Fort Henry, however, Confederates inside the fort slightly outnumbered them. Weather and water had been the scourge of the Confederacy at Fort Henry. These same phenomena now delayed the arrival of a frustrated Grant for almost four days. The Rebels used this time wisely. With ever increasing numbers inside the fort, the Rebel defenders spent hours digging trenches, constructing rifle pits, and surrounding their artillery with more pits and abatis. In four days, the fort's already extensive natural defenses were considerably strengthened.[2]

In his command of troops in the field, Grant invariably displayed audacity. Having read and appreciated Mahan, Wallace was a mirror image of Grant in this regard.[3] Three episodes from Grant's career, all perhaps colored by an author's need to exalt Grant, demonstrate the audacity with which he confronted military situations. On February 7, Grant conversed with Albert Richardson, a Northern war correspondent, telling him that "I am going over to attack Fort Donelson tomorrow." Evidencing surprise, Richardson asked, "Do you know how strong it is?" Grant casually replied, "Not exactly, but I think we can take it; at all events we can try." During the early evening hours of April 6, at the conclusion of the first day's battle at Shiloh, Lt. Col. James B. McPherson confronted a harassed and presumably defeated Grant. He inquired if his commanding general had prepared plans for the retreat of the Army of the Tennessee. Grant responded, "No, I propose to attack at daylight and whip them." Later that same night, when Grant appeared to be unusually quiet and contemplative, Sherman likened that first day at Shiloh to "the devil's own day." Grant agreed. "Yes. Lick 'em tomorrow though," he retorted.[4] On a more definitive note, after Fort Donelson, Grant wrote to Julia that his goal as the leader of the army was to avoid what he called "hard fighting." The only way to accomplish this goal was to push forward "as vigorously as possible."[5]

Just as the Romp to Romney had a formative impact on Wallace's response to how best to wage war, three episodes prior to Fort Henry appear to have done likewise for Grant. Grant evidenced thought processes derived from all three learning experiences at both Donelson and Shiloh. As colonel of the 21st Illinois, Grant had received orders in mid-July 1861 to interdict and shut down the operations of Confederate "General" Thomas Harris and his guerrillas, then operating in southeast Missouri. Grant recalled in his *Personal Memoirs* that, as he approached Harris's camp, he felt his heart leap up into his throat. He came upon an evacuated camp, however; Harris had fled to parts unknown. Years later Grant wrote, "it occurred to me at once that Harris had been as much afraid of me as I had been of him. This was a view of the question I had never taken before; but it was one I never forgot afterwards. . . . From that event to the close of the war, I never experienced trepidation upon confronting an enemy . . . I never forgot that he had as much reason to fear my forces as I had his. The lesson was valuable."[6]

The second incident shaping Grant's maturity as an officer occurred soon thereafter. Recently promoted to the rank of brigadier general, he led his command to Ironton, Missouri, to construct fortifications "intended to so strengthen the frontier as to make it tenable against any force likely to be brought against it." Two weeks after his arrival, Grant displayed displeasure with orders. "I am not fortifying here at all," he informed Frémont. He stated that upon his arrival he had found no engineer as he had been promised; had little, if any, tolerance for or expertise in the construction of fortifications; and had forgotten what little he had learned about that particular subject at West Point. Bordering on insubordination, he protested that with everything else he had to accomplish "there is but little time left for drilling. Drill and discipline are more necessary for the men than fortifications."[7] If one constantly sought the initiative in battle against his enemy, he had little time left for digging trenches. Grant would pay a near fatal price at both Fort Donelson and Shiloh for his unwillingness to entrench and fortify.

The third, and potentially most destructive aspect of Grant's development as a general officer, arose out of a series of observations he made in 1861, again from his Ironton experiences. Frémont had ordered Grant "to scour the country," to maintain a "watchful eye," and to employ "reliable spies" so as to gain information of any and all enemy troop movements in the area. Although he admitted he had been in Ironton only one day, Grant reported "from all that I have yet learned from spies and loyally-disposed citizens, I am led to believe that there is no force within 30 miles of us that entertain the least idea of attacking this position."[8] Time and again, Grant believed he was fighting an essentially passive enemy. As he responded to this bias, he perceived that the Confederates quite often displayed a fundamental unwillingness to come out into the open and fight. For example, in October, 1861, disagreeing with Smith's expressions of apprehensions voiced to Wallace, Grant reported that his "impression is there is no concerted plan to attack this place [Cairo], Cape Girardeau or Paducah for the present." Three days later, he reiterated this basic tenet of his newfound belief. He telegraphed Frémont that there were

45,000 Confederates at Columbus who "talk boldly of making an attack on Paducah. . . . My own impression however is that they are fortifying strongly and preparing to resist a formidable attack and have but little idea of risking anything upon a forward movement."[9] This construct of his enemy's passive, defensive nature and intentions almost cost Grant everything, first at Donelson and then at Shiloh.

On February 12, Grant led McClernand, Smith, and the Army of the Tennessee without Wallace to Fort Donelson. Forrest's cavalry sought to delay the advance but with limited success. Soon the Rebels retreated into the security of the fort. This only confirmed Grant's view that his enemy was more inclined to remain behind its fortifications than to seek him out for a fight. Upon arrival, Grant positioned Smith on the federal left flank directly in front of the fort. He placed McClernand on Smith's right, with orders to extend his division as far to the southeast as possible. The intention was to envelop both Fort Donelson and the town of Dover with one continuous line of Union troops. Pursuant to orders, Wallace remained at Fort Henry. Grant stated in his *Personal Memoirs* that he directed Smith to constitute a rear guard from a portion of his division to stay at Fort Henry, protecting the rear and right flank of Grant's army as well as its lines of supply. "He [Smith] left General Lew Wallace with 2,500 men." Grant was concerned that either Polk might abandon Columbus or Confederate Maj. Gen. William J. Hardee might do likewise at Bowling Green. Should either or both occur, a potentially large force of Confederates might descend upon Grant from the rear. Wallace reluctantly acknowledged that the creation of a rear guard was a military necessity. Still, he knew that the leadership of such a force was something best assigned to a colonel not a brigadier. He was distraught, mortified. He had been left behind once more.[10]

Although Grant had ordered the rear guard, Wallace was absolutely convinced that Smith had designated him for this less than glamorous and rewarding task of commanding the reserve. "Through old Smith," Wallace wrote to Susan on February 11, "I am left behind in command of this fort [Heiman] and Ft. Henry. Nice arrangement truly. I have been sick with rage ever since the order came." Afraid of being left behind, Wallace reacted with peevishness and petulance, concluding "my patience with old Smith is now 'played out'. I have been too modest and patient. He has abused both. I will change policy—in fact, have done so."[11]

Loyalty for Wallace could be a fleeting commodity. In a February 7 letter to Susan, he had noted with pride that with Smith's blessing, he had been in charge of Union troops on the west bank of the Tennessee. "I led the advance on the right [west] bank of the river . . . I directed the head of my column by a road which turned the enemy's works." The Alabamians had fled when they saw his men advancing to battle. Once inside Fort Heiman, he invited Smith to breakfast. Four days later, he had exhausted his patience with "Old Smith." He continued to harbor resentment against Smith even after Fort Donelson had surrendered. "I am now in command of these forts [Henry and Heiman]," he wrote Susan on February 19, "with fourteen regiments. In other words, I am acting Major Gen. commanding a division. All of which is not so satisfactory as the happy riddance of Gen. Smith which is at last accomplished. He is at Donelson, I hear. . . . He left me behind on the marching of the troops [to Donelson on February 12], thro' jealousy."[12]

Wallace then went one step further. He expressed his frustrations in writing to one of Grant's aides. Once more he showed flagrant disrespect for the chain of command. When Wallace believed he was a victim, he had an uncanny ability to broadcast that fact far and wide. On February 11, Capt. William Hillyer, a member of Grant's staff as well as a personal friend, acknowledged receipt of a note from Wallace, writing, "I was surprized [*sic*] to hear that you were to be left behind—and so was Gen. Grant. . . . He told me today that he would give you a Division as soon as new troops arrive and he would see that you should have a good position in the next fight." Noting that he had not anticipated that a general would be in charge of the rear guard while men of lesser rank, specifically seven colonels, were ordered to Fort Donelson, Hillyer concluded, "I should have made a more active effort to change it." In a postscript, Hillyer assured Wallace that Grant intended to give him a new division. He concluded "Donelson will be only the first skirmish. You will be in at the tug of war." Hillyer then warned Wallace, "Let me beg of you as your friend that you keep quiet for a day or two—and you will have a position that will suit you in every particular—having no intermediate commander." Keeping quiet was never a character trait Wallace possessed.[13]

The fighting at Fort Donelson on February 13 was limited and produced few results for Grant and his army. Although Grant issued no orders to either of his division commanders to engage the enemy, both Smith and McClernand did just that. Smith got bogged down in the ravines and hills to the west of the fort before retiring from his unilateral attempt to capture it. McClernand stormed the entrenched Confederate line southwest of the town of Dover, suffering heavy, unnecessary casualties. Grant did issue orders to Walke to fire upon the fort from the *Carondelet* stationed on the Cumberland River. This action, while lasting the better part of two hours, likewise generated inconsequential results. In his official report, Grant discussed only the actions of the ironclad.[14] Unofficially, he bemoaned the fact that the taking of Fort Donelson might well be more difficult than he had originally thought. In a letter to Julia, he suggested that Donelson "bids fair to be a long job. The rebels are strongly fortified and are in very heavy force." Ever the optimist, however, Grant ended on an encouraging note, "When this is to end is hard to surmise but I feel confidant of ultimate success."[15] Grant planned to send the ironclads against the fort the next day. He expected Foote to duplicate his extraordinary performance at Fort Henry. In addition, he ordered Wallace that night to come immediately to Fort Donelson. Grant told him to bring the 11th Indiana and the 8th Missouri with him.

At approximately 3:00 P.M. on February 14, Foote and his gunboats lying northwest (downriver) of Fort Donelson opened fire. His flotilla consisted of four ironclads, the *St. Louis*, the *Carondelet*, the *Louisville*, and the *Pittsburg*, supported by two timberclads, the *Tyler* and the *Conestoga*. Foote had sent two ironclads disabled at Fort Henry, the *Essex* and the *Cincinnati*, back to Cairo for repairs and abandoned the temporarily inoperable timberclad, the *Lexington*, at Paducah. Heavy rains had caused the level of the Cumberland River to rise. The new level was sufficient to nullify the obstructions and torpedoes the Confederates had spent hours planting in the river specifically to deter the progress of the gunboats. The river had not risen high enough, however, to duplicate the conditions that largely determined the outcome at Fort Henry.

Since Fort Donelson had been built on a bluff rather than in a bowl, Foote's flotilla was forced to aim and fire its guns upward rather than parallel to or down upon the Confederates as had been the case at Fort Henry. With an elevation often as much as 35°, accuracy was at a premium. Many Union shells fell not upon the Confederate shore batteries but into the fort and beyond, doing much less damage than intended. Fire from the Confederate shore batteries meanwhile rained down upon the Union gunboats, particularly as they maneuvered as close to the fort as 300 to 400 yards. Foote claimed he had learned the lessons of Fort Henry well. The trouble was that those lessons had little, if any, applicability at Fort Donelson.

Similarly to Fort Henry, however, the bombardment lasted less than two hours. This time the results were dramatically different. The Confederates

Looking north from River Battery: Fort Donelson along the Cumberland River. (Photo by author)

Fort Donelson along the Cumberland River. (Photo by author)

prevailed. Confederate guns pounded and ultimately drove both the *St. Louis* and the *Louisville* back down the river. Foote reported that the wind and the water currents had damaged the two remaining ironclads, which "soon followed us, as the enemy rapidly renewed the fire as we drifted helplessly back down the river." Foote concluded that this particular affair had been a "hotly contested but unequal fight."[16] While true, what Foote did not emphasize was that the results of the fight at Fort Donelson were the direct opposite of what the Union navy had experienced at Fort Henry. At Donelson, the Confederates not only survived but beat back the dreaded attack of the ironclads. At least for the moment, the Rebels eliminated the Union navy as an effective fighting force on the Cumberland.[17]

Three other events occurred on February 14 that would have an enormous impact upon the battle for Fort Donelson. First, Wallace arrived at Donelson a little before noon. When Wallace received his orders from Grant to come to Donelson, his mood shifted immediately to unbridled enthusiasm. As he hastily prepared his men for the march, Wallace penned a brief letter to Susan announcing, "I have just received orders to march two Regiments to Ft. Donelson. . . . If we win, this rebellion goes under at once, and there shall be no such word as fail."[18]

Upon Wallace's arrival, Grant signed General Field Orders No. 14. As directed, Wallace transferred operational command and control of the 11th Indiana and 8th Missouri to Smith's Second 2nd Division. In return, Grant gave Wallace the newly formed 3rd Division, consisting almost entirely of the raw recruits Halleck was daily sending to the Army of the Tennessee, some disembarking from their steamers at Fort Donelson the very same instant that Wallace arrived. Brand new men, few who had been in battle, few who had fired a shot in anger, and even fewer who had even seen a Butternut, filled the ranks of the newly formed 3rd Division. Wallace was likewise totally inexperienced as a division commander. Grant assigned him and his untried and untested men to a location in the center right of the Union line.[19]

Grant probably did not anticipate that the newly created 3rd Division would see much combat at Donelson. Frustrated with not having enough men to complete the envelopment of Dover toward the southeast, Grant had created the 3rd Division and given its command to Wallace. Even then, however, the new division did not possess sufficient numbers to accomplish its basic purpose. The Union right flank of which Wallace was now a part was still undermanned and too thinly stretched. As a result, Wallace found himself encamped about three quarters of a mile from Smith's right flank and over half a mile from McClernand's left flank. His flanks were not only exposed, they were bare. In addition to having no anchor point with either of Grant's other two divisions, the 3rd Division had no cavalry. Grant had not ordered Wallace to bring cavalry from Fort Henry and he had no cavalry to give to Wallace upon his arrival. Cavalry was designed to link the various units in the field together and, as importantly, to provide field commanders with battlefield reconnaissance. Wallace was in the center of the line. Comforting though that may have been, he was still isolated. He felt the sting of being the junior brigadier.[20]

The second event of February 14 important to the ultimate outcome of the battle for Fort Donelson occurred during the naval bombardment. Foote suffered a severe injury (to his foot, ironically) when a shell from the fort struck the *St. Louis*, his flagship. In his February 15 report to Navy Secretary Gideon Wells, Foote said nothing about this incident other than to list himself among the "wounded." In a later dispatch to Welles, Foote explained that "my foot is much inflamed, but, with care, the surgeon considers, will soon be better."[21] Foote's wound produced a potentially very serious problem at Donelson the next day. Wallace and then Grant would confront that problem and succeed in preventing a disaster in the making.

The third event critical to the fortunes of both Wallace and Grant took place late in the evening of February 14 in the form of a Confederate high command council of war. Pillow, the second-in-command, proposed assuming the offensive the next morning, breaking out of the Confederate defensive line south and southeast of Dover, and striking McClernand on Grant's extreme right flank. Floyd and Buckner, now third-in-command, agreed. Pillow and 8,000 Confederates intended to surprise McClernand on the Union far right, forcing a Yankee retreat in a southwest direction along the Wynn's Ferry Road, back toward Fort Henry. Once having achieved this objective, Pillow's surprise would reopen the road to Charlotte, Tennessee, and thence to Nashville. Pillow intended to create an avenue of retreat, or more precisely escape, for Confederate forces becoming increasingly bottled up inside the fort.

None of the three Confederate commanders that night disputed the tactical necessity for the proposed breakout. They believed that Union reinforcements in ever-increasing numbers were arriving daily on river transports and disembarking north of Fort Donelson. All three generals understood that with increased numbers alone, Union troops would complete the envelopment of the fort and town, dooming their occupants to a siege. Floyd, Pillow, and Buckner all agreed that the outcome of a siege was disastrously predictable. The Rebel leaders also feared the Union gunboats. Although defeated earlier that day, a least some Union gunboats were thought to be available on the Cumberland River to support a siege. If that point were ever reached, the option to escape east to Nashville would no longer exist and surrender would be the only remaining choice. Confederate high command inside Donelson thus decided to abandon the fort by initiating a breakout against the Union right flank followed by an escape to Nashville via Charlotte.[22]

Actually, the three Confederate brigadiers had agreed during the night of February 13 to execute the same tactics of breakout and retirement to Nashville on February 14. They designed this breakout to occur early in the morning of February 14 before Union forces could possibly complete the envelopment of Fort Donelson and Dover. For a variety of reasons, Pillow hesitated and then decided it was too late in the day to initiate such a maneuver. Had the Confederates attempted a breakout on the morning of February 14, it might well have succeeded.[23] McClernand did not have at his command sufficient manpower to complete, in conjunction with the Cumberland on the north, his encirclement of the fort and the town. In addition, on February 14, there was no 3rd Division as Wallace was then marching from Henry to Donelson and would not arrive at Grant's headquarters until around noon. On the night of the 13th, as they did on the night of the 14th, Floyd, Pillow, and Buckner unanimously agreed that if successful the next morning, Confederate troops were to retire immediately in an orderly fashion northeast toward Charlotte, Clarksville, and then to Nashville.[24]

During the late evening hours of February 14 outside the fort, Grant appeared unusually distracted by the idea that victory at Donelson might require more time and effort than he had originally thought. Unexpectedly, the navy had failed to destroy the fort, forcing its defenders to surrender. As a result, Grant believed he had only two viable alternatives—either to retreat from the fort and the town all the way back to Fort Henry, or to initiate a siege. To be successful, a siege would require time. For the navy to be effective once more, repairs to its damaged gunboats had to be completed. In addition, Halleck must send Grant even more men and material. The noose around the fort and the town had to be drawn as tightly as possible. This would require almost as many men as it would take to launch an effective assault upon the fort and it would take time to accomplish. Time and reinforcements, Grant reluctantly conceded, were on his side.

The other consideration that made an effective siege possible was Grant's perception of the Rebels' proven passivity. His enemy had demonstrated to him on more than one occasion that it preferred to remain inside fortifications rather than venture beyond their walls to attack him aggressively. If a siege were forced upon him, Grant believed he had already positioned his army well for the task. "We have the works of the enemy well invested," he enthusiastically reported to Collum that night.[25] For the moment, as annoyed as Grant was by having to choose between retreat and siege warfare, he regrettably understood he had no other recourse but to conduct the latter. He knew that a cautious Halleck would approve. Even so, the very idea of siege warfare was anathema to Grant, screaming as it did of defensive, not offensive, warfare.

If siege warfare was in fact imminent, Grant gave no indication he planned to use picks and shovels to construct fortifications or dig entrenchments for the protection of his troops. At this stage in his career, he disparaged the idea of fortifications. Furthermore, under present circumstances, Grant believed fortifications were entirely unnecessary, a total waste of time and energy. He told Cullum that the Confederates inside the fort "do not seem inclined to come out. They are very strong, however, being well fortified."[26] This was the same conclusion that Grant had reached as he assessed the situation first at Paducah and then at Columbus the preceding year. The Confederates at Fort Donelson, behind their strong defensive positions, were no different than the Confederates at Columbus; they would not "come out" for they had little to gain and much to lose by undertaking an "offensive."[27] Thus, a confident, albeit highly displeased, Grant determined to tighten the noose around Fort Donelson and Dover, awaiting reinforcements. There would be no fortifications or entrenchments constructed, however. That was not his way.

Very chilly winds the night of February 14 exacerbated a heavy snowstorm that was making existence on the west bank of the Cumberland River barely tolerable. "The weather was bitterly cold," Sgt. Charles B. Kimbell of the 1st Illinois Light Artillery, Battery A, wrote, "and we had orders to build no fires. As we were wet, tired, and hungry, most of us managed to get our feet near some live coals on our side of some large trees that were down." After feasting on "hard tack and bacon," Kimbell and his battery mates "rolled up in our ponchos under 'shebang's' made of evergreen boughs, and had a sound and refreshing sleep."[28] The men of Battery A would need their rest. As they hunkered down that unseasonably cold and snowy night, the three Confederate brigadiers inside Fort Donelson had just finalized plans for a breakout the next morning. As the men of Battery A sought sleep, Grant was in the process of completing the backdrop against which the Rebel breakout the next morning would nearly succeed. Fortunately for the Union cause, Grant had also just added to his command a young brigadier general who had yet to learn exactly when and how to follow orders.[29]

Early on the morning of February 15, Grant received a note from Foote requesting a personal conference on board the *St. Louis.* Foote believed it was imperative that the two men have a personal conversation, not merely an exchange of messages. He intended to tell Grant that his wound required medical attention and that the condition of three of his damaged ironclads dictated that he and at least two ironclads return to the Union construction facilities at Mound City, Illinois, at once for repairs.[30] Upon receiving Foote's request, Grant did not hesitate. He evidenced little concern for any danger that might arise while he was absent from the battlefield. "I at once made my preparations for starting," Grant wrote in his *Personal Memoirs,* "When I left the National line to visit Flag-officer Foote I had no idea that there would be any engagement on land unless I brought it on myself." Grant was reacting to the lessons his earlier experiences had taught him. Penned behind their walls and trench lines, his enemy could not retreat. The Confederates would certainly not risk an advance. He need not fear being surprised on the field of battle. He did, however, inform his headquarters staff that he was riding to the river to meet with Foote. In addition, he ordered his adjutant general "to notify each of the division commanders of my absence and instruct them to do nothing to bring on an engagement until they received further orders, but to hold their positions."[31]

CHAPTER SIX

Fort Donelson, February 15, 1862, A.M.

The Confederate breakout the morning of February 15 completely surprised Grant and the men on the Union right flank at Fort Donelson. Grant had nearly left the battlefield when the Confederates attacked. As he approached the river, he rode past the newly arrived 20th Ohio. Neither Grant nor Col. Charles Whittlesey, the regimental commander, was aware of a Confederate offensive then in progress. No one heard or reported the sounds of battle. Atmospheric conditions that morning probably contributed in large part to the absence of the sound of gunfire. In addition, Rebel forces were assaulting Union troops located some four to five miles away. Dense woodlands, two creeks, and at least two ravines sculpted the landscape separating Grant on the river from the sounds of many thousands of muskets and cannons.[1]

Grant continued on to his meeting with Foote. No one with Grant was able to share the plight of the 41st Illinois, McArthur's brigade, McClernand's division, as it unexpectedly bore the direct frontal assault of the Confederate troops advancing out of their fortifications. Pvt. J. M. Roberts wrote that when he and his comrades first became aware of the Butternuts, "our guns were stacked in line of battle." Rushing to get into formation, his company sergeant "reached out to take his gun from the stack. As he raised it up, a shot from the enemy hit the bayonet and bent it down on the muzzle of the gun. He engaged in a number of adjectives."[2] The surprise was complete and the land battle for Fort Donelson was joined.

Upon Wallace's arrival at Donelson the day before, Grant had dispatched the newly created 3rd Division into the Union line on the right. As directed by Capt. John A. Rawlins, Grant's assistant adjutant general, Wallace established his camp in a flat area of land west of Indian Creek and two large fields that were cleared but uncultivated. Wallace was elated. He was the newly minted commander of the newly formed 3rd Division, Army of the Tennessee. During his meeting with Grant, the general allegedly told him, "[y]our part will be to hold the centre, and resist all attempts of the enemy to break through. You must not assume the aggressive. Those are your orders."[3] Wallace understood that his assignment was to plug the ever-widening gap between Smith on the left flank and McClernand on the right. He might have suspected from the moment of his arrival in camp that there were not yet enough Union troops at Donelson to accomplish this objective. He might not have known that the 25th Kentucky regiment of his new command on his extreme right was sleeping that night more than half a mile southwest of the 17th Illinois regiment, occupying the extreme left of the 1st Division. He could, however, see that on his right a wide swath of flat land and uncultivated fields separated him from McClernand. He could not fail to notice that through that area ran two improved roads, the Old Pinery Road (present-day Indian Creek Road) from Dover to Fort Henry and the Wynn's Ferry Road, likewise from Dover to Fort Henry. He knew he had no cavalry. He might have wondered just how he would obtain battlefield reconnaissance or who would shield his exposed right flank in the event the Rebels attacked down either of those roads. More likely than not, Wallace did not think too long or too hard about any of these matters. He had just arrived, just been promoted to division commander, and now, shortly after going into camp on the afternoon of February 14, he heard the naval flotilla begin its bombardment of Donelson.[4]

"As the morning of the 15th crawled up the eastern sky as a turtle in its first appearance after hibernation crawls up a steep bank," Wallace later recollected that he was busy attending to his horse, John. "A burst of musketry" startled him. Under restrictive orders from Grant and lacking the necessary cavalry as scouts to provide him with up-to-date, on-the-ground intelligence, Wallace could only wait and wonder. Finally, around 8:00 A.M., Maj. Mason Brayman, a member of McClernand's staff, suddenly appeared with an urgent call from McClernand for assistance. "I am from General McClernand sent to ask assistance of you," Brayman stated. "The general told me to tell you the whole rebel force in the fort massed against him in the night. Our ammunition is giving out. We are losing ground. No one can tell what will be the result if we don't get immediate help."[5] McClernand appeared to be in serious trouble. He needed help.

Wallace's instincts would have been to move forward immediately to aid McClernand. Such an action would, after all, be totally consistent with the man whom Col. W. H. L. Wallace from Illinois described to his wife as being one with "blood in him. . . . I like his style except his profanity. He is prompt ready and exact-brief."[6] The new commander of the 3rd Division had a problem, however. Notwithstanding his robust inclination to march to the sound of the guns, he had his orders. Grant had specifically instructed his three division commanders that in his absence, they were "to do nothing to bring on an engagement." Until such time as McClernand, Smith, and Wallace received updated orders directly from their superior, they understood in no uncertain terms that it was their responsibility to "hold their positions."[7] At that moment, the commanding general was absent from the field of battle. Later paraphrasing those orders, Wallace wrote that he had been told "to hold . . . and prevent the enemy from escaping in that direction; in other words, to remain there and repel any sally from the fort. Under the orders, I had no authority to take the offensive." Appearing before the Joint Congressional Committee on the Conduct of the War on July 9, 1862, Wallace reiterated this position, informing the members of the committee that "I had no authority whatever given to me to make an offensive movement, and I accordingly held my position."[8]

Wallace now sent not one but two separate dispatch riders to Grant's headquarters seeking further clarification of his orders. His efforts were fruitless. None of Grant's staff officers wished to clarify or to interpret Grant's order. None of them believed Grant had appointed a temporary field commander to serve in his absence. The most reassuring thing they could collectively suggest to Wallace was that some staff members had already left headquarters hoping to find Grant. Smith, on the Union left, knew something was afoot on the Union right. Both Wallace and McClernand had sent messengers to Smith, a West Point graduate, requesting help from the senior and most professionally trained officer in the Union army in the field that day. The dedicated old soldier, however, likewise had his orders. They were the same ones Grant had issued to the two Union generals on his right. Thus, while others were engaged in efforts to save the Union right, Smith, on the Union left, sat under a tree facing the fort, calmly whittling. Smith knew his *U.S. Army Regulations* by the book; he knew how essential it was to respect and obey without question a superior officer's orders. Back on the right, a little after 10:00 A.M., Wallace received a second messenger from McClernand, this one more intense and desperate than the first. At this point, in direct disobedience to duly issued orders, Wallace seized responsibility and initiated his first independent act of the campaign.

Even though Confederate progress during the breakout from Fort Donelson had been marked by ebbs and flows, Brig. Gen. Gideon Pillow's tactics were sound. The Rebel breakout was gradually achieving its first stated objective, pushing the disorganized Union army down Wynn's Ferry Road as far as possible from the Dover to Charlotte to Nashville road. Wynn's Ferry Road extended south from the Cumberland River through the town of Dover for about two-thirds of a mile before turning at a right angle southwest toward Fort Henry. Dudley's Hill lay just to the east of where Wynn's Ferry Road turned to the southwest. Col. John McArthur's brigade of McClernand's 1st Division had slept the previous night on Dudley's Hill. Col. Richard Oglesby's brigade was camped immediately to the southwest of McArthur's camp, along Wynn's Ferry Road, while the camp of Col. W. H. L. Wallace's brigade lay next to it on the road moving southwest. Four to five hundred yards further southwest after passing by Colonel Wallace's camp, one came upon that half-mile swath of cleared land that separated the 1st Division from the 3rd Division.

Pillow planned to drive McArthur due west off Dudley's Hill onto Wynn's Ferry Road. McArthur's continuing retreat southwest would bring him into direct contact with Col. Richard Oglesby's right flank. Pillow intended to drive both McArthur and Oglesby back into W. H. L. Wallace's brigade until all three of McClernand's brigades were stacked literally one on top the other. This tactic was designed to exert an accordion effect on the whole Union line as one brigade was successfully pushed back into and on top of its neighbor and so on down the line of Wynn's Ferry Road. Then, when Pillow's troops had succeeded in driving all three Union brigades together, Brig. Gen. Simon Bolivar Buckner and his Confederate forces lying in wait in trenches on the south side of Dover directly north of Col. Wallace's camp would strike the flank of this disorganized mass of Union troops to hasten an already accelerating Union retreat.

Shortly after 7:00 A.M., Pillow's charge surprised McArthur. Seeking an outlet from the attacking Rebels, the entire Union right slowly began to roll down Wynn's Ferry Road as the Confederates had planned. Notwithstanding the momentary pauses in the overall progress of the attack, Pillow's troops generated confusion among the Union regiments constituting the 1st Division. Troops intermingled with each other as Union

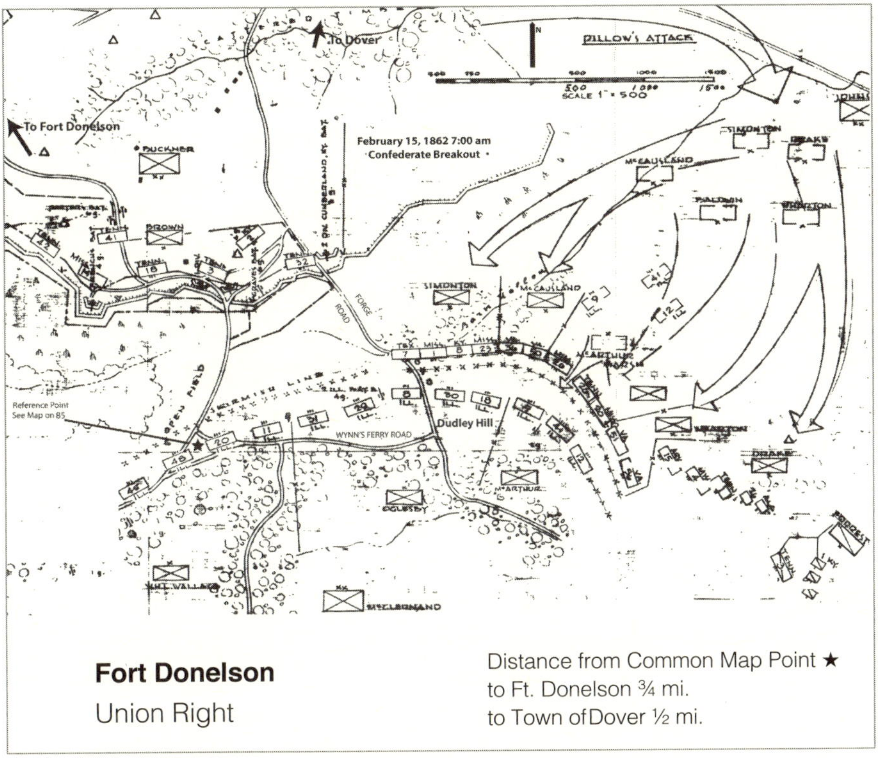

Fort Donelson, February 15, 1862, 7:00 A.M. Confederate breakout. (Troop Movement Map, sheet 5 of 11, by Edwin C. Bearss, National Park Service)

regiments often seemed to stand side by side with Confederate brigades. Companies from the same Union regiments became separated. Initiative, and the success it spawned, belonged decisively to the Confederates; both sides were running low on ammunition; and resolute Union leadership was remarkably nowhere to be found. Sometime after 9:00 A.M., a Confederate brigade, led by Col. John C. Brown, Buckner's division, charged out of its trenches. The men of the brigade rushed down a hill, crossed a field, and assaulted the center-left of the Union line, now made up of three disoriented and disorganized brigades, thereby adding more offensive weight to the breakout. The Rebels continued to drive the Union forces further southwest down Wynn's Ferry Road away from Dover. Then, almost as soon as it had started, the breakout ground to a halt. After three hours of near continuous fighting, Pillow's men paused and a lull descended on the battlefield as both sides sought to regroup. The advance had stopped near the eastern edge of the half-mile-wide swath of land that lay to Lew

Wallace's right. Wallace would soon locate his division on the western edge of that swath, attempting to seal it off against the advancing Rebels.[9]

All three of McClernand's brigade commanders blamed their battlefield plight to a large degree on an ever-dwindling supply of ammunition. This was in part true. None of the three, however, seemed to appreciate the extent to which the troops under their command had been caught so totally unaware by the Confederate breakout. None acknowledged in their post-battle reports the degree to which their troops collapsed and then ultimately retreated, even though initially the men of each brigade had met and resisted the surge of the Confederate breakout surprisingly well. Casualties on both sides were mounting and by mid-morning, the 1st Division had lost a considerable amount of its cohesiveness and effectiveness as a fighting unit.[10] The Rebels, exhausted as well and beginning to run low on ammunition, nevertheless seemed to have the advantage. With Union regiments separated from their brigade commanders, individual Union soldiers separated from their company commanders, and with the whole scene along the Wynn's Ferry Road bordering on chaos, Union forces were simply standing around. Whittlesey observed that "defeated battalions were not fleeing to the rear, but scattered without commands." As the Confederates paused for the first time in their breakout, most of the 1st Division had fallen back and was attempting to regroup in an area a good quarter of a mile further south of Wynn's Ferry Road. Depending on what happened next, a potential rout was at hand.[11]

McClernand would make his second appeal to Wallace from this position. In response, reacting to what he knew of the developing situation, Wallace acted independently. He committed a brigade. Approximately 2,500 men of the 3rd Division under the command of Col. Charles Cruft began a march to their right to find and support McClernand. In so doing, Wallace cut Cruft and his brigade off from any support from the remainder of the 3rd Division and likewise prevented them from providing any support to the division. Cruft and his men never had much of an impact in stemming the Confederate advance for two very good reasons. The scout ordered to guide Cruft to the 1st Division's front lines got lost and abandoned the brigade short of its intended destination. Then, when it did arrive, McClernand placed Cruft's brigade of fresh troops in his reserve rather than directly on the front line.

Ultimately, McClernand gave credit to Cruft for the assistance he rendered that day. Begrudgingly, he recalled that Cruft's brigade arrived in support sometime between 9:00 A.M. and 10:00 A.M. (it would have been more like 12:00 noon). McClernand was unable to acknowledge the contributions in battle of any other officer, such as Wallace, whose rank was in close proximity to his own. Thus, Wallace's decisive decision and action was portrayed by McClernand as follows: "This re-enforcement was generously brought forward by Colonel Cruft upon his own responsibility, in the absence of General Wallace, his divisional commander, in compliance with my request." Cruft soon corrected this portrayal of events, observing in his report that "[a]t 8:30 o'clock A.M. [much closer to 10:00 A.M.], General Wallace's order was received to put the brigade in rapid motion to the extreme right of our line, for the purpose of re-enforcing General McClernand's division."[12]

Wallace had dispatched Cruft to aid McClernand. In so doing, he had disobeyed Grant's orders. Because of those orders, he questioned his ability to do more. Further, with no cavalry for reconnaissance purposes, Wallace lacked the requisite battlefield intelligence necessary to make sound, critical decisions. By late morning, he knew only four things for certain: a battle was raging on his right flank; McClernand's position therein was apparently perilous; Smith was sitting firmly doing nothing; and Grant had authorized him only to stand firm to repulse any Confederate advance. Wallace knew neither the exact nature of the Confederates' intentions nor how many troops they had committed to the breakout. He was aware that things were not as they should be, but the uncertainty born of a lack of battlefield intelligence impeded his ability to do more, compelling him to continue to wait and wonder. On the other hand, an educated guess strongly suggested Wynn's Ferry Road as the probable avenue of Confederate concentration and advance. Finally, Wallace decided to wait no longer. He determined to assume the initiative at least in support of the beleaguered 1st Division and so he advanced. In so doing, Wallace knowingly and intentionally disobeyed the orders of a superior officer.

A man with Wallace's personal convictions had little concern about his own abilities in such a situation, but he was none too sure of those of his men and their officers. He had known them for less than a day and had probably not even led them in drill. There was a great deal of uncertainty involved in that fact alone. Later in the afternoon, Wallace would again command the 11th Indiana and 8th Missouri, but neither regiment was with him now. At Romney, he had known what the men of the 11th Indiana could accomplish. For a battle of the magnitude of Fort Donelson, he was frankly as untested as his men although he would never have admitted it. Further, everyone around him might soon find themselves engaged in a defensive action simply to hold onto the ground where they now stood, to prevent capture, and perhaps to save their own lives. Grant's order demanded prudence and circumspection. Exhibiting initiative and audacity often precluded a consideration of these qualities. Frankly, under the circumstances, Wallace had already violated them by dispatching Cruft. An hour before even that occurred, Wallace had talked with Rawlins. Grant's aide had offered no greater hope or assurance than a pledge to ride to find Grant to ask him what to do. Time appeared to be at a premium. As he wrote to Susan several days later, "altogether that moment tested my nerve more than ever before."[13]

Sometime before 12:00 noon, Wallace resolved his dilemma. He decided to hunt Rebels. He advanced his division in a general forward movement to and then up Wynn's Ferry Road in the direction of Dover, aggressively shifting his men to the right toward what he intuitively sensed were the advancing Confederates. This was an offensive maneuver. He was advancing, no longer holding, his position as Grant had ordered. The further to the right that Wallace marched, the more he came into contact with "broken regiments and companies, most of the men gathered in knots ready to fight on their own hook." An officer of the 76th Ohio recalled that "for the first time I saw wounded men being carried off on stretchers and in ambulances. I remember one of the Illinois boys saying to us: 'Boys, you'll catch Hell! We've just come out of there, and our regiment is all cut to pieces'."[14] Advancing about half a mile northeast of his original position, Wallace reasoned that whatever designs the Confederates had, the key was control of Wynn's Ferry Road. He therefore sought out and found on that road an excellent spot to establish a strong defensive position.

Wallace selected a place astride Wynn's Ferry Road at the crest of a small ridge southwest of the spot where the 17th Illinois, W. H. L. Wallace's brigade, had camped the night before. The ascent to the point where he established his line was not great. However, snow from the storm the night before was beginning to melt, forming puddles of water and mud at various spots in the roadway. Both the degree of ascent and the mud would cause some difficulties for the advancing Rebels, perhaps slowing the charge Wallace knew they would make. His defensive line intersected Wynn's Ferry Road at the western edge of a small, open field, approximately 400 yards southwest of a wooded area out through which

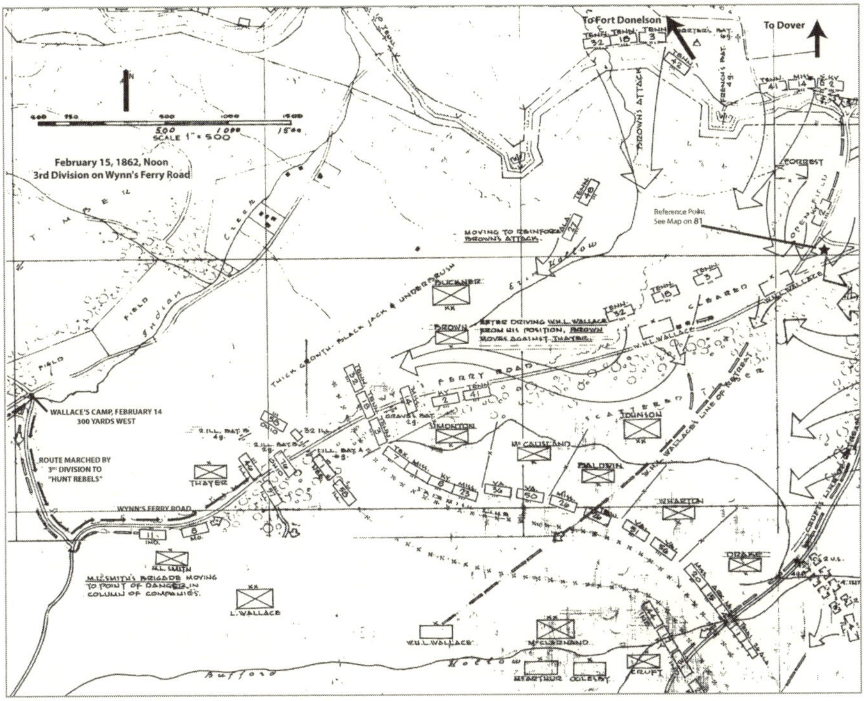

Fort Donelson, February 15, 1862, 12:15 P.M.–1:00 P.M. Wallace and 3rd Division. (Troop Movement Map, sheet 8 of 11, by Edwin C. Bearss, National Park Service)

Wynn's Ferry Road ran. He nestled his left flank close to a row of tall trees thereby partially shielding his command from Confederate artillery located high on a ridge to the north. The mere presence of the mostly disorganized remnants of the Union 1st Division about a quarter of a mile to the south protected and secured the right of his line against a Rebel flanking maneuver.[15]

In creating his defensive line, Wallace placed the six guns of Battery A, 1st Illinois Light Artillery, adjacent to and on the south side of Wynn's Ferry Road, supported on their immediate right by the 1st Nebraska, the core of Col. John Thayer's Brigade. Further to the right, Wallace located a combination of the 20th Ohio and the 58th Illinois. In the confusion of the Union retreat earlier that morning, Wallace had unexpectedly inherited command of Battery B, 1st Illinois Light Artillery. He now positioned two of the six guns of Battery B adjacent to and on the north side of Wynn's Ferry Road, supported on their immediate left by Company A of the 32nd Illinois and the 58th Ohio. Wallace assigned the 76th Ohio to a location astride the road some one hundred fifty feet or so to the rear of his first line. The remaining four guns of Battery B were located directly to the left of the 76th Ohio on a small knob, enabling this battery to pinpoint the advancing Rebels while firing over the heads of the 32nd Illinois and 58th Ohio. Further to the rear, in reserve, stood the 46th Illinois on the left and the 57th Illinois on the right. Wallace, as Whittlesey observed, "formed a new and more defensive line nearly at right angles to the first line [which had been McClernand's original position on the south side of Wynn's Ferry Road as the breakout commenced]. I was directed to the extreme right of that crotchet with energetic orders to hold it."[16] All was in readiness to confront and turn back any Rebel charge that might come down that road. Thayer clearly stated in his battle report that the location of the artillery and the positioning of the brigade had been done pursuant to orders issued by Wallace. Assuming the offensive on his own initiative, Wallace had established a strong defensive position.[17] He awaited the arrival of the Butternuts.

Shortly after noon, a Confederate offensive, commanded by Colonel Brown of Buckner's division, consisting of the 3rd, 18th, and 32nd Tennessee along with the 14th Mississippi, with the 2nd Kentucky and 41st Tennessee being held in reserve, emerged from the woods, charging down Wynn's Ferry Road. Wallace's men met them in three separate charges with steady and deliberate artillery and rifled musket fire for about forty-five minutes "when the enemy were [*sic*] completely repulsed and fled." Wallace and the men of the 3rd Division heard the Rebel yell three times that day. Each time they resisted, stopped, and finally broke the Rebel charge.[18] Lieutenant Burt of the 76th Ohio observed that Union troops under Wallace had reversed the Confederate tide. "As the leaves on the underbrush and the butternut uniforms of the rebels were nearly the same color," he recalled, "it was difficult to see the latter, but their balls whizzing about us convinced us that they were there. In less than half an hour, we had driven them from their position and their firing ceased." The combined fire of the 1st Nebraska, augmented by Lt. Peter P. Wood's Battery A and Capt. Ezra B. Taylor's Battery B, 2nd Illinois Light Artillery, "met the storm, no man flinching, and their fire was terrible." In his report, Wallace concluded that the twelve artillery pieces, supported by infantry, "repelled the charge." At this moment, near 1:00 P.M., Wallace and his men stood firm, stubborn, and proud as they, according to Sgt. Charles B. Kimbell, "succeeded in repelling the last decisive charges of the enemy as they came pouring out of the fort." The correspondent for the *Missouri Democrat* thought the turning point occurred when "Taylor's and Willard's [Lieutenant Wood had just replaced Willard in command of Battery A] batteries could be brought into action, [and] we were able to stem the tide. These two batteries outdid themselves. Grape, canister and shrapnel, and an uninterrupted musketry fire from the First Nebraska, Forty-eighth and Fifty-eighth Ohio proved too much for the so far victorious foes, and they were at last obliged to retire."[19]

As he reported the events of Saturday morning, the *Harper's Weekly* correspondent illustrated a certain amount of confusion as to the progression of the battle. For example, he reported that Smith on the left was already "inside the enemy's entrenchments" before the last desperate charge of Brown's brigade took place. That was simply not the case as it is difficult to lead a division of infantry in a frontal assault through hills and ravines while simultaneously whittling. Smith's heroic efforts came later Saturday afternoon. The correspondent also erred when he mistakenly said that Wallace had with him on Saturday morning the 11th Indiana and the 8th Missouri. He would not lead the men of these two regiments in battle until that afternoon. However, he correctly reported the formation of Wallace's defensive line on Wynn's Ferry Road and the devastating impact it had on the last phase of Pillow's breakout. "Company A, of the Chicago Light Artillery, was planted in the road," the correspondent wrote, "and as the rebels, supposing we were in retreat, came yelling out of their works into the road, the Chicago boys poured a hail-storm of grape and canister into their ranks. . . . Simultaneously with this the infantry commenced firing at will and the rebels went pell-mell back into their works."[20]

Soon after Brown's third charge was repulsed, Pillow ordered his men to retreat into the very entrenchments in front of the fort and the town from which they had commenced the breakout six hours earlier. Wallace sent out skirmishers in advance of his position and held his line, now content to wait for further orders from Grant. It had been a grand and glorious affair. The Rebels had shown their backsides to the 3rd Division. Wallace and the men he had not even known twenty hours earlier had fought their first major battle together and prevailed. Wallace always believed his contribution that day was both critical and decisive.

The Confederates on Wynn's Ferry Road wilted before a defensive line initiated and brilliantly deployed by a young general officer from Indiana. Had Pillow's well-conceived breakout maneuver succeeded, and it had come remarkably close to doing just that, neither the fighting Saturday afternoon nor the surrender of the fort the next day would probably have occurred, at least for a time.[21] Wallace salvaged the integrity of the Union right flank. He and his 3rd Division rescued a major portion of Grant's army from a serious situation, perhaps from a jolting defeat, and perhaps even from destruction. In the process, Wallace preserved for posterity the military reputation of Ulysses S. Grant.

Wallace played a limited but highly decisive role in the battle for Fort Donelson. His bold resourcefulness and audacity on the morning of February 15, 1862, had saved Grant's right flank from a possible rout. By his actions, Wallace gave Grant two tactical military elements usually common to success in any military venture—time and opportunity. Once he became the beneficiary of these two elements, Grant seized the initiative from the staggered Confederates and engineered a brilliantly conceived, spontaneous counterattack. If nothing else, the ferocity of that counterattack exerted a profoundly negative psychological effect on Confederate command now back inside Fort Donelson. In the process, armed with the two elements Wallace had given him, Grant also redeemed his military reputation. All these results would become manifest the next day. First, however, there would be more decisive action favoring the Union on Saturday afternoon. In support of Grant, Wallace would play a significant role in that action.

CHAPTER SEVEN

Fort Donelson, February 15, 1862, P.M.

In his official report of the 3rd Division's performance at Fort Donelson, Wallace was predictably frank. He detailed the three tenets of Grant's orders. Grant had instructed him first "to hold [his] position," which he identified as being in the center of the Union line with Smith on his left and McClernand on his right. Further, from this location, he was next "to prevent the enemy from escaping in that direction." Third, Wallace was "to remain there" and, if necessary, "repel any sally from the fort." Having established these assertions as indisputable facts, Wallace then enunciated the basic premise of his case: "Under these orders, I had no authority to take the offensive."[1]

Notwithstanding these specific orders as he recollected them, Wallace had assumed the offensive Saturday morning, February 15, 1862. Directly disobeying those orders, Wallace had gone off aggressively looking for Rebels. He informed Grant that, as he pondered his decision, his line was being more and more inundated by Union soldiers then in retreat, men appearing as "fugitives from the battle," men bearing in their wake the "unmistakable signs of disaster." He even recited a story of an unnamed Union colonel riding into his line shouting, "We are cut to pieces." He told Grant that in his view the situation on the ground compelled him at least "to prevent a panic among the regiments of my Third Brigade." He further justified his actions by implying he had personal knowledge that "the enemy had turned his [McClernand's] flanks, and were endangering his whole command." In the final analysis, Wallace acted aggressively and unilaterally, as "there was no time to await orders" for "the crisis had come."[2]

Wallace gave Grant some detail as to the placement of his defensive line once astride Wynn's Ferry Road. He pointed out that the charging

Rebels focused upon Company A, 1st Illinois Light Artillery, and Thayer's 1st Nebraska as the "principal points of attack." The soldiers of his division "met the storm, no man flinching, and their fire was terrible. To say they did well is not enough. Their conduct was splendid. They alone repelled the charge." Unlike McClernand's statements on the action that day, Wallace praised his men, not himself. Wallace noted that Cruft, still with McClernand, "saw the enemy retire to their works pell-mell and in confusion." By attributing this conclusion to Cruft, Wallace thus indicated his belief that not only had his men performed well that morning but he also had played a decisive role in the ultimate outcome of the battle.[3]

Wallace waited twenty years to learn what the Confederates directly involved in the charge against him on Wynn's Ferry Road had contemporaneously written about that event. In 1882, the U.S. government published volume 7 of *The Official Records of the War of the Rebellion*, which contained the battlefield reports filed by the five Confederate brigade and regimental commanders who had directly confronted Wallace on Wynn's Ferry Road. Only one said anything remotely complimentary about the 3rd Division. "The enemy opened a galling fire of shot and shell upon us," one officer remarked. The writers of each of the five accounts either implied or stated outright that the Confederates forced the 3rd Division to retreat that day, leaving the field of battle open to and in the hands of the victorious Confederates. This, of course, presents an interesting conundrum. These reports unanimously conclude that the Rebels on Wynn's Ferry Road prevailed, forcibly removing Wallace and the 3rd Division from the field of battle. If true, Pillow's ordered retreat makes no military sense whatsoever. Each of the five writers glossed over that contradiction in one of two ways. Three Confederate commanders simply stated that the order to retreat came as a surprise, concluding that as junior officers, they had no alternative but to comply. The remaining two avoided highlighting the problem altogether, failing to mention the retreat as if it had never occurred. None of the five Confederate battle reports contained much in the way of reliable information. So ill-informed were these five Rebel commanders that none of them even identified Wallace as their opponent on Wynn's Ferry Road. Wallace could scarcely have been pleased with that.

The "fog of war," accented no doubt by personal vanity and ego, hung heavy over Wynn's Ferry Road. It beguiled and misled the five Confederates as they penned their accounts. Pillow's two official reports were not much better in this regard. He did, however, indicate that he had ordered

3rd Division Artillery on Wynn's Ferry Road, February 15, 1862, 11:00 A.M. Batteries of Taylor and Wood (formerly McAllister). (Library of Congress)

a general retreat when he personally witnessed Buckner's command become thoroughly demoralized after "being repulsed by the battery."[4] Among the defeated, undoubtedly Randal W. McGavock, lieutenant colonel of the 10th Tennessee, uttered the most balanced and accurate account of that morning's events. From a battery located behind the Confederate entrenchments on the hillside north of the action, McGavock witnessed everything. He saw the three Rebel charges down Wynn's Ferry Road against Wallace's defensive line. Dispassionately, he wrote that the turning point occurred when infantry in support of Union artillery entered the fight. "While they [McClernand's division] were retreating and just as they were about crossing the ridge leading into the Central valley, a battery and several Reg's came to their aid. The battery opened upon us," McGavock wrote, "and caused our troops to falter. At this point, our forces were ordered to fall back into their pits."[5]

Grant did little better than the Rebels in acknowledging Wallace's February 15 contributions at Fort Donelson. He gave Wallace the same limited and casual praise he bestowed upon his other two divisional commanders. Grant wrote that McClernand, Smith, and Wallace had each led their respective divisions "in the midst of danger." This was a lackluster accolade, particularly when compared with the lavish praise Grant bestowed the next day upon "the men who fought the battle [who] will live in the memory of a grateful people."[6] In his *Personal Memoirs*, Grant made a slight concession to Wallace, noting that "at an opportune time," Wallace moved Thayer to the support of McClernand and "thereby contributed to hold the enemy within his lines." Such an innocuous off-the-cuff and essentially erroneous remark did little in 1885 to placate Wallace. Grant never said a word about the amateur soldier's timely, proficient, and altogether professional deployment of batteries A and B, 1st Illinois Light Artillery.[7]

Pillow's breakout had come perilously close to destroying a major portion of Grant's army at Donelson. Had this occurred, Grant's military career might well have been destroyed as well. The Rebels had surprised him with their breakout. He was embarrassed. Arguably, the less he said about the battle, the better for him. Thus, his official battlefield report on Fort Donelson was amazingly succinct. So much so that there was no discussion at all of how precarious conditions became on the Union right that Saturday morning. Grant did not intentionally mislead anyone in his account. He just kept the conversation to a minimum. Further illustrative of his efforts to dampen down his report, Grant did not embellish his official Donelson statement with accounts of his personal command activities. Nor did he criticize any of his subordinates. Instead, when he realized the time had come to disapprove of a subordinate's action, he offered such in the form of an endorsement to that subordinate's report. This did not apply to Smith, because he wrote no report. Grant did not endorse Wallace's report in any respect. When, however, McClernand attempted to assume full responsibility for virtually all of Wallace's timely command decisions, as well as one or two Grant knew he had made, Grant endorsed the report of his 1st Division commander, dismissing McClernand's exaggerated self-importance by writing, "I have no special comments to make on it, further than the report is a little highly colored as to the conduct of the First Division, and I failed to hear the suggestions spoken of about the propriety of attacking the enemy all around the lines on Saturday. No suggestions were made by General McClernand at the time spoken of." Grant employed the same tactic as at Shiloh, refusing to endorse Wallace's report "in some other particulars," none of which he ever specifically identified.[8]

Having received scant praise from Grant, Wallace justifiably felt his contributions to the victory at Fort Donelson had been grossly overlooked. He believed his actions on that Saturday morning had provided Grant with two vital commodities, time and opportunity, which Grant then exploited with clarity and celerity to produce a great victory. Yet the glory and honor Wallace believed he had won was not accorded him. Perhaps most galling of all was that Grant never mentioned anything in his official report about the activities of the 3rd Division along Wynn's Ferry Road. The Lincoln administration recommended and the U.S. Senate confirmed Wallace's promotion to the rank of major general. Lincoln also, however, sought and obtained promotions to the same rank for Buell, who had not even been at Donelson, and thus done nothing to produce victory, and for McClernand, who, Wallace was confident, had done almost everything to produce defeat. Wallace retained command of the 3rd Division but even that was a hollow achievement. Following the battle, Grant ordered the division back to Fort Henry. Thus, for a variety of reasons, Wallace simply felt unappreciated and perhaps again left behind.

Not everyone reacted to the day's events as disingenuously as Grant. To honor Wallace's accomplishments at Donelson, friends and neighbors in Crawfordsville presented him with a ceremonial sword. Wallace's acceptance was perfunctory, anything but gracious, suggesting, perhaps, how hurtful it was to be overlooked by those who really mattered. To his friend Aaron Blair, he casually observed, "I see the citizens have been getting me a sword. Good! It will be the only present I have received during the war, and all the more flattering because unsuggested [*sic*] and unsolicited. From what I have heard of it, my fear is it will be too fine for camp day use." When Wallace appeared before the Joint Congressional Committee on the Conduct of the War several months later, Congressman John Covode of Pennsylvania asked him if the situation as it unfolded on the morning of February 15 had compelled him to act upon his own personal judgment and initiative. Wallace answered in the affirmative. Covode concluded, "[a]nd in doing so you saved the army, did you not?" To this, Wallace gave a measured, but enthusiastic, response, "I am satisfied my command repulsed the enemy; I know they did."[9]

There was, however, still more fighting to do on the banks of the Cumberland and Wallace had two more significant contributions to make. By 12:30 P.M. on February 15, Wallace had blunted the Confederate breakout. The Rebels had retreated into their fortifications surrounding Fort Donelson and Dover. The contest for Fort Donelson was far from over, however. With his offensive maneuvers on the Wynn's Ferry Road, Wallace had set the table; in a moment of boldness and audacity, Grant would decide how to clear it. Wallace was certain that he and he alone of the four Union general officers at Fort Donelson had made that moment possible.

Around 1:30 P.M., having returned from his meeting with Foote, Grant arrived on the Union right. He found Wallace and McClernand on horseback analyzing the recently concluded activities. They were not debating whether either or both should lead a charge against the Confederate fortifications. That was not their prerogative. They had their orders to stand firm until Grant spoke further. Neither man had any intention of violating those orders under ordinary conditions. Each was waiting for his superior to appear.

Riding up Wynn's Ferry Road in search of Wallace and McClernand, Grant observed isolated groups of McClernand's embattled division "standing in knots," mostly milling about, while "no officer seemed to be giving any directions." Collectively, the men of the 1st Division appeared physically exhausted, confused, and low on ammunition. Grant was struck by the fact "that the enemy did not take advantage" of these conditions. Maybe it was time for him to regroup and consider himself fortunate that the Confederates had visited no more damage upon his right flank that day than initially appeared to be the case. On closer observation, Grant noticed many of the Confederate dead had knapsacks stuffed with food, ammunition, blankets, and clothing. It was conceivable that the Rebels had intended to go somewhere if their breakout had been successful. Grant began to suspect that the enemy was bone tired, as confused and low on ammunition as his own men. Having been ordered to retreat, Confederate forces might just be as demoralized as their Union counterparts. The enemy might possibly have lost their will to fight. Even so, given the overall condition of the Union right flank, Grant was inclined to assume that the tactical advantages of initiative and momentum still lay with the Butternuts. Nevertheless, he began to grasp the possibility that Wallace's defeat of the Rebel charge down Wynn's Ferry Road had produced a momentary shift in the psychology of the battle. The Rebels seemed to have abandoned the initiative. That valuable commodity was now his for the taking. Approaching his two division commanders, he hurriedly evaluated his options.[10]

In his *Battles and Leaders* essay, Wallace characterized this impromptu meeting with Grant as "the crisis of the battle." Grant appeared concerned but not overly agitated. Exhibiting a surprising degree of "calmness," Grant asked his two brigadiers to report, after which Grant told them that Foote intended to take the majority of the ironclads to Mound City for repair. He then ventured the opinion that under existing circumstances, it might be best to draw the tenuously extended Union line back behind a series of low-lying hills beyond the range of Confederate artillery. There, Union troops could initiate a siege of the Donelson–Dover area. Union reinforcements of men and materials were arriving daily. Once repaired, Union gunboats could take control of enemy activity on the Cumberland River. In time, a siege would induce surrender.

At that point, Wallace observed in Grant's demeanor that "the idea [siege warfare] was detestable to him—bitterly so." Wallace said he then observed that the Confederate breakout that morning had succeeded in reopening the road to Charlotte and thence to Nashville should the Confederates choose to abandon the fort. Upon being advised of this, Grant "flushed up . . . and ordered the assault. The flushing of the face . . . was the visible emotion natural to a man in a position of vast responsibility resolving suddenly upon a decisive action."[11] Instantly, Grant saw that a siege was not the answer. He ordered McClernand and Wallace to advance immediately and at least retake the original Union positions lost that morning during the breakout. Having made his decision, Grant then rode off to find Smith. It was time to attack the fort.

Whatever thoughts and emotions assailed Grant at that moment, he chose to be aggressive rather than passive, audacious rather than cautious. In his *Battles and Leaders* essay, Wallace focused on this meeting to assess Grant's intuitive nature as a military commander as well as his character in general. "In every great man's career," Wallace wrote, "there is a crisis exactly similar to that which now overtook General Grant, and it cannot be better described than as a crucial test of his nature." Wallace understood that an individual of lesser character might well have embraced conditions then existing on the battlefield as the new status-quo, rationalized that others, not he, had created his current dilemma, and then accepted the less threatening realities of a siege. A siege would undoubtedly have been a legitimate response to the day's developments. It was, however, the wrong decision in Wallace's opinion. "Had General Grant done so, it is very probable his history would have been then and there concluded. It cannot be doubted that he saw with painful directness the effect of the disaster to his right wing." At that moment, "his face flushed slightly. . . . But in an instant these signs of disappointment or hesitation . . . cleared away." As he galloped off to find Smith on the left, "in an ordinary quiet voice he said, addressing himself to both officers, 'Gentlemen, the position on the right must be retaken'." Penning an earlier version of these events, Wallace concluded, "[h]ad he, failing the inspiration of his own genius, obeyed that order [the order allegedly from Halleck to commence a siege], Donelson would have been in our arms the empty success that Corinth was a little later."[12]

Instinctively, Grant knew what to do. With no maps other than those that were in his head and without consultation with anyone other than himself, Grant intuitively devised a three-pronged counterattack. The recapture of the lost ground on the Union right must be coordinated with Smith's assault on the fort. Underscoring these simultaneous advances, Union gunboats on the Cumberland River must use as much force as possible even though the navy had already failed in its attempt to control the river. Grant sent a hastily written yet precise dispatch, submitting the following proposition: "If all the Gun Boats that can, will immediately make their appearance to the enemy, it may secure a victory. Otherwise all may be defeated." He further advised that "a terrible conflict [had] ensued in my absence, which has demoralized a portion of my command and I think the enemy is much more so." Now was the time to strike. Technically, the Union navy at Fort Donelson was under the command of the army. However, Grant seldom treated Foote as a subordinate. In this light, Grant's hurried communiqué was more of a request, a suggestion of action, than an order. Be that as it may, Grant believed that if the gunboats remained idle "it [would] reassure the enemy and still further demoralize our troops."[13] Without Wallace's contribution on Wynn's Ferry Road hours earlier, Grant would not have had the time or the opportunity to write that dispatch or to devise and direct any counterattack.

On the Union left, the first coordinated phase of the three-pronged counterattack began. Smith, who had earlier sat firmly before the fort whittling while obeying Grant's orders to the letter, personally led the 2nd Division against the fort. At his command, the 2nd Iowa and the 25th Indiana left the ridgeline where they had encamped the previous night and descended into the first of two ravines shielding the fort. There, confusion reigned and military formation disintegrated amid his troops' inability to penetrate heavy underbrush and fallen trees while dodging murderous fire from the Confederates above. Cursing and prodding, Smith slowly led his men out of that ravine, up the hill, and took the Confederate trench line atop the ridge sometime after 4:00 P.M. The Confederate defenders retreated down into the next ravine and back up into the trenches on the ridgeline immediately adjacent to the fort on its west side. Smith struck again. By this time, Buckner's men had returned to their original positions of Saturday morning following Pillow's unexpected retreat. They reinforced the Confederates left in those trenches, halting the advance of the 2nd Division. At this juncture, stalemate reigned. Some battlefield reports stated that this or that particular regiment actually penetrated the fort's perimeter defenses. Other regimental commanders acknowledged that their advance stopped just short of that objective. In fact, no Union regiments broke into the fort that day. Perhaps one or two Union regiments were close enough to achieving this goal to give Buckner the impression that the Yankees had penetrated the fort's defenses. In that context, Smith undoubtedly imbued his enemy with the psychological perception of defeat.[14]

On the Cumberland River, as the second prong of Grant's counterattack began, Commodore Benjamin M. Dove's guns on the *St. Louis* "threw a few shells" into Fort Donelson "and toward dark" retired downriver. This had no demonstrable impact on the two infantry battles then in progress. Just the fact, however, that one Union gunboat had gone on the offensive the day following what appeared to be a near total defeat of the Union navy made a considerable impression that night on the Confederates inside the fort. This was exactly what Grant had intended and so desperately needed.[15]

One of the first things Grant had done when he returned from his impromptu meeting onboard Foote's flagship was to detach the 11th Indiana and the 8th Missouri from the 2nd Division and send both to Wallace. At the time, Grant had at best an incomplete knowledge of what lay before him but he intuitively sensed that Wallace had a greater need for these men than did Smith. Grant recalled he had required Wallace, upon his arrival at Donelson and as a condition for being vested with command of the newly created 3rd Division, to transfer both regiments to Smith. This had been a difficult thing for Wallace to do, particularly as he had lived, trained, and fought with the 11th Indiana from the very beginning. In addition, he had come to value highly the men of the 8th Missouri and their commander, Col. Morgan Smith. Now, under the exigencies of the current situation, Grant restored both regiments to Wallace. This was a significant command decision. Both regiments arrived on the right too late to participate in the combined artillery and infantry defensive line that sent the remnants of Brown's brigade and then all of Pillow's men back into their trenches. For the pending counterattack to recapture ground lost earlier that morning, however, Wallace had his two favorite regiments under his command again.[16]

Wallace knew he could trust these men and their officers. They were trained to advance and fire, pushing forward in small, irregularly formed groups along the front of the battle line, more like skirmishers than stiff-necked marionettes marching in formal, unbending column or line. They had been taught to anticipate an enemy volley, to fall to the ground and crawl forward before the volley was discharged, and then to rise and race

3rd Division—counterattack on Union right, February 15, 1862, 3:00 P.M.–3:30 P.M. (*Frank Leslie's Illustrated Newspaper* [March 15, 1862])

toward the enemy line while the enemy reloaded. They knew how to distract the enemy and cause much of their enemy's fire to be too high to do any real damage. They had also had extensive combat instruction with the bayonet. They fought as Zouaves.[17] In addition to his personal knowledge of these men and their training techniques, Wallace knew they were psychologically prepared and ready to fight. Wallace directed them, and under colonels McGinnis and Smith they fought well. As the battle drew to a close for the day, the men of the 11th Indiana and 8th Missouri had proudly and successfully displayed at Fort Donelson the extent to which they had learned their training and battle tactics.[18] In giving these men back to Wallace, Grant propounded yet another brilliant command decision.

On the Union right, Wallace led the third coordinated phase of Grant's counterattack. By 5:00 P.M., the Union right line had advanced approximately one thousand yards northeast along Wynn's Ferry Road from the point at which the 3rd Division had stopped Brown's brigade to the intersection of Wynn's Ferry and Forge roads west of Dudley's Hill. Even before Grant arrived at Donelson, the Confederates had extended their defenses around the town of Dover by digging an eight-to-ten-foot-deep trench line about three-quarters of the way up a steep hill. The hill was located between the north edge of the field that Wallace now occupied and Dover, just a short distance further to the north. In front of that trench line, the Rebels had constructed sections of split-rail fences and one or two small abatis. At 3:00 P.M., on Saturday, the Confederates were back in those entrenchments. Wallace had to cross the field, climb the hill, and assault the entrenched Rebel defensive line.

On the Confederate left of that line, Col. Gabriel C. Wharton's brigade, supported by enfilading fire from a battery of four field guns directed by Capt. David A. French, stood ready to repulse. On the Confederate right, Col. John M. Simonton's brigade, likewise supported by enfilading fire from a battery of four field guns commanded by Capt. Rice E. Graves, occasionally identified as the "Cumberland" (Ky.) battery, prepared to pour withering fire down upon any invader.[19] Despite several attempts, the 11th Indiana and the 8th Missouri, supported by Thayer and Cruft's brigades, found themselves unable to penetrate the Confederate defenses. Zouave training notwithstanding, the attack on the Confederate defenses on the Union right that afternoon could simply go no further. For one thing, Wallace had outrun his lines of supply. As evening fell, Wallace had regained most, but not all, of the land lost to the Confederate breakout that morning.[20]

"While the fighting was in progress," Wallace wrote in his battlefield report, "an order reached me through Colonel Webster to retire my column, as a new plan of operations was in contemplation for the next day." Wallace had already retaken one hill, one field, and an intervening ravine from the Rebels that afternoon. Pondering Webster's order, Wallace realized that if it were obeyed, he would be "compelled to give up the hill so hardly recaptured," as well as a large portion of the ground that his troops had reclaimed. "Satisfied that the general [Grant] did not know of our success when he issued the direction, I assumed the responsibility of disobeying it, and held the battle ground that night."[21] Webster, Grant's chief of staff, never discussed this alleged order in his final report. He never stated whether or not Grant had issued such an order to Wallace. More likely than not, having charged across the open field in front of the Rebel entrenchments and having failed to break through the Rebel defensive line, Wallace called a halt to his advance. Daylight was waning. He realized he was thoroughly unfamiliar with the lay of the land in front of him, having been on the ground at Donelson for only twenty-eight hours. He determined that, without a greater concentration of artillery against the Rebel defensive line, not even Zouave tactics could breach it. Wallace's offensive did not fail for lack of enthusiasm or valor, just logistics.

If Wallace did disobey a second Grant order that day, he disobeyed it only to the extent that he did not withdraw his forces to the point where Thayer and the Chicago Board of Trade Battery had repulsed Brown's three charges earlier in the day. Maj. Fred Arn, 31st Indiana, unwittingly had the last word on the question of whether or not Wallace disobeyed a second order from Grant, a somewhat insignificant controversy. With the 17th Kentucky on his right, Arn, sometime around 5:00 P.M., charged "over the hills until we reached a ravine immediately below the enemy's batteries [French and Graves] where we were exposed to a terrible fire of grape, shrapnel and shells." At this point, Arn said, "we were ordered back to the position from which we charged." The 31st Indiana and the rest of the 3rd Division then retired from directly in front of the Confederate entrenchments to the south side of the field, facing the Confederate defensive line but not all the way back to the area from which Pillow had retreated shortly after noon that day. As a fitting conclusion to Wallace's participation in Grant's three-pronged counterattack, Colonel Smith supplied history with an anecdote. In his brief battlefield report, he wrote, "The gallant Eleventh Indiana would have gladly been in the lead, but kindly yielded to their brothers, the Eighth Missouri, with the understanding that it opens the ball on the next occasion, for which it is patiently waiting."[22]

CHAPTER EIGHT

Breakfast at Fort Donelson

On February 15, as the Union army broke off its attack late Saturday afternoon, Confederate commander, Brig. Gen. John Floyd called a council of war for that night at the Dover Hotel. After an hour's discussion, all three brigadiers, Floyd, Gideon Pillow, and Simon Bolivar Buckner, agreed a second breakout would be attempted the next morning. Lt. Col. Randal McGavock left the conference early, "with the impression on my mind that the battle would be renewed tomorrow with greater vigor."[1] Moments later, Rebel command decided that once the Confederates had achieved the same level of success as they had the previous day, the army would retire to Nashville by way of Charlotte.

Around 1:00 A.M., February 16, Floyd convened a second conference at the Rice House in Dover to make plans for coordinating troop dispositions for the morning's breakout. While discussing these issues, Floyd and Pillow broached the subject of the condition of the Charlotte road. Together, they speculated that the road might not be passable given the recent rains and the probable flooding of the Cumberland River and its tributary, Lick Creek. The three Brigadiers agreed to dispatch two teams of scouts, one under the direct command of Lt. Col. Nathan Bedford Forrest, to ascertain the proximity of Union troops to the Charlotte road as well as its condition. As they concluded the conference shortly afterward, Floyd set 4:00 A.M. as the time for the second Confederate breakout.[2]

Floyd, Pillow, and Buckner remained at the Rice House to receive intelligence from the scouts. The first team reported that the waters of Lick Creek had risen sufficiently to inundate the road with three feet of water. In addition, Union campfires had been observed on Dudley's Hill south and west of the road. Next, Forrest's scouts returned with information that over one hundred yards of the road was flooded at a depth roughly equivalent to the height of a saddle skirt on a cavalry horse. There was mud everywhere, but neither the water nor the mud would be a major deterrent to the retiring army. All agreed that conditions were far from optimal for the infantry but doable. Most, if not all, the artillery would be spiked and left in the fort. Still, Forrest and his scouts concluded the road was passable. Although they had seen the campfires on Dudley's Hill in relatively the same locations as the night before, none of the scouts had encountered any Union forces during their ride. It was windy the night of February 15. One or two, including Forrest, suggested that atmospheric conditions, not humans, were re-stoking the Union campfires from the night before. After all, having been so surprised the morning of the 15th, no Yankee had had the time to douse a fire as the breakout descended upon him. Forrest was convinced that very few Union soldiers were bivouacked around those fires. There was some speculation that the fires were bogus. Forrest suggested some fires might have been purposefully started to persuade the Confederates that Union troops once more occupied Dudley's Hill. Forrest believed that the fires were nothing more than a trick of nature and man. He was correct. A pitifully small number of Union wounded had started the fires that night.

The scouts departed. Forrest remained. Buckner had something on his mind. In addition to his perception that Union troops were perilously close to entering the fort on the Confederate right, he was concerned about the condition of the escape road as well as the campfires the scouts had observed. The flooding on Lick Road was decidedly an unfavorable circumstance. He was unsure if the fires on Dudley's Hill meant that Grant's troops had reoccupied that position but he felt certain that Yankees were close enough to the Rebel left flank to pose an insurmountable obstacle if the Confederates encountered any other problem carrying out the retreat. He was overwhelmed by his recollection that a few hours earlier all three brigadiers had agreed not to make this attempt if Union troops already blockaded the only avenue of escape.[3] Above all else, Buckner could not dismiss from his mind what he knew of the condition, real and psychological, of the Confederate army at Fort Donelson.[4]

In fact, Buckner knew nothing for certain inasmuch as all three Rebel generals had spent more time and energy denying their scouts' reports than accepting them. Buckner could, however, speculate. Suddenly, he stated that the Confederates must surrender the fort in the morning.[5] From then on, confusion reigned. Desperation and despair, underscored by a comical and cowardly attempt by Floyd and Pillow to pass command of the fort to Buckner, dominated the discussion. If the importance and far-reaching consequences of the subject matter had not been so serious, it would have been a burlesque worth seeing. During the remaining tenure of the conference, the structure of Confederate command within the fort broke down, sealing the fate of the Confederacy on the banks of the Cumberland River. Five or so hours later, in the early morning hours of February 16, 1862, Buckner, now in command, raised the white flag and surrendered the fort and the town.

"There was a strange silence" that morning as Union officers prepared their men for the coming day's battle, the fourth of the campaign on the Cumberland. Then, without warning, cheers erupted all along the line as the assembled Union troops suddenly became aware of an unexpected sight. Flags of surrender were now flying over the Confederate defenses at Donelson and Dover. Wilbur F. Crummer, 45th Illinois, wrote in his diary: "Soon after daybreak . . . we heard great cheering by the troops along the line and presently orderlys [*sic*] came galloping toward us, swinging their caps and proclaiming the news of the surrender of the fort. Did we shout? Well, if we didn't use our lungs then we never did."[6]

The Twin Rivers campaign, the first major Union campaign of the war in the western theater, had come to an end. As a result of Union victory, amazing in terms of the number of Confederates and the amount of war materials captured, national hero status awaited Grant. Not so for Wallace. Wallace had undoubtedly been as responsible as Grant for the appearance of the white flags over Fort Donelson. He certainly believed this to be true. In the aftermath of victory, however, he garnered minimal recognition from the Northern press, scant appreciation from his supposed political allies back home, and certainly very little of the glory and honor that he deemed he justly deserved from the public.[7] Within the military, his efforts and the results he produced were either simply not appreciated or purposefully ignored. Painfully, Wallace realized that Grant would never be prepared to acknowledge his contributions at Donelson.

Grant was, however, eloquent in his praise of the events of the day. Summarizing the impact of Donelson, he observed that "the victory achieved was not only great in the effect it will have in breaking down the rebellion, but has secured the greatest number of prisoners of war ever taken in any battle on this continent." Then, with an unusual display of enthusiasm, Grant concluded, "Fort Donelson will hereafter be marked in Capitals on the maps of our United country, and the men who fought the battle will live in the memory of a grateful people."[8] Grant did not bestow such accolades on Wallace. It is doubtful Grant ever appreciated how deeply indebted he should have been to him.

Donelson was the first major Union victory not only in the West but of the war itself. Approximately fifteen thousand prisoners, thousands of horses and mules, rifles and artillery pieces, ammunition, food stuffs, blankets, uniforms, overcoats, and medical supplies, none of which would be available to the Confederacy at Shiloh six weeks later or ever, were appropriated that Sunday morning without another shot being fired. Overnight, the initials in Grant's name took on the aura of popular legend. Even though both Foote and Smith had used the term before Grant did, "U.S." Grant became "Unconditional Surrender" Grant. Tribute for Grant now became the order of the day. For his efforts, Wallace received few, if any, national accolades. The war correspondents who had so favored him in the East now seemed to ignore him in the West.[9]

At Donelson, Grant revealed his military character. Wallace did likewise. Although Grant was more experienced and seasoned than Wallace, both made mistakes at Donelson. On the positive side of the ledger, they both performed brilliantly. As Romney had been for Wallace, Donelson was for Grant. The fort was in front of him, blocking where he wanted to go, so he took it. For Grant, the fort was just another obstacle to overcome. Both he and Wallace proved on many occasions that they could act decisively, with boldness and audacity. Wallace accomplished this midmorning, February 15. Grant did likewise mid-afternoon the same day. Nowhere the reckless and feckless soldier Halleck believed him to be, Grant was simply unwilling to sit and watch. In this respect, he and Wallace were mirror images.[10]

The two men, in at least three respects, were otherwise so dissimilar that their shared traits were secondary to their differences. Grant evidenced a greater toleration than Wallace for inactivity imposed by orders from above. Generally speaking, when Grant received an order from a superior, he did his best to comply. Wallace often had serious problems duplicating Grant in that respect. Second, while both fought with patriotic zeal to preserve the integrity of the Union, Wallace sought to win personal honor and glory in the process. Grant often emphatically denied that such accolades had any real meaning for him. Third, and most importantly, Grant was a listener, not a talker. He had his problems from within the military chain of command but invariably the only two persons who had knowledge of this were his patron, Illinois Congressman Elihu B. Washburne, and his wife, Julia. In similar circumstances, Wallace frequently resorted to the public forum to vent his anxiety and anger. These personality differences did not bode well for a continuing personal or military relationship between the two men.

It is difficult to assess objectively the impact Wallace had on events at Donelson because of two facets of his persona. First, other than in his Donelson battlefield report, whenever Wallace wrote or spoke about his role in any event, his statements were highly personalized and subjective. Regardless of the medium, he often found it next to impossible to be objective. His letters back home to his wife, in which one might suspect he could seize the opportunity to relate the unvarnished truth to a genuine confidante, suffered the same fate. A noticeable absence of personal detachment too often marred his keen analysis of the events at Donelson and Shiloh in the articles he wrote twenty-five years later for the series *Battles and Leaders*. Understandably, objectivity about his role in those two pivotal events, in particular, was not his paramount concern in his *Autobiography*, written forty years after the war. In virtually all these instances, Wallace demonstrated an unremitting passion to elevate his personal contributions to a much higher level than that assigned to them by history. His writings about himself were not intentionally fabricated; they were just liberally embellished. A thorough analysis of those embellishments might more clearly reveal the answer to who Wallace was and what his contributions to the war effort genuinely were. Last, Wallace never seemed to have been sure that his most recent attempt to explain, justify, and promote himself had been successful. Hence, he always had one more statement to make on his behalf. Wallace's passion to preserve his dignity and to parade his honor publicly more often than not stood in the way of his accomplishments.

With respect to the second facet of his persona, Wallace was obsessed that others discriminated against him unjustifiably. His greatest fear was that he would be left behind, sitting on the sidelines while the opportunity for glory and honor was played out on the field of battle by others. He was deeply fearful that through what he deemed to be no fault of his own, he would not be allowed to be a participant in the grand and glorious events in which he found himself. On this point he never ceased to let others know his true feelings.

When these two constructs of Wallace's character are combined with the simple fact that he felt he never got the recognition he believed he so richly deserved, it becomes difficult to assess accurately Wallace's role at

Donelson or in any other battle in which he fought. Following Donelson, Hillyer privately bestowed upon Wallace one coveted testimonial. In a brief note written the day of the surrender, Hillyer applauded Wallace, saying, "God bless you. You did save the day on the right." Yet, for all that it meant at the time to Wallace, this accolade was not the recognition from a grateful nation that he strongly believed he had earned.

Wallace deserved much more credit than he ever received for the tactical decisions he spontaneously made between 8:30 and 11:30 on the morning of February 15. He contributed significantly, perhaps overwhelmingly, to Union victory at Fort Donelson.[11] The issue, however, as Wallace soon perceived, was whether or not he had saved the Union that day. Wallace never hesitated to cast himself in the role of savior at Donelson. On February 19, for example, he wrote to Susan that he felt redeemed. Effective February 14, Grant had ordered him to Donelson, entrusted him with a Division and shoved him into the line between Smith and McClernand. "Next day I saved the whole army from rout. McClernand's division had been beaten and drawn back. I thrust mine between him and the enemy, and repulsed them."[12] Few, however, thought to agree with him.

Wallace's spontaneous and unilateral battlefield decisions to release Cruft's brigade to the assistance of McClernand and then to advance offensively and establish a defensive line along Wynn's Ferry Road had a major impact on the ultimate outcome of the battle. Acting upon these decisions, Wallace and the 3rd Division bought Grant time and opportunity. Grant seized both and secured victory at Fort Donelson. Had Wallace not disobeyed Grant in the first place and had he not marched his men up Wynn's Ferry Road looking for Butternuts or, alternatively, had the Rebels succeeded in driving Wallace from the defensive position he established on that road Saturday morning, it is extremely difficult to see how Grant would have had either the time or the opportunity to devise and carry out his brilliant three-pronged counterattack. Without Wallace's performance, the battle might not have come to an end Saturday morning, and a siege would have been Grant's only viable alternative. Wallace's actions were critical, and perhaps, in terms of what he bought for both the Union Army of the Tennessee as well as for Grant, could be perceived as the acts of a savior.[13]

On Sunday morning, February 16, Wallace had a unique experience of his own making. As the men of the 3rd Division were preparing for battle, Confederate Maj. W. E. Rogers came into Wallace's camp under a white flag. He carried a dispatch from Buckner to Grant. Wallace quickly

Surrender of Fort Donelson, February 16, 1862. Union troops enter fort and town of Dover, where Wallace has breakfast. (*Frank Leslie's Illustrated Newspaper* [March 15, 1862])

scanned the message from his old friend from antebellum military encampment days. He then detached two of his aides to escort Rogers to Grant's headquarters. Aware that the Confederates had "stacked their arms" inside the fort, Wallace and his staff rode into Dover in search of Buckner. He found him at the Dover Hotel.

Buckner invited Wallace to join him and his staff for breakfast. Wallace accepted because "before the war, he and I, and everyone at the table had been friends, between whom, on several occasions, military courtesies had been interchanged." Wallace did not negotiate surrender terms with Buckner. This was Grant's prerogative. The two were eating and recounting past military matters when Commodore Dove of the Union navy unexpectedly appeared. Dove asked Wallace what surrender terms had been proposed. Wallace told him he was waiting for Grant to do the honors. Shortly thereafter, Dove departed. Recalling that Foote and the Union navy had accepted Tilghman's sword of surrender at Fort Henry while Grant sloshed through ankle-deep mud, Wallace took great delight in remarking, "the navy seemed to be abroad very early: they were looking for swords, perhaps. This time I had been about three-quarters of an hour ahead of him [Dove]." Upon Grant's arrival, Wallace immediately deferred to his superior and left to return to his camp.[14] Simply by being with Buckner when Dove arrived, Wallace prevented the navy from getting to the vanquished first with all that entailed. Thus, once more Wallace had given Grant "opportunity," the privilege of accepting Buckner's sword and Confederate surrender. It is uncertain how Grant would have reacted if Dove had arrived first.

Grant never commented on this incident. For a second time, Wallace believed his contribution to Grant at Fort Donelson went unrecognized. He understood this was not a matter of great national significance. Nevertheless, he knew he had given Grant an opportunity to do something that Grant had never done before—accept the emblematic sword of surrender from a defeated foe. Wallace might have derived sufficient recognition had Grant bothered to write a word in a personal note, to insert a brief acknowledgment into a formal report, or simply to say "thank-you." Even that level of recognition would have given him something about which to crow. Instead, he received nothing. Clearly, the symbolism of participation in the formal act of surrender was more meaningful to Wallace than to Grant, further illustrating the wide gulf dividing their respective characters and personalities. In time, Wallace saw that just as Grant failed to recognize his contribution the day before on Wynn's Ferry Road, the specter of non-recognition would be his reward for preventing the navy from getting to Buckner first. Nevertheless, even without Grant, Wallace derived a great deal of personal satisfaction from the event. As his despondency over being left behind once more at Fort Henry intensified, he took great comfort in knowing, as he wrote to his wife, that "Buckner surrendered himself to me."[15]

Wallace summarized his feelings about the victories at forts Henry and Donelson in a letter to Susan. "Verily," he wrote, "the war looks over to me. When we break the centre of the rebellion, as we have done, we break the monster's heart. Don't be surprised if we all come home to sit down under our own 'vine and fig tree,' to eat, be merry, smoke and talk our battles over again, with nobody to shake a fist at but England."[16] That same day, in a letter to his wife Julia, Grant took a more prosaic approach. "'Secesh' is now about on its last legs in Tennessee," he observed. The army must continue to move rapidly toward the enemy for that would minimize having to engage in one after another pitch battles. "These terrible battles are very good things to read about for persons who loose [*sic*] no friends," he concluded, "but I am decidedly in favor of having as little of it as possible. The way to avoid it is to push forward as vigorously as possible." In anticipation of turning sentiment into reality, the Illinois Wallace wrote to his wife Ann three days after the fall of Donelson, "I do not underrate the importance of the victory. I think it is the death blow of the rebellion." Colonel Wallace cautioned, however, that the true meaning of Union success would become manifest only "if rapidly and judiciously followed up."[17]

In less than eleven days, the Army of the Tennessee, in a combined assault with the Union navy operating on the Tennessee and Cumberland Rivers, had wrenched open the gateway to the Confederate heartland. Union Blue burst through and never again looked back. To be sure, Grant and the two Wallaces were overly optimistic about the duration of the war, but with victory achieved at the two forts nothing now stood in the way of a rapid and convincing conclusion to the war, at least seemingly nothing dressed in Butternut. All three, however, failed to consider the possibility that Halleck, a devout disciple of slow and cautious warfare, might choose this very moment to reassert his influence over the army's progress toward ultimate victory.

On February 16, the day of the surrender, Wallace received orders to return to Fort Henry to command the Union reserve. Although Grant took steps in his Special Field Orders No. 10 to make it clear that this force was a necessity "to guard all points captured," Wallace believed that he had been slighted and quietly pushed aside. His concerns as well as his anger deepened when Grant specifically ordered Wallace to leave the 11th Indiana and the 8th Missouri at Donelson. Wallace overtly schemed to circumvent that part of Grant's order. The next day, he telegraphed his commanding general that by the time he received Grant's order, the two regiments were already "on their way" to Fort Henry. In a second telegram later that same day, he claimed the two had just arrived "a few minutes ago." This was not true. Both regiments had been with Wallace the whole time. Begging to keep both, Wallace petitioned Grant to allow them to remain at Henry and thought it appropriate to suggest that Grant might well "consider the 'exceeding great love' I bear them."[18] Grant patiently denied Wallace's petition.

As he marched back to Henry, Wallace still found solace in Hillyer's letter. Grant, Hillyer maintained, had no intention in any future advance of leaving Wallace behind. The only circumstance that might require Wallace's continued presence at Fort Henry would be "to defend against a threatened attack." Otherwise, Hillyer wrote, "I know Gen. Grant's views. He intends to give you a chance to be shot in every important move."[19] On the other hand, Wallace was upset. He was convinced that because Grant had demanded he return the 11th Indiana and the 8th Missouri to Smith's command, he was keeping the battle-tested regiments as a strike force for his army on the advance while sending the less capable and experienced men to the reserve to maintain the defense. Wallace feared that in giving him command of that reserve Grant might feel the same way about him, deeming him to be the least capable and least experienced of his brigadiers. Wallace could live with the broader conclusion about the men. The corollary relating to him alone was unsatisfactory and very difficult to accept. Even now, Wallace might be intuitively sensing that the older, more experienced, and decidedly more reserved brigadier named Grant was starting to feel uncomfortable in the presence of the younger, less experienced, and unquestionably more vocal and assertive brigadier named Wallace. He was convinced that since Smith had come to treat him in this manner, perhaps Grant would as well. If so, it would be logical for him to react to a changing Grant as he had to "Old Smith."

As his days at Fort Henry in charge of the reserve slipped by, Wallace became more and more convinced that his being left at Henry before the battle of Fort Donelson and his being sent back to Henry after the victory were two events with distressingly similar messages. He slowly became aware that Grant had little idea of the full story of Wynn's Ferry Road. What Wallace never understood and never appreciated was that Grant knew all he really ever cared to know on that subject. To the utter dismay of the young brigadier, the older brigadier's mind was closed on this subject. Grant had determined that if he spoke any further on the subject of Donelson, he spoke to his own personal detriment. Grant would reach a very similar conclusion with respect to certain events that would occur seven weeks later in southern Tennessee at a place called Shiloh.

Wallace remained at Fort Henry from February 16 until March 5. During this time, he never had to worry about Polk or Hardee attacking him from the rear. A few military forays were made into the countryside to secure railroads lines, repair bridges, and the like. He trained and drilled his men every day. There was not much personal glory and honor in such activities. Coordination of transport for sick and wounded Union soldiers and captured Rebels from Donelson through Henry to hospitals in Paducah and Yankee prisons further north came to be his principle daily task.[20] There was nothing to check his growing anger and frustration. On February 24, he wrote Susan that he now commanded two forts and fourteen regiments and was, if nothing else, a de facto major general. "All of this is not so satisfactory," he wrote to his wife, "as the happy riddance of Gen. Smith which is at last accomplished. He is at Donelson." In that same letter, Wallace found a new enemy to vilify. "The Illinois-ans," he wrote, "still keep up the most ridiculous stories as to what they did on that bloody Saturday. I am satisfied the whole thing was intended to be a fight and victory for that State." Wallace knew that McClernand's division was made up almost exclusively of Illinois volunteer regiments. "But alas," he gleefully concluded, "They got terribly thrashed. There was not one Illinois regiment that did not retreat or retire—some were routed outright."[21]

During his days at Fort Henry, he continued to develop his sense of being a victim. He never seemed to comprehend that he spent most of this time victimizing himself. On February 27, for example, he enigmatically proclaimed to Susan that "justice is not being done our troops, and especially those in my division." Having tossed out this somewhat obscure reference, Wallace compounded it with a firm pledge that he would "rectify this thin[g], if possible, and at all hazards: and shall endeaver [*sic*] to accomplish this end in my report."[22] Arguably, Wallace was discovering anew the extent to which he saw himself as the victim of a gross injustice. Men of lesser rank and qualification now marched to Nashville, while his only prospects for action were drill and training. His destiny was to spend his days in endless administrative battles over the proper allocation, usage, and ultimate destination of hospital and prisoner ships. It never entered his mind that with his vitriolic pen pathetically portraying his own obstinacy, he was his own proverbial worst enemy. Time and again in that brief three-week period, he forgot Hillyer's advice to be patient and keep quiet.

In another respect, while at Henry, Wallace remained true to his essential character. He revealed anew to his wife his romantic nature with simple, direct statements on the unalterable beauty of personal courage. "I find myself just as anxious to go forward as ever," he told Susan. "I find my interest in battles rather increased than otherwise—in fact, I like the excitement, and in very truth, I never heard music as fascinating and grand as that of battle."[23] He was too restive, too consumed by the spirit of adventure, and in too much of a hurry to achieve honor and glory merely to play at being a soldier. What had happened to him at Paducah began to consume him at Henry. Endless hours of camp life drifted into endless days. There was still drill and training to be conducted and Plutarch and Mahan to be read but that could only go so far for a man like Wallace.

However, before there could be another Woolfolk type event, the day to advance south from Fort Henry finally arrived. Wallace's re-kindled enthusiasm knew no bounds. Years later he described the "spectacle." Thirty thousand men in Union blue assembled on the banks of the Tennessee River amid "the cheering and braying of bands, and the waving of flags." With "drums" rolling, with weaponry "glistening," they moved inexorably forward toward seventy steamers standing "at anchor ready to haul in and take their assignments aboard." "For this," Wallace understood, "was a victorious army that knew its strength and rejoiced in it." Writing about this event in his *Autobiographical Sketch*, Wallace observed that "[i]t is difficult to conceive anything more orderly and beautiful than the movement of the army up the river. . . . Cannons fired, regiments cheered, bands played. It was indeed a sight never to be forgotten." Wallace revealed one of the most illustrative and poignant examples of his romantic nature as he concluded his remarks about the embarkation of this great armada. In his *Autobiography*, he wistfully reminisced about this day, concluding, "[a]nd in thought of it all I would grow young again, but for the other thought always waylaying the first—I cannot hope ever to see the like again, much less be a part of it."[24]

The serenity of his surroundings replaced the pomp and pageantry of the departure as the steamer *John J. Roe* churned up the Tennessee River deeper and deeper into the Southern interior. "The day has been soft and beautiful, actually sultry," Wallace wrote to Susan. "The trees are beginning to put on their mantles of green, every thing [*sic*] budding, and a little bunch of wild flowers lies before me on the table. This is indeed the Sunny South." At the same time, Wallace knew he was going into battle. With a renewed sense of eagerness and determination, he told Susan not to worry. "The expedition or rather my errand is considered hazardous, tho' I do not consider it so. The struggle is now, thank Heaven, in earnest, no child's play, but a reality. Pushed continuously, it can't last long. The rebels are ahead of us. . . . They are disorganized and, of course, demoralized. Still they will fight."[25] Grant had placed him and the 3rd Division in the vanguard of the advance, assigning him a specific objective to achieve. Then, suddenly, Halleck replaced Grant with Smith. His nemesis had returned. Smith, however, opted for the status quo. While Wallace expressed no appreciation for Smith's decision, he seemed surprisingly unconcerned about the reappearance of Smith in his life. For once, he kept silent, knowing full well he had earned the right to be in that place at that time. The Sunny South was beckoning.

CHAPTER NINE

The Mind-Numbing Caveat

In response to the firing upon Fort Sumter, the Northern press and Northern public opinion defined Union wartime goals in the East. "On to Richmond" was the strategic battle cry. There was no such similar clarion call in the western theater. There were far too many disparate voices raised over concerns centered on too vast an area to define the strategy for the West simply as "On to New Orleans," or "On to Nashville," or even "On to the Mississippi River." The conflict in the West would be an offensive war, an invasion to conquer and restore, not a defensive struggle to pacify and preserve. From the beginning Commander of the Department of the Missouri, Halleck focused on rivers and railroads as the most expeditious way to dominate the Confederacy and re-establish the Union. He seldom spoke about the destruction of the Confederate armies in the West or the Confederate will to resist as valid strategic goals. By mid-December 1861, he was beginning to see the potential for gain through the Confederate heartland. Executing the elements of the Twin Rivers campaign, Grant and the navy achieved significant Union victories at Fort Henry and Fort Donelson. In the immediate aftermath of these triumphs on the Tennessee and the Cumberland, Halleck paused to consider his next move while he sought to turn both victories to his personal advantage.[1]

On March 1, 1862, Halleck issued campaign orders to Grant. Corinth, Mississippi, was an important Southern railroad hub. Here, at a location not too far from the Tennessee River, the Memphis and Charleston Railroad intersected the Mobile and Ohio Railroad. Not too far to the north, the Memphis and Ohio Railroad crossed the tracks of the Mobile line at Humboldt, Tennessee. Halleck was convinced that whoever occupied Corinth controlled vast areas of Southern commerce and dominated important lines of military transport and communication. Be prepared "as soon as possible to move your column up the Tennessee River," he instructed his senior brigadier, "to destroy the railroad bridge over Bear Creek, near Eastport, Miss., and also the connections at Corinth, Jackson and Humboldt. It is thought best that these objects [all depots on the Mobile and Ohio Railroad] be attempted in the order named." Halleck did not tell Grant the number of men required for this task, but he thought it doable, with "strong detachments of cavalry, light artillery, supported by infantry." He implied that his campaign plan might well be nothing more than a temporary tactical deployment. "Having accomplished these objects, or such of them as may be practicable," he instructed Grant, "you will return to Danville [on the Tennessee River] and move on Paris [a depot on the Memphis and Ohio Railroad]." This was Halleck's plan now that Henry and Donelson were safely under his control.[2]

In his lectures at West Point, Dennis Hart Mahan had distilled for his students the basic tenets of what he called the "Plan of Campaign." The Plan must be kept "so limited as to comprise only the leading strategical [*sic*] dispositions." To be effective, Mahan reasoned, it had to be based upon "only the outline features," thereby providing "ample latitude for all movements of detail and their execution." Cadet Halleck undoubtedly agreed. However, Mahan enunciated a second unassailable principle. "Nothing could be more absurd than to pretend to dictate to the commanding general what he shall do from day to day," he posited. "Once within the sphere of the enemy's operations, a commanding general is no longer at liberty to do what he wishes, but what he best can. Marches, maneuvers, combats depend on circumstances for the most part imperative; decisions arrived at are often sudden, and brought about by the attitude, resources, strength, and the *morale* [italics in original] of the enemy. The commanding general should have *carte blanche* for carrying out the details of the campaign." In sum, Mahan concluded, once the strategic objective(s) for a campaign had been firmly established, most of the tactical maneuverings must be "left in the hands of him who has the whole responsibility of its execution on his shoulders."[3] As his plan unfolded, Halleck demonstrated he had no intention of limiting his personal involvement in the daily ebb and flow of the campaign as Mahan had mandated. Halleck knew that while many might soon forgot the name of a general who planned a successful campaign, few seldom forgot the name of the general who successfully executed it.

To a dedicated micromanager like Halleck, this second Mahan dictate was anathema. Halleck was ambitious. He also had a deeply ingrained belief that none of his junior officers possessed the requisite experience, knowledge, and skill that he brought to all phases of the military operation. Without his direct and uninterrupted intervention, the Union war effort would suffer accordingly, perhaps even collapse. To Halleck, the exercise of as much control as possible over a subordinate leading the campaign was the only guarantee for the plan's possible success. Based upon this belief, he embodied his continuing involvement and intervention in the campaign he had so artfully designed in the form of an often-repeated caveat. In his March 1 order, Halleck warned Grant to "avoid any general engagement with strong forces. It will be better to retreat than to risk a general battle." This requirement was meant for Grant's eyes but not his alone. "This should be strongly impressed upon the officers sent with the expedition from the river."[4] In the brief period of time Smith was in command of the plan, Halleck badgered him as well with the first version of his admonition.

For the success of the war effort and the safety of his army, Halleck was convinced that the repetitious issuance of this warning was a military necessity. Soon, he would change the phraseology from "avoid any general engagement" to "wait for Buell," but his intent remained the same. He repeated this part of his orders from St. Louis so many times in the next five weeks that the concept quickly became an openly expressed mantra for the campaign. Assuming a life of its own, it rapidly developed into the paramount dictate of the plan of campaign. Halleck's incessant repetition of this warning succeeded in paralyzing Grant, numbing his overall level of awareness and accordingly limiting his military effectiveness. In short order, it worked to prevent Grant and most of his subordinate commanders from initiating any substantive independent thought about what was happening on the ground at Pittsburg Landing. By his words alone, Halleck fabricated a mental trap of constant physical and intellectual inactivity into which Grant, many of his subordinate officers, and seemingly the entire Union Army of the Tennessee fell. Although flawed and not too well thought out from the beginning, Halleck's plan of campaign by itself did not precipitate the first major Union blunder at Shiloh. It was much too limited in scope to accomplish that. Rather, Halleck, himself, with the constant repetition of three little words, created the conditions in which this blunder took place. Utilizing the Mahan precept of "surprise," Confederate forces under Johnston and Beauregard exploited these conditions with near tragic results for Union arms.

On March 4, the day before the campaign was to commence, Halleck replaced Grant with Smith as Commander of the Army of the Tennessee. In a mere two short sentences, Halleck illustrated that he, not Grant, was in total control in the West. "You will place Maj. Gen. C. F. Smith in command of the expedition, and remain yourself at Fort Henry. Why do you not obey my orders to report strength and positions of your command?"[5] Leaving aside whatever personal responses he might have wished to convey to Halleck at that moment, Grant immediately obeyed. He dutifully informed Smith that he was now in charge of the Corinth expedition. In addition, he sent him a copy of Halleck's March 1 order as well as the March 5 revision, both containing the explicit warning to be cautious above all else.

Grant congratulated Smith on his "richly-deserved promotion." Feeling properly bound by the military chain of command and all orders previously issued by Halleck, Grant repeated his superior's warning. "A general engagement is to be avoided," Grant emphasized in his orders to Smith, "while the bridges are to be destroyed if possible. The idea probably is there must be no defeat, and rather than risk one it would be better to retreat."[6] These must have been difficult words for an offensive-minded soldier to write. Nevertheless, the last of Grant's three communications with Smith on March 5 illustrated that Halleck's binding and paralyzing caveat was beginning to work itself like a cancer through the command structure of the Army of the Tennessee. Lest his generals forget this dictate, Halleck intended to repeat it often.

Grant's reaction to Halleck replacing him and leaving him behind was entirely different from anything Wallace had ever exhibited. Had he been in Grant's place at the time, Wallace would have undoubtedly utilized any and all opportunities, including the public forum, to proclaim himself a victim. No doubt Grant was taken back and offended by Halleck's inexplicable decision. Deferring to the bounds of military propriety, Grant kept this side of his nature to himself, hidden from all except his wife and Washburne, his political ally. Immediately and with very few words, Grant accepted his new status. In three brief communiqués to Halleck following his demotion, Grant evidenced respect for Halleck, refused to posture as a victim, and, exhibiting little emotion, declined to become embroiled in an argument. He did ask to be relieved from further duty within the Department of the

Missouri.[7] Halleck refused to act upon this request. This change of leadership would have no impact on Wallace, who continued in command of the 3rd Division.

Beginning on March 5, Grant thus went about his new duties, patiently forwarding the men and materials Halleck sent to Fort Henry to Smith's new command. He gave a candid summation of his dilemma to Julia on the evening he received the news of his demotion. "I am in a very poor humor for writing," he explained. "I was ordered to command a very important expedition up the Tennessee river [*sic*] and now an order comes directing one of my junior officers to take command whilst I am left behind here with a small garrison."[8] As Wallace had demonstrated in at least two letters contemporaneous to these events, he possessed neither the strength of character nor the restraint to duplicate Grant. This is another reason why these two men, despite many similarities in their ways of thinking about warfare and then waging it, could never get along. Before this episode ended, however, Grant did reflect a bit of Wallace's independent nature. Despite a model performance while serving his purgatorial stint as a quartermaster at Fort Henry, Grant failed to address one order from Halleck. "Intrenching [*sic*] tools," Halleck instructed Grant, "should be sent to Genl. Smith to enable him to secure his position wherever he may land."[9] No tools were ever sent. Grant demonstrated he also could ignore a superior officer's order which he thought inconsequential or with which he did not agree.

On March 11, an event took place that allowed Halleck to change the persistent admonition he regularly dangled in front of Grant into a mind-numbing caveat. Lincoln appointed Halleck commander of the newly created Department of the Mississippi. Halleck now controlled not only an expanded version of the Department of the Missouri but most of the Department of the Ohio as well. Halleck finally had something he had sought for some time, command over Brig. Gen. Don Carlos Buell and the Army of the Ohio. Now, instead of having to coax or beg Buell to vacate the security of Nashville and move to join the Army of the Tennessee at Savannah, Halleck had the authority to order him to do so. The unintended consequence of Lincoln's decision was to make Grant just that much more aware of the presence of Halleck in his life. The more Halleck was unable to convince Buell of the urgency behind his joining the Army of the Tennessee, the more he badgered Grant to "wait for Buell" before undertaking any "major engagement" other than the bridge destructions previously ordered.[10]

On March 11, two divisions of Smith's Army of the Tennessee, those of Sherman and Wallace, reached Savannah on the east bank of the Tennessee River. Smith disembarked, ordering Sherman to take his 5th Division further south to Eastport, Mississippi, to destroy the Memphis and Charleston Railroad bridge over Bear Creek. The 3rd Division under Wallace went ashore at Crump's Landing on the west bank of the Tennessee about five miles south of Savannah. It then marched west on the Purdy–Bethel Road to wreck havoc on the Mobile and Ohio Railroad lines at Bethel Station. Rain, floodwaters, snow, and Confederate cavalry forced Sherman to turn back before reaching his objective. Though unopposed and not hindered by poor weather conditions, Wallace had limited success, destroying a portion of a railroad bridge over Beach Creek at Purdy as well as "a small portion of the track on either side of the bridge."[11]

Smith ordered Sherman's 5th Division to make camp at Pittsburg Landing on the west bank of the Tennessee River, approximately ten miles south of Savannah. On March 17, Brig. Gen. Stephen A. Hurlbut's recently created 4th Division joined Sherman. Smith decided to locate his headquarters at the Cherry House in Savannah. Earlier, Smith had ordered Wallace to establish his headquarters at Crump's Landing. Wallace's primary duty at Crump's Landing was to position his division along the Purdy Road to guard the right flank of the Union army at Pittsburg Landing from possible Confederate attack from Bethel Station.

On March 17, Lincoln and Stanton reversed Halleck's efforts to marginalize Grant by ordering him to restore Grant to command of the Tennessee River expedition. Even in the order reinstating Grant, Halleck felt compelled to repeat and insist upon absolute adherence to his caveat.[12] Arriving in Savannah that same day, Grant informed Sherman that he was satisfied with this disposition of the army.[13] Grant sent all his remaining forces, except McClernand's 1st Division, to join Sherman and Hurlbut at Pittsburg Landing. In this dispatch to Sherman, Grant stated he intended to keep his headquarters at Savannah. He gave Sherman the authority to organize all incoming, detached regiments presently in camp or soon to arrive into brigades and assign them to the various divisions at the Landing. In Grant's absence, Sherman was designated the de facto commander of the army on the ground at Pittsburg Landing.[14]

A flurry of telegrams between Grant and Halleck, particularly Grant's response of March 20, illustrates why Halleck's caveat had such a pervasive influence upon Grant and his army. This influence, in turn, contributed significantly to the upcoming first few hours of the Battle of Shiloh being such a bloody disaster for Grant. On March 19, Grant telegraphed a series of dispatches to Halleck from Savannah that the Commander of the Department of the Mississippi found confusing. They seemed to suggest that Grant was preparing an advance on Corinth which, in fact, he was. In one of these messages, Grant wrote that "immediate preparations will be made to execute your perfectly-feasible order. I will go in person, leaving General McClernand in command here." In an earlier telegram, Grant had announced he had intelligence that placed the number of Confederates at Corinth at no more than 20,000 and that Confederate command appeared to fear the arrival of Buell more than Grant's command alone. Now, Grant was suggesting, was the time to act. In addition, although Halleck did not know this, the very next day, Grant sent orders to Wallace at Crump's Landing and Sherman at Pittsburg Landing to put all divisions of the Army of the Tennessee, other than McClernand's, in full readiness for a march, with at least three days' rations. As he had specified in his last dispatch to Halleck, such a march would not occur until the 23rd or the 24th of March.[15]

Halleck was more than confused. He was near apoplectic. He had given no orders to march upon Corinth. In fact, he had been clear. Grant was to wait for Buell. The next day, Halleck telegraphed Grant. "I do not fully understand you. By all means keep your forces together," Halleck charged Grant, "until you connect with General Buell, who is now at Columbia, and will move on Waynesborough with three divisions. Don't let the enemy draw you into an engagement now. Wait until you are properly fortified and receive orders."[16] Halleck had moved quickly to quash his subordinate's command to find the enemy and fight him.

It was Grant's response to Halleck the same day that revealed the negative, mind-stultifying impact the caveat was beginning to exert. Grant was unwilling without at least having another word with Halleck to abandon his plans to march upon Corinth. He conceded, however, that should he be allowed to proceed, he would certainly comply with the letter as well as the spirit of Halleck's admonition. "I will take no risk at Corinth under the instructions I now have," he wrote. "If a battle on anything like equal terms seems to be inevitable I shall find it out in time to make a movement upon some other point of the railroad, or at least seem to fill the object of the expedition without a battle and thus save the demoralizing effect of a retreat upon the troops." It is quite difficult to imagine that

Grant penned these words for any reason other than to pacify Halleck. Grant did not receive a reply to this last communiqué. It was obvious that Halleck had just enunciated the final form of the caveat, taking it to a new and higher level. It was not the last time during this campaign that Halleck demanded the caveat be observed.[17]

From March 20 until the Confederates stormed out of the woods against his right flank at Shiloh on April 6, Grant waited. The impact of the caveat and the delays it mandated was virtually paralyzing Grant, his subordinates, and his entire army. As the time passed, Grant grew less and less concerned that the Rebel force at Corinth, still of undetermined size and strength, was barely twenty miles south of his position. Rather, he became more and more convinced that no fight would occur in front of him until he instigated it. "The temper of the rebel troops," he wrote to Halleck, "is such that there is but little doubt but that Corinth will fall much more easily than Donelson did, when we do move. All accounts agree in saying that the great mass of rank and file are [*sic*] heartily tired."[18]

Finally, even as he first began to sense the possibility that those same Confederates might decide to attack him, he nevertheless believed it more likely such an attack would originate from the Purdy area against Wallace at Crump's Landing. On April 4, Grant sent a dispatch to Sherman cautioning him that he had just received information from Wallace that perhaps the Rebels were concentrating in force at Purdy. Grant instructed Sherman to be alert and provide for such a contingency. He further told Sherman that he had notified General W. H. L. Wallace, commanding the 2nd Division at Pittsburg Landing, to stand ready to shift his entire division north to Crump's Landing if the 3rd Division required reinforcements. "Although," Grant concluded, "I look for nothing of the kind, but it is best to be prepared." Halleck's caveat was flourishing.[19]

From Halleck down, Union command now knew the next big battle of the war in the West would occur at Corinth. As a major hub for all Confederate railroad activity in the area, Corinth was an easily identifiable strategic objective. Since Confederate forces already occupied Corinth, Grant was convinced he must go there in order to do battle. He planned to depart Pittsburg Landing as soon as Buell arrived. Battle "was imminent," he wrote to Julia, "and its outcome certain. I do not feel that there is the slightest doubt about the result." With amazing self-assuredness, Grant concluded, "and therefore, individually, [I] feel as unconcerned about it as if nothing more than a review is to take place."[20]

Wallace agreed with Grant as to the location of the next battle but not with the waiting. The next fight, he informed Susan, would occur "in the neighborhood of Corinth, Mississippi." Lew lectured Susan that she must treat this information as "strongly confidential." Three days later, he once again identified Corinth as the site for the pending battle, concluding that it would be "another fight more serious than that of Donelson."[21] Unfortunately for Wallace during this time, he once more became apprehensive and impatient. The waiting created unendurable periods of enforced inactivity. Not moving forward was a parasite, eating at him personally as well as at the army. His response was reminiscent of Paducah. "We are lying on our oars," he complained, "here awaiting orders, giving the enemy abundant time to build up new Donaldsons [*sic*] and Columbuses [*sic*]."[22] Halleck's caveat had created the atmosphere out of which the first Union mistake at Shiloh occurred. Grant and his army had been immobile much too long. The Confederates seized the initiative and surprise now awaited Grant and the Union army.

The second major mistake at Shiloh was an inevitable corollary to the mind-numbing attributes of the first.[23] Under the frustrating strictures not to engage the enemy offensively without Buell, Grant became complacent and passive. Upon his arrival at Pittsburg Landing, Grant unwisely chose comfort over prudence. He established his field headquarters not with his troops on the ground at Pittsburg Landing but with Smith ten miles downriver at the Cherry House in Savannah. After all, he did not fear his enemy would advance against him. Moreover, he could wait for Buell in greater comfort in Savannah than in a tent at Pittsburg Landing. It really did not matter where his headquarters were. Depending on the strength of the current of the Tennessee River on any given day, he and his staff were only twenty-five minutes to perhaps an hour away from his army. The Rebels were twenty miles away at Corinth. They would still be there when he and Buell marched out to do battle with them.

As importantly, having had the caveat made into a major facet of his daily life, Grant at times seemed in no particular hurry for Buell to arrive. Coming from Nashville, his army would have to be transported from the east to the west bank of the Tennessee River. There would be time to arrange and implement that when the day came. They would even make time, perhaps, for a joint conference or two to plan the advance on Corinth. The Confederacy had insufficient physical resources and manpower to rebuild from the losses of men and materials experienced in

February at Henry and Donelson. Union victory was certainly all but assured although the two generals must attack and take Corinth by force to secure that victory. In part under the influence of Halleck's persuasive dictate and in part because he appeared oblivious to any constructive lessons that might be learned from his Donelson experiences, Grant really did not seem to mind the wait that much.

As mid-March blended into early April, Halleck sat in the comfort of his headquarters in St. Louis. From there, he demanded that Grant and his field commanders do nothing to get involved in any major engagement with the enemy until he, Halleck, determined the moment was appropriate to do so. Until Buell arrived, a prerequisite for such a determination, Grant and his lieutenants had to be satisfied spending their time raiding and destroying railroad rolling stock, caring for the sick and injured, transporting both down the Tennessee to Fort Henry or Paducah, providing food for the army and forage for the animals, and engaging in drill and still more drill. The same enforced boredom seemed to be affecting even Halleck. He had yet to dispatch a formal order to Grant designating Corinth as the next Union strategic objective for the continuing plan of campaign. Everybody knew this to be the objective; it had yet to be ordered on a formal basis. It almost seemed as if nobody was in any hurry to do anything.

At Shiloh, Charles Morton served in the 25th Missouri Volunteers, 1st Brigade, Prentiss's 6th Division. He and many others in this newly formed division had never before been in battle. In fact, he arrived at Pittsburg Landing the day before the battle began. Thirty-five years later, on October 6, 1897, Morton addressed the New York Commandery of the Military Order of the Loyal Legion of the United States, a group of Civil War veterans, with reflections entitled "A Boy at Shiloh." He told his compatriots that the common soldier alone fought and won at Shiloh. He praised the men he had fought side by side with for their "fierceness," "persistent determination," and "determined resistance." "The battle," he maintained, "was simply a series of fierce combats." There was no leadership at Shiloh, either before or during the battle. "We had no generals but in rank and authority." The events that occurred in the weeks preceding Shiloh, Morton believed, were nothing more than a series of random acts, some connected, more disconnected, in which "dense ignorance" was the prime player. "The almost absolute necessity that no battle should be fought before the arrival of Buell's army," he concluded, "seemed to forbid scouting or anything that might appear aggressive. Ignorance of the resources, energy, and enterprise of the enemy lulled our commanders into fancied security." Unequivocally, Morton concluded, the officers that Grant and Sherman had become by 1864 "would have relieved for utter inefficiency generals of no more skill than the Grant and Sherman at Shiloh."[24]

"The complete absence of the ordinary precautions, always taken by military commanders since the beginning of history, is inexplicable." The year was 1889. Warren Olney, 3rd Iowa, 2nd Brigade, Hurlbut's 4th Division, speaking to the California Commandery of the Military Order of the Loyal Legion of the United States, revealed his thoughts about his days at Shiloh. "The only reason I can conjecture for it [this lack of ordinary precaution]," Olney stated, "grows out of the character of General Grant and his distinguished subordinate [General Sherman], and their inexperience. They had had then little practical knowledge of actual warfare." Collectively, Olney would group these mistakes under the heading of "a want of preparation" as well as "an exhibition of unsuspicious security in the presence of a hostile army." Because of these mistakes, the Union failed to administer "a crushing defeat upon the South" during that two-day battle. For a period of time thereafter Grant lost "the confidence of the army and country." Most damning of all in Olney's mind, because of these inexcusable mistakes, "every village and hamlet in the West had its house of mourning."[25]

These two indictments of Grant and Sherman at Shiloh were severe but incomplete. Neither took into account the negative influence Halleck had upon Grant prior to Shiloh. In this regard, both presented an incomplete story. In the immediate aftermath of Fort Donelson, Halleck several times proved himself to be ambitious, duplicitous, and devoid of loyalty to all but himself.[26] He feared that an unchecked Grant would commit an error that might be ruinous to the Union cause as well as Halleck's career. Grant must be restrained from acting impulsively. Halleck decided he must do all he could to insure that Grant acted with more circumspection than rashness. Grant must continue to be a doer but only when Halleck alone determined it was time. In his attempts after Donelson to keep Grant on a very short leash, Halleck had even gone so far as to demote Grant for failing to obey orders. In justifying his actions to McClellan, he had raised once again the allegations of Grant's excessive drinking.[27] Halleck even suggested to McClellan that he had considered having Grant arrested for dereliction of duty. After having been obliged to reinstate Grant, Halleck hounded him relentlessly not to be overzealous and not to engage the Rebels under any circumstances until his numbers were decidedly superior to those of his enemy. Perhaps Halleck was more successful than he intended to be. At any rate, before Shiloh there were times when Grant no longer appeared to be wary of his enemy presence or potential. His attitude in time came to affect Sherman negatively as well. To his discredit, Grant failed to appreciate the impact that Halleck's imperative was exercising upon his thoughts and actions. Under its influence, he allowed himself to become too complacent, little realizing that Halleck's caveat continued to work as Halleck intended it to do.

The third major mistake at Shiloh belonged to Grant alone. As one of his first acts upon reinstatement, Grant reaffirmed Smith's dispositions for the Army of the Tennessee at Pittsburg Landing. As he had done before, he made this decision without first personally inspecting the site. Sherman had assured him that topographically the landing was a good location to occupy. Smith, his old friend and mentor, had ordered the encampment at Pittsburg Landing. Smith had also decided to establish his headquarters at Savannah. Having been commanded to wait for Buell, Grant saw no compelling reason to counter either decision. Thus, Grant chose to remain in the comfort of Savannah rather than join his army at Pittsburg Landing. Moreover, Grant had decided that Pittsburg Landing, with its lengthy shoreline at which to dock federal steamers laden with men and materials, was also an excellent locality from which to launch his offensive against Corinth.[28] Beyond Owl Creek on the western boundary of the camp, the ridge line opened up for an unobstructed march south into Mississippi. Grant understood this. He failed, however, to appreciate, in the words of one who fought at Shiloh, that "the open way to Corinth was also an open way from Corinth to the Landing."[29] Grant made no plans in the event this contingency became a factor at Shiloh.

Having affirmed Pittsburg Landing as his camp site, Grant did not take any further action to alter or redress the haphazard manner in which the camp had developed. Sherman's 5th Division contained the first Union soldiers to arrive at Pittsburg Landing. Sherman positioned his 2nd Brigade under Col. David Stuart on the left of the Hamburg–Savannah Road at its junction with Lick Creek, fronting and covering the actual landing site. He had the rest of his men make camp about a mile and a half to the west of the landing on the Corinth Road a short distance east of a church meetinghouse called Shiloh. This portion of Sherman's 5th Division constituted the Union right flank. The men of Hurlbut's 4th Division, the second contingency of the Army of the Tennessee to settle in, pitched their tents to the northeast of Sherman, much closer to the Tennessee River, but with no common points of connection between them.

W. H. L. Wallace's 2nd Division troops then moved into the northernmost area of Pittsburg Landing, nearest to both Snake Creek and the 3rd Division at Crump's Landing but at a point confoundedly remote from Sherman's rear. In this location, these battle-tested veterans of the attack on the Union left at Fort Donelson on Saturday afternoon would be among the last Union soldiers to confront a Rebel attack from Corinth if such occurred. The soldiers of McClernand's 1st Division, who had borne the brunt of Pillow's breakout at Donelson, filed in between W. H. L. Wallace and Sherman, providing some continuity of men and line with the latter but none with the former. McClernand's men, as well, were unreasonably far removed from the point of any possible Rebel attack from Corinth. The men of Prentiss's 6th Division, the unit still being constituted when the battle actually began, all totally untested in combat, made camp furthest to the south at Pittsburg Landing and thus closest to the enemy.

The layout of the camp had neither internal rhyme nor reason. No plan controlled its development as a camp. Each division commander sought and established his own ground. Proximity to a clean source of drinking water was the guiding principle for determining where to pitch a tent or locate a division headquarters. The Confederates were known to be at Corinth. It was presumed they would remain there in all circumstances. Grant seemed unconcerned, even unaware, that his greenest, most inexperienced, and hence most vulnerable officers and men slept each night along a line that lay closest to the enemy. No one seemed to notice; no one seemed worried.[30]

Last, Grant did not order the construction of any entrenchments. No division commander thought or acted to do so. Hence, no fortifications, no trenches, no earthworks, no abatis, no log fences, no walls, wood, or brush—nothing defensive or protective in nature—marked the landscape. Olney certainly realized in 1889 that the work that should have gone into the construction of some minimal defensive precautions at Pittsburg Landing was ultimately expended in the aftermath of Shiloh in the construction of those "houses of mourning."[31]

In addition to foregoing any changes or modifications of troop emplacements within the camp at Pittsburg Landing, Grant chose not to have any input as to the placement or divisional organization of the newly arriving replacements. He vested Sherman, a subordinate with whom he had had little prior association, with full authority to make such decisions. There was no need for him to be involved in such matters. In May 1887, Lt. Alfred T. Andreas, 12th Illinois, 2nd Brigade, W. H. L. Wallace's 2nd Division, speaking to the Illinois Commandery of the Military Order of the Loyal Legion, observed, "I think I can say, without much exaggeration, taking everything into consideration, that our army at Pittsburg Landing was camped, distributed, and guarded with as little thought of danger from the enemy as though that great camping-ground had been situated in the State of Illinois."[32]

In the days before Shiloh, Grant exhibited an inexplicable casualness about his position and his enforced waiting. Thus, for example, when he finally received word as to Buell's whereabouts, he responded by suggesting that whoever was leading the advance column might just take his time on the last part of the march to Savannah. On April 3, he sent a telegraph to "the Officer in Command of the Advance of General Buell's Army" stating that whereas he expected the march to Savannah to continue on an uninterrupted basis, "there is no need for haste; come on by easy marches."[33]

One of the more egregious examples of this newfound casual and almost indifferent behavior occurred when advanced elements of Buell's Army of the Ohio finally appeared at Savannah on the east bank of the Tennessee. Grant was compelled to admit he lacked the immediate ability to transport these troops across the river to the west bank for the continuation of their march to Pittsburg Landing. From the time he told Buell's advanced elements on April 3 to "come on by easy marches," Grant had a minimum of two days to arrange for the necessary transport. He seemed totally oblivious to the fact he had not accomplished this task. This was another indication of the defensive mode of thinking and acting to which Grant had succumbed. He appeared quite nonchalant about his role in this mistake. He later explained to his father that his failure on April 5 to have the necessary steamers available for Nelson's advanced units resulted from his having been distracted even though "it was important that I should have every arrangement complete for his [Buell's] speedy transit to this side of the river." His time had been consumed, he wrote, constantly receiving new regiments at Savannah and allocating them among existing brigades and divisions at Pittsburg Landing. Grant failed to mention to his father that he had earlier assigned this task to Sherman. Ultimately, as Grant stated in a dispatch to Buell on April 5, the pontoons necessary to construct a bridge for Buell to cross the Tennessee River at

Savannah did arrive. It is not recorded if and when that bridge was ever built, but it certainly was not operational the next day, April 6, when the Confederates struck and the bridge was no longer a convenience but a necessity. As to the steamers, Grant never did arrange such transport for Buell. Thus, in the early afternoon of April 6, Buell crossed the Tennessee at Pittsburg Landing utilizing many of the same steamers that had brought Grant's army there in the first place.[34]

On Saturday afternoon, April 5, the soldiers of Col. Jacob Ammen's 10th Brigade, Nelson's 4th Division, were the first of Buell's men to reach Savannah. Finding no transports, Ammen asked Grant if he should take his men immediately on to Pittsburg Landing. Ammen wrote in his diary that Grant responded, "you cannot march through the swamps [on the east bank]; make your troops comfortable." Grant promised Ammen that boats would be available to ferry the 10th Brigade across the Tennessee on Monday or Tuesday or "sometime early in the week." According to Ammen, Grant then added, "[t]here will be no fight at Pittsburg Landing; we will have to go to Corinth, where the Rebels are fortified. If they come to attack us, we can whip them, as I have more than twice as many troops as I had at Fort Donelson." Less than eighteen hours later, as the guns announced the advent of battle at Shiloh, Grant hurriedly sent a written message to Nelson ordering him to march his brigade immediately along the east side of the Tennessee to a point directly across from Pittsburg Landing through the same swamp land he had told Ammen the day before was too troublesome to navigate. Despite having waited for him for three weeks, Grant was totally unprepared for Buell's arrival. In this matter in particular, Grant demonstrated either incompetence or the ultimate impact of the mind-numbing caveat upon his psyche. It was probably the latter; it might have been both.[35]

A problem surfaced during the last week of March in the person of McClernand. On March 29, nine days before the battle, McClernand wrote to Grant that "our proximity to the enemy makes it, at least proper, that the various camps here should be formed upon some general and connected plan. Such a precaution might be necessary to avoid confusion and self-destruction in case of a possible night attack. Your presence, here, too, as Commander-in-Chief of the Army, would tend to avoid differences between Subordinate Commanders, and to secure uniformity and efficiency in their several administrations." Regardless of how officious McClernand appeared in his communication and the extent to which McClernand owed his current military position and rank to his political status, Grant knew his arrogant 1st Division commander was correct.[36]

In 1903, Captain Andrew Hickenlooper, 5th Ohio Light Artillery, Prentiss's 6th Division, addressed the members of the Ohio Commandery of the Military Order of the Loyal Legion. He briefly joined the ongoing discussion about the absence of a defined relationship between one Union division and another within the camp structure at Pittsburg Landing and what that meant in terms of how the Battle of Shiloh was fought. Then, he spoke directly to the very issue McClernand had raised with Grant, noting that a major blunder at Shiloh arose out of the fact that "there was no common directing head or superior officer beyond the rank of division commander placed on the firing line whom [*sic*] all recognized and promptly obeyed. There was nothing to give the whole a cohesion and unity of action, which would have resulted in the judicious use of reserves and the shifting of positions to counteract partial reserves." To emphasize his point, Hickenlooper forcefully concluded that "there was no battle plan, no strategy, no tactical maneuvers, and but few commands—certainly none that had any important bearing upon the final results."[37]

In 1903, Wallace also joined the argument, stressing the same point as Hickenlooper. Stating that the Army of the Tennessee had begun the Battle of Shiloh without its commander who was then downriver at Savannah, Wallace observed that "the five divisions on the field had each its chief, to be sure; but none of the five chiefs was in general command. Instead of one supreme governing will, nowhere so essential as in battle, there were five officers each independent of the others. Between them things were done by request, not orders. No one of them was responsible for what the others did."[38] For many contemporaries who deplored the loss of life at Shiloh and sought answers, responsibility for the fourth major mistake likewise belonged to Grant. His absence from the field every night and early morning had drastic, unintended consequences.

Last, at least because of his West Point classroom experiences, Grant should have been familiar with an observation that Mahan often emphasized. Mahan propounded the belief that basic familiarity with the terrain in which one is operating is essential to making sound command decisions. One could never underestimate the value of reconnaissance. When an army was in the field in an essentially stationary position, it was even more critical that its commander be thoroughly informed with respect to conditions on the ground and the nature and character of the surrounding terrain.[39] Wallace made an effort to become well-informed about the various roads to and from Crump's Landing and Pittsburg Landing. There is little evidence to suggest that Grant did likewise. Rather, it seems clear that Grant lacked even a basic familiarity with the terrain in and around Pittsburg Landing as well as the location and condition of the roads leading to and from his camp. This ignorance would play a critical role in what transpired between Grant and Wallace on April 6 when, in response to Grant's order, the latter marched from Crump's Landing to the battlefield. In the time leading up to the fighting, there is no evidence that Grant ever discussed with Wallace the roads in and around Pittsburg and Crump's landings. Wallace apparently never initiated any communication with Grant on this subject either, although he did with W. H. L. Wallace.

It is difficult to ascertain exactly what Grant was focused on during the three weeks prior to April 6. While it may have been Corinth, it certainly was not the possibility of being compelled by the enemy to fight at Pittsburg Landing. On April 5, he telegraphed Halleck, "I have scarcely the faintest idea of an attack (general one) being made upon us, but will be prepared should such a thing take place." He never defined for Old Brains how or what he planned in the event such an attack occurred. In addition, he revealed to Halleck his plan to send Buell's arriving divisions to Hamburg, Tennessee. "From that point to Corinth," he noted, "the road is good, and a junction can be formed with the troops from Pittsburg at almost any point."[40] Despite his claims that he was prepared for any possible contingency, Grant made few, if any, tactical decisions designed to defend his staging area. He was intent upon capturing Corinth and its railroads because that was what Halleck had ordered him to do. He knew he would find a defensive-minded Rebel army there. The Confederates certainly were not immediately in front of him in any significant numbers. If they were, he either could not see them or refused to admit the existence of such a possibility.

Early on the morning of April 6, 1862, Confederate forces under Albert Sydney Johnston coming north from Corinth surprised, smashed into, and nearly overwhelmed the five divisions of Grant's army at Pittsburg Landing. More than 44,600 Confederates joined battle that morning with approximately 41,300 Union troops. After what was for that time an epic struggle, the two armies renewed the fight the next morning. Now, as the second day of fighting dawned, with the arrival of Buell's three divisions from the Army of the Ohio and for the first time Wallace's 3rd

Division, Grant had an additional 23,800 fresh troops at his command. By late afternoon, the Confederates were in retreat to Corinth while Grant and his men regrouped.[41]

The casualties were staggering. Of the Union soldiers, 1,754 lay dead, 8,404 were wounded, while 2,885 were missing in action. The total number of casualties for the North alone—13,043 sons, fathers, brothers, and friends—was nearly incomprehensible. When the total Confederate loss of 10,699 men killed, wounded, and missing in action was factored in, few could fathom or appreciate the reality of what had just occurred. Northern public opinion was as nearly overwhelmed by the statistics as its army had been by Rebel surprise. Even fewer understood exactly how and why it had happened but from that day until this, opinions on the whys and the wherefores of the Battle of Shiloh have been formulated and enthusiastically propounded.

CHAPTER TEN

Shiloh, Surprise, Aftermath

Intentionally or otherwise, Halleck had lulled his field commander to sleep with his incessant, nagging caveat that he wait for Buell before taking any action. Grant and the Army of the Tennessee were prime candidates for "surprise" at Shiloh as Baron Antoine Jomini had defined that term. As a participant and keen observer of Napoleon and his methods of waging war, Jomini believed that an attacking force achieved surprise when those being attacked realized that the enemy was in their midst "before [its] presence is known." Jomini further believed that surprise was possible only to the extent that "the first duties of field service are forgotten." "To surprise an army," Jomini wrote, "it is not necessary to take it so entirely unawares that the troops will not even have emerged from their tents, but it is sufficient to attack it in force at the point intended, before preparations can be made to meet the attack."[1] Johnston more than just attacked Grant on April 6; he administered a Jominian surprise.

Up to the very last moment when the Confederates surged out of the woods, Sherman was actively aiding and abetting Grant's myopic view of the situation on the ground. Maj. D. W. Reed, 12th Iowa, 1st Brigade, 2nd Division, later to become one of the premier historians on Shiloh, related an April 5 incident involving Capt. I. P. Rumsey, a member of W. H. L. Wallace's staff. Rumsey and Col. T. Lyle Dickey, 4th Illinois Cavalry, had reentered the 5th Division's camp, having returned from a brief reconnaissance mission. Both men went directly to Sherman's tent. Rumsey told Sherman that they had made contact with a sizeable body of Confederate cavalry. According to Rumsey, Sherman responded, "I know they are out there, but our hands are tied; we can't do a thing." Colonel Dickey then offered to take the 4th Illinois out to investigate further. To this, Sherman retorted, "Dickey, if you were to go out there with your regiment you would bring on a battle in less than an hour, and we have positive orders not to be drawn into a battle until Buell comes."[2]

That same day, April 5, Sherman sent a dispatch to Grant. "I have no doubt," Sherman trumpeted, "that nothing will occur today more than some picket firing. The enemy is saucy, but got the worst of it yesterday, and will not press our pickets far. . . . I do not apprehend anything like an attack on our position." The next morning, April 6, moments after personally criticizing one of his regimental commanders for being too distracted as he confronted a few scattered Rebels lurking nearby, Sherman looked up and exclaimed, "My God, we are attacked."[3] By that singular statement alone, Sherman defined the effect that Halleck's mind-numbing caveat had exercised upon Union high command at Shiloh.

The Confederate surprise at Shiloh was deadly but not fatal.[4] As Lt. Alfred T. Andreas, 12th Illinois, speaking to the Illinois Commandery after the war, and others had observed, the camp at Pittsburg Landing developed over time as five semi-detached sites rather than one contiguous, cohesive entity. Grant failed to address and correct this error. In the end, ironically, the camp's layout was a saving grace for him and his army. Even though the Confederates surprised them, their numbers were insufficient to overwhelm all the Union camps on the right-center because of the distances between the camps. When the Rebels first confronted the troops of Prentiss and Sherman, the distance between these troops and those of Hurlbut and W. H. L. Wallace gave the latter a little extra time to organize in line of battle. Had the five Union camps been closer to each other, it is doubtful that there would have been time to prepare a defense. It was not a great deal of time but it was enough to sound the long roll of the drums and to give the men an additional moment or two to grab their muskets and form under their company and regimental commanders. The unsupervised, haphazard location of Union troops on the ground, working in conjunction with the type of attack formation that Beauregard had chosen to use that morning, prevented the Rebel surprise from penetrating any deeper and causing any more destruction than it did. At the same time, however, the camp layout and the formation or type of the Rebel attack worked together to give Grant a little time, as the morning wore on, to react.

On the other hand, the Rebel surprise at Shiloh created, as Jomini suggested any such tactic might, a great and seemingly endless confusion on the battlefield for the entire first day. This quickly and seriously limited

Grant's ability to confront the advancing Rebels with a unified defense and a coherent counterattack. Capt. Charles Morton, 25th Missouri Volunteers, commenting several decades later, observed that "the battle was simply a series of fierce combats. So many brigade and regimental commanders fell, and their successors knew so little as to what orders had been received, or whence they came, that the reports simply defy a tangible connection for an accurate account of the struggle." In 1898, Col. George F. McGinnis, 11th Indiana, 1st Brigade, Wallace's 3rd Division, stated the obvious when he told the members of the Indiana Commandery of the Military Order of the Loyal Legion of the United States that "we were not prepared that morning." "The fight at Shiloh," McGinnis explained, "was not a fight of divisions; it was not a fight of armies; it was not a fight of brigades; it seemed to me a strife between regiment and regiment, company and company."[5]

More than a decade and a half earlier, writing in 1881, Lt. Col. Manning J. Force, 20th Ohio, 3rd Brigade, Wallace's 3rd Division, summed up that first day as well as anyone. Force believed that "surprise" that morning thrust Grant onto the defensive, where he remained all day. The enemy's tactics deprived Grant of the ability to choose his field of battle, causing him to react rather than act. He did not command that first day, Force concluded, but directed men from where chance and the first Rebel assault wave had driven them. "Combat made up of numberless separate encounters of detached portions of broken lines, continually shifting positions and changing directions in the forest and across ravines" characterized that "entire day" and produced a stalemate.[6]

More than thirty years later, veterans of Shiloh were still articulating the same theme. One such veteran of the first day stated that "after the first assault in the morning, regiments, brigades, and divisions had to a great extent lost their identity. 'The Boys' realized that they were there to fight, and they fought without waiting for commands." Another stated that ordinary men fought and won the Shiloh battle, men who under intense fire became soldiers—"a heterogeneous mass, representing various degrees of courage, from reckless daring to ignominious fear. . . . It was a private soldier's battle, fiercely fought by unskilled, uninstructed and inexperienced volunteers, supported by the indomitable energy, desperate courage, and marvelous staying qualities of the rank and file."[7]

Contemporary commentators on Shiloh quickly realized that early morning Confederate successes were made all the more possible, glaring, and costly because Grant had failed to obey a common-sense directive that an army in camp must entrench for its own protection.[8] Sherman rationalized this mistake by suggesting that the Army of the Tennessee was on an offensive mission. The army had neither the time nor the inclination to construct defensive fortifications, not even trenches. To act upon such a directive, Sherman maintained, would have negative psychological ramifications that would surely destroy the army's morale. Sherman's argument overlooked the salient fact that on the eve of battle, the Army of the Tennessee had remained under Grant's command in one place for more than two-and-a-half weeks. During that period of time, a growing inclination to think defensively rather than offensively compromised the leadership of Grant and many of his field commanders. Jomini would undoubtedly have charged that Grant had "forgotten the first duties of field service." Long after the war, Grant would argue that the use of the pick, axe, and spade had not yet become a part of the thinking of the army in the West in early 1862. That might read well in his *Personal Memoirs* but it was far too many words to put on the tombstones of so many fallen soldiers or to inscribe on the front door of Olney's "houses of mourning."[9]

There was no scarcity of words during and after the war criticizing the failure of Union command to fortify its position at Shiloh. Capt. Andrew Hickenlooper, 5th Ohio Light Artillery, Prentiss's 6th Division, undoubtedly set the record for concentrated criticism when he characterized Grant's reasons for not entrenching as "lame," "unjustifiable," "insufficient," and "unsatisfactory," requiring only two sentences to do so. Less vitriolic but no less damning, Lt. Patrick White, Medal of Honor winner at Vicksburg, 1st Illinois Light Artillery, Taylor's Battery, Sherman's 5th Division, wrote in his diary, "I will repeat again, it was gross carelessness. A little earth works thrown up would have given our raw troops more confidence."[10] A significant number of the men who fought at Shiloh believed that had Grant constructed at least some fortifications on the battlefield, the results of the first day's battle would have been significantly different. This is probably true, although the thesis must remain in the realm of historical speculation. As opponents of his performance at Shiloh focused on this particular point, no doubt Grant suffered a great deal of personal frustration. His embarrassment was a major reason for his intentional lack of response to Wallace on the question of the march to Shiloh as well as Grant's self-imposed general silence on the entire affair.

In the wake of the two-day battle, a wave of negative press criticizing Union command at Shiloh, particularly Grant, rolled out of the Northern states. One such highly exaggerated example will suffice. War correspondent Whitelaw Reid led the onslaught with his commentary, most of which was sensational in nature and dubious in authenticity. "Here began scenes," Reid wrote, "which, let us hope, will have no parallel in our remaining annals of the war. Some, particularly our officers, were not yet out of bed. Others were dressing, others washing, others cooking, a few eating their breakfasts. Many guns were unloaded, accoutrements lying pell-mell, ammunition was ill-supplied—in short, the camps were virtually surprised—disgracefully it might be added." Reid was graphic in his portrayal of the horrors of Shiloh. He made a point of suggesting that Confederate soldiers indiscriminately slaughtered Union soldiers that morning even though many "were trying to impress on the cruelly-expectant enemy their readiness to surrender." He highlighted for his readers one of the more disgusting stories of the day: "officers [who] were wounded in their beds and left for dead through the whole two days' fearful struggle, lay there grasping in their agony." Reid was intent on telling his readers just how badly Union general command had performed at Shiloh, and he had the imagination to do so. Nevertheless, his writing had a profound impact upon the nature as well as content of other press reports and the formation of Northern public opinion about the battle.[11]

The presence of three phenomena, unique at that time to the American military experience, caused major problems for those who sought to minimize the impact of Shiloh on Northern public opinion. The first was the horror, disbelief, and disgust slowly engulfing the home front over the extraordinary number of dead and wounded suffered by both sides at Shiloh. Inexorably, these feelings collided with the heretofore innocent view held by many Americans that war was a pursuit both romantic and glorious full of military parades and balls with an occasional small battle fought here and there. The numbers certainly were at odds with the notion still prevailing that the conflict would be a short and decisive one. The second phenomenon, the sensationalist, rancorous journalism about Northern military ineptness at Shiloh and the inordinate number of casualties resulting therefrom accelerated the impact of the first. Last, survivors of the battle and then visitors to the battlefield began writing letters to their loved ones, friends, neighbors, and constituents back home, relating stories and conclusions specifically targeted and starkly drawn. On April 16, for example, a veteran, signing his name only as "H.S.," 2nd Iowa, 1st Brigade, W.H.L. Wallace's 2nd Division, wrote to the editor of the *Gate City* (Keokuk, Iowa) newspaper that "the smoke of battle has cleared from the bloody field. The terrible visit we received from our brethren, *the Corinthians*, [emphasis in original] will not soon be forgotten. . . . I have ridden over the whole field, in every direction, and am a frequenter of Grant's headquarters, and speak the sentiments of the army when I say that Gen. Grant is responsible for much of the terrible sacrifice of life on the 6th." Dr. A. Ady of West Liberty, Iowa, visited Iowa troops on the battlefield in late April. Ady wrote to a newspaper editor back home that "[i]t is the sheerest folly to claim for the General in command on that day that he exhibited any of the characteristics of a prudent, still less, of a great commander. . . . The name of Grant really has no magic for the soldier."[12] The American military establishment now had a new and essentially onerous task to perform; it had to unite in order to marginalize this newly emerging national consciousness. The powers quickly determined that silence was the best response. Neither Halleck nor Grant had any reason to object.

Late in the afternoon of April 7, having watched the Confederates under Beauregard commence a withdrawal toward Corinth, the Union Army of the Tennessee sought to regroup. Quite surprisingly, though his troops were probably less exhausted than their Confederate counterparts, Grant did not order a general pursuit of the retreating Rebels.[13] On April 11, Halleck arrived at Pittsburg Landing to take field command of the army. As the guns grew silent, Halleck and Grant each demonstrated their acute awareness of just how closely they had courted disaster. Both, in their separate ways, initially attempted to divert the impact of the resulting criticism by denying the reality of what had occurred. Neither was wholly successful. It would not be long before both understood that silence was indeed the best policy for them to pursue.

Initially, Grant kept his thoughts to himself. When he finally spoke, not in the public forum to which Wallace undoubtedly would have resorted, but to a close confidant, he disavowed reality so imaginatively that his comments bordered on the farcical. In late April, he wrote to his good friend, George P. Ihrie, "[a]s to the surprise spoken of, we could not have been better prepared had the enemy sent word three days before when they would attack." Had that been the case, all else notwithstanding,

Grant certainly would have been on the field of battle at Pittsburg Landing quite early on Sunday morning. He might even have spent Saturday night around a campfire at Pittsburg Landing. He did not. Grant initially wanted neither scapegoats nor excuses. As he did after Donelson, he only wished to be left alone, hoping that the outrage would soon die down. In that same letter to Ihrie, Grant explained his tactics for handling the matter. "By the way," he wrote, "the papers are giving me fits for the last [Shiloh]. This matter will all be understood after a while, without any explanation from me, and will appear much better than at present."[14]

Halleck's efforts to explain to Stanton what had happened at Shiloh revealed that Grant's rationale, whether credible or not, would be offered time and again as the "official" military version. "The newspaper accounts that our divisions were surprised are utterly false. Every division had notice of the enemy's approach hours before the battle commenced," Halleck wrote on May 2. This did not appease Stanton, who dispatched another inquiry to Old Brains. To this, Halleck responded with a statement equally without substance. He characterized the reports of Confederate surprise on April 6 as "entirely erroneous." As the result of "a patient and careful inquiry and investigation," Halleck informed Stanton on June 15, he had satisfied himself "that all our troops were notified of the enemy's approach some time before the battle commenced."[15]

Halleck never revealed with whom he had consulted during this alleged "patient and careful inquiry." Surely, he had not discussed the matter with Maj. John Foster, 25th Indiana, 2nd Brigade, 4th Division. Late in the afternoon of April 7 after two days of continuous fighting, Foster wrote to his father. He explained that in the early morning hours of April 6, the 25th Indiana was camped about as far away from the point of initial Confederate contact as any other Union force that day. Having heard heavy firing at a distance and immediately gotten his command into line, "we had hardly left the camp, before we saw the roads full of our flying men, and all along the route for the two miles we passed over were strewn guns, knapsacks, and blankets, and we found to our dismay, that our front had been completely surprised, our whole division scattered, and retreating in utter confusion, and the enemy in force already a mile within our camps." Notwithstanding such first-hand accounts, Stanton satisfied himself that Halleck's explanations told the truth of what happened at Shiloh those two days in early April, 1862. The administration had decided to let the matter lie, refusing to initiate any further official inquiry.[16]

On April 11, Halleck arrived at Pittsburg Landing from his desk in St. Louis. He assumed field command of the Army of the Tennessee and immediately moved to reorganize it. In the process, three Union generals were shuffled off the front line into secondary roles. Arguably, they were the three most qualified and experienced field commanders in the Union army in the West at that time—Maj. Gen. Ulysses S. Grant, Maj. Gen. Lew Wallace, and Maj. Gen. John A. McClernand. Each, however, had irritated an ambitious and fundamentally paranoid Halleck. Despite what the reports to Secretary of War Stanton said, Halleck understood that Shiloh had been concluded one step short of a disaster. He knew that someone had to be held accountable. Halleck responded to this challenge in several different ways. One of his first acts was to demote Grant to second-in-command of the Army of the Tennessee.

It was much less complicated to dispose of civilian amateurs like Wallace and McClernand. Halleck refused to consider any facts or theories that might challenge a long-held professional conviction that no civilian, amateur, politician-playing general merited holding any position of significance within the Union military command structure. Following Shiloh, Halleck was even more convinced that Wallace and McClernand lacked the credentials necessary to bring the army back onto the road to victory. He would surround himself with qualified, dedicated, trustworthy, West Point–trained professionals.[17] Thus, he concluded that Wallace and McClernand would do quite nicely somewhere in the rear, out of the way, perhaps in the newly created reserve. Halleck intended to lead the Army of the Tennessee in the conquest of the Confederate railroad hub at Corinth, the glorious completion of his plan of campaign.

Once again, Wallace responded to a perceived injustice. On May 10, he wrote to Susan that in Halleck's recently reorganized Army of the Tennessee "nobody but West Pointers have high command in the front." He claimed that this Halleck-led group of officers amounted to "a closed corporation," which, along with its leader, had decided that he and McClernand were "interlopers." "So he and I (particularly myself)," Wallace wrote, "are undergoing the process of shelving." He continued by telling Susan that he was "conscious, too, of being an object of jealousy." Furthermore, he was painfully aware "that my progress is being carefully watched by those who, having the power, stand ready to push me the instant I topple." Wallace concluded with the forlorn remark, "Heavens, if I should fail."[18] Several weeks earlier, he had broached the same subject in a letter to his brother-in-law, U.S. Senator from Indiana Henry S. Lane, noting that there existed in the army "a clique that has given me nothing but opposition and ridicule, simply because I was not a West-Pointer." With a touch of romantic wistfulness, he concluded, "So, I will yield not a bit. . . . Tho' I am 'young, gallant, and unselfish'."[19] His acute sense of being a victim, whether justified or not, was pervasive and growing stronger each day.

On May 3, now free from the direct influence of three subordinate major generals, Halleck began the campaign against Beauregard at Corinth, some twenty miles to the south. He sent a telegraph to Stanton announcing that the Union army would "be before Corinth to-morrow night." Almost immediately, he confronted unexpected and, in his estimation, well-nigh insurmountable obstacles. Some were even imagined. On May 13, he complained that heavy rains had produced mud-clogged roads running through "thick forest, with numerous streams and deep marshes," impeding his advance. "Our progress," he concluded, "is necessarily slow." By May 18, he reported that he was "within two miles of [the] enemy's works," even though the "country is so wooded and marshy that we are obliged to feel our way step by step."[20]

Halleck himself was an obstacle to the march. Sounding much like McClellan and Buell, he frequently complained that he lacked a sufficient number of men to undertake the task. He clung to the chessboard of war. He was so fearful of being visited by another "surprise" that he had his army entrench its way south from Pittsburg Landing on a daily basis. On May 22, he told Stanton he was waiting for much-needed reinforcements. "I hear nothing of the Kansas troops," he protested. Even the arrival of these troops did not comfort him, as he constantly envisioned and frequently proclaimed that his enemy outnumbered him several times over. A distraught Lincoln sought to mollify his general. "I beg you," he telegraphed Halleck on May 24, "to be assured we do the best we can." The next day, a highly disingenuous Halleck claimed "I have asked for no re-enforcements, but only whether any were to be sent to me."[21]

On May 30, after a twenty-one mile march lasting twenty-six days, Halleck marched into an abandoned Corinth. He took possession of a major Southern railroad hub, some materials of war, a few Quaker guns, a small amount of usable rolling stock, and many burned-out railroad boxcars. He did not fight, capture, or destroy Beauregard's army, which had departed the night before, heading east into Alabama.[22] Halleck's plan of campaign had floundered in the mud of Tennessee and in his tortured imagination.

He had produced a laughable failure. Wallace spent the entire time in and around Monterey rebuilding "bridges" and corduroying "roads."[23]

Wallace thought he saw at least one more opportunity for honor and glory arising out of Halleck's failed Corinth campaign. Retreating from Corinth, Beauregard had slipped out of Halleck's grasp. Wallace reasoned that Halleck had no alternative but to order his reserve, the divisions of Wallace and McClernand, to chase after, defeat, and capture the fleeing Rebels. With characteristic caution, Halleck refused to pursue. Bewailing his fate once more, Wallace wrote Susan, "Now it appears that the reason which forbids my participation also forbids my taking part in the pursuit. Hence, I bid fair to say in all likelihood, I shall be left to garrison Pittsburg Landing or Corinth." Wallace's obsessive fear of being left behind had resurfaced.[24]

Two weeks later, from Union Station near Raleigh, Tennessee, Wallace issued another protest, coloring his anger with sarcasm. "McClernand and myself [*sic*], being volunteer generals," he wrote to Susan, "will be left to guard and repair the railroad while sundry Brigadier Generals go marching on to glory, they being of the regular army." Wallace perceived that the campaigns, the endless quests for glory and honor, all seemed to be ending in failure. He had always known that at least one of his foes in this war did not wear Butternut but was garbed in Union Blue. That foe was the elitism of West Point. Wallace was just beginning to appreciate that his dreams for the battlefield were fast falling victim to this phenomenon. Perhaps for the first time, he was also becoming aware that there was really nothing he could do to alter this situation, or at least nothing he cared to do.[25]

Wallace's dreams continued to fade before his eyes. He was floundering, unable to identify precisely either the problem or who his enemy was. Following Corinth, it appeared to be Halleck. However, in an earlier incident shortly after Shiloh, the hand of Grant seemed poised against him. In late April, Grant had ordered Wallace to Adamsville, on the Purdy Road, "to cut off the railroad."[26] Wallace did not budge from Stantonville. He feared he had insufficient cavalry to accomplish his task. He telegraphed his concerns to Grant. "Shall I look for more Cavalry?" he asked. Furthermore, if Grant were prepared to send him additional mounted reinforcements, Wallace wished to know "who will command it?" This was not what Grant wanted to hear from his subordinate. His reply was succinctly damning: "Your instructions are plain. . . . You were not to await the arrival of Cavalry, but the Cavalry was to follow and report. Too often my orders and instructions are misunderstood or totally disregarded by you."[27] Wallace continued to be a source of aggravation for Grant; perhaps he was fast becoming a major irritant.

The days drifted by without much change. In mid-June, Halleck ordered Wallace to take and occupy Memphis. He secured his objective on June 17 with little or no fighting. Grant arrived on June 23. By virtue of seniority, based upon date of commission, Grant took command of the city from Wallace. Wallace was upset by this turn of events. He was getting restive. He had seen no major fighting for almost three months. Then,

Clockwise from top left: Major General Lew Wallace. (Library of Congress); Major General Halleck, author of the Mind-Numbing Caveat. Currier & Ives, c. July 1862. (Library of Congress); Lieutenant General Ulysses S. Grant. Johnson, Fry & Co., c. 1866. (Library of Congress)

in late June, another incident occurred that once more demonstrated to Grant that Halleck had little regard or tolerance for Wallace.

Halleck was upset that Wallace failed to execute an order with the specificity and timeliness that Halleck expected. Wallace had been ordered to Grand Junction, Tennessee, "to protect the railroad [Memphis and Ohio] against marauders." Fearing a Rebel attack against Memphis, Wallace had delayed several days before executing the order. As a direct result of Wallace's lack of timeliness, or so Halleck believed, a Rebel force had captured not only a train but also some Union troops engaged in repairing the telegraph lines. "There was culpable neglect in sending out the train from Memphis till the road was properly guarded," Halleck telegraphed Grant on June 29, seeming to imply that Grant, more than Wallace, was responsible for this unfortunate state of affairs. Grant immediately retorted that "certainly no blame can attach to me." In fact, Grant proclaimed, "your orders have countermanded mine." Halleck apologized to Grant on July 3, informing his subordinate that "I made no insinuation that there had been the slightest neglect on your part." In an artlessly worded conclusion, Halleck took exception to "the tone of your dispatch and the ill-feeling manifested in it, so contrary to your usual style, and especially toward one who has so often befriended you when you were attacked by others." Although Halleck felt compelled to be contrite with Grant, he was hardly happy with Wallace. Grant had seen just how disingenuous Halleck could be. At the same time, he could not have missed the import of Halleck's exceedingly clear message. Halleck believed Wallace to be unpredictable and unreliable.[28]

Grant survived this scrape with Halleck but he clearly saw that Halleck deemed Wallace a pariah. Whether or not Grant shared this view at this time is uncertain but it is a good possibility that he did. At least he was coming to that same conclusion. This train event and the correspondence it engendered undoubtedly went far to convince Grant that he had better things to do than spend his time and energy dealing with and then defending Wallace. Neither this, nor the Adamsville incident of April 28, boded well for the continuation of a cordial military relationship between the two men. A decided change in that relationship was in the making. In addition, the Grand Junction train matter only served to confirm for Grant another decision respecting Wallace that he had made a week or so earlier. Wallace had alleged he had unresolved financial matters at home. He noted further that he had been absent from the Hoosier state for almost a year. Based upon this, Wallace asked Grant for a twenty-day leave of absence effective immediately. Grant did not hesitate to approve the request.[29]

CHAPTER ELEVEN

Before the Committee

After being at home in Crawfordsville for less than two weeks, Wallace journeyed to Washington. His mission was to persuade Secretary of War Stanton to give him a field command in the eastern theater. This would free him from the influence and control of both Halleck and Grant. He failed to achieve his objective.

On July 9, 1862, Wallace gave sworn testimony before the Joint Congressional Committee on the Conduct of the War, then engaged in gathering testimony "in relation to the administration of affairs in the department of the West, more particularly while under the command of General John C. Frémont." Earlier, on August 30, 1861, Frémont had issued a Proclamation declaring martial law throughout Missouri. In addition, Frémont confiscated the property of all Missourians who had taken up arms against the United States as well as those "who shall be directly proven to have taken an active part with their enemies in the field." Should such persons own slaves, then "their slaves, if any they have, are hereby declared freemen." The Lincoln administration saw these policies, particularly the statement freeing any slaves, as completely at odds with its evolving policy of "conciliation" toward Southerners and their property. On the other hand, for a variety of reasons, the members of the Joint Committee were decidedly in favor of Fremont's action. The committee's strong bias against the Lincoln administration was revealed not only during its examination of Wallace but in its final report, which accompanied the assembled testimony. The majority report conceded that Frémont might have lacked the authority to issue his proclamation. His timing might have been suspect. There was, however, no doubt that in

The Congressional Inquisitors, left to right: John S. Covode, U.S. Congressman, Pennsylvania. (Library of Congress); Daniel W. Gooch, U.S. Congressman, Massachusetts. (Library of Congress); George W. Julian, U.S. Congressman, Indiana. (Library of Congress)

calling for emancipation in the Department of the Missouri, Frémont had identified "the most effective means of subduing this rebellion."[1]

For Wallace's appearance, the members of the committee sought any evidentiary statements pertinent not only to its main purpose with Frémont but in two other areas as well: the course and conduct of military operations in the West and an assessment of the overall efficacy of current administration governing policies there. Wallace welcomed the opportunity to testify on both matters. In addressing the first, he would have free rein to lay out his side of the Fort Donelson story. At this juncture, he really had no reason to suspect he needed to make any particular statements about Shiloh. The controversy concerning his march to the battlefield on April 6 had not really surfaced yet. With respect to the second line of inquiry, he would be enthusiastic and direct in his comments on the administration's policy of dealing with the property of Southern whites. He would not hesitate to give the committee members the benefit of his observations, opinions, and wisdom in all the detail they might desire. Just months earlier, Wallace had written to his wife's brother-in-law, Aaron Blair, that "[a]fter being a Major General in the Great Rebellion, I am satisfied. More than that, I am fully determined never to be a candidate for any thing [*sic*]. I joined the army because I thought possibly I could be of service to the government and win an honorable place in history; not to pass any way [*sic*] to a set in Congress." With Shiloh behind him, he continued to further his personal military agenda. On the other hand, as he appeared before the committee that day, Wallace had an inexorable belief that he knew what was necessary to win this war. He was further convinced that the administration's current policies were falling far short of achieving that objective.[2]

With U.S. Congressman John S. Covode from Pennsylvania skillfully leading him, Wallace agreed that he had in fact "saved" the army at Fort Donelson.[3] To Wallace's surprise, Covode then quickly moved him beyond Donelson to Pittsburg Landing. He did not need to ask Wallace for his opinion concerning the Rebel surprise at Shiloh inasmuch as Wallace volunteered information. He noted that he was aware "there is a great debate as to whether General Grant was surprised or not." Declaring that he was not personally making such an allegation, Wallace nevertheless observed, "I am satisfied that some of the regiments were surprised." Even so, he testified, the responsibility for permitting the enemy to launch an unexpected attack that morning did "not properly attach to him [Grant]. If anyone could have gone to his headquarters and seen the immense mass of details that he had to attend to, he would readily have understood how absolutely impossible it was for him to go around the picket lines and see whether they were all right or not." It was Grant's staff and junior field officers, but not Grant himself, who were to blame for the Confederate surprise. In other words, in Wallace's opinion, the mistake was real; it was costly; it was merely a heretofore unanswered question just who had made it. Wallace claimed he was attempting to protect Grant from further criticism. It would have been much better for Wallace to have said nothing at all.[4]

As he rendered his opinion, Wallace overlooked two important considerations. Invariably, the man at the top of any chain, particularly the military chain of command, bears ultimate responsibility for whatever occurs, certainly for being surprised by the enemy on the field of battle. Second, Wallace failed to appreciate that the man at the top had subordinate officers devoted to insuring that their man remained at the top. Furthermore, such officers were usually beholden to the man at the top for their position on the chain. As he gave his testimony about "surprise" at Shiloh, Wallace directly attacked these men, particularly as he concluded, "[f]rom the very nature of his [Grant's] situation he had to confide much in the officers." Wallace erred in discounting any subsequent impact the men on Grant's staff, Rawlins, Rowley, McPherson, and Hillyer, might exert upon Wallace personally. He apparently did not appreciate the degree of influence they might have in molding and shaping any future relationships he might have with Grant. Wallace had gratuitously made three mistakes at one time: he answered a question not asked of him; he failed to comprehend that his method of exonerating Grant was lame and ineffectual; and in his zeal to absolve Grant, he laid the blame for surprise at Shiloh squarely at the feet of Grant's subordinates, particularly his staff.

Wallace, more recklessly than otherwise, continued to enjoy his day before the committee. His responses to questions were more the unrestrained acts of an unusually cooperative witness than the cautious calculations of an experienced attorney. Wallace never allowed a short, concise answer to get in the way of disgorging volumes of information while enjoying immensely every minute of the lengthy discourse. He did not force others to extract a statement from him; he gave his opinions freely. For example, in response to Covode's very singular and pointed question, "to whom," referring to General Smith, Wallace responded with an uninterrupted monologue lasting at least three to five minutes commencing chronologically with Grant's reinstatement to command in mid-March through the first and second days at Shiloh. It also included a somewhat detailed weather report for the night of April 6.[5] What Wallace was really doing that day before the committee was telling its members what he thought would best serve their purposes as well as his own.

As with the question of surprise, Wallace initiated the discussion of the failure of the Union army to pursue the battered Confederates as they retreated to Corinth. He concluded his summary of the second day's events at Shiloh by informing the committee members that "the next morning [April 8], I formed line of battle, expecting an order to pursue the enemy; but no order came." He intimated that this was most unusual because the results of the second day were "in our favor" and the Rebels "were routed." Covode did not hesitate to accompany Wallace through the provided opening, asking "could not our army have driven the enemy from Corinth at that time, routed as they were, if we had pursued them?" Wallace responded, "There is no question about that, in my mind." With this exchange, Wallace had openly criticized Grant for one of his command decisions at Shiloh. Wallace continued, observing he was as certain he would have issued orders to pursue as he was positive "I was then a living man." He waited, he said, for such orders in vain but "they never came. Why they did not, I do not know, nor did General Grant ever inform me. I have heard it stated that it was on account of orders that he had." When asked from whom such orders would have come, Wallace quickly answered, "from General Halleck; but General Halleck was not on the ground at that time.

. . . I knew of no telegraphic communication with General Halleck."[6] With this piece of misdirection and innuendo, Wallace transferred the decision not to pursue from one made solely by Grant to a decision shared by Halleck. It did not really matter, however, who made the decision not to pursue; Wallace had succeeded in ciriticizing them both.

For a second time that day, Wallace demonstrated he did not understand the concept of the military chain of command. Further, he displayed ignorance as to what his failure to acknowledge the basic tenets of that chain of command, even in passing, could do to his career. In the first instance, his testimony paired the name of Grant with the reality of Rebel surprise at Shiloh. In the second, he associated both Grant and Halleck with the post-Shiloh failure to pursue a defeated enemy. Earlier in his responses, Wallace had stated his goal was "to do justice to General Grant." He never comprehended that in the final analysis what he had done to Grant was exactly the opposite. Further, by his attacks on his field commander, Wallace succeeded only in doing harm to himself and his military career. The committee did not really seem to be that interested in the issue of Grant's or even Halleck's military expertise. For them, Lincoln, and then Halleck as his errand boy, was the prize. Notwithstanding this, as he several times criticized both superior officers, Wallace never quite grasped that the damage he was doing that day was to himself. He would soon come to realize such damage was well-nigh irreversible.

Wallace afforded himself one more opportunity to criticize his superior officers. Again, he did so as part of a larger answer to an unasked question. Covode had inquired, "to what place did you go?" Wallace correctly answered "Savannah." He then unexpectedly used the rest of a lengthy response to praise his old nemesis, Gen. Charles F. Smith. He stated that in the first several days following their arrival at Savannah, he and Smith were engaged in gathering intelligence about the enemy. Surprisingly, Wallace then added, "he was very frank with me." Without another word of explanation, Wallace commented that for the first time ever, he felt comfortable in Smith's company and command. Without going into any further detail, Wallace concluded, "and I frankly state my opinion that if General Smith had retained his health we would have had Corinth, and there would have been no battle at Pittsburg Landing." Wallace probably failed to cleanse his soul with respect to the now-deceased Smith with this unwarranted and rather strange epitaph. With it, however, he earned the simmering wrath of Halleck and Grant. As a military officer, Wallace's testimony was inexcusable, not only with respect to his superior officers and the revered chain of command but with respect to himself as well.[7]

Wallace answered the committee's questions concerning Halleck's role in the Twin Rivers and Shiloh campaigns in the same manner. For example, when Covode sought confirmation that the fighting encompassed by these two campaigns "was not done in accordance with any general plan from Washington," Wallace stated, "[n]ot that I know of." Surely Wallace would limit his answer to this simple, unambiguous, and direct response. Such was not to be the case. "It was not done, as I understand it," he facetiously maintained, "in accordance with any plan from anywhere." Then, when he was asked if he could "account for the long delay in making the attack on Corinth, thus permitting the rebels to get away," Wallace retorted, "[o]f course I can . . . he [Halleck] thought it wiser to approach the place cautiously . . . systematically." Wallace told the committee that in his opinion the time involved in reaching Corinth could only have been warranted if the Rebels "were in superior numbers, or even equal to us in numbers." In his judgment, the Union army "was larger than theirs by 10,000 to 15,000 men." He characterized Halleck's advance as "slow. But it was very safe."[8] Wallace must have been having a good time; his answers were speculative and self-serving but not designed to advance his career.[9] A simple "no" would have served Wallace's career interests much better, but not his personality or his anger against Halleck.

Wallace had his best opportunity to damage Halleck when Codove and then three other members of the committee, U.S. Senator Zachariah Chandler from Michigan, U.S. Congressman George W. Julian from Indiana, and U.S. Congressman Daniel W. Gooch from Massachusetts, all took him exactly where he wanted to go. Wallace had definite views on how to fight and win a war. He was among the first Union general officers to advocate using Southern slaves who had escaped bondage and were now behind Union lines as laborers in the army. Under certain limited circumstances, he proposed arming them for the strictly defensive purpose of self-protection. He was in the forefront of those advocating the use of the draft to increase the size and striking power of the army. Wallace acknowledged that his demands were "radical." In certain respects, he was one of the first in the Union army to speak passionately about "total" war.[10] The committee gave Wallace the opportunity to express his opinions on this subject as its members turned their focus away from the battlefield to examine how best to deal with the captured property of the Southern whites. Halleck, author of the military's General Orders that had superseded Frémont's earlier proclamation in Missouri, was a good target for those who passionately disagreed with the Lincoln administration's policy of "conciliation."

In early November, 1861, Lincoln had appointed Halleck to replace Frémont as commander of the Department of the Missouri. Lincoln was angry that in issuing his August 31 proclamation, with its emphasis upon confiscation and the freeing of certain slaves, Frémont had exceeded his authority and encroached upon the privileges of the executive branch. Lincoln had repealed Frémont's proclamation on November 4. He then replaced this upstart political general, the first Republican presidential standard bearer in the election of 1856, with Halleck.[11] On November 20, consistent with presidential bidding, Halleck issued General Orders No. 3. Fugitive slaves in the Department of the Missouri were now forbidden to escape their owner's pursuit by entering behind Union lines. The committee now had a golden opportunity to attack Halleck for his by-the-book espousal of Lincoln's views on captured Southern personal property. A man of decided inclinations and few inhibitions, Wallace was perfect for the task.

Covode first had Wallace confirm that current Washington policy made no distinction when it came to the protection of combatant and non-combatant property. The property of each, Union or Rebel, was protected from confiscation and was to be returned to its original owner if it were subsequently determined to have been unlawfully taken. Codove then asked Wallace "in your judgment, will a continuance of the policy we have pursued ever subdue the rebellion?" Wallace ardently proclaimed, "[n]ever, on earth."[12] Next, Julian wondered if treating Southerners and their property so magnanimously had ever transformed one Johnny Reb into a Billy Yank? Mockingly, Wallace responded, "The secessionist whose property is protected by our troops is a secessionist still . . . the moment the column [of Federal troops] is gone, he is as much of a secessionist as ever, and laughs at your clemency."[13] Gooch stated he was unable to criticize the idea that an ex-slave having escaped into a Union camp should be used "to relieve our own soldiers and promote their efficiency" by doing such work as digging entrenchments, constructing fortifications, cutting firewood, pitching tents, loading wagons, and the like. Wallace agreed, treading heavily on administration policy by observing that "[h]ad I been President of the United States I would have issued that order a year ago."[14]

Wallace believed that the slave who escaped from the plantation and came into Union lines voluntarily seeking protection was "our best friend." As he had written to Susan on June 8, 1862, "The deeper we penetrate Southward [*sic*] the more I become satisfied that the boasted love the negro has for his master is a fable. . . . There is no denying the fact that negroes believe we come as their deliverers. Sight of us affords them absolute joy." Committed to this belief, Wallace was convinced that the slave who sought and achieved sanctuary behind Union lines should be allowed to remain under the protection of the Union army and not be tossed aside only to be re-enslaved. Wallace condemned the idea of elevating the slave to a status of equality with the Northern soldier. He strenuously advocated arming the fugitive slave for the sake of his self-protection, "as a means of defending himself." He who refused to arm the slave under these circumstances, Wallace concluded, "would be an idiot."[15]

In addition to humanitarian motives for treating the escaped slave in this manner, Wallace underscored a practical, economic reason for opposing the administration's policy of "conciliation." Present efforts by the Lincoln administration to be conciliatory toward Southern whites and their property served only to impede the Union war effort as it simultaneously aided and abetted the Confederacy. "Is not the inference inevitable?" he exclaimed. Each time a slave escaped from the plantation, there was one less person to produce food for the Rebel army. "I would take every negro from every secessionists' farm," Wallace observed, "if for no other purpose than to prevent him from being able to work his farm, for just so far do I deprive that Southern army of food." "I propose to use the negro," he summarized, "purely as a military instrument."[16] True to his belief that war robbed humanity of its greatness, Wallace further exclaimed, "I do not want to set our soldiers to murdering people; all the ordinary amenities of war should be observed; but for God's sake do let our armies make war."[17]

With more panache than perhaps common sense, Wallace had said his peace.[18] As he concluded his testimony, he gave no indication he recognized he had been used by others to further their agenda. He had no idea of the enemies he made that day or of the influence Halleck and particularly Grant would exercise in opposition to him during the remainder of his military career. He never rejoined Grant and the Union army in the West. Two days after Wallace's appearance, Halleck was called to Washington as General-in-Chief of all the Union armies. Within the year, Grant and Sherman were enjoying the fruits of their efforts at Vicksburg. Had Wallace known how to refrain from excessive jawing and how to observe and perhaps even respect certain military proprieties and protocols such as the chain of command, he might very well have been there with them on the Mississippi River.

While he may have believed he won a victory on July 9, Wallace never thought it probable or even possible that he had lost a war. In very large measure, he had determined his own destiny. It was most unlikely he would ever again be a major participant in the war effort as long as Halleck and Grant loomed above him. Several more months would pass before he began to grasp the reality of that situation. He had evidenced passion as he spoke his mind, but he also had been arrogant, condescending, and more than foolish. In sum, through his own efforts, he had wasted an opportunity for further adventure and glory. He forgot that day that in speaking as he did and saying what he thought he must, he had criticized the army in the person of both Grant and Halleck. To make matters worse, he had done so in a forum controlled by certain members of the U.S. Congress who were not necessarily his friends. The professionals would not quickly forgive or forget. Neither, specifically, would the members of Grant's staff.

As he concluded his testimony, Wallace failed to understand that he had just concluded a major frontal assault on the established traditions of military command. A professional politician like a Covode, a Julian, or a Chandler could attack the citadel on the Hudson and live to fight another day. A soldier, like Wallace dreamed of being, could not. Only an inordinately obtuse individual would have thought otherwise. In particular, Wallace sealed his fate with Grant. As Grant subsequently became aware of what Wallace had said on July 9, the conclusions he drew from that event could only have accelerated the unraveling of his willingness to accept and work with Wallace. His young Hoosier general was fast becoming a nuisance. His freely given comments easily trumped any favorable opinion Grant might have had concerning Wallace's ability to perform on the field of battle.[19]

Wallace had a tragic flaw. He was too much a product of an unrestrained family and frontier environment, too aggressive, arrogant, cocksure, too much of an adventurer, too obsessed with attaining glory and honor, and too possessed of an unquenchable Romantic spirit to comprehend that there were many military men who neither practically nor philosophically agreed with him. The day of the domination of the professionally trained and educated soldier was fast approaching. Wallace could not grasp the implications of this transition.

He had been frank and terribly naïve in his testimony. Everything he disagreed with he dismissed as trivial or insignificant. He fervently believed that the one who possessed and exhibited certain definable character virtues always prevailed. He had believed this all his life. Thus, he would not play anybody's game for in his mind there was no game to be played. He explained this philosophy to Susan by quoting nearly verbatim two stanzas written by a Baden-born German poet of the early nineteenth century, Johann Peter Kebel: "D'ye know what road to honor leads, And good old Age?—a lovely sight! By way of temperance, honest deeds, and trying to do y'r duty right. And when the roads forks, any side, And you're in doubt which one it is, Stand still, and let y'r conscience guide, Thank God, it can't lead much amiss!"[20] After his sojourn in Washington, Wallace remained obtuse to the fact that he had been his own worst enemy. With each passing day, he reluctantly came to see that he no longer had any future in the West. Even that process took a long time to complete. In the end, he simply could not understand why he had failed. Even as late as October, 1862, he refused to admit that such a possibility genuinely existed. In his own inimitable way, he would keep trying to make that connection with his destiny. He never ceased in his efforts to maintain his honor.

Wallace's Washington sojourn had sealed his fate with Grant. It had undoubtedly done so with Halleck as well. Yet Halleck had reached this conclusion long before Wallace's appearance before the committee and frankly long before he knew the first thing about Wallace. Halleck neither knew nor cared that Wallace had read extensively in the realm of military matters. Neither the Montgomery Guards nor Romney meant a thing to him. Men like Wallace had never been required to present a command solution to a question posed by a West Point instructor; had never put the slowmatch to the touch hole of a Napoleonic six pounder pointed out across the Hudson River; had never walked demerit punishment across the Commons. Therefore, by definition, a civilian amateur was incurably deficient in military matters and potential. The civilian amateur's inability to exercise command could only be rectified by an extended tour of duty at West Point during which he would either fail or become a professional. In fairness, Halleck had probably never seen Wallace's April, 1861, proposal to Cameron aimed at rectifying this deficiency for the civilian, amateur volunteer. It is difficult to conclude that even if he had seen the plan, he would have approved it. He would have undoubtedly dismissed it as poppycock, not because it lacked merit but rather because it was the product of the brain of other than a West Point professional. Why bother even to argue the point, Halleck might have suggested, for certainly, in the current crisis, the Union had neither the time nor the capacity to train such men. Furthermore, he undoubtedly would have concluded that three months of training paled in significance when compared to the knowledge and traditions imparted to Cadets during four years on the Hudson.

Halleck had never led more than two hundred men in battle. He had done so executing a cavalry chase on the Baja in California in 1847 during the War with Mexico. Wallace led eight hundred soldiers to Romney; he directed the movements from Henry to Donelson of more than twenty-five hundred soldiers; he commanded almost seven thousand in a major engagement at Fort Donelson; the 3rd Division he fought beside at Shiloh was at least thirty-five times larger than Halleck's Baja contingent. Halleck would have viewed such facts as irrelevant. He would have spent little time thinking, let alone analyzing, what these numbers and actions might tell him about Wallace, the man, or Wallace, as a potential leader. Halleck believed that only he and West Pointers like him would win this war. First, however, he had to get and keep those pesky, civilian, amateur generals out of the way before they destroyed his army. He had already secured Wallace's temporary leave. Perhaps his ill-timed appearance before the Joint Committee would help Halleck make the temporary permanent. He would certainly try to make it so.

It was apparent that Wallace was intent upon making Halleck's task in this regard just that much easier. For example, he told the committee a charming little story that was undoubtedly very amusing to the Washington politicians but could only have been an annoyance to Halleck. Shortly after Halleck arrived at Pittsburg Landing, Wallace stated that he went to Halleck's headquarters to advocate the reinstatement of one of his officers whom he believed had been wrongfully discharged at Shiloh. Wallace recalled he spent "about five minutes" with Halleck. This was probably the first time the two men met face to face. Wallace made his argument on behalf of his subordinate. "The reply of the general to my application was very unsatisfactory to me." So, Wallace informed the committee, "I got on my horse and rode off, and never went near his headquarters after that. I remained in my own camp, and when he sent orders to me I executed them to the best of my ability."[21]

In his *Autobiography*, Wallace presented, or perhaps invented, a fascinating story about three officers who visited his camp one day shortly after

Halleck began the advance against Corinth. Literary license aside, and whether apocryphal or not, the incident illustrates why each time Wallace interacted with Halleck, the relationship went from bad to worse. Wallace told how three mid-level Union officers, total strangers, appeared in his camp one day shortly after lunchtime. As a matter of courtesy, Wallace invited the three gentlemen to enjoy his coffee and biscuits. The group soon graduated to "some good rye whiskey from a cut-glass decanter, and cigars of a brand Grant loved best." One of the strangers asked Wallace how he thought the Corinth campaign was going. "The question," Wallace said, "though natural as could be, was like a spark on loose powder in a magazine. I went off in a flash." Wallace did not repeat specifically what he said that day but he did point to the obvious. "To ridicule General Halleck's plan of operations was to ridicule the man himself; and that was what I did. When under headway, I saw the folly, and tried to stop. In vain I had become a loaded car with broken brakes rushing on a down-grade." No sooner had the three officers departed than it struck Wallace that these strangers had to be members of Halleck's newly arrived staff. "The consequences rose before me in an electric glare. I had made an enemy, and he was in high place and going higher."[22]

CHAPTER TWELVE

Speechifying and One Last Adventure

As Wallace departed the committee hearing room on July 9, he was far from certain what lay in his immediate future. Around 11:00 that evening, flanked by Lane, Colfax, and several other political and military dignitaries, Wallace stood on the balcony of the National Hotel in Washington as the Marine Band honored him with a serenade. At the appropriate moment, Wallace presented what one listener called "not only the best [speech] he ever made, but for compactness, point, and as a whole, for logical demonstration of the necessary and proper conduct of the war, has had no equal as yet among war speeches either in Congress or out of it."[1]

Wallace began, characteristically enough, on a highly personal note. He reminded his audience that the 11th Indiana, his men, had fought and won, and thus they had "remembered" Buena Vista.[2] He further stated he had been a "willing witness" to the courage, discipline, gallantry, and "the devotion to death" of all brave Union soldiers who fought the Rebels whether at Shiloh in the West or on the Peninsula before Richmond in the East. The audience loved him and his high-powered, patriotic rhetoric.

Wallace quickly gravitated to his second theme of the evening, a reprise of a portion of his testimony before the Joint Committee that day. Wallace wanted to make sure that people heard his call to the Lincoln administration to allow those Union soldiers now engaged in the war to be allowed at least to fight it. "He would be a poor soldier," Wallace shouted, "who would fail to use every element of war which God Almighty gave him if he could use it to his advantage." Wallace explained to his listeners exactly why it was necessary to convince the Lincoln administration to permit Northern armies to use in the war effort the Southern Negro whenever and wherever possible, excluding combat. He enumerated for his audience the considerable advantages accruing to the Northern war effort from the adoption of such a policy. The army's use of the fugitive slave would diminish the effectiveness of the Confederate effort as its plantation labor force dwindled. Integrating the fugitive slave into the war effort as a work force advanced the Northern cause by freeing Union white soldiers from the drudgery of military life—digging entrenchments, erecting fortifications, cutting and gathering firewood, loading and driving wagons, cooking meals—allowing them to focus their efforts, energies, and talents on fighting.

In addition, utilizing escaped slaves for such work as this would put the Union war effort on an equal footing with that of the South. Wallace said he had personally seen many Southern plantations where the "man of the house" was in the army while "stalwart negroes" continued to farm these plantations as if their male owners were present, reaping an abundant harvest, supporting themselves, the owner's family, and, more importantly, the Southern war effort. Wallace used humor to emphasize his point. He told his audience "do you suppose if we went humbly" to say to Jefferson Davis personally, "You have 4,000,000 operatives belonging to your people in the South; under our policy we may not touch them—not molest them. [If] we will leave them upon your farms to work, will you agree to leave us 4,000,000 operatives at home on our farms, in our shops, unmolested?" Wallace mocked Davis's obvious refusal. The absurdity of Davis agreeing to such a suggestion only served to underscore the inequality in war footing that existed between the North and South. Wallace proposed, therefore, with respect to the ex-slaves who did the menial work of the Union army in the field, "I would feed them, I would organize them, and to each one who did good service, I would at the end of the war give him or her freedom." However, at this time, Wallace believed that arming the Southern blacks was too sensitive an issue to broach. The very thought contained the potential for offending the Northern soldier, who might look upon arming the ex-slave as questioning his ability to fight the war as well as an affront to his dignity. Nevertheless, Wallace stated, if the work the ex-slave was doing for the Union war effort put his life in peril, then he should be armed.[3]

In making his third point that evening, Wallace ventured into somewhat new territory as he asked his listeners, "what do you think of the legislator who will sit in the halls of our Congress and be afraid to use the power of the Government to sustain the Government?" Wallace quickly acknowledged his pointed question was intended to reveal to members of Congress the absolute necessity of passing a draft law. Congressmen and Senators must reject "affectations" and "summon to the battle field every man who can carry a gun or stand beneath the flag." Although Wallace considered a draft a wartime necessity, he said he doubted that Congress had the courage to legalize and implement such a law. "Oh," he lamented, "if I could get a little backbone into those who are governing us. . . . If I could but stimulate them to the point of courage . . . [if] I could induce them to let us make war, that is all I ask." "Understand me," he cried, "I would not make war barbarous. I would cultivate every amenity that belongs to civilized warfare. . . . But I never again want to lead a column of troops through a land rich with comforts and luxuries belonging to the enemy of my Government without having the privilege of giving a portion of them at least to the gallant soldiers who follows me."[4] Wallace had certainly taken on the president on several points, which undoubtedly did not win him many friends in the administration. Halleck and Grant had escaped his direct wrath that night, but to the extent both supported the government's policy of "conciliation," neither would be very happy with Wallace.[5]

The next morning, Lew and Susan left Washington. They toured Philadelphia, New York, and Boston, and visited their dear friends, the Lossings, in Poughkeepsie.[6] At the end of his second consecutive twenty-day leave, realizing he still lacked a field command, Wallace returned to Crawfordsville. Perhaps, he thought, he might even go fishing and hunting on his beloved Kankakee River. Indiana Governor Oliver P. Morton had other plans.

The governor wanted Wallace to make recruiting speeches throughout Indiana. Stanton and Halleck agreed. Starting July 31, and for the next two weeks or so, Wallace made the recruiting trail his home. He was none too happy; but he had his orders. Even though he knew he belonged in the field in command of troops, he could not persuade Morton otherwise. The Indianapolis *Daily Journal* reported that Wallace spoke in Terre Haute on August 6, in Princeton on August 7, and in Evansville on August 8.[7] As ordered, he was focusing his efforts and talents in that part of Indiana where pro-South sentiment was substantial. At all three stops, and three or four more during this period, Wallace "addressed large, enthusiastic audiences on the inadequacies of the Administration's war policy and the necessity of strengthening our arms in the field."[8] On at least one occasion, however, he was met with an altogether different response. Covering Wallace's speech in Terre Haute on August 6, the writer for the Evansville *Weekly*

Gazette, "a Democratic Family Newspaper," stated that Wallace's audience was "rather disappointed than otherwise, having anticipated something grand and patriotic, but only got a commonplace speech."[9]

In the end, Morton got what he wanted and needed from Wallace: powerful assistance in fulfilling Lincoln's call for additional volunteer troops. Wallace remained restless without men to lead in battle. He became increasingly frustrated as it slowly dawned on him that Morton had no intention of helping him secure that command. Despite the political machinations of Morton and Halleck, Wallace would soon get that opportunity. First, however, he had to introduce himself to the people of Cincinnati. A rousing political speech would serve the purpose.

In the company of Morton and others, Wallace had actually begun his recruiting tour with a speech in Cincinnati at Market Street Square on July 31. The *Vincennes Gazette* noted that "the crowd present, considering the short notice given, was large . . . his speech was eloquent, earnest and impressive." The correspondent for the *Cincinnati Gazette* stated unequivocally that the Market Street Square affair was the largest war rally ever held anywhere. Furthermore, it was not just for the men that night, as "the ladies of Cincinnati, whose hearts beat strong in the cause of their country, were there in considerable numbers." Wallace was the first speaker of the evening. His appearance at the podium was "the signal for the most enthusiastic, continuous and deafening cheers." When Wallace concluded his remarks, the spontaneous outbreak of applause was "immense" and "showed that what he had said had told well on his listeners."[10]

Enunciating a theme he had used on several prior occasions, Wallace began by telling his audience he would speak to them not as a politician but as a soldier. The times demanded unity, not political factionalism. It would be best for the country, he believed, if all political parties were temporarily abolished. Then, the people as one could rise up to protect and defend their Constitution and restore their country to its former glory. Men, he exclaimed, who constantly talked about the present conflict being "an Abolition war," or "a Republican war," or "Abe Lincoln's war" were nothing less than traitors to the cause. Wallace fervently declared that if, in fact, there was not a special place in hell for those who put political party and personal ambition above country, there should be.[11]

He briefly cajoled Winfield Scott for believing in April, 1861, that the rebellious South could be quelled with only 70,000 men. Thus, Lincoln's call for 75,000 three-month volunteers had been grossly inadequate, resulting in the necessity for subsequent calls of 500,000 and then 300,000 additional troops. That was the North's and the administration's first "great" mistake made in the prosecution of the war. Wallace moved on from this point by casually observing that "[w]e have all made mistakes."[12]

He had already spent some months discussing the administration's second "great" mistake in the conduct of the war, including a discourse on the subject before the Joint Committee in Washington three weeks earlier. The road to victory could not, and did not, lie down the path of "conciliation." "There were many," Wallace observed, "who thought, when this trouble first commenced, that we could win back the rebels by kindness." Compromise and conciliation were ineffective tools against the rebellious Southerner, however. "Nothing," he concluded, "but war, real, terrible, earnest war, ever can be successful in quelling this unholy and infamous rebellion."[13]

Wallace continued by discussing the third "great" mistake committed in the prosecution of the war. He identified it as failure by Northerners to realize both before the war broke out and at the present moment that, contrary to popular belief, the Negro was a not an "element of weakness to the South but . . . that slavery is one of the main elements of strength to the South at the present time." Slavery represented a 4,000,000-person-strong workforce that was both untouchable by the North and a bulwark of abundant resources to the Southern war effort. The North did not possess such a "luxury." Undergirded economically by the institution of slavery, the South had an unequal advantage over the North when it came to prosecuting the war. He fervently claimed he was not an abolitionist. He candidly acknowledged his prejudice, stating that he never saw "a negro [*sic*] pass me in the street, without thinking: there stands the cause of all this trouble." With passion, he stated that he personally would never "permit" equality between the two races. "It never shall be done. I will fight myself, if ever it comes to that," he shouted. The *Gazette* added, parenthetically, that "loud and prolonged cheering" accompanied this last series of remarks.[14]

However, Wallace stated, such a situation would never develop. Nevertheless, the rebellion would be put down only if the North fought the war as it should be prosecuted. "I hold it to be our duty in the field," he proclaimed, "to do all we can to weaken the enemy, and if in so doing we can strengthen ourselves, in the name of God, why not do it? If slavery is the base of the rebellion," he triumphantly asked, "why not knock away the foundation?" He added that it was a mistake for the administration to permit "trade to follow the flag." If he commanded, Wallace proclaimed, he would immediately stop all trade with the South, with "these people." He declared unequivocally that if anyone was then found to have disobeyed such an order, that person would and should be "instantly hung as a traitor to his country." [15]

Having identified the mistakes made to date by the North as it attempted to quash the rebellious South and having proposed solutions to correct those inadequate policies, Wallace spent the rest of his time in patriotic, pep-rally mode. "If the country is lost," he exclaimed, "the people alone are responsible. . . . If you will come forward as you ought, then Uncle Sam will soon get well again." The struggle was noble. This was a war fought "not for conquest, not for aggrandizement, but . . . for the one sole object of once more restoring to the land of our fathers the blessings of an abiding peace." He concluded his remarks by thundering, "Let not posterity point jeeringly at us and say that we lacked the will and capacity to maintain the freedom that our fathers purchased for us at the cost of so much noble blood." According to the *Vincennes Gazette*, "shouts of applause" resonated throughout Wallace's speech.[16]

Wallace was proving on the home front to be as much of an asset to the Union war effort as he had already demonstrated himself to be on the battlefield. At the same time, he was doing little to make friends and inspire mutually beneficial alliances among both the military and the politicians in Washington and Indianapolis. In fact, if he realized he needed the support of men like Lincoln, Stanton, and Morton to achieve his restoration to command, he did little in his days of giving recruiting speeches to reveal his awareness of that possibility. Again, as on the battlefield, his unwillingness to do things in any other way than his own stood as a seemingly impenetrable impediment to achieving his ambitions. He would soon have another opportunity, however. Little more than a month later, the people of Cincinnati would again welcome Wallace to the banks of the Ohio, but this time as a soldier and not an orator.

Near the end of August, with a crisis at hand, Halleck permitted Wallace, as the highest-ranking general officer available in the area for emergency service, to come out of exile. As part of Confederate general Braxton Bragg's invasion of Kentucky in the late summer of 1862, Confederate generals E. Kirby Smith and Henry Heth threatened Cincinnati. Given emergency command of the city, Wallace organized a bold and decisive defense, which, as he implemented it, helped save Cincinnati from an actual attack.

The city council of the Queen City of the West gratefully issued a proclamation bestowing upon Wallace the title "Savior of Cincinnati."[17]

Halleck's response to Wallace's accomplishments on the banks of the Ohio was to send him to Camp Chase outside of Columbus, Ohio, to organize and command paroled but not yet exchanged Union prisoners of war. Halleck knew that this particular tour of duty included the possibility that Wallace might be banished forever from the two primary theaters of war. These prisoners stood a good chance of being sent to Minnesota to chase after renegade Sioux Indians. Amid rumors that many of them might be destined for such duty, Union prisoners at Camp Chase deserted in droves. Wallace surreptitiously encouraged this, thereby delaying everyone's departure for Minnesota, including, perhaps, his own. Then, in early October, Halleck learned that Union forces already present in Minnesota had defeated and disbursed the rebellious Sioux. Although Halleck might well have relished the possibility of Wallace visiting that Northern state, Wallace was not destined to go there.[18]

To his surprise, Wallace unexpectedly received orders to join Grant once more in the West. On October 30, Special Orders No. 320 was issued "by command of Major-General Halleck," instructing Wallace to "report in person to Maj. Gen. Grant at Corinth." If Grant had any reservations about this curious turn of affairs, he had a strange way of showing it. On November 8, he telegraphed a brief dispatch to one of his protégés, Brig. Gen. Grenville Dodge, noting that "General Wallace will probably relieve you in a day or two. A division then awaits you here."[19]

On November 10, as Wallace switched trains in Cairo for the trip further south, he received new instructions to return to Cincinnati. The telegram, "signed" U. S. Grant, had originated in Washington. Grant, however, was not in Washington but in Corinth. It is uncertain whether Halleck or Grant initiated the change. It is possible that Lane secured the original order but then either Halleck, Grant, or Morton engineered its reversal. One thing is certain. Halleck had the ability, the means, and the mindset to append Grant's name to telegraphic order. Whether the hand of Grant can be seen in this event as a direct participant is an interesting question.[20]

Halleck's personal quest to rid himself of Wallace was far from over. On November 20, Halleck appointed Wallace president of the military commission organized to hear charges against Buell for alleged incompetence during the Confederate invasion of Kentucky. Wallace was angry. Glory and honor were achieved on the battlefield, not in a military courtroom.[21] Nevertheless, as directed, he departed Cincinnati to do his duty.

Finally, on December 14, Grant put his views on Wallace down on paper for the first time. Halleck had recently had a conversation with Grant's mentor, Congressman Washburne, offering to help Grant resolve any possible staffing issues. In response, Grant told Halleck he was satisfied with the men he now had as his "wing and division commanders." He expressed his hope that "no officer will be sent into the department who rank those who are now with me." He went on to say that he "would regard it as particularly unfortunate to have either McClernand or Wallace sent to me." Calling the former "unmanageable and incompetent," Grant told Halleck that "the latter [Wallace] I could manage if he had less rank." Grant made no attempt to explain why he made this distinction between the men who had commanded his 1st and 3rd Divisions at Donelson and Shiloh. In addition, Grant did not indicate exactly how he proposed to reintegrate Wallace into his military family even if his Hoosier general, voluntarily or otherwise, was willing to accept a reduction in rank.[22]

As vague as his statement to Halleck appeared, Grant had resolved the dilemma Wallace created for him. He made no mention of Wallace's testimony before the Joint Committee. Such criticism, openly delivered by a subordinate officer, undoubtedly infuriated him. He would not, however, discuss it in writing. Lingering recollections of the devastations at Shiloh certainly gave him pause as he considered the desirability of going forward with Wallace. The overt antagonism of several of his staff members toward Wallace did nothing to soothe and improve Grant's relationship with him. Moreover, Grant knew his man. He understood that for Wallace there would always be another Smith to question; there would always be another hospital ship to direct against orders "out of district;" and there would always be another contentious matter such as who would command the 11th Indiana and the 8th Missouri to beat to death until perhaps he reluctantly gave Wallace what he wanted. To be sure, Grant knew his man. He also knew he wanted little else to do with him. Thus, even though he told Halleck he would not even consider taking Wallace back unless Wallace accepted a reduced rank, Grant was undoubtedly confident that a man of Wallace's passions and proclivities would never accept such an arrangement.

It is highly probable that Grant was impressed with Wallace's abilities as a fighting soldier and officer. Wallace had led and fought as well, if not better, than any of his other subordinates at Donelson and on the second day at Shiloh. It was not in Grant's nature, however, to say so. On the other hand, Grant also knew that with the passage of each day in the western theater many others were coming to the fore perhaps as well qualified to lead men in battle as Wallace. Many were yet to be tested but had the qualifications. He already had a number of such men on his staff and under his command in the field. Grant finally realized in late 1862 that he had no intention of welcoming Wallace back into his close-knit military family. For once, he and Halleck found themselves in agreement. In his December dispatch, Grant diplomatically established that the personality issues and conflicts between him and Wallace had grown so great that he could not accept and would not deal with Wallace in any direct capacity. He may have expressed himself somewhat ambiguously but he had more than adequately defined his objective.[23]

Wallace, however, had friends in high places. On September 20, an editorial in the Indianapolis *Daily Journal* called his removal from Cincinnati, "where he did all that the emergency required," and his subsequent posting to Camp Chase, "an intentional disappointment of his desire for active duty, and a slight for which there is no excuse." Further labelling the possibility of Wallace going to Minnesota to chase renegade Sioux "an indignity, apparent, open and most unjust," the *Journal* castigated the War Department whose fate appeared to be "to keep in service those who either do nothing, or do worse, and keen [*sic*] under or out of service all who have been successful." Earlier, on October 7, J. B. Purcell, Archbishop of Cincinnati, urged fellow Ohioan Salmon P. Chase, Lincoln's Secretary of the Treasury, to exert his influence to obtain a field command for Wallace "at the head of even a small division, and if necessary, under Generals whom he outranks." Purcell believed Wallace "now longs for an opportunity" to serve his country by commanding in battle once more. "This brave and intelligent officer" deserved no less for he had done "so much to organize an effective force for the protection of Cincinnati in its hour of peril."[24] On December 9, Lane secured a total of forty-eight signatures from fellow U.S. Senators and Congressmen on a petition addressed to the president requesting that Wallace once again be given a field command. Lincoln refused to get involved, although he did forward the petition to Halleck for further consideration. Halleck filed the petition away for safekeeping, hoping no one would notice it had disappeared.[25]

In mid-February 1863, Julian exhorted his colleagues in the House to remember "we must have commanders . . . whose whole hearts are in the work, and who believe, religiously in the rights of man." Julian proceeded to identify Wallace by name as one of seven Union general officers who were "heartily for their country, and as heartily despise the Democratic leaders who gabble about compromise with rebels." The country required the services of men like Wallace, Maj. Gen. Benjamin Butler, Brig. Gen. William Rosecrans, and others who acted as they talked, men of "action, instant, decisive, defiant action, scourging faithless men from power, sweeping away obstacles, and kindling in the popular heart the fires of a new courage and hope." Arguably, however, Julian was merely using the plight of Wallace and the others as a pretext for haranguing those Democrat politicians who were reluctant to arm "the colored men of the free States as well as the slaves of the South."[26]

Some two months later, in *Harper's Weekly*, Wallace's name was again linked with that of Rosecrans. Both men were featured in an advertisement endorsing a mess kit sold by Milligan Brothers, a New York City–based wholesale dealer in army equipment. Wallace noted his approval of this product, calling it "the most complete article of the kind I have seen. Its compactness commends it for transportation." Milligan Brothers reciprocated by boldly stating that their officer's mess kit was "endorsed by the best Military Talent in the Country." Milligan Brothers' endorsement was flattering to Wallace in both a personal and a financial sense. It would never have secured for him that which he fervently desired, a return to active battlefield command, but at least he was not being forgotten. Unfortunately, Wallace's friends and patrons exerted less influence on Lincoln and events than did Halleck, Grant, Stanton, and Morton.[27] Then, again, perhaps Lincoln and even Lane were growing weary with the factious general.

Wallace served throughout most of 1863 on Halleck's shelf. He did get some time to fish and hunt on the Kankakee. And, usually against his will, he responded to Morton's call to continue giving recruiting speeches at various times throughout the state. In July of that year, Confederate Brig. Gen. John Hunt Morgan took his cavalry on a raid into southern Indiana. Basically caught unaware by Morgan's actions and lacking experienced front-line troops with which to confront Morgan, Indiana governor Morton petitioned the War Department to transfer Wallace temporarily to state duty under his control. On July 9, Wallace led approximately 1,300 Indiana clerks and militiamen, hastily formed into a new regiment, south chasing after the elusive Morgan. The adventure lasted less than a week. For Wallace, a significant amount of bureaucratic confusion and mismanagement as well as many hours riding on trains in hot pursuit of Rebel cavalry characterized this campaign, but little else. Literally hours before Wallace had a genuine opportunity to engage Morgan and perhaps drive him out of Indiana, the Rebel cavalryman crossed into southern Ohio. Wallace's services were no longer required. Once more, at least in Wallace's estimation, he had successfully responded to Morton's plea for help and in return received little, if any, consideration from the governor.[28]

Throughout the early months of 1863, Wallace traveled to Washington, Cincinnati, and New York seeking audiences receptive to his arguments for reinstatement. Unless there was a Cincinnati or John Hunt Morgan type of emergency, he was nothing more than Don Quixote tilting at windmills. During one such trip, however, he achieved a degree of national recognition. *Harper's Weekly* again featured the general on the cover of its national news magazine. Following a dinner discussion in Washington with two friends, the poet-artist Thomas Buchanan Read and the actor-elocutionist, James E. Murdock, the eclectic Wallace penned a thirty-line poem entitled "The Stolen Stars." Reflecting both his love of country and the spirit of abolitionism which he was rapidly embracing, Wallace wrote in part, "When good old Father Washington/Was just about to die/He called our Uncle Samuel/Unto his bedside nigh/This flag I give you, Sammy dear/Said Washington, said he/Where'ver it floats, on land or wave/My children shall be free." Wallace's poetic and lyric abilities aside, "The Stolen Stars" demonstrated a fierce and steadfast patriotism that could not be denied.[29]

In early 1864, Lane and Colfax were politicking Lincoln to give Wallace a command. At the same time, Halleck sought to convince Lincoln not to give Wallace anything. In fact, Halleck was still attempting to rid the service of Wallace and several others forever. On January 14, Secretary of War Stanton submitted to the U.S. Senate a list of twenty major generals who were either excluded from active service because of wounds received or were "without commands equal to a Brigade." In this endeavor, Halleck undoubtedly gave Stanton enthusiastic support. The list, "formidable to taxpayers, and odious to soldiers who live in the front," featured as well the names of forty-seven brigadier generals who fit into the same categories as their listed superior officers, along with thirty-eight junior officers who largely constituted the staff members of the aforesaid general officers. Stanton claimed that the total monthly salaries paid to these one hundred and five individuals "exhibit an immense expenditure of public money, which the Senate will probably decide shall be in the future saved to the National Exchequer, or appropriated to increase the well-earned pay of fighting men." The message was clear. To prosecute the war more efficiently, some, if not all, of this excess baggage must be permanently

THE STOLEN STARS.

BY GEN. LEW. WALLACE.

GREAT WESTERN SANITARY FAIR.

DEDICATED TO THE SOLDIERS OF THE UNION.

WHEN GOOD OLD Father Washington
Was just about to die,
He called our Uncle Samuel
Unto his bedside nigh:
"This flag I give you, Sammy dear,"
Said Washington, said he;
"Where'er it floats, on land or wave,
My children shall be free."

AND FINE OLD Uncle Samuel
He took the flag from him,
And spread it on a long pine pole,
And prayed, and sung a hymn.
A pious man was Uncle Sam,
Back fifty years and more;
"The flag should fly till Judgment-Day,"
So, by the Lord, he swore!

AND WELL HE KEPT that solemn oath;
He kept it well, and more:
The thirteen stars first on the flag
Soon grew to thirty-four;
And every star bespoke a State,
Each State an empire won:
No brighter were the stars of night
Than those of Washington.

BENEATH THAT FLAG two brothers dwelt;
To both 'twas very dear;
The name of one was Puritan,
The other Cavalier.
"Go build ye towns," said Uncle Sam,
Unto those brothers dear;
"Build anywhere, for in the world
Ye've none but God to fear."

I'LL TO THE SOUTH," said Cavalier,
"I'll to the South," said he;
"And I'll to the North," said Puritan—
"The North's the land for me."
Each took a flag, each left a tear
To good old Uncle Sam;
He kissed the boys, he kissed the flags,
And, doleful, sang a psalm.

AND IN A GO-CART Puritan
His worldly goods did lay;
With wife, and gun, and dog, and axe,
He, singing, went his way.
Of buckskin was his Sunday suit,
His wife wore linsey-jeans;
And fat they grew, like porpoises,
On hoe-cake, pork, and beans.

BUT CAVALIER a cockney was;
He talked French and Latin;
Every day he wore broadcloth,
His wife, so gay, wore satin.
He went off in a painted ship—
In glory he did go;
A thousand niggers up aloft,
A thousand down below.

THE TOWNS WERE BUILT, as I've heard said;
Their likes were never seen;
They filled the North: they filled the South,
They filled the land between.
"The Lord be praised!" said Puritan;
"Bully!" said Cavalier;
"There's room and town-lots in the West,
If there isn't any here."

OUT TO THE WEST they journeyed then,
And in a quarrel got;
One said 'twas his, he knew it was;
The other said 'twas not.
One drew a knife, a pistol t'other,
And dreadfully they swore:
From Northern Lake to Southern Gulf
Wild rang the wordy roar.

AND ALL THE TIME good Uncle Sam
Sat by his fireside near,
Smokin' of his kinnikinick,
And drinkin' lager beer.
He laughed and quaffed, and quaffed and laughed,
Nor thought it worth his while,
Until the storm in fury burst
On Sumter's sea-girt isle.

OER THE WAVES to the smoking fort,
When came the dewy dawn,
To see the flag he looked—and lo,
Eleven stars were gone!
"My pretty, pretty stars!" he cried,
And down did roll a tear.
"I've got your stars, Old Fogy Sam;
"Ha, ha!" laughed Cavalier,

I'VE GOT YOUR STARS in my watch-fob;
Come, take them, if you dare!"
And Uncle Sam he turned away,
Too full of wrath to swear.
"Let thunder all the drums!" he cried,
While swelled his soul, like Mars;
"A million Northern boys I'll get
To bring me home my stars."

AND ON HIS MARE, stout Betsey Jane,
To Northside town he flew;
The dogs they barked, the bells did ring,
And countless bugles blew.
"My stolen stars!" cried Uncle Sam—
"My stolen stars!" cried he.
"A million soldiers I must have
To bring them back to me."

DRY UP YOUR TEARS, good Uncle Sam;
Dry up!" said Puritan,
"We'll bring you home your stolen stars,
Or perish every man!"
And at the word a million rose,
All ready for the fray;
And columns formed, like rivers deep,
And Southward marched away.

AND STILL OLD Uncle Samuel sits by his fireside near,
Smokin' of his kinnikinick, and drinkin' lager beer;
While there's a tremble in the earth, a gleaming of the sky,
And the rivers stop to listen, as The Million marches by.

"The Stolen Stars," a patriotic poem penned by Wallace, 1863. (Library of Congress)

eliminated from the national rolls. Not surprisingly, a significant number of the twenty major generals, including Wallace, had come into the service as volunteer, civilian amateurs, not as West Point professionals.[30]

The *Weekly Vincennes Western Sun* reported on January 30, 1864, that an unidentified source had given President Lincoln a list of fifteen major generals who, according to the source, should be dismissed from service.[31] None of the newspaper reports gave a reason why any of the fifteen should be dismissed or why such a list was being circulated to the president in the first place. At least three of the fifteen major generals specifically named were men Halleck could neither trust nor tolerate: Don Carlos Buell, Franz Sigel, and of course Lew Wallace. Wallace was garnering some national attention on the very level he most wished to avoid.

However, this time in the political/Lane vs. military/Halleck campaign to determine the fate of Wallace, the senator from Indiana prevailed. In March, 1864, Lincoln appointed Wallace to the post of top administrative official of the Middle Department at Baltimore as well as commander of the VIII Army Corps. Baltimore was not a prestigious military command, nor did it exhibit much potential in that regard. Yet, Wallace was once again in the field and in command. In late April, 1864, the always tenacious but now even more frustrated Halleck bemoaned the fact that "it seems little better than murder to give important command to such men as Banks, Butler, McClernand, Sigel and Lew Wallace."[32]

Then, in early July, Wallace got another chance for glory and honor. As Confederate Lt. Gen. Jubal Early hurried up the Shenandoah Valley, Wallace became overnight one of the few to realize where exactly Early was and where he was heading. Grant had no idea. In a number of telegrams from City Point, his headquarters located at the confluence of the James and Appomattox rivers, Grant stated repeatedly his conviction that Early was one of those Confederates still under siege at Petersburg. Halleck evidenced little idea about anything related to Early or his whereabouts. Sensing a crisis at hand, on his own initiative, Wallace quickly assembled "an army" made up of approximately 2,500 nearly ancient veterans, Union officer clerks, quartermaster personnel, and the like. Marching them out of Baltimore before any superior officer could object, Wallace fought Early's 20,000-man invasion force on July 7 on the banks of the Monocacy River in northwest Maryland. Fortunately, 3,500 veterans of the Richmond campaign sent by Grant from Petersburg arrived literally at the last moment to supplement his command. At the end of the day-long Battle of Monocacy, Early had significantly defeated Wallace and just as significantly precipitated his late-afternoon retreat from the battlefield. However, as at Donelson, once again Wallace had secured for Grant both "time" and "opportunity." Grant now had the ability to send reinforcements to the Capitol. Up to that point, only Wallace and John W. Garrett, president of the Baltimore and Ohio Railroad, had suspected that Washington was Early's ultimate objective.[33]

On July 9, just two days after Wallace's outnumbered, outgunned, and cobbled-together force turned Union defeat and retreat into tactical victory, Halleck and Stanton collaborated to remove Wallace as field commander of the VIII Corps, allegedly for dereliction of duty. Neither man had the authority to get rid of Wallace as political administrative head of the Middle Department. Grant initially agreed, but soon came to regret whatever involvement he had had in the issuance of that order. Ultimately, albeit quite belatedly, Grant fully acknowledged Wallace's services at Monocacy, writing that Wallace had moved from Baltimore to Monocacy with "promptness" in a "forlorn hope" to face an "enemy in force far superior to your own . . . where you could scarcely hope for a victory." Grant concluded that Wallace had indeed acted "in time to save the city [Washington, D.C.]." After Monocacy, however, Wallace never again led troops in battle.[34]

As a military man, the self-taught Wallace had thoroughly demonstrated his abilities. At Romney, he had exhibited a keen appreciation for spontaneous thinking and action. At Kelly's Island, he had proved that men drilled and trained properly could prevail in battle even against overwhelming odds. At Donelson, he displayed independent thinking and audacity, seizing the initiative. He took untested, untried, and unfamiliar men into battle at a decisive moment and prevailed. The Union, and particularly Grant's military future, benefitted immensely from his actions. At Shiloh, on April 7, he once again led men in battle successfully. He had a natural ability for such a task. At Cincinnati, he had revealed a superb skill for defensive organization. At Monocacy, when others refused to listen to and analyze what little intelligence they had, when others failed to act, Wallace moved, and moved rapidly, showing an uncanny knack for getting the job done, despite the odds.

Yet commanding men in battle and commanding himself were two entirely separate matters. He was quite accomplished at the former, not so proficient at the latter. Whether he recognized it or not, his mindset from the beginning of his military adventures was such that he must always be at the top, unfettered and unrestrained, able without reservation to do what he deemed best in any given situation. From the very first day in that Frankfort, Indiana, courtroom when he received Morton's telegram, all his thoughts and actions were directed toward winning the war for his country while simultaneously being acknowledged and honored as the one among many who brought that splendid moment of victory into being. As he pursued his adventure, it seemed that first one man, and then another, blocked and ultimately destroyed his ability to achieve his goal. In the end, however, neither Halleck nor Grant did this to Wallace. He did it to himself. At times, he hardly knew how to stay out of his own way. His participation in the controversy his actions at Shiloh had precipitated proved that beyond a doubt.

CHAPTER THIRTEEN

The Genesis of the Shiloh Controversy

From March 13 through April 5, 1862, Wallace and the 3rd Division operated from Crump's Landing on the west bank of the Tennessee River six miles downriver from Pittsburg Landing. Smith, in the initial thrust up the Tennessee River under Halleck's plan of campaign, had sent Sherman to destroy the Confederate railroad infrastructure in the vicinity of Eastport, Mississippi. He ordered Wallace from Fort Henry upriver to destroy railroad bridges, track, and rolling stock along the Mobile and Ohio Railroad around Bethel Station (now Bethel Springs) twelve miles west of Crump's Landing.

On March 13, Maj. Charles S. Hayes, 3rd Battalion, 5th Ohio Cavalry, 3rd Division, reported the destruction of fifty feet of bridge and trestlework plus a small amount of track on both sides of a bridge at Beach Creek, Tennessee. Wallace cancelled any further bridge and railroad destruction work when his scouts observed Confederate Brig. Gen. Benjamin Franklin Cheatham, with allegedly 10,000 troops in the area.[1] Pursuant to Smith's previous orders, Wallace then established his divisional headquarters at Crump's Landing. Unseasonable wintry weather stopped Sherman short of his objective at Eastport and the 5th Division returned downriver to set up camp at Pittsburg Landing. Brig. Gen. Stephen A. Hurlbut's 4th Division joined it there several days later. Thus divided into two armed camps, the Union army secured its positions at its deepest point of penetration to date into the heartland of the Confederacy.

Smith had little problem agreeing with Halleck that Confederate Maj. Gen. Albert Sydney Johnston might advance his Rebel army north from Corinth by train to Bethel Station and then march along the Purdy Road southeast toward Pittsburg Landing. Plans for such a contingency had to be devised, although it was an unlikely possibility. Equally improbable but nevertheless still a potential threat, Polk might transport his army on the Mobile and Ohio Railroad south from Humboldt to Bethel Station to initiate a similar move southeast against Union forces camped at Pittsburg Landing. Hence, Smith stationed Wallace and the 3rd Division at Crump's Landing to provide an early warning and a possible short-term deterrent to such a prospect. Reinstated to command, Grant affirmed Smith's decision. Until the day of battle at Shiloh, therefore, Wallace and the 3rd Division remained at Crump's Landing, protecting the right flank of the Union army camped at Pittsburg Landing, engaging in isolated and localized pursuits of Rebel cavalry, drilling, staging reviews, and experiencing endless daily bouts of "ennui," "inactivity," and "typhoid fever."[2]

Wallace pitched his headquarters' tent at Crump's near the landing on the east side of the Purdy Road, just south of the point where the road turned to run west to Purdy. As he placed his three brigades, Wallace demonstrated that he understood the nature and scope of his mission. He further exhibited his knowledge of the key points of egress from Crump's Landing—Purdy Road area south, either to Pittsburg Landing or to Corinth.

He posted Col. Morgan L. Smith's 1st Brigade at Linton Farm on the north side of the Purdy Road about three-quarters of a mile northwest of the landing and about one-quarter of a mile east of the intersection of the Purdy and River roads. Wallace's three favorite and most experienced regiments, 11th Indiana, 8th Missouri, and 24th Indiana, constituted Smith's brigade. Wallace deemed this brigade his best and ultimate defense against a Rebel advance from Bethel Station. He further recognized that Linton Farms provided one possible means of access to Pittsburg Landing by marching south onto the River Road and thence along that road, paralleling the Tennessee River, to the landing.

Approximately two miles further west on the north side of the Purdy Road at Stoney Lonesome, Wallace stationed Col. John M. Thayer's 2nd Brigade. This location gave Wallace three important tactical advantages. It provided an intermediate line of defense in the event the Rebels attacked from Bethel Station. Stoney Lonesome was also a starting point for a march to the Pittsburg Landing area that was equally as convenient as the River Road and under certain conditions more expeditious. Wallace had maps indicating he could march from Stoney Lonesome several miles southeast along the Hamburg–Savannah Road, merge onto the River Road, cross the aptly named Wallace Bridge at Snake Creek, and continue to the landing.

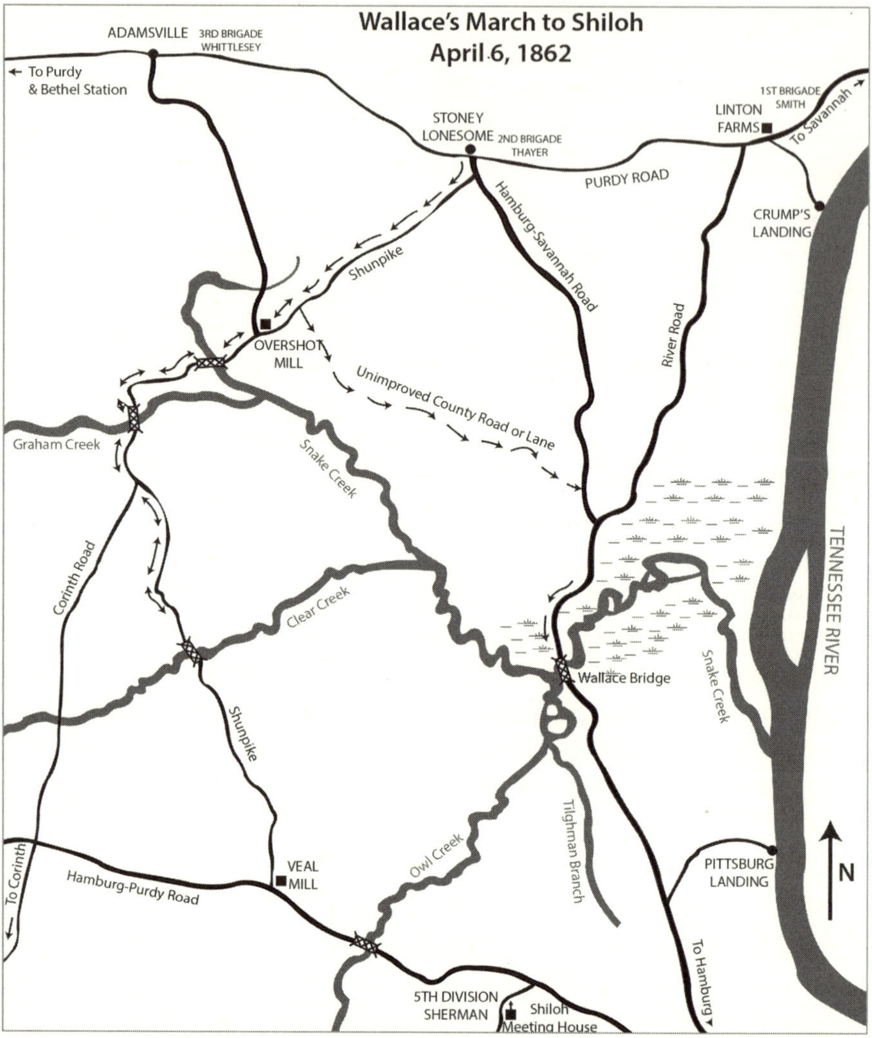

Wallace's March to Shiloh. April 6, 1862. (Map by George Ferguson, gfgraphics, Waynesville, N.C.)

A third tactical advantage existed at Stoney Lonesome. Those same maps showed that the 3rd Division could move quickly over a shorter distance from Thayer's camp south toward Corinth. The 3rd Division would march south from Stoney Lonesome a quarter of a mile on the Hamburg–Savannah Road to a point where an old country road known as the Shunpike bore off to the right, or southwest. Continuing down the Shunpike, Wallace's soldiers would march past the Overshot Mill, crossing Snake Creek at an unnamed bridge upstream and northwest of the Wallace Bridge, and then crossing a second bridge over Graham Creek, a tributary of Snake Creek. About one-third of a mile south of Graham Creek, the road to Corinth intersected with the Shunpike, the former bearing off to the right due south to Monterrey and Corinth.[3] This was without question the most expeditious route of march for the entire division to take once a move against Corinth was ordered and initiated.

The Shunpike also provided the best and quickest access to another part of the Union camp at Pittsburg Landing: the right flank held by Sherman, approximately two miles southwest of the actual landing area. The 3rd Division, after refusing to bear right on the road to Corinth, would cross a bridge over Clear Creek, another tributary of Snake Creek, and continue to the intersection of the Shunpike with the Hamburg–Purdy Road near Veal Mill. Turning left, or southwest, the men of the 3rd would cross yet another bridge over Owl Creek and continue on to the intersection of the Hamburg–Purdy Road and the Pittsburg–Corinth Road just north of the old Shiloh Meeting House and the encampment of the right flank of Sherman's 5th Division.[4]

Wallace placed his 3rd Brigade, Col. Charles Whittlesey commanding, at Adamsville, a hamlet on the Purdy Road some eight miles west of Crump's Landing. The 3rd Brigade was the Union's first line of defense in case the Confederates attacked from Bethel Station. When the day came to advance either on Corinth or on Pittsburg Landing, Whittlesey's brigade would march east on the Purdy Road to join Thayer's brigade at Stoney Lonesome. Smith's brigade would be ordered to march west on the Purdy Road to the same location. Whatever orders Grant might issue in this regard, Wallace intended to march south from his point of concentration at Stoney Lonesome to his ultimate destination.

By the beginning of April, Wallace and the other division commanders of the army at Pittsburg Landing were essentially tied to their respective campsites waiting for Buell. The martial pomp and enthusiasm that had so clearly defined the departure of the troops from Fort Henry on March 10 had largely dissipated into the dullness of inactivity. No one seemed to have any genuine sense of when this might change. There had been some adventure and danger. On March 18, Wallace boasted to Susan that for "two nights and a day," he had tricked Cheatham into not attacking him. "Of course," Wallace wrote, "nothing saved me from attack but an exaggerated idea of my force; which exaggeration I kept up by such little tricks as changing my lines in the day and multiplying my fires by night." On

March 21, three days later, Wallace informed Susan that the entire army had been put under orders with ten days' ration in preparation for a march upon Corinth. Halleck had in fact rescinded this order just the previous day, undoubtedly at the very moment he discovered Grant had issued it. On March 20, Halleck again emphatically instructed his subordinate that the Army of the Tennessee must wait for Buell. Wallace did not record his reaction to the stand-down order, but for a man of his temperament and love of adventure it must have been exceedingly frustrating.[5]

A study of the tactics and audacity with which Wallace had executed his Romp to Romney demonstrated to all who might observe that Wallace possessed military skills. His proposal to Lane just days before the war broke out illustrated a mind actively at work attempting to resolve military problems. At Fort Donelson, he had executed a spontaneous decision to disobey his superior. Seizing the initiative, he had embarked upon the offensive and stood tenaciously astride the Wynn's Ferry Road. Even in his maneuverings against Cheatham near Adamsville, Wallace revealed a fair degree of ingenuity combined with sound military instincts. Intuitively, he sensed, as he told Smith on March 13, that Cheatham "is more afraid of me with exaggerated numbers than I am of him." Smith offered no recorded response.[6]

Nevertheless, Wallace had proven that he had earned the right to be where he was. Halleck, because he despised all things not West Point, passionately disagreed. Grant, because his and Wallace's basic natures were so terribly out of tune with each other, had serious doubts. Both Halleck and Grant could have looked to Dennis Hart Mahan to support their attitudes and conclusions. At West Point, Mahan had made an excellent case against the civilian amateur ever becoming a competent military leader. "Let no man," he had noted, "be so rash as to suppose that, in donning a general's uniform, he is forthwith competent to perform a general's functions; as reasonably might he assume that in putting on the robes of a judge he was ready to decide any point of law." Mahan understood, however, there were exceptions. Summarizing his conclusions on the characteristics of a nonprofessional exercising sound military judgment, Mahan observed that "[j]ust in proportion as he has read, has reflected, has had opportunities for action, will his judgment lead him to take right measures; whilst still more certainly, if he has wanted these aids to forming an enlightened judgment, will he take wrong ones." Undoubtedly, Wallace had had insufficient time and military experience to acquire "enlightened" judgment. However, there is no question he had spent the last six or so years of his life reading and then translating his newly acquired military thoughts and knowledge into action.[7]

In early April, while Wallace whiled away his time at Crump's Landing, approximately 35,000 men, divided among five divisions, constituted the left flank of the Army of the Tennessee at Pittsburg Landing. Grant, as field commander, had concluded that the business of his army could best be conducted from neither location. Thus, he had chosen to spend a significant amount of his time at Savannah, five miles downriver from Crump's Landing and another five miles downriver from Pittsburg Landing. By sleeping overnight at his Savannah headquarters and then spending perhaps as much as two hours a day on the river, he was fairly well removed from both troop dispositions. Halleck had issued his caveat to wait for Buell; Grant intended to be bound by it.

Writing years later, one Shiloh participant pondered the wisdom of this state of affairs. An army had been assembled, deep in enemy territory "within striking distance of the enemy," wrote Joseph Rich, 12th Iowa, W. H. L. Wallace's 2nd Division. It collectively lay "in a state of suspended animation for nearly three weeks. The army was expected to cut the Memphis and Charleston road, but it was not permitted to fight for the purpose; it must do it without disturbing the enemy." Grant failed in his duties and obligations at Shiloh, Rich believed, by becoming as passive in thought and action as Halleck's order appeared to dictate he should be. One of Grant's greatest errors at Shiloh occurred because even though there was ample time and opportunity, he failed to make Pittsburg Landing "a camp of organization and instruction, as an Army."[8]

On April 4, Wallace got Grant's attention. He informed him that Rebel reinforcements were moving into his area. Wallace's scouts reported having seen as many as eight regiments of infantry and twelve hundred cavalry at Purdy with that many, or more, at Bethel Station. Wallace told Grant he had no idea yet exactly what the Rebels intended but "as a measure of precaution I would respectfully ask the General to hasten down to me the Batteries newly assigned to my Division."[9] That same day, Grant directed W. H. L. Wallace to send the missing artillery batteries to Lew Wallace immediately. In addition, he informed the Illinois Wallace that he agreed the possibility existed that the Rebels might be sending reinforcements to

Purdy and that "it may be necessary to reinforce Gen. Wallace to avoid his being attacked by a superior force. Should you find danger of this sort, reinforce him, at once, with your entire Division."[10]

Grant followed this up the same day with a dispatch to Sherman alerting him to this potential source of danger. He told Sherman that he had instructed W. H. L. to be prepared to reinforce Lew as necessary. He told Sherman "to keep a sharp lookout in that direction . . . and give all the support of your division and General Hurlbut's, if necessary." Still Grant hesitated. He was unsure just where any Confederates were and more importantly in what numbers. He concluded his dispatch to Sherman with the casual and confident observation, "although, I look for nothing of the kind, but it is best to be prepared."[11] Strangely enough, Grant never acknowledged to the Indiana Wallace directly that his request for artillery batteries had been received or that he had acted upon that request both favorably and immediately. More importantly, Grant never told Wallace that based upon information gathered by his 3rd Division commander, he had in fact shared those concerns with both W. H. L. Wallace and Sherman or that he had issued orders to the commanders of both the 2nd and 5th Divisions to be prepared to reinforce the 3rd Division should a significant Rebel threat arise against it. Quite interestingly, Grant did not pass on to either Wallace the same cavalier conclusion that he had communicated to Sherman.

The next day, April 5, Grant reported to Halleck that there were Rebels at Bethel Station, Jackson, and Humboldt, but "the numbers at these places seem to constantly change." The overwhelming bulk of the Confederate forces, Grant stated, remained at Corinth, at least 80,000 strong. All was well, however, for "one Division of Buell's column arrived yesterday [April 4]. Gen Buell will be here himself today [April 5]."[12] The waiting was over.

From the beginning, Wallace recognized that his primary task was to secure the flank of the main army at Pittsburg Landing until the day the army advanced on Corinth. He knew that at some point in time, the move against Corinth would occur. He was all too well aware that even with the defensive line he had established along the Purdy Road, he and the 3rd Division were very much isolated on that road. Depending on the numbers actually sent against him by the Confederates from either Corinth or from Humboldt through Bethel Station, he would require as easy and expeditious access as possible to Pittsburg Landing to escape that isolation and possible annihilation. His second objective at Crump's Landing was no less important. He was to stand ready to deploy the 3rd Division as reinforcements to Pittsburg Landing as rapidly and efficiently as possible in the event a Rebel attack against Grant came directly from Corinth. Altogether, he wrote in his *Autobiography*, "the need most pressing was knowledge of the country."[13]

Snake Creek, a small tributary of the Tennessee River, meandering west from the river before diverging to flow from northeast to southwest, separated the 3rd Division from the main army at Pittsburg Landing at all reasonably direct points of connection. His men, Wallace wrote years later, were totally separated from all other Union divisions in Grant's command by "a sheet of dead backwater, its shores a bog of unknown depth." Communication with the main army then on the south and east sides of Snake Creek was closed "except by boat on the river."[14] From early reconnaissance, Wallace discovered that two bridges crossed Snake Creek. Locals called the southernmost bridge on the Hamburg–Savannah Road the Wallace Bridge, named for some unknown Wallace who lived in that area long before 1862. The northernmost bridge on the Shunpike bore no name. Located some three to four miles northwest of the Wallace Bridge, near a gristmill known as the Overshot Mill, this second bridge on the Shunpike was as "dismantled and impassable" as the first. Wallace recognized that repairs had to be made to either or both bridges in order to facilitate the movement of his division in the event either the leisurely movement on Corinth or the frenetic rush to Pittsburg Landing became the order of the day.

Wallace received word that troops of the 2nd Division were in the process of repairing the Wallace Bridge. Then, one of his scouts reported to him that while the Wallace Bridge had been rebuilt and was structurally sound for a division of troops on the march access to the bridge itself was difficult and that "backwater covering the approaches was still belly-deep to his horse. Infantry could go through it, but not artillery." Wallace received this reconnaissance on April 5, the same day that Grant informed Col. Jacob Ammen, in command of the 10th Brigade, 4th Division, Army of the Ohio, the first of Buell's brigades to arrive at Savannah, that the road on the east bank of the Tennessee River would be difficult to traverse since it ran through swampland. Years later, Pvt. Richard J. Fulfer, 24th Indiana, 1st Brigade, 3rd Division, did not describe the actual conditions on the River Road as it meandered to the Wallace Bridge as he encountered them on April 6. He did recall, however, that at Crump's Landing on the evening of April 5 "the rain was falling as fast as I ever saw rain fall . . . the water was from shoe-top deep to knee deep, all over the road." In his report, filed April 10, Col. Valentine Bausenwein, 58th Ohio, 2nd Brigade, 3rd Division, described how he and his men marched all afternoon on April 6 through "ravines and swamps," crossing Wallace Bridge an hour or so after dusk. As he and his brigade reached the River Road at its juncture with the Hamburg–Savannah Road north of the Wallace Bridge, they encountered "mud and mire and backwater from Snake creek and the river to the high ground beyond Wallace Bridge at the lower crossing of Snake creek." Col. George F. McGinnis, 11th Indiana, 1st Brigade, 3rd Division, called the approach to Snake Creek where the Wallace Bridge had been rebuilt an "almost bottomless morass."[15]

Wallace had marched through the rain and mud to Fort Heiman on the Tennessee River. He had commanded at Fort Henry for several weeks from late February to mid-March while the rains still fell. He had experienced firsthand the effects of the winter rains on troop movements during the Twin Rivers campaign. Based upon his actual experiences, Wallace knew that even now, in early April, the rainy season had not quite come to an end. He appreciated what that might mean in the event he was required to move his division in an emergency. The last thing Wallace wanted was a recurrence of the marching conditions he had experienced on his way to Fort Heiman. He had seen enough mud for the moment. To that end, he sought an alternative route reasonably distant from the lowlands of the Tennessee River over which to travel to either Corinth, Sherman's right, or wherever at Pittsburg Landing Grant might direct him to go. He needed to find a road, or series of roads where weather conditions did not determine and limit accessibility. Hence, he sent his 5th Ohio Cavalry on a reconnaissance mission.[16]

On March 22, Maj. Charles S. Hayes, 5th Ohio Cavalry, reported to Wallace that he had found and traveled an old farm road known as the Shunpike. Hayes noted that the bridge over Snake Creek on the Shunpike would require some reconstruction. This would necessitate the expenditure of "some few hours' labor by a strong force" after which the road and the bridge would be made "passable." Hayes made no reference to the bridge over Owl Creek. Presumably, he found this particular bridge on the Hamburg–Purdy Road in a passable condition even for a division with horses, wagons, and artillery.

One major factor for Wallace favoring the Shunpike route was that his ability to use the Shunpike did not depend upon weather conditions. For one thing, the Shunpike ran across land elevated above the boggy lowlands bordering Snake Creek.[17] Anticipating the possibility of using this road at some time during his stay at Crump's Landing, Wallace ordered some men of the 3rd Division to duty corduroying and improving the Shunpike as well as reconstructing the unnamed bridge over Snake Creek.[18] When the project was complete, the Indiana Wallace sent a dispatch to the Illinois Wallace inviting him to send a troop of his 2nd Division cavalry to Stoney Lonesome the next day, April 6. The commander of the 3rd Division indicated he intended to send some of his cavalry to report to the camp of the commander of the 2nd Division. In this manner, the Indiana Wallace wrote, both detachments could familiarize themselves with the Shunpike–Hamburg–Purdy road connections so that each division could then "act promptly in case of emergency as guides to and from the different camps."[19]

The evidence, therefore, strongly suggests that while at Crump's Landing, Wallace sought out and obtained more than just a passing knowledge of the topography, terrain, and roadways in the area. He also took steps to improve at least one of those roads, the Shunpike, as an alternative route designed to fulfill whatever orders Grant might issue to him. At all times, his thoughts appeared to focus more upon the "Shunpike" than the "River Road." The problem he encountered because of his election to use the Shunpike arose from the fact that apparently neither Wallace nor Grant ever initiated any communications with the other about this road. It is highly probable that when the first guns of battle were fired, Grant had never heard of the Shunpike and certainly did not know its location or potential value. Grant seemed to allude to this possibility in the note he appended on June 21, 1885, to his *Personal Memoirs.* Quite begrudgingly, Grant agreed that had Sherman's position on the ground not been altered by Confederate surprise, "the road which Wallace took would have been somewhat shorter to our right than the River Road."[20] That advantage to be had by taking the Shunpike had Sherman not been pushed back the morning of April 6 toward the Tennessee River was probably in the neighborhood of two plus miles or perhaps forty minutes to an hour under the worst of conditions. This would have been significant for Union arms under the actual conditions of April 6. The correspondence between Wallace and Grant during this time was astoundingly limited. What there was continued to focus on the question of where to send the sick and the wounded and whether or not Wallace had exceeded Halleck's orders by sending them to Evansville and Cincinnati, two locations "out of district."[21]

Perhaps Wallace did not initiate any discussions about roads with Grant, but surprisingly neither did Grant. If knowledge of the roads between the two parts of Grant's army was at any time a concern or a priority for Grant, the records are silent. There is nothing to indicate that Grant made any attempt, in person, by dispatches, or even through aides, to examine, evaluate, or discuss the road systems between the two camps other than his terse, written comments to Halleck on March 25. Understandably but unfortunately, both Grant and Wallace abhorred spending their time discussing hospital ships, medicines, blankets, fodder, grain, bullets, and the like. Both were fighters not administrators. The fact that neither man saw fit to communicate his thoughts with the other on such an important issue as roads, their physical condition, their accessibility, strongly suggests that the relations between the two, while not openly hostile, were far from cordial, cooperative, or trusting.

Wallace filed his only official report on the battle of Shiloh on April 12, five days after the guns fell silent. Well over three-quarters of that report was devoted to the battle that raged on the second day, April 7. The 3rd Division, constituting the right flank of the Union army, started the morning of April 7 from its bivouac on Tilghman Branch of Owl Creek, south of the Wallace Bridge, advancing in a generally southwest direction. It initiated the second day of battle with an artillery barrage and led the slow and steady advance of Union forces all along the line. Wallace's performance was solid and successful. The steady, pounding advance of the Army of the Tennessee severely dampened the Confederate will to continue the fight. Grant's audacious response to the previous day's events, made possible by the force of his personality as well as the addition of Wallace's 3rd Division and Buell's four divisions, made Maj. Gen. P. G. T. Beauregard's decision to retreat all but inevitable. Johnston had been taken from the field of battle on Sunday afternoon, the recipient of a mortal wound. Beauregard now commanded the Confederate army. By mid-afternoon Monday, the Confederate retreat to Corinth began. On the night of April 7, Wallace and the 3rd Division camped on Owl Creek near the Hamburg–Purdy Road. They lit their cooking fires in a place not too far from where Sherman's 5th Division had slept the night of April 5. In that respect, it was a place not too far from where Wallace had intentionally sought to bring his 3rd Division to the field of battle on April 6.

In his April 12 report, Wallace forthrightly discussed all the events of April 6 germane to the 3rd Division's march to the field of battle. He distilled all his thoughts into one lengthy paragraph. For him, every statement contained absolute fact and truth beyond contradiction. Furthermore, throughout the decades of controversy fashioned by these events, Wallace never deviated from these factual statements as he had recounted them on April 12 except in one relatively minor matter. He related (see map on page 172) the following ten statements to Grant: (1) he heard "continuous cannonading in the direction of Pittsburg Landing early Sunday morning"; (2) in "anticipation" of orders from Grant, he directed the 1st and 3rd Brigades to concentrate upon Thayer's 2nd Brigade at Stoney Lonesome; (3) "at 11:30 o'clock," he received an order from Grant to advance; (4) by this order, Grant instructed him to march the 3rd Division to a position "on the right of the army and form line of battle at a right angle with the river"; (5) acting forthwith and pursuant to this order, he chose "a road that led directly to the right of the lines as they were established around Pittsburg Landing on Sunday morning"; (6) his advance began "immediately" upon receipt of Grant's order although later he amended that statement to say he paused for half an hour so that his men could have a quick meal to fortify themselves, beginning the march at 12:00 noon; (7) at all times during the march, he was within the sound of the guns and "the cannonading, distinctly audible, quickened the steps of the men"; (8) at all times during the march until the appearance of Grant's aide, Captain Rowley, Wallace intentionally kept Snake Creek on his left because Snake Creek was "difficult of passage at all times, on account of its steep banks and swampy bottom"; (10) he ordered the 3rd Division to initiate a countermarch across country to take the River Road to the battlefield only upon learning for the first time from Rowley that "our lines had been beaten back; that the right [Sherman], to which I was proceeding, was then fighting close to the [Tennessee] river, and that the road [that he was then on, the Shunpike] would take me in the enemy's rear."

At this point, Wallace departed from the realm of fact to engage in one significant moment of conjecture. He wrote that soon after Rowley arrived and gave him the "news" about Sherman being driven from his original campsite northeast over a mile toward the river, he began to speculate that if he continued on his original path "in the unfortunate condition of the battle, my command was in danger of being entirely cut off." Reluctantly, he concluded that it would be "prudent" to countermarch to the River Road. He would then cross Snake Creek at the Wallace Bridge and, advancing further south of that point, join with whatever remained of the

Union army. Rowley said he carried no order from Grant to that effect. He believed, however, that if Grant were personally present, this would be the order he would issue. Grant, he postured, was expecting Wallace on the River Road. Wallace unenthusiastically consented and gave the order. The 3rd Division did not arrive on the field until night was falling. It took no part in the battle on April 6. Over time, Wallace experienced profound regret for that moment of speculation, which had caused him to deviate from his original path.[22]

Grant's initial report to Halleck, dated April 7, merely stated that early on the morning of April 6, the Rebels attacked Pittsburg Landing "with an overwhelming force, driving our troops in from their advanced position to near the Landing." The only reference to Wallace was that he had been "immediately ordered up from Crump's Landing." The next day Grant informed Halleck in a second statement that the "enemy [was] badly routed and fleeing toward Corinth." Wallace was not mentioned in this report. In his third communiqué, Grant offered slightly more information, telling Halleck that there had just been concluded "another battle . . . between two great armies, one contending for the maintenance of the best government ever devised, the other for its destruction. It is pleasant to record the success of the army contending for the former principle." Grant then portrayed a fight on Sunday morning where "the battle soon waxed warm on the left and center, varying at times to all parts of the line. The most continuous firing of musketry and artillery ever heard on this continent was kept up until night-fall, the enemy having forced the entire line to fall back nearly half-way from their camps to the Landing."[23]

Despite the fact that at least thirty-six hours had passed since the last gun had been fired, Grant was having difficulties comprehending the truth of what had just happened. He was not yet prepared to tell Halleck that under the pressure of Confederate "surprise," thousands of Union soldiers had broken and fled ranks early Sunday morning to cower under the protective bluffs at Pittsburg Landing. He was unable or unwilling to explain to Halleck that as the result of Confederate surprise, he had lost for the better part of that first day all tactical initiative and all semblance of cohesion. Furthermore, he was simply unwilling to explain why so many men in his "great army" on the Union right and center had so readily collapsed in the face of that surprise.

In this third report, dated April 9, Grant informed Halleck that late in the afternoon of April 6, the Confederates made a bold and "desperate effort" to turn the Union left. Naval fire from two Union gunboats on the Tennessee, the *Tyler* and the *Lexington*, the fortuitous arrival of Nelson's 4th Division of the Army of the Ohio, and the creation by Col. J. D. Webster of Grant's Last Line, a concentration of artillery, had all combined to break the last Rebel charge that day. Finally, Grant got around to discussing Wallace. He informed Halleck somewhat circumspectly that Wallace had been told "at an early hour in the morning to hold his division in readiness to be moved in any direction to which it might be ordered. At about 11 o'clock the order was delivered to move it *up to Pittsburg* [emphasis added], but owing to its being led by a circuitous route did not arrive in time to take part in Sunday's action." There was certainly nothing in this report to lead one to believe that Grant, thirty-six hours after the conclusion of the battle, blamed Wallace in any way for what had happened at Shiloh. Concluding this third report, Grant grouped Wallace with McClernand, Hurlbut, Prentiss, and W. H. L. Wallace as division commanders who "maintained their places with credit to themselves and the cause." Grant gave Sherman special plaudits.[24]

Over the years, as the controversy surrounding Wallace's march took root and grew, its most crucial question never received the attention it deserved. Everybody acknowledged that a Wallace aide had lost Grant's original order. Seemingly everybody had their own idea about what that order contained. Nobody, however, offered proof of any sort to sustain their conclusion. In fact, throughout the controversy until the very end, when Wallace retained the services of a professional land surveyor, offerings of proof about anything from either side were scarce. Both sides to the argument usually seemed content to state their case and rest judgment solely on the degree to which public opinion accepted "the facts" as each advocate had presented them.

For example, one Grant aide looking back on that day stated that Grant had ordered Wallace to march from Crump's Landing "up the river and into the field on the right of our line as rapidly as possible." This statement seemed to suggest that when Rowley found the 3rd Division mid-afternoon on April 6 on the Shunpike, Wallace was in the process of executing Grant's intentions to the letter. However, the statement was too vague. As a result, it received little, if any, consideration from either side. Later, it was essentially repudiated by never being mentioned again. A second Grant aide wrote that Grant had ordered Wallace to "move up immediately by the River road and take a position on our right." That contention, perhaps because it specifically identified the route to be taken as the "River Road," achieved some traction among Grant's advocates. Yet, it further added to the confusion for it failed to identify what the writer specifically meant by "a position on our right." Grant's adjutant general, Capt. John A. Rawlins uttered the most persuasive and acceptable of all the Grant statements when he wrote with unimpeachable certainty that Grant ordered Wallace to proceed "to Pittsburg Landing, on the road nearest to and parallel with the river, and form in line at right angles with the river, immediately in the rear of the camp of Maj. Gen. C. F. Smith's [W. H. L. Wallace's camp] division on our right." Rawlins certainly had the best credentials for making this argument, even though he penned this statement nearly a year after the battle. Seemingly none of the combatants that day knew for certain what Grant had ordered Wallace to do. Grant finally confessed he did not know or remember either; Wallace was, and always remained, cocksure and confident he knew but he was never able to convince Grant's supporters of his assertion.[25]

The engaging question of this controversy, therefore, is not what anyone involved thought they remembered Grant having ordered Wallace to do that morning but what in fact or reasoned supposition Grant had actually instructed Wallace to do. In pursuit of an answer, Grant proved to be of little or no help. His first three reports to Halleck on April 7, 8, and 9 shed no light on the issue. Grant never really attempted to answer the question. In his fourth report, dated April 25, he stated only that Wallace was ordered "to march by a flank movement to Pittsburg Landing." He concluded his statement to Halleck by characteristically noting that "this report [Wallace, April 12] in some other particulars I do not fully endorse." In his fifth and final statement, dated April 13, 1863, Grant said nothing specific about his order to Wallace. He merely endorsed the narratives of his three aides, which became the heart of the cover-up.

In fact, Grant never could recall exactly what he had ordered Wallace to do. Writing his *Personal Memoirs* twenty years later, he demonstrated the same mindset. He stated his belief that all else notwithstanding, the route by which Wallace chose to come to the battlefield was indeed Wallace's choice alone. He then commented, "but this is not where I had ordered him nor where I wanted him to go." Incredulously and almost pathetically, a dying Grant could only conclude "I never could see and do not now see why any order was necessary further than to direct him to come to Pittsburg landing [*sic*], without specifying by what route."[26]

Grant never had any appreciation for the fact that Pittsburg Landing was much more than simply a point on a map. It was, in fact, a boat landing on the west bank of the Tennessee River. Even that precise geographical point, however, might mean by itself very little. Pittsburg Landing was surrounded by acres of mostly unimproved land, some of it flat and sparsely cultivated, most of it hilly, filled with ravines, creeks, underbrush, and mature trees. Over thirty-five thousand men were camped within five distinct, noncontiguous areas within that acreage. Even in the context of ordering Wallace to "Pittsburg Landing," Grant never acknowledged that this simple geographical designation might mean different things to different people. Grant had ample time and opportunity on April 6 to be quite specific in what he wanted Wallace to do. He failed to do so. Grant's confusion during those earliest hours at Shiloh underscored and highlighted his genuine lack of appreciation for what constituted the situation thrust upon him that day by Confederate surprise and illustrated the extent to which Halleck's mind-numbing caveat had exercised its stultifying influence. His three-pronged counterattack at Donelson on the afternoon of February 15 had been brilliantly clear in its inception and implementation. His order to Wallace on the morning of April 6 was muddled, imprecise, born of and fashioned by confusion, poorly transmitted, and for all that quite capable of producing tragic results.

In his fourth report on April 25, Grant informed Halleck for the first time that he had instructed Wallace "to march by flank movement to Pittsburg Landing." When Rowley found Wallace that afternoon, Wallace appeared to be doing just that. More specifically, he was advancing to join Grant's army on its right flank, to join Sherman near the Shiloh Meeting House near Pittsburg Landing. According to the most recent information Wallace possessed, a march down the River Road would not be a flank movement but a direct march to fall in behind Grant's rear guard, or the rear echelons of an advancing 2nd Division. Grant's use of this phrase "a flank movement" was a mistake. Further, he used the phrase only this one time. Eighteen days after the battle, Grant remained uncertain as to what had occurred on April 6. His use of this phrase, "by flank movement," illuminates his perplexity and its continuing hold on him. It demonstrates that almost three weeks after the battle, Grant had little grasp of what his own circumstances and those of his surprised army were that day. His April 25 statement magnifies the real possibility that on April 6, Grant demonstrated a lack of clarity as to how best to deal with events that threatened to engulf him; that he experienced a period of glaring indecision with respect to the actions necessary to be undertaken;

and he evidenced an inexplicable imprecision of thought as he issued critical instructions to Wallace.

For Grant, Wallace, and the cause for which they fought, it was regrettable that Grant did not spend the time to write out an order to Wallace telling him to bring the 3rd Division down "the River Road," cross "Snake Creek" at the "Wallace Bridge," and there await further instructions, assuming, of course, this is what Grant wanted Wallace to do that morning. It is unknown if even this limited amount of precision would have saved many lives that day. What is known is that Grant gave orders to Wallace that morning that were utterly lacking in specificity and clarity.

Grant had made a host of mistakes since arriving at Savannah, including one that attracted little attention then or now. He had agreed with Smith's decision to locate a division of men at Crump's Landing on his right flank. Having done so, however, Grant then seems to have forgotten the division was there. The evidence of communication between Grant and Wallace in the days before the battle is astoundingly sparse.[27] This lack of interaction arose through the interplay of two factors. First, the personal relationship between the two men had been strained by weeks of Wallace questioning and bickering over Grant's and Halleck's orders. Understandably, Halleck did not appreciate Wallace's actions in this regard and on several occasions he vented his frustrations upon Grant. Wallace and Grant simply did not relate well on most levels. More often than not, it appeared that Grant preferred tolerating Wallace to working with him.

Second, neither man evidenced any appreciation for the fact that under the circumstances then prevailing, each genuinely needed the other. Each reacted to Halleck's mind-numbing caveat in his own fashion. Grant had little appreciation for how his orders affected his subordinate officers. Wallace never comprehended the extent to which Halleck's caveat had boxed in a man of Grant's aggressive temperament. Even to Susan, he never expressed any sympathy for or understanding of Grant in this regard. Wallace was, however, personally restive and disgruntled. He wrote to Susan that "we are doing nothing just now, unless it be waiting fresh arrival of troops."[28] Neither man thought twice about extending a cordial hand to the other within the bounds of military propriety. One huge difference between Wallace and Sherman was that while the latter strove to work with Grant, the former was never a team player. Wallace, regardless of his military talents, could never have become a "Grant man." It is equally true that Grant had little appreciation for how his own remoteness affected his subordinates in the field.

As he sat waiting, Grant repeated several of the errors he had made at Donelson. Prior to the battle on the Cumberland, Grant neglected to familiarize himself with the terrain over which his army would have to maneuver. Never expecting to fight on the banks of the Tennessee, he failed to do this at Shiloh as well. Even though he was on the ground for almost three weeks, Grant deemed reconnaissance to be an unnecessary task for other than a subordinate to perform.

At both Donelson and Shiloh, he grossly underestimated the character and intent of his enemy. A battle was not imminent unless and until he personally took the initiative to make it so. Thus, on February 15, the day of the breakout at Donelson, Grant was absent on Foote's gunboat without providing contingency plans to cover any movement by his enemy in his absence. On both April 4 and 5, despite having acknowledged to both Sherman and Halleck that Confederates in some undeterminable force had been encountered in the area, Grant spent those two nights, like all the others, ten miles downriver at Savannah. He made no plans or special preparations for anything his enemy might unexpectedly unleash in his absence. True, Foote had been injured on February 15, necessitating Grant's visit on his flagship. Grant was also much more comfortable at Savannah, following a bad fall from his horse on April 4. But those coincidences merely obscure the fact that in both instances Grant truly believed there was next to no chance the Confederates were about to assume the offensive against him.

As he had experienced at Donelson, Grant had another moment of personal greatness at Shiloh. A man of lesser military experience, insight, and expertise, a man of lesser character, tenacity, audacity, and courage than Grant would undoubtedly have ordered a retreat the night of April 6. Confederate surprise had badly bloodied, though not beaten, Union troops that day. Grant, however, understood that the same conditions and circumstances he faced that night were equally pervasive among the various Confederate forces he was fighting. If for no other reason than this most basic of understandings, Grant was prepared to "lick-em tomorrow."

With the arrival of Wallace at Tilghman Branch of Owl Creek, adjacent to the 2nd Division, and the successful completion of the transport of all of Buell's men across the Tennessee river that night, Grant did just that the next day. As at Donelson, Grant was undeniably and profoundly embarrassed by the events of the first day at Shiloh. As he had also done in the aftermath of Donelson, he quickly assessed that for him personally the less said about Shiloh the better. This explains, except for his rhetorical flourishes in his third dispatch, why there is such a paucity of information in his five dispatches to Halleck. Not only on April 7 but for the rest of his life, Grant adopted and reflected this attitude with respect to Shiloh. For example, by all accounts, when Grant first met Wallace on the morning of April 7, he almost casually told him to advance his division against the Rebels by moving in a general southwesterly direction. According to Wallace, after acknowledging Wallace's presence at the head of his division, a friendly and outwardly cordial Grant merely pointed in the direction Wallace was to move that morning. Notwithstanding Wallace's late arrival the day before, Grant did not appear to be displeased, agitated, angry, or even prepared to remove Wallace from command.

With the firing of the last shot on April 7, the battle that was more a tactical draw than a Union victory came to an end. Beauregard's Confederates, however, had begun their retreat to Corinth by mid-afternoon, leaving the Army of the Tennessee in possession of the battlefield. Whether they truly appreciated it or not, the participants had witnessed in those early April moments a battle titanic in nature and beyond their comprehension as to its size and scope. Not too long after the war, a resident of New Orleans attempted to capture the tragic essence of those events by observing "the South never smiled again after Shiloh." Later, a modern-day historian distilled in the very title of his work a nation's response to those two days on the west bank of the Tennessee River in southern Tennessee, a turning point fittingly and forever known as *Shiloh. Bloody April.*[29] But all this would come later. On April 7, no one in Union blue or Confederate butternut had a clue as to the amount of "explaining" and "arguing" that would be required before the reality of what had transpired at Shiloh would begin to be known and thus laid to rest. Grant did make one victorious decision in the aftermath of that battle. As the controversy of Wallace's march to Shiloh evolved and intensified around him, Grant consciously chose to remain as far above and aloof from the fray as he possibly could. Wallace never had that luxury.

CHAPTER FOURTEEN

The Controversy Begins

On March 14, 1863, while in Washington, Wallace hand delivered a letter addressed to Halleck. "General: I have heard," he wrote, "of prejudices against me at your headquarters, relative to my failure to participate in the first day's battle at Pittsburg Landing. I have also heard that you yourself entertain them." With those two brief sentences, round one of the Wallace march to Shiloh controversy escalated in earnest.[1]

As he went to the War Department that day, Wallace held the rank of major general of volunteers in the U.S. Army. Other than briefly at Cincinnati, and then as he chased after John Hunt Morgan, he had not had a battlefield command since late June of the preceding year. Conversely, he was not the object of official censure. No one in the military had requested a court of inquiry concerning any of his actions at Shiloh or sought a court-martial to adjudicate formal charges. In fact, the professional military establishment was strangely silent as to his worthiness to command and hence his future. Halleck had simply made Wallace disappear from the ranks of active field commanders.

On the other hand, perhaps Halleck was not his sole antagonist. Wallace had only recently read Grant's endorsement of his Shiloh report. He was no longer just suspicious; he was now convinced that Grant had played a decisive role in countermanding his orders the previous November, sending him back to Cincinnati, away from the battlefield. Grant now took center stage as Wallace's principal foe. By this time, Wallace knew that Halleck stood there as well. Halleck had to have had prior knowledge of Grant's decision and obviously approved it. As he sought reinstatement to battlefield command, therefore, Wallace again consciously disregarded the chain of command. It dictated he should be talking and corresponding directly with Grant; Wallace chose rather to begin at the top with Halleck.

His letter to Halleck was more clarifying than confrontational. It was written "as an official explanation, solely to vindicate my conduct from unjust aspersions." Under the circumstances, Wallace was unemotional and remarkably terse. He detailed specific facts for Halleck to consider. He took it upon himself only once or twice to interpret those facts. For example, he stated he knew well the route he actually followed to the battlefield pursuant to and in execution of "General Grant's order." In fact, his men had "by my order" spent several days in early April working to improve that road.[2]

Wallace refused to argue with Halleck over the military soundness of the decisions he had made on the banks of the Tennessee River. Although Grant himself had not offered much in the way of explanation, enough had been said and written about the battle to afford Wallace a good idea of Grant's position. Expressing surprise and indignation that Halleck might likewise entertain "prejudices" against him, Wallace sought confirmation from Halleck as to exactly why Grant had refused to endorse his report. From the manner in which he presented his arguments, Wallace clearly suspected that Grant had two problems with his April 6 performance: (1) he had not marched from Crump's Landing that morning on the road that Grant intended and thought he had instructed him to take, resulting in Grant's conclusion that Wallace was lost; and (2) when Grant's aide found and directed him onto the presumptively correct road, he repeatedly exhibited a hesitant, confused behavior, producing an inexplicable slowness of movement. Grant appeared to believe that as a result of these factors, Wallace arrived too late to take part in the first day's fighting. His inexcusable errors had done nearly irreparable harm to the Union that day. Wallace knew that both of Grant's contentions were invalid. He certainly wondered why Grant had never, including on the morning of April 7, said a word to him about these alleged serious errors and the near fatal harm they might have caused. In time, being so desperate for answers, Wallace would even come to toy with the idea that Grant thought him a coward.

Proving exactly what Grant had ordered him to do on the morning of April 6 was problematic. After Wallace and three of his aides had read Grant's order, his adjutant general had lost it. Thus, Wallace had only his recollections, those of his officers, and the briefly stated generalities of Grant's early reports and endorsement upon which to rely. To be sure,

Grant had criticized his subordinate with vague statements about Wallace having taken a "circuitous route" to the battlefield and had dismissed him with innuendo about "some other particulars" being in Wallace's report with which he could not agree.[3] What all that meant was still conjecture. Grant either knew nothing more or he was being too cautious to say anything else. While Grant had said just enough to bring into question the nature and intent of Wallace's activities that day, he had not said enough to allow Wallace much room to maneuver in rebuttal.

Therefore, in his letter to Halleck, Wallace focused his attention first on making sure Halleck understood exactly what he and the 3rd Division had done that day. Second, he identified and then countered Grant's few vague pronouncements for their total lack of clarity and substance. He intended to demonstrate to Halleck that he was quite familiar with the roads running south and southwest from Crump's Landing. His goal was to prove he always knew exactly where he was going and why. It was ridiculous even to think he had been lost. Never once on that fatal day had he acted indecisively, laggardly, or cowardly. In approaching Halleck that day, Wallace had clearly decided to advance into a looming war of words with audacity.

There is no record if the two men met face to face that day. Even if they did, nothing is known of what they said. Halleck did receive and accept Wallace's letter.[4] For what he perceived as the good of the service and undoubtedly his own good, Halleck simply refused to respond in writing, thereby frustrating Wallace's intent. Several months later, following a period of deafening silence, Wallace reluctantly felt compelled to ask Secretary of War Edwin M. Stanton to convene a court of inquiry. Shortly after that, he permitted Maj. Gen. William T. Sherman to persuade him to withdraw the request and seek some other avenue of redress "for the good of the army." All of this, however, lay in the not-too-distant future. On March 14, Wallace yearned only to command again. To regain his lost honor, he marched once more. Though no fatalities were recorded as the result of his action, Wallace spent the rest of his life fighting the battle he initiated that day. He died believing he had failed in this adventure. In fact, he had not.

Following his introductory two sentences concerning "prejudices" held, Wallace told Halleck that the 3rd Division was prepared to advance that morning the moment Grant gave him an order to do so. He affirmed that Grant had instructed him to leave all his superfluous military baggage at Crump's Landing with a sufficient reserve from the 3rd Division to "guard the public property." The much-anticipated order was presented to him "at exactly 11:30 A.M.." Grant's version consistently insisted that Wallace received the order at or before 11:00. As the day's events unfolded, this half-hour difference became trivial and inconsequential. Wallace insisted that Grant's order was "unsigned by anybody." Grant's version maintained that either Rawlins, who dictated the order, or Capt. Algernon S. Baxter, an assistant quartermaster, who wrote it out and delivered it, signed it.[5] This, too, was an insignificant difference of opinion.

Wallace reminded Old Brains the original order had been lost. Therefore, he explained that Grant had instructed him to "form junction with the right of the army; after junction, I was to form line of battle at a right angle with the river."[6] Wallace had stated eleven months earlier in his Shiloh report that he had received essentially these same instructions. He was in the process of obeying those orders promptly and exactly when Capt. William R. Rowley found him on the Shunpike. Wallace's problem was that he had only hearsay and second-hand statements from which to deduce Grant's belief as to what the order contained. Halleck had taken steps to ensure that Wallace never saw Grant's official Shiloh reports. He had little desire to be of any further assistance to Wallace in this regard.

Halleck had a problem as well. He probably sensed Grant's reports presented an odd array of confusing statements and explanations, ranging from "Wallace was immediately ordered up from Crump's Landing," to "move it [3rd Division] up to Pittsburg," and finally "to march by a flank movement to Pittsburg Landing." Grant had made his statements in the immediate aftermath of a terrible battle but so had Wallace. Wallace insisted that his recollection of the contents of Grant's order was nearly flawless. On the other hand, Grant's memory and the words he used to explain his actions lent themselves collectively to an unflattering portrait of a man who did not know what was occurring around him and of an officer who did not make and execute enlightened command decisions. To Halleck, this was not a flattering picture of the alleged hero of Fort Donelson. It was potentially damaging as well. Frankly, Halleck must have suspected that Wallace exhibited a greater understanding and clarity of the substance of Grant's order that morning. Even though he was now ensconced in Washington with a new task and a new title, Halleck had to be concerned that if too much of what Grant had written and might in the future say about the order became public knowledge, the entire command structure in the West, including Halleck's previous position atop it, might suffer. Thus, seeing Wallace's dilemma, Halleck saw one for himself as well. Perhaps it might be best for several reasons for him not to say or write too much to Wallace at this time. Let Grant resolve the matter. Better yet, enshroud the problem in flinty silence.[7]

Wallace continued to his second point with Halleck. Upon receiving Grant's order from Capt. Algernon Baxter, Grant's courier, he directed his men to fortify themselves with a hasty meal. Exactly at 12:00 noon, he initiated his march with approximately 5,000 men. Wallace insisted that the road upon which he embarked was "well known to my cavalry since, in anticipation of a necessity for retiring upon the main army, it [Wallace's cavalry] had, by my order, corduroyed the road to the very point of junction." This statement, taken together with the later revelation of Wallace's April 5 dispatch to W. H. L. Wallace, was more than sufficient to demonstrate that all else notwithstanding, Wallace was never lost. Halleck, unfortunately, knew nothing of the correspondence between the two Wallaces.[8] If he had, no doubt he would have classified it as irrelevant.

Wallace then offered Halleck two reasons why he and the 3rd Division arrived on the battlefield "a little after night-fall." The first was that he had received his orders to march only at 11:30 that morning. Wallace's second reason was more substantive. His march had taken him "within a short distance of the point of junction." For Wallace, that "point" was, as it had always been, near the Shiloh Meeting House, where his 3rd Division would join with Sherman's 5th Division to fight together on Grant's right flank at Pittsburg Landing. As he neared this "point of junction," Grant's messenger, Rowley, found him. From Rowley Wallace learned for the first time that "our army had been beaten back from the position it held in the morning and was then fighting a desperate and losing battle close to Pittsburg Landing."[9] Grant's order as received from Baxter at Crump's Landing had "made no provision for such a contingency [the possibility of a Union retreat]."

Exercising his "own judgment," Wallace told Halleck he ordered the 3rd Division to execute a countermarch. The men retraced their steps along the Shunpike and then moved toward the river over a narrow and windy unimproved pathway that joined the "lower or river road." Turning south, the men crossed Snake Creek, finally arriving on the field of battle "a little after sunset." Wallace told Halleck that his men had marched approximately fifteen miles in all and that "the column was brought in in perfect order and without a straggler." In addition, Wallace correctly stated, given the total distance of his march, "certainly there could have been no idling on the way." Wallace had addressed the second issue of the controversy, giving Halleck a succinct and accurate summary to the effect that "at no time during that afternoon's march was my column halted longer than to allow it to be closed up."[10] Halleck simply had no interest in believing Wallace. Wallace had been a laggard. To conclude otherwise would run counter to Halleck's prejudices against the amateur civilian soldier.

Halleck decided to duck the allegation that he had prejudices against Wallace by taking no further active part in the controversy. He saw no need to dignify the contents of Wallace's letter or its writer with a reply. In fact, to respond might exacerbate the problem and connect him irrevocably to it. Thus, he could perceive no benefit accruing to him from engaging in further discussions of the subject with this meddlesome civilian amateur. Although the letter had been addressed specifically to him, Halleck would avoid possible confrontation and embarrassment for the professional establishment in Washington by forwarding Wallace's letter to Grant "for his remarks."[11] Grant, ostensibly too busy planning the campaign for Vicksburg and still quite uncomfortable with the prospect of resurrecting the specter of Shiloh, likewise sidestepped any direct involvement. He ordered three of his aides to reply to Wallace. The three men Grant designated to respond were Rowley, McPherson, and Rawlins. Grant forwarded their individual responses to Halleck on April 13, 1863, noting how closely the three reports collectively mirrored his memory of the day. He did not hesitate to "vouch for their *almost entire accuracy* [emphasis added]." Not to anyone's great surprise, Grant never revealed exactly what he meant by that statement.[12]

On April 13, 1863, Grant transmitted the three narrative reports to Halleck at the War Department. He included a personal communication to the Commander-in-Chief of all the Armies. Among other things, he expressed regret that he had not relieved Wallace on the morning of April 6 and given command of the 3rd Division to Brig. Gen. Morgan L. Smith. Had he done so, he wrote, "I do not doubt but the division would have been on the field of battle and in the engagement before 10:00." Grant fancied that with Smith in command of the 3rd Division, all the burdens of Shiloh and all the criticism of him arising therefrom would simply vanish. Astonishingly, even under the impossible time constraints Grant had so carelessly imposed upon Smith, Grant seems to have convinced himself that Smith could and would have done what Wallace did not do. Then, without any corroborating evidence whatsoever, Grant concluded that "there is no estimating the difference this might have made in our casualties."[13]

Halleck had sent Wallace's letter directly to Grant. He never informed Wallace he had done so. Illustrating the same bias, Halleck did not forward any portion of Grant's collective correspondence to Wallace. In time, it became clear that Halleck had no intention of talking to Wallace if he could avoid it. He did not even respond to Wallace's specific request for a court of inquiry. Old Brains had decided to consign all Wallace matters to the dust-covered throw-away bins of the War Department.[14] To Halleck's consternation, Wallace frustrated this design by corresponding directly with Grant on June 27.

With sincerity and candor, Wallace first told Grant what the latter already knew. He had filed "an official explanation" with Halleck several months earlier. He informed Grant that he had initiated correspondence with Halleck "solely with a view to relieve myself from aspersions which had been circulated to my great injury." Wallace said he had been previously unaware that Grant held "any erroneous impressions about my conduct that day." Then, he stated, he had recently seen for the first time Grant's endorsement of his Shiloh report. "It would be uncandid [*sic*] of me to deny," he wrote, "that the sight of it mortified me quite as much as it astonished me, and that it left me at a loss whether to ask a Court of Enquiry [*sic*] or attempt privately to satisfy you that you were mistaken."[15]

Wallace told Grant he had resolved his dilemma. He had decided to deal directly with Grant "to obtain a complete acquittal at your hand. . . . My confidence in my ability to satisfy you is equal to my confidence in your justice." Wallace wrote to Grant as if he believed Halleck had not corresponded with Grant concerning this matter. Inasmuch as he did not write a word about the narratives Grant had authorized, Wallace certainly appeared ignorant of the fact that Grant had made any response of any kind to Halleck.

Wallace announced his intentions to show Grant through careful factual analysis and reasonable argument the origin of the error that others so cavalierly exploited to condemn his conduct that day. Wallace said he looked to Grant only to receive "your simple statement of satisfaction on the points" he thought relevant to the issue at hand. Such a straightforward explanation from Grant "would, as far as public opinion is concerned, relieve me entirely." Not content to leave his opening statement at that point, Wallace then mildly rebuked Grant, observing, "[i]f you have done me injury through a wrong impression, you can certainly have no motive for refusing to right me as far as you can."[16] Wallace did not intimate that any public attacks against Grant might be forthcoming. He wished to confine this situation to his factual input so that when Grant further analyzed it he would then produce a personal note of exoneration. He never discussed with Grant what he intended with respect to the circulation and publication of this written exoneration should Grant do the honorable thing and give it.

Wallace then restated his position on the Shiloh march. On June 27, he essentially reiterated what he had said in his 1862 battlefield report and in his recent letter to Halleck. He did introduce two new themes. Both spoke to his growing anxiety and desperation to resolve the Shiloh matter and regain a battlefield command as soon as possible. Neither theme was in the least way flattering to Wallace's character or his honor. First, revisiting a statement he had made several times in 1861 to General Patterson, Wallace pleaded with Grant to understand that upon receiving his orders, "I marched promptly to obey it," being both "anxious" and "impatient" to do so. Further, throughout the day, he marched incessantly toward the sound of the guns. "I feared you would defeat the Rebels without giving me a chance to be present," he wrote. Wallace dreaded the thought of being left behind. He stated that he led his division from Stoney Lonesome within half an hour of receiving Grant's order "by the directest [*sic*] road to the precise point indicted in the order Baxter gave me." Wallace's second new theme flowed inexorably from the first. A mistake had been made that day, but "that mistake was neither yours nor mine, but Capt. Baxter's."[17]

The man who had gratuitously paraded his concept of personal honor the preceding July before the Joint Committee now sought to blame the messenger. Wallace had little evidence to support his claim. So, he conceded the point that Grant had instructed Baxter to order Wallace "to march to Pittsburg Landing": "Since you say you sent it to me, I have no doubt that you did." He then betrayed Baxter by stating that the message he received that day directed him "to *march and form a junction with the right of the army, without specifying that any change of its position had occurred* [emphasis in the original]."[18] Baxter had made the mistake and it possessed a double edge. Not only did it place the blame squarely on the captain from the quartermaster corps, it showed that the message read as Wallace had always maintained it did—"form a junction on the right of the army." Baxter had either not heard Grant's directive clearly or he negligently failed to add in that message that Sherman had been beaten back and no longer occupied the line he held the night before. "Capt. Baxter," Wallace concluded, "while liable for the consequences, is to be excused, since he took pains to convey the order correctly, as is proven by the fact that he attempted to reduce it to a memorandum."[19]

Wallace was convinced that he had solved the Shiloh problem for all parties. By blaming Baxter, Wallace had provided an explanation that was both "simple" and "affords a solution without impinging your official statement or mine either." A man of intense passion, Wallace had permitted his emotions to trump his sense of honor. He so desperately wanted to regain Grant's confidence, favor, and a battlefield command that for the moment it made little difference to him if Baxter was sacrificed in the process. Grant did not respond to Wallace. It is not known what he thought of Wallace's fabricated attempt to solve the problem by shifting responsibility for its origins to a third party. Rather, Grant characteristically elected to sit silently while others who so desired had a say on his behalf. He had already "called upon" Rowley, McPherson, and Rawlins for that purpose. He resolved not to participate actively any further in this affair, a resolve he steadfastly maintained until 1868.

In this particular instance, Grant was not necessarily taking a higher moral ground than Wallace. It is very probable he recognized that to accept Wallace's proposal that a mistake had been made for which neither of them could be blamed might well have unacceptable consequences. For example, merely the fact of censuring Baxter for incorrectly stating his order would reopen the Shiloh story and expose the mistakes that had been made that day. The book on Shiloh was better left closed. In addition, if he accused Baxter, he would also simultaneously be implicating Rawlins for the same failure. Grant undoubtedly remembered that it was Rawlins to whom he had given the Wallace order orally. It was Rawlins who had then dictated that order to Baxter and signed it at Baxter's request. Grant was not about to disavow a good friend and indispensable junior officer for the sake of a man like Wallace, who now appeared ready to resort to gratuitous condemnations for the sake of his own career. Furthermore, Grant could afford to remain cool and detached. Wallace had not made any attempt to refute any portion of the three narratives that Grant's aides had written. Halleck had not informed Grant that he would not be sharing these reports with Wallace. Perhaps, Grant surmised, Wallace would never be made privy to those reports unless a court-martial board or a top administrative official such as Stanton ordered them released. Grant suspected he held a much better hand than Wallace. Reacting accordingly, he refused to respond to Wallace.[20]

As he sought to open discussions with Grant, Wallace transmitted copies of several letters originally sent to him. Col. (at Shiloh, Capt.) Silas A. Strickland, 56th Ohio, 2nd Brigade, 3rd Division, wrote Wallace on June 24 1863, expressing two opinions about the march. First, Strickland affirmed that Wallace did not receive orders from Grant to march from Crump's Landing until between eleven o'clock and noon. Second, having received that order, Wallace and his division then "moved off rapidly." Strickland, who was Col. John M. Thayer's aide at the time, claimed that Thayer's 2nd Brigade "was in motion for Shiloh in just ten minutes after the order was received." Such a response, notable for the energy and enthusiasm it conveyed, was at odds with a great deal that Rawlins and Rowley had believed.

Wallace included a copy of a June 26 letter from Capt. James Ross. Rather than write a letter of his own, Lt. Ad Ware Jr, like Ross an aide to Wallace at Shiloh, attested under oath that Ross's letter was a true copy of his own best recollections. Ross recounted that upon receipt of Grant's order shortly before noon, Wallace had moved promptly toward the field of battle. Ross further stated that he had read Grant's order as Baxter brought it to Wallace before it was lost by Knefler. According to Ross, Grant directed Wallace "to move your Division up and form a junction with the right of the army on the Purdy Road [Hamburg–Purdy Road] at right angles with the river." Now, it appeared, at least three people had read Grant's order: Wallace, to whom it was issued; Knefler, who lost it; and Ross, who, by mere chance, had first encountered Baxter that morning. In addition, Ware's affidavit acknowledged that he had also read it.[21]

Grant also received a copy of a June 24 letter from Knefler. Knefler stated that when Rowley first came upon Wallace, the 3rd Division was then on the Shunpike at a point some "1½ or two miles" distant from the Union's right flank. The reference was to the location where Sherman had camped on the night of April 5. At this point in the march, Wallace learned for the first time from Rowley that advancing Rebels had pushed the Union right flank back from its original position well over a mile toward the Tennessee River. Grant saw a brief note dated June 24 from Lt. G. W. Simson, 6th U.S. Cavalry, advising Wallace, "I agree perfectly with Col. Knefler in the within Statement in regard to the movement of your Division on Sunday, April 6, 1862."[22]

The new information that Grant garnered from these letters was as follows. Strickland was convinced that had Wallace continued and not countermarched to the River Road as Rowley presumptively suggested, "we would have went [*sic*] in behind the left of the rebel army." Ross, supported by Ware's affidavit, concurred. Ross stated that had Wallace not "retraced" his steps upon Rowley's arrival, the 3rd Division would have marched "right into the enemy's rear." Knefler, with Simson agreeing, stated that when Wallace first discovered "our forces had been repulsed by the enemy," he halted his march upon the road that would have led "the Division in the midst of the enemy."[23] Grant undoubtedly recognized that the conclusions the Wallace men and any court of inquiry might draw from these statements was at best speculative. He sensed, however, that collectively these statements might create a perception that Wallace, being on the Shunpike, was on the right road after all. Collectively, these letters suggested that Wallace might well have spent the day attempting to do the right thing for Grant and the Union army. This conclusion would be both wearisome and difficult to refute.

Reading these letters, assuming he did, Grant perforce became aware that possibly Wallace had not wandered at all. For the first time, Grant had reason to consider the possibility his allegedly "lost" general had unwittingly presented him with a golden opportunity. If so, Grant had failed to exploit it. Grant began to suspect that had he not sent Rowley and then McPherson and Rawlins to find and redirect his presumed errant general, Wallace might have succeeded in striking the exposed Rebel left flank in the rear of the Confederate advancing line. If so, Wallace might well have administered a crushing defeat to the Rebels. True, Wallace would first have had to cross the bridge at Owl Creek on the Hamburg–Purdy Road. Undoubtedly, the Confederates had done something to secure an exposed flank. The crossing would not have been unopposed, yet, it would have been possible.[24]

Based on the inference that could naturally be drawn from all this pro-Wallace correspondence, Grant now perhaps began to suspect that although far from certain, it was nevertheless possible that Wallace could have successfully crossed the bridge at Veal's Mill on the Hamburg–Purdy Road and made contact with the left rear of the Confederate army. Wallace had over five thousand fresh, mostly veteran, troops under his command. If Wallace had been successful, it would have been a coup; it would have been the Confederates who experienced surprise. The ramifications appeared endless. Taken altogether, the information contained in Wallace's correspondence suggested things might have gone very differently that first day. Wallace might have been right even to the extent of correctly identifying exactly what Grant wrote in his order. If enough of this were true, or if any of it were true, or if only some of it were perceived to be true, Wallace might once again become an embarrassment. This time, however, he would be an embarrassment because he had been right. Grant undoubtedly found this proposition provocative and highly disconcerting. With this additional information at hand, Grant found his reasons to remain silent all the more compelling.

Wallace was perplexed that neither Halleck nor Grant responded to his entreaties. His tone had not indicated that he viewed the issues and the conflict as irrevocably adversarial in nature. As far as Grant could tell, Wallace was under the impression that a simple error, a miscommunication of information and intent, had been made. On the other hand, Wallace had revealed most, if not all, of his arguments. Grant thus made his determination. He need not be hostile, only guarded, and preferably silent.

Unbeknownst to both Wallace and Grant, Halleck was continuing to pursue his own agenda outside the framework of the controversy. In late July, 1863, he wrote to Stanton informing the secretary that in order to be an effective and efficient fighting force, the army required more major generals than federal law would permit. In Halleck's mind, there were a number of well-qualified brigadier generals deserving of advancement. In addition, he informed Stanton that there were a few major generals who currently had no commands and little chance of gaining one. These, Halleck offered, should either be asked to resign their commissions or dismissed from the service. Most of Halleck's candidates for resignation or dismissal were civilian amateurs. Not surprisingly, Halleck included Wallace on his list of dispensable commanders.[25] At the time, Stanton appeared not to be interested in Halleck's scheme. If Grant knew anything about it, he said nothing. It was not his position to comment. Furthermore, he sensed it was decidedly in his best interests to concentrate on fighting the war.

Receiving no response from Halleck or Grant, Wallace realized he now had little choice in the matter. He had accommodated both of his superiors with documents, reason, and arguments. Silence had been his reward. He was desperate to redeem his name and to regain his honor. He had insured that his beloved Indiana 11th had "Remembered Buena Vista." Now, he understood that his personal honor had to be remembered and restored as well. The "attempt privately" to discuss and resolve the issues had failed. Halleck and Grant, not he, had made the matter adversarial. His only remaining option was to request a court of inquiry. On July 18, 1863, Wallace wrote to Stanton with his reasons for demanding that such a court be convened.[26]

Alleging the same "facts" as before, Wallace informed Stanton that there were two interpretations as to the content of Grant's April 6 order. Grant's version maintained he had ordered Wallace "to march by a flank movement to Pittsburg Landing." Wallace insisted the order actually directed him "to march to the right of the army and form junction there." Wallace noted that this point was "nearly, if not quite, 3½ miles from Pittsburg Landing." Wallace then increased the stakes. Either Grant had correctly represented his order or he had not. If Grant had spoken the truth, the Hoosier general concluded, then Wallace was wrong and was "guilty of making a false report in a very material matter." He must be formally charged.[27]

That particular charge, however, was trivial and inconsequential compared to the second conclusion that would flow from a finding that Grant's order was as Grant depicted it. If such were the case, then it would be equally true that Wallace had marched that morning in direct "disobedience of orders." "In the disastrous turn of the battle at that time, there can be but slender apology." If true, Wallace wrote, his actions were inexcusable. He should be charged accordingly. On the additional count that Wallace's march to the battlefield was negligently slow, Wallace stated categorically that if this were true, he was "unfit to hold a commission of any kind in the United States Army." Even worse, if indeed Grant felt the necessity not once but twice of sending aides to find Wallace and hurry him to the battlefield, then "the imputations can be easily shaped into charges of cowardice and treachery." Charges must be filed and an investigation pursued, all under the auspices of a military court.[28]

On July 24, 1863, Stanton referred Wallace's petition to Halleck. The general-in-chief's response was classic Old Brains. He appended Wallace's letter with the following cryptic notation: "I do not think Genl. Wallace is worth the trouble or expense of either a Court of Inquiry or a Court Martial. His only claim to consideration is that of gas."[29] He then unceremoniously filed another Wallace letter away. Stanton did not object and like both Halleck and Grant, chose to remain silent. He undoubtedly thought he already had one too many argumentative irons in the fire with Halleck to add another. Neither Grant nor Halleck nor Stanton wanted anything to do with Wallace. By this juncture, Grant and Stanton viewed him with a significant degree of detachment and indifference. Halleck still sought, unsuccessfully, to ruin him. Now it appeared that silence would best serve their disparate motives and similar interests.

Wallace became disturbed when he received no response to his court of inquiry demand. Desperate to command once more, he wrote to Sherman seeking his personal intervention with Grant. As he had done many times before with Morton, Wallace again demonstrated his inability to assess that one who seemed at first to be a reliable friend and ally might in fact have motives diametrically in conflict with his. He never understood that Sherman might just have a pro-Grant–pro-Sherman perspective concerning Shiloh and that Sherman might just conclude that what was good for Grant in this instance was equally good for him. Wallace never appreciated that this was exactly what motivated Sherman. Being second-in-command to Grant in the West and having his fate at Shiloh inextricably interwoven with that of his superior officer, Sherman indeed had little room in his career for any pro-Wallace sentiments, particularly none expressed at Grant's expense.

Sherman's response left little doubt that Wallace had confided in and sought help from the wrong person. On August 27, with the ink hardly dry on Wallace's August 16 letter, Sherman sent a "confidential" evaluation to Rawlins. He noted that he had just received a "long and very proper letter" from Wallace. In it he found expressions of "great respect" for Grant. These, Sherman believed, were quite genuine as were several other sentiments that Wallace felt "evidently restrained from expressing" directly to Grant. Sherman suggested to Rawlins he might write immediately to Wallace evidencing "a kind tone and holding out to him a hope of again serving with modified notions." Sherman suggested waving a meaningless carrot in front of Wallace. He told Rawlins that he knew that at Shiloh Wallace had been a "laggard." Having expressed his belief that Wallace had to accept "modified notions" and that at Shiloh Wallace had been a "laggard," it would now seem impossible for Sherman to proceed in good faith. Nevertheless, he rhetorically asked Rawlins "has he no good qualities which with proper cultivation might serve his honor and be of use to the service?"[30] Sherman was equally bent on averting a court of inquiry even to the extent, perhaps, of offering Wallace some form of partial vindication. (Interestingly, Rawlins never provided a written answer to Sherman's question.)

That same day, and without waiting for such, Sherman wrote a very folksy letter to Wallace filled with accolades. He thanked Wallace for his expressions of good wishes on the recent success of the Vicksburg campaign. "I assure you," he wrote, "that I regret exceedingly that Gen. Grant has not carried with him throughout his entire campaign the Generals with which he opened it, and Donelson was as important a beginning as the capture of Vicksburg, the end of the one Great Design." He noted that he would soon talk with Grant and would "endeavor to convey to him your proper expression of confidence, without in the least compromising your delicate sense of honor." He flattered Wallace, telling him that both he and Grant recognized Wallace's military talents and that he believed Grant "would readily aid you to regain the high position you held in the estimation of the country." He spoke magnanimously of finding one's place in a system in which every general officer performed his duties for the "common cause of our country" and wherein each could "only gain a permanent fame by subordinating ourselves, and our peculiar notions, to that of the common Commander." If Wallace ever recognized those words for what they were, damning criticism, he never indicated that fact to anyone.

Sherman was now done with indulging and flattering Wallace. Hence, he turned to his true intent in writing. For the sake of Grant and undoubtedly himself, Sherman cautioned Wallace against pursuing his designs for a court of inquiry. "Subsequent events may sweep that into the forgotten of the past," he advised. Wallace should "keep quiet as possible and trust to opportunity for a becoming sequel to the brilliant beginning you had."

Suggesting that Grant harbored no ill feelings, Sherman portrayed himself as "an unselfish friend," who willingly gave Wallace "honest unselfish advice." The war was far from over. Opportunities still abounded. Sherman promised to help Wallace "in regaining your true place."[31] Sherman concluded by advising Wallace to "avoid all controversies, bear patiently temporary reverses, get into the current events as quick as possible, and hold your horses for the last home stretch." In other words, according to Sherman, Wallace must withdraw his request for a court of inquiry ("avoid all controversies"); he must accept and remain in forced inactivity ("bear patiently temporary reverses"); he should stay properly active ("get into the current events as quick as possible," although neither Halleck nor Grant would approve); and, most importantly, not write to Grant again, for, when appropriate, Grant would communicate with him

Benson J. Lossing, American historian, personal friend, and confidant. (Collection of Mrs. Blair Miller)

("hold your horses for the last home stretch").[32] Wallace was gratified. Sherman, however, had hoodwinked him.

Once before, Hillyer had cautioned Wallace to be patient and keep quiet. For a very brief time, Wallace had taken this advice. This came to a resounding end in a flood of self-pity after Donelson when Wallace was ordered to return to Fort Henry with the rear guard. Undoubtedly out of a misguided sense of personal honor, Wallace accepted Sherman's advice to be patient and keep quiet. On September 16, he wrote to Stanton asking for a "suspension" of his request for a court of inquiry. "It is possible," he stated, "that I may satisfy General Grant upon the points involved and thus save further trouble." This round of the controversy was over. Wallace had capitulated. Grant, Halleck, Stanton, and now Sherman had won. Rawlins possibly breathed a sigh of relief.[33]

At this time, one of Wallace's most sympathetic and supportive friends was Benson Lossing. Earlier, Lossing sought to encourage Wallace by reminding him that the Ohio Legislature had recently called him "a sensational General." "I like that," Lossing wrote. He then compared Wallace to British Maj. Gen. James Wolfe, the hero of Quebec during the French and Indian War. One of King George II's ministers, Lossing wrote, had intemperately exclaimed "Wolfe is mad!" The English King retorted "Mad! Mad! Wolfe mad! I wish he'd bite some of the rest of my Generals."[34] There is a certain irony here. Lossing was defending Wallace with a story that was remarkably similar to one that Lincoln allegedly employed about this time on behalf of Grant. "Grant is a drunkard. I can prove it," someone intemperately shouted in Lincoln's presence. The president calmly replied, "Well, you needn't waste your time getting proof; you just find out, to oblige me, what brand of whiskey Grant drinks, because I want to send a barrel of it to each one of my generals."[35] Lossing, a historian by craft, could offer Wallace no assistance other than loyalty and friendship. Wallace needed and gladly accepted both; but it would not be enough to help him realize his burning ambition.

Life and the war went on for Wallace. All his efforts to regain what he had lost went wanting. Not even his incredible success in defeat against significant odds at Monocacy in July, 1864, changed Grant's mind. As the highest-ranking officer in the Union army, Grant simply could not bring himself to acknowledge that Wallace's efforts in northwest Maryland had saved him embarrassment and provided him with "time" and "opportunity" to right a mistake he and several others had made. Based upon this lack of recognition, it was Fort Donelson all over again. Several months later, Grant wrote to Wallace expressing gratitude for his performance at Monocacy. He further requested Wallace visit him at his headquarters at City Point. Wallace journeyed to the south bank of the James River in early September, 1864. He was not restored to battlefield command as a result of that meeting. In April, 1865, the war came to an end. Wallace's dream of battlefield glory evaporated with the advent of peace.[36]

CHAPTER FIFTEEN

The Cover-Up

Wallace had gone to Washington seeking a forum in which to tell his version of the April 6 events that transpired on the banks of the Tennessee River. With little hesitation, Halleck had decided that it would be best for him to remain as far removed from the fray as possible. He wasted no time sending Wallace's letter to Grant for a reply. Grant avoided further participation in this pending war of words by ordering three members of his staff, Capt. William R. Rowley, Lt. Col. James B. McPherson, and Capt. John A. Rawlins, to address Wallace's statements and allegations.

Each of the three men Grant chose was a trusted member of his military family. Two had been Grant's personal friends and sometime business acquaintances before the war. Each had more than a passing familiarity with the events concerning Wallace and his march to Shiloh inasmuch as each had been dispatched by Grant to find the missing Wallace and hurry him and his 3rd Division to the battlefield. Wallace had argued his case. Grant, however, saw no need to dignify the Hoosier general with a personal response. In fact, unlike Wallace, he wished to remain silent. His men could speak quite adequately for him. He believed their participation would first balance and then offset any influence the various letters written by Wallace's officers in support of their general might have. There was a convincing symmetry to be gained from complying with Halleck's request in this manner.

McPherson wrote first from Lake Providence, Louisiana, on March 26, 1863; Rowley wrote his report from Galena, Illinois, on April 4, 1863; and Rawlins wrote his account from Grant's field headquarters at Vicksburg on April 1. On March 30, Grant invited a fourth officer, Capt. Algernon S. Baxter, to "send me [a] Statement at your earliest possible convenience,

The Men Who Manufactured the Cover-Up, clockwise from top left: Captain John A. Rawlins. (Library of Congress); Captain William R. Rowley. (Galena History Museum); Lieutenant Colonel James B. McPherson. (Library of Congress)

of the time and circumstances at and under which you delivered my order to Maj Genl Lewis Wallace at Crump [*sic*] Landing to move to the field of battle at Pittsburg Landing on the 6th day of April 1862 and the time that I passed Crup [*sic*] Landing on the way to Pittsburg Landing." Baxter did not reply. Grant did not appear concerned that Baxter had turned down his "invitation."

Years later, Baxter granted a newspaper interview in which he suggested a compelling reason why he refused to prepare a written summary of events at Grant's request. Baxter told the newspaper that he had written Grant's order down as Rawlins had dictated it to him. Rawlins then signed the written statement as Baxter had asked him to do. Baxter made no comment on the crucial question of where Grant directed Wallace to march the 3rd Division, but what recollections he made decidedly contradicted Grant's view of the event. Baxter said in 1886 that when he delivered Grant's communication, Wallace "was waiting for orders, had heard the firing all the morning, and was ready to move with his command immediately—knew the road and had put it in good order." This last part of Baxter's statement to the New York *Mail and Express* offered an excellent indication of what Grant might actually have told Wallace to do that morning. The only road that Wallace "had put in good order" while waiting at Crump's Landing was the Shunpike. Perhaps, Grant had indeed instructed Wallace "to form junction with the right of the army"[1] and Wallace had led his men down the only road that would expeditiously accomplish this objective. Baxter concluded by noting he had been with Rawlins preparing the order "between the hours of 8 and 9 o'clock A.M."[2]

All three of the men who answered Grant's call in the spring of 1863 were members in good standing of Grant's military family. All three owed their current military status and rank to his continuing favor. Rowley initially served with the 45th Illinois Volunteers as a 1st lieutenant. In late February 1862, he joined Grant's staff with the rank of captain. After brief service as a major in the same Illinois regiment, Rawlins was promoted to the rank of captain in the regular army and appointed to Grant's staff. At the end of the war, still a member of Grant's military family, Rawlins was Chief of Staff of the Army with the rank of brevet major general. In civilian life, Rawlins and Rowley had been business associates with Grant in Galena as well as with each other. On the eve of the Twin Rivers Campaign, McPherson, a West Point–trained engineer, was a lieutenant colonel on Halleck's staff. Grant requested Halleck to transfer McPherson to him. McPherson drew detailed maps of Fort Henry and Fort Donelson for Grant, ably assisting him in his offensive thrust against both forts. His service at Shiloh was not unusually noteworthy, though presumably it was quite competent. In late March,1863, less than a year later, as he wrote on behalf of Grant, McPherson was a major general leading the 17th Corps, the first and only one of the three to hold a major field command.[3]

During the controversy over Shiloh, several staff and field officers in Wallace's command put their recollections of events of April 6 into writing. Collectively, their accounts had a greater amount of consistency than did those written by the men who advocated for Grant. At times, however, Wallace's supporters were equally guilty of advancing theories too loosely based in fact and frankly too unbelievable.[4] Their errors in this respect, however, occurred with much less frequency and with significantly much less pushing, prodding, and stretching of the truth than characterized the efforts of the Grant men. For another thing, the men who wrote for Wallace exhibited a greater degree of personal courage and fortitude than did the Grant men. To support a division commander currently out of favor with the War Department's commanding general, thereby potentially earning the enmity of that general, was more than a mere act of faith and friendship. One could easily jeopardize and ruin one's own prospects and career by doing so. The more time that elapsed after Shiloh the greater Grant's career appeared to be in the ascent. In 1863, when Wallace first sought support from a few of his aides, Grant had become the highest-ranking Union officer in the western theater. Wallace and his career prospects seemed to be moving in the opposite direction. Nevertheless, the men who supported Wallace in this controversy proved to be as fiercely loyal to Wallace as those who spoke for Grant. The difference lay in just how far the men on each side went to demonstrate that loyalty. Rawlins and Rowley, and even McPherson to a lesser degree, formally participated in the controversy by manufacturing a cover-up. Rawlins and Rowley consistently punctuated their reports with half-truths as well as intentional distortions and fabrications. It is difficult to level and sustain the same charge against any of the men who wrote on behalf of Wallace.[5]

The first thing to be noted about the Rowley, Rawlins, and McPherson written reports is that they did not attain the status of common, public knowledge until at least the mid-1880s. Halleck received them and immediately hid them away in the War Department. Collectively, they first saw the light of day only in 1884 when the government published volume 10 of *The War of Rebellion: A Compilation of the Official Records of the Union and Confederate Armies*, focusing on events, correspondence, and written orders from Shiloh. By that time, Rawlins, Halleck, and Stanton were dead and Grant was dying. There were few then still living who could objectively and dispassionately examine them. The second relevant observation is that Rawlins and Rowley, undoubtedly under the leadership of the former, collaborated in fabricating a detailed cover-up of the events surrounding Wallace and his ill-fated march to the Shiloh battlefield. When, in 1884, the reports finally surfaced to become public knowledge, there were few who cared to analyze them with respect to their authenticity. The third and last fact of interest about these reports was that both individually and collectively they had minimal impact on the Wallace march to Shiloh controversy. If nothing else, the reports themselves came to light much too late to exert much influence on the thoughts of the men who waged the war of words constituting the controversy.

On the other hand, following the preparation and submission of these reports, their respective authors, with the exception of Rowley, then spent many subsequent hours living, working, and fighting the Rebels. To that end, correspondent Sylvanus Cadwallader suggested a point at which the cover-up intersected with Grant's growing aversion, then antipathy, toward Wallace. "I knew the esteem—or rather lack of esteem—in which Wallace had ever been held for his conduct at Shiloh," Cadwallader wrote in 1886. "Every member of Grant's staff at Shiloh were hot and outspoken whenever the subject was introduced. I have heard Gens. McPherson, [William R.] Rowley, [William S.] Hillyer,[6] Rawlins, and others rehearse the affair many times, in Grant's presence. He always assented to their criticism of Wallace's behavior."[7] As Cadwallader observed, Grant permitted his aides to voice anti-Wallace sentiments openly around his campfire although he himself probably did not participate in such discussions. Over time, such free and frank verbal sessions undoubtedly damaged Wallace's relationship with Grant by helping to create in Grant the realization that he did not care to welcome Wallace back as a member of his military family. In addition, making frequent speeches after the war, particularly in the context of his new position as president of The Society of the Army of the Tennessee, Rawlins often spoke to the very same points he had set forth in his 1863 report. Since many of these speeches were given in 1866 and 1867, prior to Adam Badeau's publication of his political biography of Grant, it can be reasonably assumed that even after the war, Rawlins had a continuing anti-Wallace influence on the controversy.

Therefore, these reports should be examined in some detail to reveal the nature and scope of the cover-up, the extent of animosity the name of Wallace apparently inspired among those who supported Grant, and the lengths to which a few would go to keep some of the basic truths of the matter from surfacing. Lastly, scrutiny of these reports will disclose just how far removed Grant intentionally positioned himself from the realities and truth of that eventful day.

Each author designed his report so that he could set the stage for Grant and the issuance of the order to Wallace. In so doing, each made a series of admissions contrary to Grant's interest. For this reason alone, any Wallace supporter would have been delighted to see these reports in 1863 or 1868, but they remained secreted away until 1884. Rowley began by describing Grant upon his steamer, the *Tigress*, churning upriver toward Pittsburg Landing on the morning of April 6, 1862. As Grant came to Crump's Landing, he ordered his steamer to pull toward the bank of the river to allow him to communicate with Wallace. Grant verbally instructed Wallace to "get his troops under arms immediately and have them ready to move at a moment's notice." Wallace yelled back that "the necessary orders had already been given." Grant was, according to Rowley, uncertain whether a major battle was then raging at Pittsburg Landing or if the Rebels were executing a feint there to distract him from concentrating his army for a major Confederate attack down the Purdy Road. As Grant continued his journey upstream toward Pittsburg Landing, Rowley stated that the *Tigress* met the steamer *Warner*, carrying a dispatch from W. H. L. Wallace to the effect that "a battle had commenced" at the landing. Acknowledging this communication, Grant ordered the *Warner* to turn about and accompany him to Pittsburg Landing.

It will always remain a mystery why Grant, armed with this new intelligence, failed to direct the *Warner* to continue downriver to Crump's Landing to carry this message to Wallace along with orders for Wallace to commence his march south immediately. Artillery barrages and rifled musketry fire had been heard to the south. No such ominous warnings came from the Purdy–Bethel Station area to the west. Wallace had not conveyed to Grant that he possessed any information from anywhere or anyone that the Rebel army had descended upon Adamsville and was now moving east. One might have thought that this was sufficient to allay Grant's fears of a major Rebel attack against Wallace. If Grant thought this, he said nothing. He simply steamed south. He appeared to be more bewildered than in charge. Altogether, this recitation of the encounter with the *Warner* appeared more damaging than beneficial to Grant.[8]

Rawlins, as he commenced his narrative, also conveyed conflicting and potentially damaging information about Grant's initial behavior at Savannah. Rawlins simply knew that he had to find reasons why Grant did everything possible to get from Savannah to the battlefield as quickly as possible. Although much will be said about this shortly, it is interesting to note that Rawlins made a point of stating that prior to departing his Savannah headquarters, Grant took the time to write out two dispatches. The first was sent to Brig. Gen. William Nelson, newly arrived with advanced elements of the Army of the Ohio and now encamped on the east bank of the Tennessee River. Grant ordered Nelson in writing to march his division forthwith from Savannah to a spot opposite Pittsburg Landing where steamers waited in readiness to ferry his men across the river. Rawlins appeared to have overlooked the fact that less than eighteen hours earlier Grant had told Col. Jacob Ammen, commanding the 10th Brigade of the Army of the Ohio, that the road on the east bank of the Tennessee River ran through a "swamp." Rawlins did not explain why Grant now believed that Nelson's men could move south rapidly along the road paralleling the east bank of the Tennessee early in the morning of April 6 when he had told Ammen he could not do the same late in the afternoon of April 5.

Second, Grant wrote out Nelson's order before he departed Savannah. It can be deduced from Rowley's report that upon arriving at Crump's Landing some twenty to twenty-five minutes later, Grant was still uncertain where the brunt of the Confederate attack would fall. Rawlins's account concurred. Rawlins went so far as to state that at Crump's Landing, as Grant and Wallace shouted at each other from their respective steamers, Grant ordered Wallace to "send out and ascertain if there was any enemy on the Purdy Road, apprehending as you [Grant] did, that the real attack might be intended against this position."[9] Just two days earlier, Grant had created a reserve for Wallace by ordering W. H. L. Wallace and his 2nd Division, plus Sherman and his 5th Division to stand ready to go to Wallace's relief should the Rebels attack in force at Crump's Landing. In this context, his act of ordering Nelson to Pittsburg Landing before he knew exactly where the Rebels were was surprising. If the Rebels were then flying down the Purdy Road threatening to overwhelm Wallace by sheer numbers alone, Nelson could do little to stop that onslaught if he and his men were wading through muddy swamps on the east bank of the Tennessee on their way to Pittsburg Landing. Grant had really not thought that through. As he concluded his report on this incident, it was obvious Rawlins had not done so either. In reality, Grant's command decisions were inconsistent and mutually contradictory. He had ordered Wallace to wait at Crump's Landing until he, Grant, obtained more information about Confederate intent. He had done so, however, literally within the hour after sending Nelson scurrying through a swamp without having such information, Grant had acted precipitously. He looked somewhat foolish. That conclusion would not be revealed in Rawlins's report.

According to Rawlins, Grant then took even more time before departing Savannah to write a dispatch to Maj Gen. Don Carlos Buell, commanding the Army of the Ohio, stating essentially the same thing he had just told Nelson. Buell at Pittsburg Landing, like Nelson at the same location, could do little for the cause of Union arms if the Rebels were attacking Crump's Landing. True, if the Rebels were attacking in force at Pittsburg Landing, both Buell and Nelson were desperately needed there. Yet, neither command, whether still at Savanna or at Pittsburg Landing, could aid and assist anybody if they were still located on the east bank of the Tennessee. Grant's first consideration with respect to both should have been to get his entire army on the west bank of the Tennessee River. He wrote to Buell and Nelson to move immediately whether he had the information or not. Rawlins was attempting to create an image of a decisive commander; the image he developed was one of a confused and perplexed general decidedly unsure what his next step should be. Perhaps he should have ordered those steamers, which he told Buell awaited him at Pittsburg Landing, to get to Savannah to pick up both Nelson and Buell. By that time, surely, Grant would know where the Rebels were.

It should not be lost sight of that Rawlins had stated that Grant's orders to both Nelson and Buell were written. Yet, on a subsidiary point, Rawlins offered no explanation why, during the twenty minutes or so that elapsed as Grant steamed upriver from Crump's to Pittsburg Landing, he failed to take the time to prepare two written dispatches to Wallace. In one, he could have given Wallace specific, detailed instructions in the event the Rebels were attacking in force at Pittsburg Landing. In the other, he could have afforded Wallace equally specific orders what to do in the event the attack was descending upon Crump's Landing. In the latter, he might even have taken a moment to inform Wallace that two days before he had put Sherman and W. H. L. Wallace on notice that in such an event, both were ordered to go to Wallace's aid immediately. True, as he paced the quarterdeck of the *Tigress*, he still may not have known exactly where the primary Confederate attack had struck. Arguably, he already possessed that information from the dispatch given him from the *Warner*. Assuming, for the sake of argument, Grant required more precision in the information than he had at that moment, he nevertheless had ample time to take the simple precaution of writing out alternative orders.[10] Grant, however, did nothing. No one knows exactly what consumed his time and energies during the twenty or so minutes he spent steaming upriver from Crump's to Pittsburg Landing, but he failed to do anything to ameliorate the picture of a surprised, confused, and altogether perplexed leader. He did not appear to be in control.

Interestingly, all this rather unflattering information appeared in Rowley's report and to a lesser extent in that penned by Rawlins.

McPherson initially implied that perhaps Wallace knew exactly what he was doing on April 6 when he avoided marching on the River Road. Wallace had asserted that the only road south from the Purdy Road–Crump's Landing area that his division could expeditiously use was the Shunpike. A year later, McPherson substantially agreed. The engineer noted that upon his arrival at Savannah in mid-March, all the tributaries of the Tennessee River were backed up "from 2 to 6 feet," thereby "making Lick and Snake Creeks impassable. As soon as the water subsided sufficiently the bridge across the creek was reconstructed." McPherson identified this as the Snake Creek Bridge on the River Road south of its junction with the Hamburg–Savannah Road. Locals knew it as the Wallace Bridge. McPherson wrote that immediately upon completion of the work, he sent out "a detachment of cavalry" to communicate this fact to Wallace. Last, he wrote that Wallace was not likely to forget about the repaired bridge quickly. The work had been completed on April 3, "on Thursday, previous to the battle."

McPherson had thus specifically contradicted Rowley's assertion that when Rowley finally "found" the allegedly wayward 3rd Division commander, Wallace claimed that the road he was then travelling, the Shunpike, was "the only road he knew anything about." Rowley claimed that Wallace then retained him as a guide, purportedly informing him "none of us know the River road you speak of." According to McPherson, Wallace "knew" about the River Road and the repairs to the Wallace Bridge that had been completed three days before the Sunday battle.

Unfortunately, McPherson omitted from his report any statement regarding the condition and accessibility of the River Road leading to and from the Wallace Bridge over Snake Creek. By this omission, McPherson made the condition of the road in that vicinity, and not the bridge itself, a highly debated issue in the controversy.[11] Rawlins stated in his narrative that marching conditions along the River Road to and from the Wallace Bridge were "fine." McPherson neither affirmed nor contradicted that assertion. In fact, having discussed the condition of the bridge as well as the depth of the backed-up Snake Creek just weeks before the battle, arguably McPherson's unwillingness to discuss this subject further implied that he likewise found the condition of the road to be "fine." That simply was not the case. Several accounts from the men of the 3rd Division who actually traveled the River

Road across Snake Creek that day offered sharp, dissenting contrasts to the opinion advanced by Rawlins and perhaps by McPherson.

In their desire to portray their general in the most favorable light possible that morning, both Rawlins and Rowley contradicted a statement Grant had made almost a year earlier. Grant had written to Halleck on April 25, 1862, that Baxter had given his order to Wallace "certainly not later than 11 A.M." Rawlins wrote that Baxter left Pittsburg Landing to find Wallace with orders in hand at 9:00 A.M. Rowley stated the time for this event was "about the hour of 8 o'clock." If one could ascend the Tennessee River between Savannah and Pittsburg Landing against the most benign of currents in forty-five minutes or so, then travelling downriver from Pittsburg Landing to Crump's Landing, a trip of less than half the distance with the same speed of current now flowing favorably, would require less than half that time. Thus, had Rawlins completed his computation, Baxter would have arrived at Crump's before 9:30 that morning. According to Rowley, Baxter would have disembarked at the landing before 8:30. Yet Wallace, according to Grant, did not get his orders until 11:00. Rowley does not explain what Baxter did from 8:30 until 11:00 nor does Rawlins describe his activities between 9:30 and 11:00. Having arrived at the landing, surely it did not take Baxter two and a half hours or one and a half hours to find Wallace. In fact, in this instance, the reports of both men revealed major inconsistencies that no one seemed to notice other than Grant who, as noted earlier, had rather casually told Halleck that the three reports read together substantially represented the facts as he, Grant, knew them. Wallace had stated in his battlefield report that although he had consolidated his force at Stoney Lonesome even before he met with Grant the first and only time that day, he and several of his aides remained at Crump's Landing awaiting a message from Grant. Upon his arrival at Crump's Landing, Baxter should have found Wallace almost immediately.

Before moving to the substance of each report as it relates to the controversy and the cover-up, it should be noted that on two points, all three evidenced a well-rehearsed agreement. Each narrator included at least one statement Wallace allegedly uttered seeking to explain and justify his actions. Each report advanced the inescapable conclusion, without regard for its accuracy, that Wallace said someone else was to blame for all his misfortune. For instance, Rowley wrote that upon meeting Wallace on the Shunpike, Wallace told him he "was on the road his cavalry brought him." This was absolutely true as far as Wallace was concerned; his cavalry knew that road and from the information Major Hayes had previously conveyed to him, Wallace knew it as well. Wallace trusted Hayes and his cavalry. In the hands of an advocate like Rowley, this statement was spun in an attempt to show that Wallace was blaming his own mistakes on a third party. Both McPherson and Rawlins claimed that Wallace blamed "his guide" for directing him onto the wrong road. From that day to this, no one has ever seen fit to substantiate this innuendo by identifying by name just who "his guide" was. Nevertheless, the implication in all three reports was that Wallace was inexcusably ignorant of the terrain, topography, and roads and that he trusted the leadership of his command to some equally uninformed third party such as "his cavalry" or "his guide." As attributed to Wallace, these statements are unadulterated fabrications. Wallace was not the kind of man to suffer fools gladly. Nor was he inclined to incur anyone's disrespect or wrath by casually admitting to a subordinate that he was ill-prepared and uninformed.[12] From the outset, as his first and only battlefield report clearly indicated, Wallace always knew where he was and where he was going.

All three reports, moreover, either stated directly or with unmistakable implication that during the march, Wallace acted more like a irresolute follower than a leader. This, too, was either the creation of each narrator's imagination or the product of a well-rehearsed conspiracy. The writer of each narrative stated that once Rowley succeeded in correcting Wallace's first mistake and getting him to reverse his march to the River Road, the 3rd Division marched with excessive caution and pitiful slowness. None of these three writers knew Wallace as the man who had "Romped to Romney." Regardless of that fact, they were aware that they must characterize and portray Wallace as a man exhibiting little appreciation for quick and decisive movement. It was not difficult to put words in Wallace's mouth illustrating that if nothing else that afternoon, he was engaged in a complete repudiation of Mahan's demand for celerity of thought and action. All three agreed Wallace finally began to march "to the sound of the guns." All three further wrote that as he did so, however, he appeared at best lackadaisical, at worst indifferent. The three reports collectively picture Wallace, as he retraced his steps that afternoon toward the River Road, as utterly lacking in competency, conviction, and courage.

Specifically, Rowley stated that for the entire time he personally was with the 3rd Division, Wallace's march "appeared intolerably slow resembling more a reconnaissance in the face of an enemy than a forced march to relieve a hard-pressed army." He drove his point home with a dash of hearsay that suggests that the three reports together represented a well-rehearsed conspiracy. "The same idea," Rowley wrote, "seemed to have taken possession of the minds of Colonel McPherson and Major [Captain] Rawlins." McPherson suggested that when he first came upon Wallace, he could not contain his anger over Wallace's apparent apathy. He wrote that his first words to Wallace constituted a desperate plea to the man—"for God's sake to move forward rapidly." "I knew very well," McPherson concluded, "unless we arrived before sunset, we could be of no use in that day's battle and would not be able to retrieve the fortunes of the day."

Rawlins did his utmost to portray Wallace as a man displaying unjustified as well as unacceptable actions and attitude that day. He stated that Wallace continually called a halt to the march to ask questions of him and McPherson. At one point, according to Rawlins, a flurry of artillery activity suggested the Confederates had worked their way between the 3rd Division and the Tennessee River. "General Wallace here asked," Rawlins wrote, "if such was the position of the opposing forces, what had best be done?" Rawlins stated here that "Colonel McPherson said 'Fight our way through until communication can be had with General Grant'." To this, Wallace inventively replied "'That is my purpose.'"[13] To anyone who knew anything about Wallace or the audacity with which he had marched to fill the gap at Donelson, all these conversations were absurd. It is incomprehensible that Wallace would have used such words when communicating with subordinates. Furthermore, Rowley and particularly Rawlins were doing all that they could to make Wallace appear to be an incompetent buffoon. Above all else, Wallace was never that.

Arguably, standing alone, each writer succeeded to one degree or another in casting aspersions on Wallace and his level of competency and patriotism. This appears to be the case even when one reads only Rawlins's report. Further, the less one knew about specific events leading up to April 6 the more credible Rawlins's report became. All three were written, however, pursuant to the same request. All three were written at essentially the same time and since both Rowley and McPherson wrote directly to Rawlins, all three were submitted together. Therefore, all three must be read together as one. At this point, the collective story begins to unravel in a plethora of erroneous statements, outright conjectures, contradictions of what others, including Grant, had written as well as contradictions of what the author himself had written earlier, and a rather substantial amount of hyperbole. It is at the point where intentional deceit surfaces that one clearly sees a cover-up in the making and the end to which it is intended to lead. McPherson's role in all this is undoubtedly limited to filing a report at the request of a senior officer for the purpose of describing a specific task he was ordered to undertake. In several instances, his statements result more from sins of omission than commission. As McPherson himself concluded, the emotionalism that colored his report was genuine but was inspired only by a sense of trying to do the best for his country. McPherson should be taken at his word. The same cannot be said either for Rowley or Rawlins.

CHAPTER SIXTEEN

The Cover-Up Continues—"Oh! The Lies"

Each of the three reports failed initially to create the impression desired by their respective writers. To varying degrees, each writer had as his purpose to pose serious questions concerning Wallace's command abilities, casting doubts on his credibility, and then to answer those questions in a manner designed to diminish Wallace while elevating and exonerating Grant. However, each writer had begun his report with statements, undoubtedly unintentionally, that to varying degrees discredited Grant. The time had come for Rowley and particularly Rawlins to accelerate their anti-Wallace points of view. To accomplish their purpose, Rowley and Rawlins seized upon the idea of introducing a third party into the events of the day. They each created a straw man to lend, by introducing certain "truths" into the narrative, a new substance and credence to their respective opinions of Wallace. For Rowley, this character was simply "a cavalry officer." Rawlins dignified his creation slightly by designating him "an officer of the Second Illinois Cavalry." Neither gave their straw man a name and McPherson must have missed being introduced to this particular individual altogether for he never mentioned him.

Rowley had his cavalry man appear on the Shiloh battlefield from nowhere shortly before noon. Rowley's creation was intended to serve only one function. He reported to Grant that in his presence, Wallace had announced he would not march from Crump's Landing without a "written" order. Wallace had previously laid out his understanding of Grant's order in some detail. Never once had he mentioned that before obeying, he required a written order. Wallace had stated the order he received was not "signed." Since Rowley found Wallace around 2:00 P.M., obviously marching toward the battlefield, Rowley would have had a serious problem making something out of an allegation that Wallace had said he would march only with "signed" orders. This problem underscored the necessity for the straw man. Rowley knew for a fact that Wallace and Grant had conversed several hours earlier and that Wallace expected to receive an order from Grant. What Rowley neither knew nor appreciated was that Wallace was not the kind of man who required such an order to be in writing. Given the exigencies of any emergency type situation, such a demand would contradict Wallace's most basic instincts.[1]

However, for Rowley's purposes, the issue of a "written" order was fundamental. First, it would demonstrate that Grant was in control and that Grant had issued a specific order to Wallace. Rowley implicitly suggested that such an order would have been uncharacteristically incomplete without the inclusion of certain details, unambiguously stated, such as road names and their locations. Second, the "written" order issue would give a reason why Grant then sent Rowley to find and "correct" Wallace. Therefore, upon learning about the "signed order" from the straw man Rowley had placed on the scene, Grant allegedly uttered, in Rowley's words, the following: "Captain [Rowley], you will proceed to Crump's Landing and say to General Wallace that it is my orders that he bring up his division *at once* [emphasis in original], coming up by the River road, crossing Snake Creek on the bridge (which General Sherman would protect), and form his division on the extreme right, when he would receive further orders; and say to him that it is *important* [emphasis in original] that he should make haste."[2] Rowley was obviously attempting to have Grant say with great specificity what he had failed to say, or write, on April 6. Whatever else Grant's order to Wallace did say, it should be apparent that if Grant had been as detailed in his first order to Wallace as Rowley now represented him to be in his second order, there never would have been a controversy or a cover-up. Had Wallace received such unambiguous orders from Grant in the first place yet still marched down the Shunpike, he would have been court-martialed. He would have deserved it.

To embellish his tale further, Rowley stated that Grant next purportedly stated that if Wallace still refused to march without a written order that he should "give him one."[3] Rowley recalled that Grant then asked him if he "had writing materials." Rowley indicated he did and immediately wrote out Grant's order. Then, Grant told Rowley to take the unnamed cavalry officer with him "and two orderlies, and see that you do not spare horse flesh." This scenario suggests an interesting point. Grant might have resolved all prospective problems by spending a minute or two to take those writing materials from Rowley's "haversack," scribble out the basic details of his order, sign it, give it to Rowley, instructing him to thrust it, bodily if necessary, upon Wallace. The reason why Grant never did any of these things is simply that this incident never occurred, certainly not in the form and manner invented by Rowley. This episode, the words purportedly spoken, and indeed the presence of the straw man were all fabrication, designed to enhance Grant's stature as the general in command and to discredit Wallace as the ill-informed and obstinate subordinate.

Rawlins, in devising a more significant role for his straw man to play, also made the same mistake. According to Rawlins, Grant suddenly came upon the 2nd Illinois cavalry straw man on the battlefield. Grant then sent him, after Baxter but before Rowley filled this same role, to find Wallace and give him an order to hurry forward "with all possible dispatch." Like Rowley, Rawlins maintained that when this messenger returned from his mission, he reported to Grant that Wallace would "only obey written orders." However, Rawlins overlooked the fact that earlier in his own report he had stated that because Baxter was fearful "of some mistake in the delivery of the orders," he had obliged Baxter's request by dictating and then signing a "written memorandum" setting forth Grant's orders.[4]

Rawlins had a much greater purpose in mind for his straw man than simply using him as Rowley had. Rawlins intended his "officer of the 2nd Illinois Cavalry" to be the vehicle by which he, Rawlins, expressed his own personal views about Wallace's failures. Thus, according to Rawlins, the straw man allegedly informed Grant that "he [Wallace] should have been by this time [1:00 P.M.] on the field. His presence then would have turned the tide of battle, which was raging with great fury; saved the lives of many brave men, and ere the setting of that crimson spring day's sun secured to us certain victory."[5] Rawlins neither quoted nor paraphrased his creation in this instance; he merely put words into his straw man's mouth. The words Rawlins wrote and the ideas his straw man supposedly uttered were in fact Rawlins's own views and opinions now cleverly put on paper. Like the character created, the conclusions Rawlins had him offer were fiction. It was irrelevant to Rawlins that there was simply neither substance nor proof for his speculations. Rawlins had a task to perform on behalf of his general.

Grant had asked Rawlins to respond to Wallace. As he considered what to include in his report, Rawlins had the advantage of knowing exactly what Wallace had told Halleck. Old Brains had obliged them by forwarding Wallace's March 14 letter to Grant. In that letter, Wallace had implied he was disappointed with Grant following their first conversation that day. "Very early in the morning," Wallace had written, "I became satisfied that a battle was in progress at Pittsburg Landing." Wallace explained he set about immediately to organize his men and to concentrate his three brigades at Stoney Lonesome. He was prepared "for moving instantly upon receipt of an order from General Grant." He then awaited Grant's arrival from Savannah. "My expectation," he stated, "was that he would give me marching orders as he passed upriver to the scene of the action." "Instead of an order to march," he lamented, Grant verbally issued only a general directive "*to hold myself in readiness* [emphasis in original]."[6]

Rawlins understood that with these few words, Wallace had artfully drawn a detailed picture of a subordinate division commander instantly ready and completely prepared to execute any orders he might be given by his superior. In defense of Grant, Rawlins would be compelled to assail and destroy Wallace's self-portrait by creating an equally incontrovertible picture of his general, likewise prepared for any contingencies and ready to act decisively. Wallace might have known what he was about that morning, but so, too, did Grant. Or, at least he would once Rawlins completed his report.

For obvious reasons, Rawlins did not use the word "surprise" in his narrative. Instead, he pictured Grant as a commander acting, not reacting, with promptness and certitude. At the same time, Rawlins portrayed Wallace as a man fast succumbing to indecision and hesitation. The contrast between the two was inescapable and decidedly in Grant's favor. Whatever the costs, Rawlins intended to create with his pen a series of inferences all to Wallace's detriment. Rawlins knew it was imperative that Grant decisively win this particular battle.

Rawlins began his report, and thus the essence of the cover-up, with his personal decision to make the morning of April 6, long before the first guns were heard from the south, different than any other morning during Grant's preceding three weeks at Savannah. A reason must be invented for why Grant was prepared on that particular morning, literally as he arose from his bed, to travel to Pittsburg Landing. That reason had to be time specific.

Thus, Rawlins began his narrative by reciting General Orders No. 30, dated March 31, 1862, pursuant to which the Army of the Tennessee announced the physical transfer of its military headquarters from Savannah to Pittsburg Landing. The order did not establish a date certain for this to occur. Suffice it to say, this was a unique way to begin what was intended to be Grant's response to Wallace's report. "Up to the 5th day of April, 1862, from the date of said order," Rawlins wrote, "you had run up every morning to Pittsburg Landing and returned at night on the steamer *Tigress*, used for your headquarters boat and on which boat steam was continually kept up."[7]

With those last eight words, Rawlins initiated his cover-up. He implied that previous to the date of General Orders No. 30, the soldiers who maintained the *Tigress* in a state of readiness apparently allowed the fires in its boilers to die out overnight. Now, commencing on the night of March 31, those boilers were to be maintained at maximum steam level throughout the night.[8] Rawlins did not bother to explain the circumstances that led to General Orders No. 30 being drafted in the first place. He did not find it necessary to detail how McClernand's dispatch of March 27 to Grant had disclosed anew the 1st Division commander's proclivity for creating command problems. In addition, Rawlins had seen no reason to establish that when Grant learned that McClernand, but not Sherman, had been promoted, he realized how his overnight absences from Pittsburg Landing had acerbated the realities of his command problem at the landing. The transfer of headquarters to Pittsburg Landing was an administrative task pure and simple. In the light of what the Rebels caused to happen on the morning of April 6, Rawlins thought that creating a story around this simple task might serve a very useful purpose.

Thus, a year later, when called upon to explain and sustain his general's performance at Shiloh, Rawlins represented fiction as fact as if all along Grant had ordered the transfer of headquarters to take place early on the morning of April 6. In so doing, Rawlins hoped he could demonstrate that when the sounds of the guns at Pittsburg Landing were first heard at Savannah, Grant and all his staff literally jumped aboard the *Tigress*, and with steam-up arrived on the field of battle in less time than anyone else might have taken, totally prepared to face whatever might occur that day. The fiction that General Orders No. 30 was to be executed that very day served Rawlins quite well, or so he thought.

The immediate question Rawlins failed to address was how the mandate of General Orders No. 30 explained the alleged decision to keep the *Tigress* under full steam each night beginning March 31. Rawlins did not address that issue; he merely stated that such a decision had been made.

Grant could obviously allocate his resources as he saw fit. Nevertheless, keeping his river transportation under a full head of steam in conditions hardly amounting to an emergency was an unusual and costly response to what then was a nonexistent problem. Rawlins's mission was to lay the foundation and thereby make the conclusion inevitable that on this particular morning, Grant appeared more in command of his army, events, and any looming emergency than he had ever seemed to be since first arriving at Savannah. To plant this suggestion, Rawlins had Grant's means of travel to Pittsburg Landing ready to speed upriver.

To enhance this proposition, Rawlins embellished his initial scenario. He stated that "the horses" for the men scheduled to make the trip early on the morning of April 6 were "in readiness, as per orders of the night previous." To round out and finalize his portrait of Grant being totally prepared for any eventuality, Rawlins added so "that there might be no delay in getting off (and consequent detention in moving the office) to Pittsburg Landing, directions were given for breakfast and horses to be in readiness at an earlier hour than usual."[9] Therefore, whether the sound of cannons emanating from upriver surprised Grant or not, he wasted no time getting to the battlefield. Rawlins had made it so. For reasons completely unrelated to anything other than resolution of a minor, albeit thorny, administrative problem, Grant had fortuitously prepared for an early departure from Savannah. With Rawlins employing his capable and imaginative pen, any criticism of Grant being slow or dilatory in arriving at Pittsburg Landing simply lacked substance and merit. The comparisons between Grant and Wallace as Rawlins drew their respective pictures were quite striking. Once initiated, all the remaining items constituting Rawlins's cover-up flowed as naturally as the currents of the Tennessee River.

In concocting this scenario, Rawlins overlooked two additional considerations that made his story all the more implausible. First, in publishing General Orders No. 30, Grant had stipulated that at some point a physical transfer of headquarters would occur. No other documentation exists that suggests that any of his field commanders were ever given any date for the move. For example, Wallace never indicated that on the evening of April 5 he possessed any knowledge that the transfer of command headquarters was scheduled to occur the next morning. No other divisional commander did either. An entire army could not be expected to relocate its official residence without, at an absolute minimum, specific notice of the date of the transfer being dispatched at least to its division commanders. Rawlins was, if anything, dedicated to detail. It is quite unlikely that he would have failed to give some form of written notice or order of this event's scheduled occurrence to at least these six men. On perhaps a comical note, Rawlins failed to explain why Grant was directly involved with the purely physical act of moving in the first place. His presence was neither necessary nor required for the process to occur. Surely Rawlins was not suggesting that implementation of General Orders No. 30 required the direct involvement and participation of the highest-ranking field officer in the Army of the Tennessee?

Second, when Rawlins created his fiction that the morning of April 6 had been designated as the date for the headquarters transfer, he either overlooked or sought to marginalize an important fact. Once Buell arrived in Savannah, the overriding reason for the transfer of command headquarters immediately ceased to exist. With Buell coming into camp, Pittsburg Landing instantly became a way station. The combined armies would immediately march on Corinth. Grant would be with his army at every step. Rawlins created his fiction little appreciating that the rational for its existence was no longer relevant. He overlooked the fact that one usually does not undertake to move ledger books, ink wells, papers, maps, tents, tables, chairs, and so forth to another location when one is poised to initiate an offensive and the often-repeated impediment to doing so has just disappeared. On April 5, a dispatch, dated April 4, was received at Grant's headquarters announcing that Buell, accompanied by two divisions, would be in Savannah the next day. Nelson with three brigades had already arrived. Grant responded to Buell the same day: "I will be here to meet you to-morrow." Rawlins failed to recognize that having Grant go to Pittsburg Landing as early as possible April 6 to move his headquarters was totally inconsistent with Grant scheduling a meeting with Buell. In fact, no one was now thinking about moving headquarters just to Pittsburg Landing. The headquarters tent would accompany the army to Corinth. Grant had been waiting for this news for three long weeks. Halleck's mind-numbing caveat was about to disintegrate.[10]

In creating his myth about the transfer of headquarters, Rawlins had crafted a perception for Halleck that Grant had been neither "slow," "tardy," nor "dilatory" in his response to the events of the early morning of April 6. From there it was but a small step for Rawlins to imply it made little difference whether or not Grant had been surprised that morning. Immediately upon his arrival at Pittsburg Landing, Grant had seized control of the situation and pursued it to a victorious conclusion. The contrast between

Grant's and Wallace's alleged performances that first day was stark. Grant, as molded by Rawlins, was superbly confident and absolutely in control. By contrast, Wallace appeared supremely irresolute, lost, and slow. Rawlins seemed unconcerned that the picture he had drawn was based upon a lie.

Upon receipt, Halleck buried the three reports, along with everything else relating to Wallace's requests for answers. Had Rawlins's story ever been scrutinized contemporaneously, there is a decent chance it would have unraveled swiftly based upon his failure to note something quite unusual that day about his friend and mentor. Everyone acknowledged that Grant lacked pretense. Contemporary observers used many words to describe Grant, but among the more common were "modest," "low-keyed," "unassuming," and "no nonsense." For one thing, Grant apparently disliked wearing the trappings of his rank. Charles A. Dana, Assistant Secretary of War and Stanton's special envoy in the west, described Grant as "a simple-hearted, unaffected, unpretending hero, whom no ill omens could deject [*sic*] and no triumph unduly exalt." After the war, a member of the 33rd Illinois recalled that Grant was "one of the most modest and unpretending officers we have served under." Albert O. Marshall observed that Grant usually rode with one or two orderlies, in contrast to "officers of less rank [who] often appear in grand style attended by a full staff and cavalry body-guard. By the careless way he goes among them, Grant evidently thinks that every Union soldier he meets is part of his body-guard." The war correspondent for the *New York World* saw in Grant's bearing a man who shunned "Napoleonic displays," avoided "ostentation," and had little time for "superfluous flummery." Extending these attributes to his manner of dress, the correspondent for the *New York Times* observed that Grant's normal attire consisted of "a plain blue suit, without scarf, sword or trappings of any sort, save the double-starred shoulder straps—an indifferently good 'Kossuth' hat, with top battered in close to his head."[11]

Yet, Lt. Douglas Putnam Jr., who rode the steamer *Tigress* with Grant to Pittsburg Landing, had difficulty containing his surprise on April 6 when he observed Grant on the field of battle attired in "full uniform, with the major-general's buff sash, making him very conspicuous, both to our own men and also to those of the enemy." According to Putnam, both McPherson and Rawlins "remonstrated" with Grant "for so unnecessarily exposing himself, as he went just in rear of our lines of battle." In juxtaposing Rawlins's report concerning what Grant anticipated doing that day with Putnam's observations about his dress, one might reasonably ponder the significance of Grant wearing one of his best dress uniforms merely to supervise the transfer of his command headquarters. If Putnam's observations were correct, Grant seemed poised to welcome Buell to Savannah, not to move his headquarters and certainly not to fight a battle. Putnam might possibly have exaggerated or actually been mistaken as to the quality and dignity of Grant's uniform that day. On the other hand, it is equally possible that Grant had dressed himself up in such proper attire specifically to welcome Buell to Savannah. Overwhelmed by the surprise of Confederate artillery at Pittsburg Landing and in the resulting confusion of rushing to the battlefield, Grant hardly had the time to change his attire.[12]

Rawlins's narrative might also have dissolved upon closer examination in another respect. Rawlins claimed that when he first found the 3rd Division leader, Wallace told him that his guide had misled him. Rawlins thus joined forces with McPherson and Rowley, claiming Wallace, by his own admission, knew he was on the wrong road and was lost. If all three accounts had not sought to magnify this point, had not sought to make Wallace something he was not, namely the arch-personification of Halleck's bungling, witless, incompetent civilian amateur soldier, their collective impact could have been quite damning to Wallace. However, Rawlins, in particular, sought to demonstrate just how lost and just how unhurried Wallace had been that entire day. At this point, the cover-up floundered in a flurry of unnecessary, boring, and largely suspect details.

For example, Rawlins stated that he informed Wallace in general terms of the status of the fighting and urged him "with all the earnestness I possessed to hasten forward." Wallace allegedly responded that "there was no danger; he would yet reach there [the battlefield] in good season, and with his fresh troops would soon end the fight in a victory for us." Wallace did in fact speak and write with a Romantic flair. It is absurd to think, however, that his retort to Rawlins at this highly charged moment was similarly cloaked. Rawlins also suggested that Wallace was so ridden with doubt that he could scarcely move. To amplify this image, Rawlins said he suggested to Wallace that he might send a detachment ahead to make sure the bridge over the Snake River was secure. Wallace responded, "capital idea." Wallace was many things; he was not a witless fool.[13]

Rawlins continued by picturing a doubt-ridden Wallace being uncertain if he were on the right road even though at the time he had nearly completed his countermarch to the River Road. Hence, according to Rawlins, Wallace stopped his march in order to send McPherson to inquire at a local farmhouse if he was indeed going in the right direction. Rawlins characterized this as a blatantly unnecessary act that only took valuable time away from the march. It is doubtful that Wallace thought such an action by McPherson or anyone to be necessary. Rawlins was aware that by the time he and McPherson "found" him, Wallace had already backtracked; had already turned onto the old country dirt road that intersected with the Hamburg–Savannah Road; and that Wallace was in the company of Rowley. Surely Rawlins was not suggesting that Rowley, his good friend and fellow storyteller, was likewise "lost?"

The unnecessary details continued. Rawlins accused Wallace of moving "coolly and leisurely forward until we reached the main Pittsburg Landing road." There, he dismounted and sat while his artillery was transferred to the rear of the column off the road, permitting his infantry to move along more quickly to its destination. Rawlins labeled this, as well, "an excuse for considerable delay—I should say for full half an hour." Neither Rawlins, nor Rowley, nor McPherson had ever commanded a large number of men in battle under circumstances remotely like those that prevailed that day. It is doubtful any of the three had any appreciation for Wallace's motive or intent in this regard. It was potentially suicidal to arrive on the field of a raging battle in column with artillery preceding infantry. Next, Rawlins complained that Wallace's column came to a halt while Wallace allegedly checked out a report that the bridge over Snake Creek was now in enemy hands. Rawlins acknowledged this turned out to be a rumor. He still complained that Wallace hesitated to march, allowing his men time once again to close ranks "and his troops to rest." When Rawlins officially protested this delay, "General Wallace still gave no orders to move, but manifested the utmost coolness and indifference." There is no evidence other than Rowley's and Rawlins's comments to indicate that Wallace, the man who had not hesitated, despite the apparent danger, to insert himself and his command, onto the Wynn's Ferry Road, inexplicably experienced such a fundamental change in character and courage.[14]

Rawlins concluded his report amid a flurry of wild, speculative assertions. Wallace demonstrated an abysmal "want of knowledge of the road"[15]; Wallace "should have been perfectly familiar with all the roads leading to and from his camps"[16]; "the roads were in fine condition"[17]; during the march, Wallace and the men of the 3rd Division "did not make a mile and a half an hour, although urged and appealed to push forward"[18]; and, finally, had Wallace only proceeded that day "with the rapidity his command was able and anxious to have moved after we overtook him, he would have reached you in time to have engaged the enemy before the close of Sunday's fight."[19] Rawlins could not and did not offer a scintilla of proof for any of these assertions and charges, but they remained an uncontested part of the record he had created.

The cover-up was penned and it was real. However, its contents did not see the light of day for over two decades. Grant sent all three reports with his summation dispatch to Halleck. Old Brains, perhaps with the connivance of Stanton, was not going to allow Wallace to have his day in court or with the public at large through the newspapers. Upon receipt of Grant's response, Halleck merely "shelved" it all as he had so unceremoniously done with the person of Wallace the year before.

In the summer of 1884, Wallace returned to the United States, having served three years as U.S. Minister to the Ottoman Empire. That was the year the government published volume 10 of *The Official Records of the War of the Rebellion*, devoted to the Shiloh campaign. In a letter to Grant, Wallace stated that he had just read the reports of Rawlins, Rowley, and McPherson for the first time. "I shall regret all my remaining days," Wallace lamented, "not previously knowing their tenor; for I think I could have explained to the satisfaction of those gentlemen every mystery of my conduct during their ride with me the afternoon of the 6th April." It is doubtful that Wallace would have influenced the writers of the three narratives one whit. What is most striking about this letter to Grant is that Wallace refrained from labeling the reports of Rowley and Rawlins as overtly defamatory and libelous. If in doing so he had been guilty of losing his temper, his reaction would have been completely justified.[20]

Halleck's role in this cover-up was at best cowardly. By his actions in sending all of Wallace's correspondence to Grant and none of Grant's to Wallace, Halleck denied Wallace the right to confront his accusers. Secreted away, the three narratives constituting the written cover-up thus never significantly impacted the controversy during the war or immediately thereafter so far as the public or most officers in the Union army were concerned. When released, the veterans and the historians altered this by jumping headlong into the fray. The irony is that ultimately, Halleck's act of shelving these three narratives had made neither Wallace nor his controversy go away.

Rawlins seldom missed an opportunity after the war to tell the Shiloh story. Speaking on November 11, 1866, at the first annual meeting of the

Society of the Army of the Tennessee, he denied that Union forces at Shiloh had been surprised. "We had sufficient notice, before the shock came, to be under arms and ready to meet it." Rawlins had once again drawn the Grant-Halleck chestnuts from the fire and pried them wide open. Grant had left Savannah "about seven o'clock," Rawlins said. He repeated his invented remarks from the cover-up that upon his arrival at Crump's Landing, Grant had instructed Wallace "to send out and ascertain if the enemy might not be making a move on his position." Rawlins continued to do all he could to make Grant look crisp, efficient, and totally in command of the situation. Arriving at Pittsburg Landing "about eight o'clock," Grant sent back orders to Wallace "to move with all dispatch to Pittsburg Landing." It had never been proven that Grant ordered Wallace to "Pittsburg Landing." Rawlinjs had just turned a speculation into a gospel fact. A second new fabrication was now deemed gospel fact. When Rawlins next mentioned Wallace to the assembled veterans, he was just getting to the field of battle "after dark." Brief, biased, and flagrantly riddled with falsehoods, Rawlins concluded his address with the following subtle but scathing indictment: "had he [Wallace] got upon the field with his splendid Division at the time his orders contemplated, we might have turned the tide of battle; we certainly would have staid it much earlier than we did."[21]

The three narratives, however, did have an immediate impact on the participants. Collectively, they and their respective authors, particularly Rawlins, did irreparable damage to Wallace's relationship with Grant.[22] Perhaps it would be more accurate to say they simply put an end to the relationship. In that respect, the narratives, particularly those penned by Rowley and Rawlins, achieved their purpose. McPherson seemed not to have had any specific agenda in mind other than to report his experiences as ordered. One must wonder if Grant ever read any of these accounts. If he did, it is difficult to believe he read them in any depth or detail. On the other hand, if Cadwallader is correct, Grant did not have to read them as the ideas and images they created were often discussed openly around Grant's campfire. It is clear that when Grant invited Wallace to meet him at City Point in September, 1864, following Wallace's brilliant "tactical defeat" at Monocacy, Grant had become inflexible. His mind was closed. There was to be no further discussion of Shiloh. Wallace would no longer command in the field. Three factors had become cemented together to form the foundation for Grant's decision: Wallace's personality; the innuendos, misrepresentations, and outright lies of the cover-up; and the degree to which both had fashioned and then destroyed Grant's relationship with Wallace.

Maj. Gen. Grenville Dodge observed years after the war that Grant habitually evaluated not only his subordinates' actions but also their intent. If he found them wanting in either respect, if any of his subordinates failed to meet his expectations, then, Dodge believed, Grant "dropped them so quickly and efficiently that the whole country could see and hear their fall."[23] This was certainly true in Wallace's case.

In the final analysis, Wallace's entire military career and whatever identity he achieved as a general officer in the American Civil War were shaped and defined by the events of April 6, 1862. For Wallace, the facts of the April 6 journey that lay at the heart of the controversy—from the Purdy Road down the Shunpike to near the bridge at Owl Creek, the partial return by countermarch cross country to the River Road, over the Wallace Bridge spanning Snake Creek, finally to arrive on Tilghman Branch as night fell—only had relevance in the context of who was telling the truth. He understood that those events could never be undone or relived. Truth and honor, however, could be exhumed from the decay of the battlefield and given a proper burial. Over the next four decades, during this last great military adventure, Wallace focused with great intensity on recapturing his honor. Only a man who had labored so many decades to save and restore that which he believed had so unjustly been stolen from him could have written at the turn of the century with such tortured pathos, "O, the lies, the lies that were told to make me the scapegoat to bear off the criminal mistakes of others in connection with that awful first day! It took General Grant about a quarter of a century to work himself up to an admission that I was blameless. But think, my brave comrade, think of what I suffered in the meantime! Think, too, that the slanders have gone into history, and may never be corrected."[24]

CHAPTER SEVENTEEN

"Except in Sympathy and to Defend"

Initially, all the participants in the controversy had been very successful internalizing it to the army. It was a common goal for most, although the reasons behind the desire varied widely. Then, in 1868, Adam Badeau, another Grant aide, wrote and published a two-volume presidential campaign biography of Grant. It immediately ignited the ire of Wallace and his supporters. Badeau's book initiated round two of the controversy by reopening the subject of Wallace's march and thrusting it into the national arena. As a matter of personal honor, inextricably associated with his feelings toward Grant, Wallace would refuse again to argue and debate the controversy in the public forum. Grant likewise avoided public pronouncements, but, for the first time, he felt compelled to participate. Finally, after years of silence, he responded in print to Wallace. In so doing, he indicated he had not changed his position on any of the particulars. He did, however, make a sincere suggestion to Wallace. "In view of the assaults made upon you now," he wrote, "I think it due you that you should publish what your own Staff and other subordinate officers have to say in exoneration of your course."[1]

Wallace might have been wise to accept Grant's proposal as the best possible resolution of the issues. Perhaps Grant sensed Wallace could not do this. Still seeking exoneration only from one man not the public at large, Wallace refused to fight this battle other than solely with Grant himself. Wallace believed Grant did not deserve public disparagement on any level. After all, he still considered Grant his general and his general was soon to become the Republican standard bearer for the presidency of the United States. Wallace's sense of personal honor prevented him from addressing the public with his version of the specifics of the controversy.

The difference between 1868 and times past with respect to the controversy was that the opposing sides now heard for the first time on a grand scale the voices of many veterans of Shiloh. They alone kept the controversy very much alive for at least the next three decades.

Badeau claimed that on April 6, once Rowley turned Wallace "in the right direction at one o'clock," it then "took him [Wallace] till seven that night, to march five miles in the direction of the battle."[2] Badeau's accusation that Wallace marched his command a total of five miles in approximately six hours was both ludicrous and personally hurtful. Wallace was incensed. Wallace knew there was no basis in fact for such an accusation. He would write yet another letter to Grant, thereby doing the best he could to keep the controversy internalized.

As he had done in 1863, Wallace sent a number of letters from his supporters, all still within his military family, along with his letter to Grant. Grant did not call upon his advocates to say or write anything. To a certain degree in 1868, the pro-Wallace faction merely rehashed the verbiage of 1863. There was, however, a greater emphasis given in 1868 than before to Wallace's use of the Shunpike to approach the battlefield. Wallace seized the opportunity to reaffirm that he had known from the very beginning of his march exactly where he was going. For the first time, he added that his men knew as well. "*Not only did I know the road,*" Wallace proclaimed to Grant, "*but every step my division took from the initial point of the march up to the moment of the change of direction, was, as well known to every soldier in the column, a step nearer to the firing, and therefore a step nearer to the battle* [emphasis in original]."[3]

Interestingly, Wallace did not attempt to substantiate this statement with any comment that prior to April 6 his command had improved the condition of the Shunpike. He did not utter a word about his April 5 dispatch to W. H. L. Wallace. This was an unusual tactic to take inasmuch as his knowledge on either or both points would go far to vindicate him and his actions that day. He might, upon the presentation of such evidence, succeed in justifying to Grant the road he took that morning. At the same time, however, Wallace knew that if those "facts" became public knowledge, they might also do irretrievable harm to Grant in the political arena. Wallace refused to condone such conduct.

Neither Badeau's book nor the correspondence it generated changed anyone's thinking on the issues involved. Basically, Wallace once again made it clear he was seeking "an exoneration" from Grant, "a simple act of justice," nothing more than "a note of acquittal from blame, plainly enough, to allay the suspicions and charges to which I have been so painfully subjected." Grant need only recognize that Wallace was neither "lost" nor "late" that day because he had marched in strict accord with the order that Baxter handed to him. Wallace never made it clear how Grant was to recant his version of that order without in some manner involving the public. In addition, Wallace never explained how his myopic resolution of the matter would not do the very harm to Grant that he seemingly sought to avoid.

Badeau concluded his discussion of Shiloh with an acknowledgment that on April 7, Wallace and his men "fought well on the extreme right relieving themselves from any responsibility for the laggard movements of the preceding day." Wallace viewed this attempt at exoneration to be grossly insufficient when compared to Badeau's claim that his march lacked celerity and that as a consequence he had been so very late the day before.[4] Badeau had also unapologetically employed that dastardly word "laggard."[5]

Wallace overlooked several statements in Badeau's book that, if properly examined, could have been turned to his advantage. On one very important matter, which went directly to the crux of the controversy, Badeau made contradictory statements. In the first instance, he wrote that Grant had given Wallace "verbal directions . . . to march by the nearest road parallel to the river." That was basically the Grant version of the lost order. Then, not more than a page later, Badeau authoritatively stated, "Lewis Wallace was directed to come up and connect with Sherman's right." That was the Wallace version of the controversy. Knowingly or not, Badeau had drawn the very issue of the controversy into the public eye. Surely, Wallace recognized the contradiction for what it was. If he brought that point to the forefront of the conversation, if he pursued the truth that the contradiction exposed, he could destroy Grant. Again, Wallace refused to countenance this possibility. Thus, as a practical political animal during a national election year, Wallace chose not to exploit Badeau's contradiction. Wallace wanted only a modicum of exoneration. A simple note from Grant would suffice. The issues involved were not matters for the public forum at this time.

The second round of the controversy altered few, if any, opinions, and the documents constituting the cover-up remained at the War Department hidden away from everybody's view. Seventeen years later, however, a more conclusive piece of evidence surfaced attesting to the idea that Wallace knew exactly what road he wished to travel on April 6. Sometime in early 1885, Ann Wallace, widow of W. H. L. Wallace who had fallen mortally wounded on the first day of Shiloh, sent Grant a letter found in her husband's coat pocket as he was being carried from the battlefield. It was dated April 5, 1862. Lew Wallace, commanding the 3rd Division, had written from Adamsville to W. H. L. Wallace, commanding the 2nd Division. Lew had informed W. H. L. that because the 3rd Division had three camps strung out along the Purdy–Bethel Road, including the westernmost at Adamsville, "I thought it would be better to open communication with you from Adamsville." The Indiana Wallace told the Illinois Wallace that the next day, Sunday, April 6, he would send Major Hayes of the 5th Ohio Cavalry to the latter's camp "and, if you are so disposed, probably, you had better send a company to return with him, that they may familiarize themselves with the road, to act in case of emergency as guides to and from our camps." Confederate surprise on April 6 prevented that event from taking place. The letter illustrates that the Hoosier general in fact knew a great deal about the road systems in and around Crump's Landing and Pittsburg Landing, particularly the Shunpike.[6]

This new information combining with Grant's growing awareness that Wallace had been unwilling to expose the issues of the controversy to public scrutiny finally led Grant to make a small but significant concession. As a "Note" in his *Personal Memoir,* Grant extended partial and begrudging exoneration to his 3rd Division commander. He still used words such as "mistake" and "dilatoriness" and characterized Wallace as a man with minimal military "experience." He acknowledged, however, that "if the position of our front had not changed, the road which Wallace took would have been somewhat shorter to our right than the River road."[7] It was a small and heavily veiled admission but a victory nonetheless.

One aspect of the controversy that amazingly failed to capture the imagination of most of the Shiloh participants as well as the American public had its origins in an observation Wallace made in his battlefield report. Wallace stated that he first learned from Rowley mid-afternoon on April 6 that Rebel surprise had driven the commands of Sherman, McClernand, and W. H. L. Wallace back toward the Tennessee River, more than a mile northeast of their original campsites. Wallace stated correctly that for him, this was new and provocative intelligence. He now understood for the first time that Confederate troops, not Union divisions, were massed in and around the destination to which he had been intentionally marching his men. The road he had been taking with a very specific purpose in mind—to join with Sherman on Grant's right—would now take him into the enemy's rear on its unsupported left flank. Quite reluctantly he was compelled to concede that if he continued down that road, the 3rd Division "was in danger of being entirely cut off." Wallace thus deemed it prudent to act consistent with Rowley's "representation" to seek out the River Road. He then initiated a countermarch to that location.

On several subsequent occasions, beginning as early as March, 1863, when he wrote to Halleck, Wallace speculated on the wisdom of that decision without reaching any definite conclusion. Then, on April 7, 1881, retired Brig. Gene. Ralph P. Buckland, who as commander of the 4th Brigade, Sherman's 5th Division, bore the brunt of Rebel surprise nineteen years earlier, publically reopened the issue. After attempting, rather unsuccessfully, to repudiate the idea that Grant and his army had been caught unaware that morning, Buckland suggested to the assembled veterans of the Society of the Army of the Tennessee that "if General Wallace, with his division of eight thousand men [5,500 effectives], had continued on the road he started upon, which I think he ought to have done, and struck the enemy on his left flank and rear by 2 or 3 o'clock P.M., the tide of victory would have been turned against the enemy; it would have saved the disaster to Prentiss' Division, and I think would have driven the enemy from the field on the first day." In 1899, Wallace finally took a public stand on the issue, agreeing respectfully with Buckland's assessment. His conclusion was that had he only continued with his march along the Shunpike to the Hamburg–Purdy Road and fought to cross the bridge at Veal's Mill, he would have captured a "great part of the Confederate army. The surprise would have been to them, not our people."[8]

Although the fog of war has been known to play amazing tricks on one's recollections, the Buckland perspective has considerable merit. By mid-afternoon, April 6, a temporary stalemate had been reached on the Union right. Most, if not all, of the Union right still lay on or slightly west of the Hamburg–Savannah Road, about a mile or so north of the Hamburg–Purdy Road. As events during the rest of that afternoon amply demonstrated, Union troops on the right had plenty of fight left in them. If Wallace had continued his march, his division would have encountered a Rebel force certainly in less than brigade strength at the bridge at Veal's Mill. The 5,500-plus soldiers of Wallace's relatively fresh 3rd Division more likely than not would have swept that Rebel resistance aside. Then, the 3rd Division would have descended upon the left rear flank of the

Confederate army. With a strong and unanticipated blow, Wallace might well have hammered the now-surprised Rebels against the anvil of Union forces under Sherman, McClernand, and W. H. L. Wallace to their front in the area generally west-northwest of the Sunken Road. It was then, as today, a very delicious "what if."[9]

The controversy about Wallace getting lost, taking the wrong road, and thereby being late that first day at Shiloh has continued from its inception to the present day. The controversy has never been at a loss for participants. Isabel Wallace, the daughter of W. H. L. Wallace, when she published her father's letters in 1909, criticized Lew Wallace for arriving late to the battlefield as the result of his "misunderstanding of orders." Douglas Putnam Jr, as a member of Grant's quartermaster corps on April 6, rode the steamer with Grant as it left Savannah and descended the Tennessee River to Pittsburg Landing. On a February evening in 1889, Putnam informed the assembled members of the Ohio Commandery that once Grant arrived at Pittsburg Landing and determined that the attack there was a general one, "an order was sent immediately by Captain Baxter to Wallace, merely telling him to come up." Putnam observed that the order was neither written nor did it specifically give a name to the road over which Wallace was to march to the battlefield. In that same year, however, Olney noted simply but eloquently that Wallace's "failure to reach us was fatal." In 1899, Brevet Lt. Col. William Hemstreet, addressing his comrades in the New York Commandery, stated that he personally observed Wallace sitting "on a log smoking a cigar and holding the reins of his horse, with five thousand splendid soldiers, five miles from Shiloh, all day long in the sound of our guns, while our Southern brethren were drubbing us soundly, and he never lent a hand."[10] The list could easily go on and on. The Wallace detractors are, even today, legion. Like so many controversies, the Wallace march to Shiloh story appears based in fact only to the extent that one selects one's facts. It was, at the time, a controversy well grounded in personalities, cliques, and a cover-up.

Years later, Wallace himself said it best. In 1903, at the dedication of the Indiana monuments at Shiloh National Battlefield Park, he spoke with his usual eloquence. He pondered the answer to a question that he had asked himself often. Why, he inquired of his audience, if he were guilty of any of the charges leveled against him arising out of the march of April 6, 1862, had not any of the members of the 3rd Division spoken against him, then or in the intervening years? He might have added that while certain officers like Morgan L. Smith and Alvin P. Hovey had gone forward with Grant following Shiloh, neither officer ever publicly criticized Wallace's April 6 conduct.[11]

In his speech, Wallace made no excuses. He merely observed, "Had I been guilty of any military offense while with them marching to the assistance of comrades in distress that black Sunday; had I been laggard in the march; had I led them from the musketry and peals of cannon sounding in our ears all the day from dawn to dusk, like the monotone of the ocean spreading its infinite energies upon a stony beach, would these men have not seen it?" The men of the 3rd Division were not then or ever subservient dolts. "Eager, anxious, sharp of discernment, keen in the discovery of mistakes or misconduct, and more than independent enough to expose them, how was it possible for me to deceive them?" Of course, the answer to this rhetorical question was that it was not possible. What Wallace really evidenced in that speech was infinite pride, not bitter remorse. In the final analysis, "not one man of the division, officers or privates, ever raised his voice in the controversy except in sympathy, and to defend me."[12]

In the presence of his assembled audience that day, Wallace discovered anew his personal legacy from Shiloh. He found it as he recalled the names and faces of the men who had participated in his adventure; he recognized it in the faith they had had in him and the loyalty they had so unhesitatingly conferred upon him. He realized they, too, had remembered.

CONCLUSION

On July 1, 1864, Lt. Benjamin Marshall Mills, who, like Wallace, was from Crawfordsville, Indiana, wrote to his father Caleb. The younger Mills was then stationed at Vicksburg, Mississippi, second in command of Company F, 49th U.S. Infantry (Colored). He had been mustered-in only a month and a half earlier. He explained to his father he was just beginning to learn a very valuable military lesson. "Keep all your dislikes," he wrote, "to your self [*sic*] and you will make no enemies. One learns a great deal in the army, here he learns to be obedient, *to obey orders without stopping to enquire why such orders were given and what the use of them are but he has to obey and in obeying discovers their utility* [emphasis added]. I think sometimes myself that I would very much like to know what such and such an order is, but don't care that much."[1]

Maj. Gen. Lew Wallace once gave a nod to the same military truths that young Mills was exploring in 1864. "You understand," Wallace said in response to a question posed by Covode during his July, 1862, appearance before the Joint Committee, "that it is the duty of an officer to obey his orders without questioning." Wallace was not at that moment thinking about Paducah. "Suppose I issue an order to a subordinate," he continued, "it would be very improper for him to demand to know the reasons for it." This, Wallace concluded, "would result in having a general council of war consisting of all the officers and all the soldiers: a thing impossible in itself."[2] Wallace respected the concept of the military chain of command from the top down, but usually only when he was at the top dealing with subordinates. Mills, on the other hand, understood the operation of the same chain, but as a recipient of orders. The philosophical difference in the two viewpoints is illuminating.[3] A comparison of the two is much more than merely a statement of the perspectives of a general officer juxtaposed against those of a subaltern. One can only wonder how much differently the career of the older, civilian amateur soldier might have been written if he had had the willingness to listen to, honestly evaluate, and perhaps accept the wisdom of his Hoosier colleague and hometown neighbour.

A quarrel with fortune, great or small, neither dictated the course of Wallace's military career nor destroyed it. Virtually on his own, with unrestrained self-assurance and unfettered arrogance, Wallace did more than enough by himself to achieve Halleck's objective of ridding his army of at least one civilian amateur. Wallace had used adventure, audacity, and an unbounded patriotic spirit to educate himself in things military and to succeed on the field of battle. He accomplished this in much the same way as he had earlier fathomed the marvels of Dickens without much outside assistance. In the final analysis, however, he was too independent, too unrestrained, too self-assured, too brash ever to have succeeded within the confining parameters of the newly emerging American military system. Whether it was Woolfolk and Paducah, or an argument about hospital ships, or a plea to a superior officer as to the disposition and whereabouts of the 11th Indiana and the 8th Missouri while he simultaneously misled that officer, or a failure to protect a train at Grand Junction, Tennessee, or the desire to speak his mind virtually whenever and wherever he wanted, Wallace would always be Wallace. All this undoubtedly fashioned and underscored his greatness as a nineteenth century literary figure. All this inspired his highly successful and enduring Renaissance quest for knowledge—to make a violin simply because he wanted to learn to play the instrument. All this in his military career, however, defeated him.

Wallace's fatal military flaw did not surface during battle. He invariably performed at his best amid shot and shell. The fatal flaw in his military character became manifest rather in his reaction to the boredom and the seemingly senseless purpose of ordinary, everyday military life. It surfaced without fail as he was forced to react to the formal order and structure supporting and sustaining the professional military establishment. Try as he might, the independent and self-reliant Wallace could neither live with nor escape the strictures, formalities, and absolutisms that characterized the establishment's unquestioned obedience to the military chain of command. When he agreed with an order, or at least found it to be neither distasteful nor incompetently issued, he forged ahead. With skill, he performed quite well and usually achieved the purpose of that order. On the other hand, when an order offended his definition of common sense, or ran counter to his standard of personal values, or lacked military wisdom and practicality as he personally defined these concepts, he became reticent, then reluctant, and finally found at least one reason to disobey.

The consummate irony of Wallace's military career occurred at Shiloh when he scrupulously obeyed a particular order from Grant. Marching southwest from Crump's Landing down the Shunpike, Wallace never doubted he was leading his men into battle in direct obedience to an order Grant had given him through Baxter. Then, in response to Rowley's pleas and what certainly under the circumstances was a direct order from Grant, he obeyed once more, countermarching his division back along the Shunpike to the River Road and then to Pittsburg Landing. It was unquestionably against his ingrained nature to obey that second order; but he did so. He paid a terrible price for his allegiance to the chain of command that day. From that point onward, far too many would characterize his performance at Shiloh with words like "lost," "late," and "laggard."

The best and most damning evidence of Wallace's fatal flaw came from his constant squabbles with Halleck and Grant. The same problems, however, existed for Wallace in virtually all his military relationships. His relationship with C. F. Smith resembled a bouncing ball. He once blatantly criticized Maj. Gen. George B. McClellan in writing to a superior officer. It is not surprising that Wallace clashed with the professionals since, like most of the knuckleheaded schoolmasters he had encountered in his youth, they dominated and controlled the system in which he found himself. Neither is it surprising that in such clashes, he invariably lost. He never grasped that there simply were times when a major general, or even a young schoolboy, should keep silent and follow orders to the best of his abilities. To be sure, Wallace had friends with influence, but very few of them were in the military. Of those who wore Union blue and could be counted as friends, they, too, lacked influence. Like Wallace, they were mostly civilian amateurs.

In a rare moment of self-examination, Wallace recognized the pitfalls of his particular personality. Writing in his *Autobiography* concerning an incident that had occurred during Halleck's Corinth campaign, Wallace observed that "one day, however, I opened my mouth and let my opinions fly; this, too, under circumstances so discreditable to my good sense that I hesitate writing them . . . I make no apology for my foolishness, except the very general one that it is not in nature for any man to be always good and always wise."[4] Even as he scourged his soul, Wallace still managed to rationalize his actions.

In the final analysis, the ever-increasing size and scope of the war his country waged from 1861 to 1865 necessarily dictated the emergence of a corps of professionally trained military officers and the solidification of the status of that group within the military command structure. The trend had begun very slowly during the Mexican War. By 1865, the evolution away from the civilian, amateur officer to the professional was progressing virtually unimpeded. The keystone to this process was the growing membership in a highly exclusive club, the West Point Corps of Cadets. Wallace's father had belonged to that club; he did not. He highly resented that fact. Moreover, he failed to appreciate that the members of this club shared a common bond simply by virtue of having spent four years together on the banks of the Hudson River. He never quite recognized that membership in the club by itself made the West Pointer separate and distinct from the volunteer, civilian, amateur soldier of the nineteenth century.[5]

Even though Wallace knew that this exclusive "clique" had become a legitimate factor in his military life, he persisted in following an illogical course of action. Time and again, he refused to make any concessions that might allow him to co-exist peacefully with the elite. Rather than keeping his mouth closed at times, rather than striving for some sort of accommodation without sacrificing his principles, both for the sake of achieving self-preservation, Wallace spent his time and energy bemoaning the fact that certain officers were elevated in rank or opportunity over him simply because they belonged to the club. Rather than accept this West Point exclusivity as a fact and seek common ground with his self-appointed nemeses, Wallace never hesitated to tell others that many of these so-called professionals were inferior in thought, skill, and action to him. Indeed, many were, but he never recognized that that fact was irrelevant to his existence. Furthermore, he was not alone in his prejudice. Fred Knefler, Wallace's adjutant at Donelson and Shiloh, and later colonel of the 79th Indiana Volunteers, echoed the thoughts of his mentor: "The people are being educated to the lamentable fact that our highly educated West Point officers are an abominable humbug and nuisance to the country." Writing one day before the Union defeat at Second Manassas, Knefler sought to encourage Wallace by concluding, "the latest dispatches received will not improve the impression so rapidly gaining hold upon the minds of the people."[6]

As a result of his refusal to seek peaceful co-existence with members of this exclusive club, Wallace ultimately became a casualty of its influence. Had Wallace desired to deal with those West Point professionals rather than oppose them at virtually every turn, the history of his participation in the war might well have been written differently. On more than one occasion, Wallace proved he was a very competent, self-educated, civilian, amateur soldier. He demonstrated he was as knowledgeable and capable in the art and science of warfare as some of the very best professionals his army had to offer. He certainly possessed the intuition and the audacity of thought and action that Lincoln prized but often found wanting in his generals. After Shiloh, had Wallace been able to retain his status as a primary player in the western theater, principally by using discretion in what he said and when he said it, it might well have been Wallace and his men who scaled Lookout Mountain or who witnessed the dynamite explode at Petersburg creating the crater.

Wallace's military career lacked permanent traction primarily because he was not, and never would be, a team player. He was forever at the center of one controversy or another. The professionals like Grant had things to worry about other than Wallace's temperament and the often inexplicable problems he caused. In time, Grant simply grew weary of Wallace the man. This weariness had little to do with the value he may have placed on Wallace's military abilities. In the end, Grant's acknowledgment of Wallace's military performance at Monocacy suggests he might have preferred to have had Wallace with him throughout the war. This, however, is speculation. What is clear is that whereas Halleck put Wallace on the shelf following Shiloh, in the final analysis Grant kept him there.[7]

The controversy over events at Shiloh was both real and damaging to Wallace. The cover-up and the effect it had upon Grant, particularly in the situations and events Rawlins fabricated, were likewise real. Both did damage to Wallace's military career but not to the extent that Wallace did himself. To be sure, Badeau's campaign biography had brought the controversy into the public arena. That was 1868, however, and nothing could or would be settled other than Grant's victory at the national polls. More importantly, for the continuation of the controversy, Badeau had given it some new life by shifting the paradigm of the debate from being "lost" and taking the "wrong" road to the parameters of time and distance, along with words like "slow," "tardy," "dilatory," and even "cowardice."[8]

With Badeau's two volumes, those who believed Wallace acted that day as a man indifferent to the task at hand, as a man wasting a tragic amount of time sitting on a log,[9] as an officer marching his men at too casual a rate of speed toward the battlefield, as one who frequently rested his troops while thousands of his comrades fought against surprise and the Rebel yell just a few miles down the road—all who held such a view now had proof of their claims in the public forum. It was easy to blame it all on Wallace. His critics could now maintain he was responsible for the tragedy that was Shiloh, particularly for all of Olney's "houses of mourning." Yet, at the same time, the controversy was starting to lose its appeal. Only the veterans and the historians seemed to care.

The cover-up manufactured in 1863 had never gained any traction with the public at large and thus, beyond how it influenced Grant, it never had much impact. By the time the cover-up documents became public in the mid-1880s, Halleck, Stanton, and Rawlins were dead. Grant was dying. Few seemed interested in analyzing Shiloh in the specific light suggested by the cover-up.

In the spring of 1895, Wallace sought scientific evidence to attack the content of Badeau's new paradigm.[10] Joined by three wartime comrades, Brig. Gen. George F. McGinnis, Lt. Col. James R. Ross, and Lt. James Brown, Wallace walked and "chained the route" taken by the 3rd Division on April 6. Recounting this adventure, Wallace observed, "We did not merely step the route. I employed the surveyor of Hardin County and paid his chain and consulted his compass as he followed us." The result was clear and convincing. "Instead of six miles," Wallace proudly exclaimed, "by actual chain measurement, my division moved full seventeen miles from half-past eleven in the forenoon till dusk in the evening. Instead of going from the fight, every step was toward it." He noted that any soldier would agree that under the best of physical conditions, a march of fourteen miles a day would be average. "Yet that day we moved over eighteen miles, under disadvantages seldom encountered."

Wallace was now convinced he had confirmed the truth of his day at Shiloh. He had empirical evidence to sustain his position, evidence in the form of a recreated march measured with precision by an old-fashioned surveyor's tripod and chain. His demonstration and the indisputable mathematical verification it produced had little impact on the controversy. For one thing, no one sent out a second surveying team seeking either to verify or to contradict Wallace's findings. None of those still participating in the controversy, other than Wallace, gave the impression they cared in the least about this new evidence. If now, more than thirty years after the guns had fallen silent, one were going to continue to engage in discussions concerning the march, all one needed to do was choose—either you were or you were not in the Wallace camp.

Back in 1868, when Grant finally corresponded with Wallace, he had given Wallace not one but two openings. The first was his suggestion that Wallace publish his collection of supporting letters. Wallace rejected this. Second, Grant made two startling admissions. He disclosed to Wallace that "my orders to you were given verbally to a Staff Officer to communicate." The aforementioned officer, on his own initiative, "made a memorandum of the order he received. That memorandum," Grant stated, "I never saw."[11]

One must wonder where Wallace's military reputation might stand today if he had publically confronted Grant in early 1868 using both this letter and his April 5, 1862, letter to W. H. L. Wallace as the basis for his arguments. His sense of personal honor simply precluded that possibility. He had no intention of publically challenging his general in any fashion; no desire to argue in public with, and potentially damage, the man who would be the next president of the United States. Nevertheless, Grant had acknowledged he had never seen anything remotely resembling a written order addressed to Wallace. He admitted he could say with much less certainty than Wallace what the contents of that order were.

At this time, Wallace surely was aware that before leaving Savannah, Grant had issued written orders to both Nelson and Buell. Hence, Wallace might also have confronted Grant with two questions: "First, would it not have been more beneficial to retain Nelson in readiness at Savannah, as you had done with me at Crump's, until you had fully assessed the situation?" "Second, if in fact the Confederates were concentrating against me at Crump's Landing, what earthly advantage would accrue to me, you, or to the cause if the Army of the Ohio was then marching toward Pittsburg Landing five miles to the south and on the wrong side of the river?" Had Wallace truly been interested in exonerating himself regardless of the expense to Grant, there was an appropriate third question he could have asked—"Once you encountered the *Warner* and then left it to continue your trip to Pittsburg Landing, what were you doing for the thirty minutes or so it required to complete that trip?" Wallace refused to ask these questions. In one respect, his actions were quite honorable; for him personally, they were overwhelmingly tragic.

That last question illuminates one of Grant's greatest mistakes at Shiloh. He had left Wallace at Crump's with instructions to stand ready waiting future orders. He then encountered the *Warner* with its messenger from W. H. L. Wallace. After receiving that information, he instructed the *Warner* to follow him to Pittsburg Landing rather than continue downriver to deliver that news to Wallace, accompanied, perhaps, by new orders from Grant. During the next half hour or so as the trip wound upriver to Pittsburg Landing, Grant apparently did nothing to resolve the issue of where to order Wallace to march. He failed, for example, to spend any portion of his remaining time on the *Tigress* drafting two written, alternative orders for Wallace, one to apply if the Rebels were attacking Pittsburg Landing, the other if they were advancing against Wallace at Crump's Landing. He certainly had the time and opportunity to do this.

His failure or inability to act in this regard is inexplicable as well as inexcusable. While confined to the quarterdeck of the *Tigress*, Grant had an absurdly abundant amount of time to do something with Wallace. He did nothing and that failure constituted a major mistake. Had he responded differently to the uncertainty of the situation confronting him, had he valued precision in communication as a means of addressing the doubts assailing him at that moment, conceivably the course of the battle at Shiloh, not to mention Wallace's military career, might well have gone very differently. He seemed to be weak, indecisive, and confused. Based upon prior experience, Grant knew that fortune favored audacity. In the early morning hours of the first day at Shiloh, Grant abandoned this precept. Wallace would do the same several hours later on the Shunpike.

Buckland suggested that had Wallace only continued his march down the Shunpike and struck the attacking Rebels in their rear, left flank, Shiloh might easily have been a one-day battle, producing an overwhelming Union victory. Initially, Wallace had seen it otherwise. In his battlefield report, he commented that if he had disregarded Rowley's instructions, his advance would have come to an end "in the enemy's rear, where, in the unfortunate condition of the battle, my command was in danger of being entirely cut off." He characterized Rowley's new directive to countermarch as being the more sensible thing to do. In his 1863 letter to Halleck, Wallace expressed doubt that this had been the correct decision.

He was certain that Grant would never have given him the authority to "continue my march and unsupported, form line of battle on the ground his whole army had been beaten from." Even though he might "have successfully cut my way through the enemy, fighting superior forces over that space," he gave Halleck the only conclusion Old Brains would accept. Had he continued, he asked rhetorically, "in what condition would my regiments have been to give the general the assistance he so much required?" A countermarch was simply more "prudent."[12]

As the years passed, Wallace rethought and redefined his position on the advisability of his decision to countermarch. As early as 1884, as he reassessed his decision, Wallace boldly suggested to Grant that when Rowley found him "the enemy had used the last of his reserves. I would have taken the bluff on which Sherman had been camped in the morning and, without opposition, effected my deployment." Forgetting that by the time he consulted with Rowley, the Rebel early-morning pillaging of Union campsites had largely ceased, Wallace nevertheless told Grant that he would have then descended "upon the horde plundering the sutlers and drinking in the streets of the camp. Their fears would have magnified my command."[13] By 1896, Wallace enthusiastically conceded that his decision to retrace his steps back to the River Road was ill-advised. He now believed he should have proceeded apace to the rear of the Confederate battle line notwithstanding Rowley's entreaties to the contrary. Hence, he pointedly asked Gen. James B. Wilson, "who shall tell the result had I been permitted to go on in my march?" He then described how he had been so badly served by events that day. "Many a time," he wrote to Wilson, "seeing as we see in dreams, I have beheld Thayer's deployed regiments moving through those tented streets [Sherman's overrun camp], a wave crested with bayonets, and heard the demoralized hordes [Confederate rear guard] rushing panic-struck upon their engaged lines."[14]

This was much more than the ramblings of a man grown old in the resolution of a controversy. These were the heart-wrenching expressions of a man who finally realized that he had made a terrible mistake at Shiloh. At a critically decisive instant, he shunned and turned away from "l'audace." Like Grant had done just hours before, Wallace denied his innermost instincts. He had obeyed orders and turned from one portion of the battlefield to countermarch to another. He had acted defensively with caution rather than offensively with audacity and celerity. He had not continued forward to that very place where he knew he should be. In so doing, he had failed his state, his country, and his men. As importantly, he had failed himself. His reward for making that decision on the Shunpike to follow his superior's orders was anything but honor and glory. "And still," Wallace concluded, "in moments when personal ambition gets the better of me, I hold Rowley's coming my greatest quarrel with Fortune. Oh, if he had remained lost in the woods an hour longer."[15]

Wallace spent the first year of his military service pursuing adventure, defending his country, seeking the restoration of the honor of his state, and striving for personal honor and glory. Because of his efforts, all would remember "Buena Vista." At Romney, Fort Donelson, the second day of Shiloh, and Monocacy, he convincingly proved he understood how to lead men in battle. Honor and glory were elusive, however. One minute both were his; the next both instantly evaporated in a plethora of tasteless and unbecoming words such as "lost," "late," and that damnable "laggard." He had defeated the Rebels at Donelson but he was powerless before the enemies that massed against him after Shiloh—Halleck, Grant, Morton, Stanton, the professional military establishment, and most certainly himself.

He spent the years after Shiloh until his death re-marching Shiloh. As he pursued this adventure, he sought to restore his honor in the hope he would be remembered. Upon his death on February 15, 1905, he was still battling the specter of Shiloh. He died believing his personal campaign for exoneration and thus redemption had ended in failure. Not so was the near universal opinion of the men of the 11th Indiana, the 8th Missouri, and the men of Wallace's 3rd Division, the Army of the Tennessee, who had marched with him to preserve the Union, first at Romney, then at Fort Henry and Fort Donelson, and lastly at Shiloh.[16]

NOTES

Introduction

1. Wallace to Grant, September 16, 1884, "The March of Lew Wallace's Division to Shiloh," *Battles and Leaders of the Civil War*, vol. 1 (New York: The Century Company, 1887), 610. All future references to articles appearing in this series will be cited by author, title, *Battles and Leaders*, with appropriate volume and page numbers.

2. Wallace to Col. John Thomas Smith, undated letter, in John Thomas Smith, *A History of the Thirty-first Regiment of Indiana Volunteer Infantry in the War of Rebellion* (Cincinnati: Western Methodist Book Concern, 1900), 197.

3. Wallace first used this phrase in 1896 in a letter to James G. Wilson. He believed his "greatest quarrel with fortune" occurred when Rowley found him in the mid-afternoon of April 6, interrupting his march to the battlefield. Wallace to Wilson, November 6, 1896, *William P. Palmer Collection* (copy in *Wallace Collection*), 34. Wallace further suggested that fortune had already deserted him once that day. Grant's order to Wallace was in writing but his adjutant, Capt. Fred Knefler, after three other of Wallace's staff officers had read the order, lost it when he stuck the paper in his sword belt for safekeeping. Later that day, something jarred the paper loose and it fell to the ground and was lost. This paper contained the only written evidence of what Grant had instructed Wallace to do. Wallace never blamed Knefler for this cruel twist of fate. "We could not foresee," he wrote to Wilson "what all its subsequent production would have saved me." Ibid., 23.

4. Wallace to Aaron Blair, April 3, 1862, *Wallace Collection*.

5. Lew Wallace, *An Autobiography* (New York: Harper & Brothers, 1906), 1:244.

6. Ibid., 1:242–43.

7. Lew Wallace, "Fifth-Street Market Square Speech," Cincinnati, July 31, 1862, *New York Times* 11, no. 3388 (August 3, 1862), 8; Wallace to Susan Elston Wallace, July 10, 1861, *Wallace Collection*. Wallace never deviated from his belief that the war was being fought to preserve the Federal Union. As early as December, 1861, he added an abolitionist component to his perception. He summarized his recently formed belief in a letter to Susan, noting, "However we may go into the war, we shall come out of it abolitionists." Wallace to Susan, December 22, 1861, ibid. Federalism and Abolitionism came together in his testimony before the

Joint Congressional Committee on the Conduct of the War on July 9, 1862 (see Chapter Eleven). Here he confronted, challenged, and in so many ways lost to both the professional military establishment as well as the professional political establishment. An analysis of Wallace's testimony that day is critical to an understanding of the man as well as the subsequent rapid decline in his military fortunes, which, at the time of this testimony, was just beginning.

8. The one possible exception was in his marriage. His wife, Susan Elston Wallace, was more likely than not the dominant figure in the relationship.

9. Lossing to Wallace, March 17, 1863, *Wallace Collection.* Actually, Lossing wrote that Wallace appeared "to ride Pegasus and Buscephalus with equal ease and grace." Pegasus was the winged stallion of Greek mythology said to have been sired by the God Poseidon. Buscephalus was the stallion, trained and ridden to military glory by Alexander the Great.

10. Edward M. Coffman, "The Duality of the American Military Tradition: A Commentary," *The Journal of Military History* 54 (October 2000) 972–75. While the U.S. army in the Mexican War was filled with volunteers led by officers culled from the ranks of state and local politicians, it was the Regular Army, led by professionally trained soldiers like Winfield Scott and Zachary Taylor, aided by younger West Point graduates like Lee, Grant, and Jackson, that was victorious. Throughout the 1850s, Americans largely forgot the Regular Army and its professionals. They remembered the minutemen of Lexington Green, the "rude bridge that arched the flood" at Concord, and Old Hickory's frontiersmen at New Orleans. In the latter part of the decade, Americans turned their attention to the glitz and glamor of volunteer militia companies organized throughout the United States, of which Wallace's Montgomery Guards was but one example. When war finally came in 1861, North and South of necessity turned to volunteers and the politically appointed officers to fill their armies. As the war dragged on, the transition to the ascendancy of the professional Regular Army over the volunteer military was completed on the battlefield. Coffman identified only four volunteers who survived the war near the top of the military ladder—Nathan Bedford Forrest, John B. Gordon, John A. Logan, and Nelson A. Miles. In 1865, at war's end, Wallace remained a major general but was without a battlefield command. Perhaps that is why Coffman overlooked him. See also: Theodore G. Gronert, "The First National Pastime in the Middle West," *Indiana Magazine of History* 29 (September 1933): 171–86.

11. Wallace to David Wallace, December 19, 1846, in Oran Perry (comp.), *Indiana in the Mexican War* (Indianapolis: William Burford, 1908), 127–28; Wallace to Susan, February 27, 1862, April 17, 1862, *Wallace Collection.*

12. Alexander D. McCook, "Six Weeks in the Mud," *Overland Monthly: An Out West Magazine* 2 (March 1869): 217.

13. Wallace to Grant, September 16, 1884, in Wallace, *Battles and Leaders,* 1:610.

14. Wallace to Susan, December 8, 1862, *Wallace Collection.* Reacting to Burnside's defeat at Fredericksburg, Wallace told Susan "I am fast falling into the belief that we no longer have any such thing as pure patriotism. Everything is politics. Even the blood of soldiers is a subject of political traffic." Then, he then addressed a recurring complaint—"The fault is not with our soldiers, but with our generals." Wallace to Susan, December 22, 1862, ibid.

15. When the 11th Indiana arrived in Paducah in the fall of 1861, Capt. Issac C. Elston, Jr., Wallace's brother-in-law, learned that the U.S. Senate had confirmed Wallace to the rank of brigadier general. When the novelty of that news wore off, the dullness of everyday camp life returned. Wallace confronted this directly with an ever-increasing number of written complaints mailed back home. Either to quiet anxiety on the home front or to snipe at his brother-in-law, Elston wrote to his sister that "Lew is full of complaints because he has no brigade assigned him commensurate with his abilities." Elston to Mary Elston, December 14, 1861, *Wallace Collection.*

16. See: Shelby Foote, *The Civil War: A Narrative* (New York: Random House, 1958), 1:343 ["Wallace 'at last' arrived"]; Bruce Catton, *Grant Moves South* (Boston: Little, Brown, 1960), 241 [Wallace had a "complete misunderstanding about the roads he was supposed to take. He had marched his division off on a wrong road"]; General Sir James Marshall-Cornwall, *Grant as Military Commander* (New York: Van Nostrand Reinhold Company, 1970, republished New York: Barnes & Noble Book, 1995), 76 [Wallace was on the "wrong road"]; William S. McFeely, *Grant: A Biography* (New York: W. W. Norton, 1981), 113 ["The only problem was that he had taken the wrong road"]; James M. McPherson, *Battle Cry of Freedom. The Civil War Era* (New York: Oxford Univ. Press, 1988), 409 [Wallace "took the wrong road"]; Jean Edward Smith, *Grant* (New York: Simon and Schuster, 2001), 196 [Wallace never appreciated "the urgency of the situation"]; John Keegan, *The American Civil War: A Military History* (New York: Knopf Doubleday, 2009), 132 (Wallace "lost his way"). The only agreement between these viewpoints is that Wallace did not arrive on the field of battle until darkness had fallen and therefore did not participate in the first day's fighting.

1. The Adventure Begins

1. Chelsea L. Lawlis, "Migration to the Whitewater Valley, 1820–1830," *Indiana Magazine of History* 43 (September 1947): 232; Irving McKee, "The Early Life of Lew Wallace," *Indiana Magazine of History* 37 (September 1941): 205–6; George S. Cottman, "The Whitewater Valley," *Indiana Magazine of History* 1 (December 1905): 206; Robert E. Morsberger and Katharine M. Morsberger, *Lew Wallace: Militant Romantic* (New York: McGraw-Hill, 1980), 1–2; Irving McKee, *"Ben-Hur" Wallace: The Life of General Lew Wallace* (Berkeley: University of California Press, 1947), 1–30; Dorothy Riker, ed., *Messages and Papers relating to the Administration of David Wallace, Governor of Indiana, 1837–1840* (Indianapolis: Indiana Historical Bureau, 1963), 4; George W. Cullum, *Biographical Register of the Officers and Graduates of the U.S. Military Academy at West Point, N.Y.*), 2nd ed. (New York, 1868), 1: 214.

2. Riker, *Messages and Papers,* 5. William, the eldest son of David and Esther, was born in 1825, John, who died in 1832, was two years younger than Lew, while Edward, the youngest, was born in 1831.

3. McKee, "The Early Life of Lew Wallace," 205–7.

4. Cottman argued that when the land office opened in Brookville, thousands of people intent on purchasing land, accompanied by "the presumable surplus of travelers," visited the town annually. This was the origin of Brookville's unexpected

prosperity. When the state legislature moved the land office to Indianapolis, the community plummeted overnight into a time of "sorry decadence" during which "money became all but extinct." David moved his family to Covington where he built a modestly successful law practice and joined his brother's "merchandising" business as a silent partner. Undoubtedly, the onset of Brookville's localized depression strongly influenced David's decision. Cottman, "The Whitewater Valley," 206–7; Riker, *Messages and Papers*, 7–9.

5. Summing up his early formative experiences, Wallace wrote that "When I was a boy, I ran wild in the great woods of my native State. I hunted, fished, went alone, slept with my dog, was happy, and came out with a constitution." Wallace to Bainton, November 22, 1887, *Wallace Collection*, in Morsberger and Morsberger, *Wallace: Militant Romantic*, 1.

6. Wallace, *An Autobiography* (New York: Harper & Brothers, 1906), 1:10.

7. It is interesting to note that in his epic, *Ben-Hur: A Story of the Christ*, Wallace named his secular heroine Esther. In later years, Wallace developed a son's love and respect for his stepmother, Zerelda.

8. Wallace, *An Autobiography*, 1:9, 32, 45.

9. Ibid., 1:73–77.

10. Ibid., 1:27. Here Lew was talking about his mother, Esther, not his stepmother, Zerelda. Lew reported that Esther often tied him to a bedpost or required him to wear "a woman's frock or petticoat." Wallace implies that this last punishment was the most effective of any administered by his parents. He was so annoyed and embarrassed by it that for the moment he lost all thought of continuing his bad behavior.

11. Wallace, *An Autobiography*, 1:14–15.

12. Ibid., 1:37–42. At the time, his father David was away actively seeking to become governor of the state. His mother had died several years earlier and his father had yet to remarry. His older brother William had been formally admitted to the preparatory school and Lew, being lonesome, followed him to Crawfordsville. Wallace later claimed that being recognized as the son of the governor (or perhaps the Whig gubernatorial candidate) readily gained him admission to the school at the tender age of nine.

13. Ibid., 1:55–59. Hoshour introduced Wallace to Lord Byron, Oliver Goldsmith, and Isaiah of the Old Testament as well as the four Gospels of the New Testament. Wallace recalled how he marveled at "the small part given to the three wise men" in the story of the birth of Christ. "Little did I dream then," he wrote years later in his *Autobiography*, "what those few verses were to bring me—that out of them *Ben-Hur* was one day to be evoked." Unfortunately, Wallace never explained why he spent only a year with Hoshour. The reason might have been financial. David's term as governor had recently ended. Although now practicing law in Indianapolis, he might have lacked the financial resources to fund another year at the Centreville academy.

14. Ibid.,1:63–72.

15. Ibid., 1:81–84.

16. Ibid., 1:77–79. Unfortunately, the only first-person account of this incident appears in Wallace's *Autobiography*. It is consistent with young Wallace's desire to be free of all artificial constraints.

17. McKee, *Ben-Hur Wallace*, 19–20; Morsberger and Morsberger, *Wallace: Militant Romantic*, 39. When Susan completed her husband's *Autobiography* after his death, she added Clemmer's observations written when Lew was twenty-one. Wallace, *An Autobiography*, 1:199–200. Clemmer's description of Lew's beard and mustache, which both McKee and the Morsbergers accept, is problematical. In most known photographs of Wallace before the war, he appeared clean-shaven.

18. Maurice Nicholson, "The Provincial American," *The Atlantic Monthly* 107 (March 1911): 313–14.

19. Wallace to William Wallace, August 23, 1850, *Wallace Collection.*

20. Ibid.

21. Wallace to William Wallace, February 17, 1853, *Wallace Collection.* A "clipeding" is a nickname.

22. Wallace, *An Autobiography*, 1:226–27.

23. Ibid., 1:226–27, 247. So far, Wallace's *Autobiography* has been the source for much of his early life. This might be a suspicious approach since self-indulgence and flattery are two words commonly associated with memoirs. The intent is not to cast Wallace in stone but to describe him and detail some of his formative experiences as he saw himself. This should give the reader some input into deciding who Wallace was and why he acted as he did. Embellishments aside, Wallace lived the events he recounted. Perhaps it is the embellishments that accurately describe Wallace best. He alluded to this in his "Note" to *The Fair God*, when he suggested that if only history could be taught by the persons actually engaged in living it the retelling of such events would be "more attractive" to its listeners. "If the makers of history, contradistinguished from its writers, could teach it to us directly, one telling would suffice to secure our lasting remembrances. The reason is, that the narrative so proceeding derives a personality and reality not otherwise attainable, which assists in making way to our imagination and the sources of our sympathy." Lew Wallace, "Note by the Author," *The Fair God or, The Last of the'Tzins: A Tale of the Conquest of Mexico* (Boston: Houghton, Mifflin and Company, 1888), iii. See also: Lee Scott Theisen, "The Public Career of General Lew Wallace, 1845–1905" (unpublished Ph.D. dissertation, University of Arizona, 1973), 1–26; Morsberger and Morsberger, *Wallace: Militant Romantic*, 3–19; McKee, "Early Life of Lew Wallace," 205–16; McKee, *"Ben-Hur" Wallace*, 25–30.

24. Wallace to Davis, December 11, 1860; January 3, 1861; January 25, 1861; February 25, 1861, *Wallace Collection.*

25. Wallace, *An Autobiography*, 1:200; W. H. H. Terrell, *Indiana in the War of the Rebellion: Report of the Adjutant General* (Indianapolis, 1869), 1:6, 564. Wallace often misjudged the motives of others. In late 1862 and 1863, he turned to Morton as a friend and ally and received surprisingly little in return. Margaret Stephenson wrote that John C. Nelson, Shiloh veteran and former Mayor of Logansport, Indiana, personally told her that Morton "wanted all the honor and glory in war for himself, and he would not consent to there being any great Hoosier generals. . . . Lew Wallace should have been a general but Governor Morton wouldn't permit it." Margaret Stephenson, "Reminiscences of Logansport Civil War Veterans," *Indiana Magazine of History* 27, no. 4 (December 1932), 271. In April, 1861, Morton appointed a West Point graduate from Indiana Thomas A. Morris as the senior

Brigadier General of the Indiana Volunteers. In August 1861, Morton gave that post to another Hoosier graduate of West Point, Joseph J. Reynolds. Both times he passed over Wallace. Joseph A. Parsons, Jr., "Indiana and the Call for Volunteers, April, 1861," *Indiana Magazine of History* 54, no. 1 (March 1958), 2–23.

2. A Meteoric Rise

1. R. C. Burley, "Indiana in the Mexican War," *Indiana Magazine of History* 15, no. 4 (December 1919): 293–307; 16, no. 1 (March 1920): 48–68; Steven E. Woodworth, *Manifest Destinies: America's Expansion and the Road to the Civil War* (New York: Knopf, 2010), 221–34; David A. Clary, *Eagles and Empire: The United States, Mexico, and the Struggle for a Continent* (New York: Bantam Books, 2009), 271–84. See Burley, "Indiana," 15:307, and 16:46, 60–61. Nearly sixty years after Buena Vista, Wallace demonstrated the degree to which Taylor's judgments still offended him. "In all American history," he wrote, "there is not another sentence which, taken as a judgment of men in mass, equals that one for cruelty and injustice—none so wanton in misstatement, none of malice so obstinately adhered to by its author, none so comprehensive in its damage, since it dishonored a whole state. . . ." Lew Wallace, *An Autobiography* (New York: Harper & Brothers, 1906), 1:177.

2. Wallace, *An Autobiography,* 1:271–72; *Harper's Weekly* 5, no. 315 (June 22, 1861): 388–89.

3. Lew Wallace, *Autobiographical Sketch,* August 16, 1863. Lossing requested Wallace write a letter to him containing this autobiographical information. Wallace to Lossing, August 16, 1863, *Wallace Collection* (Indianapolis: Indiana Historical Society), 14–15.

4. Wallace proudly told Lossing that the 11th Indiana was "an assembly of mechanics, farmers, lawyers, doctors and ministers. They were all young, and full of life and ambitious . . . quick, shrewd, and enterprising, just the material for Zouaves." Wallace, *Autobiographical Sketch,* 13, 16.

5. Wallace to Lane, April 6, 1861, in *The War of the Rebellion: A Compilation of the Official Records of the Union and Confederate Armies,* series 3, 1 (Washington, D.C.: Government Printing Office, 1899), 65, hereinafter cited *OR,* with all citations being to series 1 unless otherwise noted as above. All volumes in series 1 were published between 1880 and 1898. "Ninety-day Wonders" is World War II nomenclature. It is nevertheless an apt description of what Wallace sought to create. Lane endorsed Wallace's proposal and forwarded it to Cameron, noting that "the writer of the above letter is one of our best military men, and entirely reliable in his devotion to the Union." Gronert found that over time many militia companies founded in the 1850s lost their inclination to be military units and became more social in nature. This was certainly not the case with outfits like Ellsworth's Chicago Zouaves and Wallace's Montgomery Guards. Theodore G. Gronert, "The First National Pastime in the Middle West," *Indiana Magazine of History* 29 (September 1933): 171–86.

6. Wallace to Susan, May 6, 1861, *Wallace Collection;* Wallace, *Autobiographical Sketch,* 17.

7. Wallace to Susan, May 6, 1861, May 11, 1861, *Wallace Collection*. Wallace pictured his campsite as "the most romantic encampment in the State. . . . From the hill-top imagine our band of twenty-five players making music to listeners in Kentucky, on the river, and in the city, the latter just far enough off to catch the strains melted into the mellowest music."

8. Wallace, *Autobiographical Sketch*, 17; Wallace to Susan, May 11, 1861, *Wallace Collection*. Wallace had asked Lane to intervene. Morton acknowledged his awareness of this in a telegram to Secretary of the Interior Caleb B. Smith, a fellow Hoosier politician. On June 5, he angrily informed Smith that he knew that Lane, Smith, and others "have procured Wallace's regiment to be sent to Cumberland." This exertion of political influence on Wallace's behalf without consulting Morton first produced "great dissatisfaction" because "Col. [William P.] Benton's and Col. [Mahlon D.] Manson's regiments, being the 8th and 10th . . . are still in camp." Morton to Smith, June 5, 1861, *Morton Telegraph Book*, 1:66 (http://www.in.gov/icpr/2566.htm). Wallace never hesitated to ask Lane for help, particularly after Shiloh. In this sense, Wallace was a "political general." This fact seemed to bother only Morton and Halleck. It is doubtful that Wallace appreciated the problems he might encounter as the result of Lane's intervention or the preferential treatment Lane had secured for him. He certainly gave no indication he knew how angry Morton was. See: Gail Stephens, *Shadow of Shiloh* (Indianapolis: Indiana Historical Society Press, 2010), 22–23.

9. Wallace to Patterson, June 14, 1861, *OR*, 2:123–24; *New York Times* 10, no. 3048 (June 28, 1861): 2–3. The correspondent for *Harper's Weekly* 5, no. 235 (July 6, 1861): 423, identified Romney as "another of those brilliant skirmishes which have marked the progress of the war so far." Hereinafter, as appropriate, the author will identify Wallace's first offensive effort of the war as the "Romp to Romney." The fact that the march was probably more like seventy-five miles, of which thirty-three were on foot, should not diminished the accuracy of the label. It is not only highly descriptive of what actually occurred on June 12–13 but also served, at least in Wallace's mind, as a point of comparison with one other Union officer's excessive caution in the face of the enemy. As representative of that unfortunate affair, the author has created a second tag, the "Creep to Corinth."

10. *Frank Leslie's Illustrated Weekly* 14, no. 342 (May 17, 1862): 53–54.

11. Wallace and his men extended their mastery over the battlefield by practicing Zouave fighting methods at all times even during routine camp training exercises. One month after Romney, Wallace described a friendly camp competition between the 11th Indiana and "the pet Massachusetts regiment." The latter, according to Wallace, had begun its daily drill in two parts, with one group of Bay State men on one side of a road and a second group on Wallace's side of the same road. "In ten minutes," Lew triumphantly announced to Susan, "the whole body, officers and men, quit that they might match us in the Zouaves, and stood so for more than an hour. They surrendered completely." Wallace to Susan, July 15, 1861, *Wallace Collection*.

12. Patterson to Wallace, June 6, 1861, *OR*, 2:668.

13. Wallace to Patterson, June 13, 1861, *OR*, 2:123–24. What actually happened at Romney may not have been beyond what Patterson intended for Wallace to

do. On June 12, Lt. Gen. Winfield Scott dispatched a series of orders to Col. C. P. Stone. Accompanying those orders, Scott sent a copy of Patterson's June 11 report to Scott in which Patterson stated that Wallace had arrived at Cumberland on June 10 and that "He will call to-day on small parties of secession militia in his vicinity." *OR*, 2:105, 675–76. It all depends on whether or not one agrees with Wallace's very broad interpretation of "call," "militia," and "vicinity."

14. *Philadelphia Inquirer*, June 14, June 17, 1861, 3; Wallace to Lane, *Wisconsin Patriot* 8, no. 13 (June 27, 1861): 4.

15. *Wisconsin Patriot* 8, no. 15 (June 29, 1861): 4.

16. *Philadelphia Inquirer*, June 17, 1861, 3; ibid., June 14, 1861, 4; *New York Herald* 26, no. 171 (June 21, 1861): 5; *New-York Daily Tribune* 21, no. 6287 (June 13, 1861): 1. There can be no question that the possibility of personal glory and honor that awaited him at Romney was a major factor in propelling Wallace down that dark, windy, mountainous road the night of June 12.

17. Johnston to Cooper, October 14, 1861, *OR*, 2:471–72; in *Lincoln Finds a General: A Military Study of the Civil War* (New York: The Macmillan Company, 1949), 1:71–72, mathematician turned historian Kenneth P. Williams wrote that when Johnston learned what actually transpired at Romney he recognized he had made a mistake by abandoning a tactically superior position to McClellan. Williams attributed Johnston's pullout from Harpers Ferry and relocation to Winchester solely to Wallace's success at Romney.

18. Wallace to Patterson, June 27, 1861, *OR*, 2:134–35; *New York Herald* 21, no. 182 (July 2, 1861): 8.

19. *Philadelphia Inquirer*, July 8, 1861, 8; *New York Times* 10, no. 3049 (June 29, 1861): 1.

20. *Wisconsin Patriot* 8, no. 15 (June 29, 1861): 4; Wallace to Lane, *Wisconsin Patriot* 8, no. 43 (July 27, 1861): 4. In his *Autobiography*, Wallace reproduced a letter dated June 28, 1861, from Schuyler Colfax, then a member of the House of Representatives from Indiana. Colfax called the Kelly's Island affair "splendid," and further noted that President Lincoln "in a conversation with me, alluded especially to our splendid dash on Romney." Wallace was indeed becoming known beyond the boundaries of his native state. Wallace, *An Autobiography*, 1:306–7.

21. Wallace to McClellan, June 27, 1861, *OR*, 2:134.

22. McClellan to Scott, June 27, 1861, *OR*, 2:726–27; McClellan to Scott, June 28, 1861, *OR*, 2: 134.

23. Dennis Hart Mahan, *An Elementary Treatise on Advanced-Guard, Out-Post, and Detachment Service of Troops and the Manner of Posting and Handling Them in the Presence of an Enemy* (New York: Wiley and Putnam 1847), 171, 199, 198, 200, 202, 203. The "dictum" referenced herein was a favorite saying of the illustrious eighteenth-century military commander, Le Marechal de Saxe, a favorite of Louis XV of France. Wallace claimed, in his *Autobiographical Sketch*, to have received and read ["studied them carefully"] all the books he had requested from Davis. In addition to Mahan's *Outposts*, Wallace owned copies of Hardee's *Light Infantry Tactics;* Ellsworth's *Manual of Arms for Light Infantry;* Kelton's *Manuel on the Bayonet;* Mahan's *Field Fortifications;* and the U.S. War Department's *U.S. Infantry Tactics*, among others. Undoubtedly, from the way he pursued and waged war, Wallace

had read Mahan and was at Romney subjecting that knowledge to the test of practicality. Larry Paarlberg, Director of Lew Wallace Study, to author, November 13, 15, 2014. Romney made it clear that one observation Mahan made seemed to strike a responsive chord in Wallace. "In looking back on military history," Mahan wrote, "it may with truth be said that nothing is impossible to a determined will." Mahan believed that such a will consistently recognized and applied certain immutable principles of war. All winning strategic campaigns and the tactical maneuvers incident thereto were based upon the successful application of concepts such as "speed," "mobility," "surprise," "pursuit," "initiative," "activity," "audacity," and "vigor." Having no cavalry at Romney, Wallace could not implement "pursuit."

24. Mahan, *Outposts*, 207. One place where Wallace will be in the proverbial "right place" at the equally celebrated "right time" will be Saturday morning at the battle of Fort Donelson.

25. The cautious approach of these men to the battlefield could perhaps best be described as a case "of the slows." Wallace had proved at Romney he was aggressive, a man of action. Halleck preached that war was a methodical and deliberate chess game. Movement on the chess board was at some point imperative, but only after thoroughly examining all the possible options. Halleck would make no move before its time. Carl von Clausewitz, the illustrious Prussian commentator on the Napoleonic Wars, aptly described a Halleck-type thinker when he wrote in the early 1830s that "this glueing down of a great offensive plan of attack on a geometrical square is losing one's way in the regions of fallacy." Carl von Clausewitz, *On War*, trans. J. J. Graham (London: Kegan Paul, Trench, Trübner & Co. , 1908), 3, 164. For a different point of view, particularly with respect to McClellan, see: Joseph L. Harsh, "Battlesword and Rapier: Clausewitz, Jomini, and the American Civil War," *Military Affairs* 38 (December 1974): 135, 137.

26. Porter to Cadwalader, June 15, 1861, *OR*, 2:687–88; Wallace to Porter, June 15, 1861, *OR*, 689.

27. Porter to Cadwalader, June 15, 1861, *OR*, 2:687–88; Wallace to Porter, June 15, 1861, *OR*, 689; George W. Cullum, *Biographical Register of the Officers and Graduates of the U.S. Military Academy at West Point, N.Y., from its Establishment, March 16, 1802* (New York: D. Van Nostrand, 1868), 2nd ed., 118, 140, 753; Cullum, *Biographical Register* (Boston: Houghton, Mifflin and Company, 1891), 3rd ed., 568. Why Wallace chose to employ the word "fair" in his complaint or to include McClellan in this tirade is unclear. Perhaps unfortunately for him and his future career, Wallace suffered no adverse consequences from these complaints. This is a good example of the peevishness with which Wallace could respond to an order he deemed to be not only wrong but also a personal attack.

28. Johnston to Cooper, October 14, 1861, *OR*, 2:473; various telegrams from Patterson to Scott, and Scott to Patterson, July 12–18, 1861, *OR*, 2:164, 2:165, 2:166, 2:168, 2:170; on July 18, Patterson informed Scott that "the men are longing for their homes, and nothing can detain them." On July 19, Porter appealed to Wallace "He [Patterson] knows, too, that as long as danger threatens the regiment will not leave. Can you give him assurances they [the 11th Indiana] will remain till he can safely relieve them, which he thinks cannot exceed ten days, and may be much less?" *OR*, 2:171. Wallace agreed to this request.

29. *Frank Leslie's Illustrated Newspaper* 7, no. 299 (August 10, 1861): 201, 199.

30. *Harper's Weekly* 5, no. 238 (July 20, 1861): 453, 463. Both national magazines, *Harper's* and *Leslie's*, appeared to be in competition to determine who could do more to make Wallace and the 11th Indiana into national heroes. No doubt, Hoosier politicians like Lane and Colfax had a greater influence persuading Lincoln to create brigadier generals than either of these two national newspapers. However, one cannot ignore the close temporal proximity of these events on July 20, August 10, September 1, all on the heels of the Romp to Romney.

31. Special Orders No. 124, July 23, 1861, *OR*, 51:423; General Orders No. 46, July 19, 1861, *OR*, 2:171.

32. Gayle Thornbrough, Dorothy L. Riker, and Paula Corpuz, eds., *The Diary of Calvin Fletcher, Including Letters to and from Calvin Fletcher* (Indianapolis: Indiana Historical Society, 1980), 7:162.

33. Evansville *Journal*, August 15, 1861, reprinted in the *Philadelphia Inquirer*, August 19, 1861, 4. Interestingly, this same appeal appeared under a dateline of Indianapolis without editorial comment in the *Memphis Daily Appeal* 12, no. 185 (August 15, 1861): 2.

34. W. H. H. Terrell, *Indiana in the War of the Rebellion: Report of the Adjutant General*, (Indianapolis: Douglass & Conner, 1869), 1:564.

35. Thornbrough, *Diary of Calvin Fletcher*, 7:190.

3. Paducah

1. Lew Wallace, *An Autobiography* (New York: Harper & Brothers, 1906), 1:328–32.

2. "Proclamation to the Citizens of Paducah," September 6, 1861, in John Y. Simon, ed., *The Papers of Ulysses S. Grant* (Carbondale: Southern Illinois Univ. Press, 1967–2000), 2:194. Also found in *The War of the Rebellion: A Compilation of the Official Records of the Union and Confederate Armies* (Washington, D.C.: Government Printing Office, 1899), 52:189, part 1, hereinafter cited *OR*. Grant to Frémont, September 6, 1861, Simon, *Papers of Grant*, 4:197.

3. Grant to Paine, September 6, 1861, Simon, *Papers of Grant*, 4:198. On that same day, Frémont informed Grant that he had appointed Brig. Gen. Charles F. Smith to command at Paducah. Frémont to Grant, September 5, 1861, Simon, Papers of Grant, 3:471.

4. Wallace's letter was to be read to the assembled Democrats of Johnson County at their meeting in Franklin, Indiana. "The Duty of Democrats," *New York Times* 10, no. 3096 (August 25, 1861): 2. Wallace was undoubtedly pleased that the *Times* announced that "Col. WALLACE, the distinguished leader of the Eleventh Indiana Regiment" was the author.

5. Ibid.

6. The Lincoln administration indentified three categories of Southern white civilians specifically with respect to their property—committed secessionists, known sympathizers, and neutrals. The official Washington policy from April 1861, until late 1862, was labeled "conciliation." Many believed that if occupying

Northern armies treated Southern whites and their property with respect Southerners in great numbers would sever their ties to the Confederacy and rejoin the Union. In his Fifth Street Market Square speech in Cincinnati on July 31, 1862, Wallace characterized the Paducah-type expression of "conciliation" [Wallace mistakenly called it "reconciliation"] as the second of three great mistakes the federal government made in waging the war. Wallace, "Market Street Square Speech," July 31, 1862, *New York Times* 11, no. 3388 (August 3, 1862): 8. Wallace had proclaimed these same ideas to the Johnson County Democrats almost a year earlier. In the wake of a succession of battlefield losses in the East culminating with the "stand-off" at Antietam, the administration gradually abandoned conciliation and adopted a more pragmatic approach. Specifically, Union military commanders were encouraged to appropriate the property of Southern white civilians if such property had a discernible use in the prosecution of the war. Beginning in February 1864, the actions of the Lincoln administration and military initiated the transition to the "hard hand of war." Mark Grimsley, *The Hard Hand of War: Union Military Policy Toward Southern Civilians, 1861–1865* (Cambridge: Cambridge University Press, 1995), 2–6, 106.

7. Wallace to Susan, October 27, 1861, November 9, 1861, *Wallace Collection* (Indianapolis: Indiana Historical Society).

8. Leisure hours were spent primarily in three pursuits—reading, playing chess, "both essentially military," and evening visits from his junior officers. Wallace's military family included his brother-in-law, Maj. Isaac C. Elston Jr., or "Ike." Since his father-in-law was also known as Maj. Isaac C. Elston, Wallace mischievously wondered how the family would adjust to having two "majors." "What confusion is going to be entailed. . . . How are we ever to distinguish one Major Elston from the other?" Wallace inquired if "the older Major" ever voiced any pride in the "younger Major's" accomplishments? Earlier, Wallace had described his new headquarters in Paducah, where he was "beginning to live—like a General," to Susan, demonstrating that even in the midst of war, he still found time for beauty. "My quarters are in a house, one story, pleasant yard and shade trees about, flower patches in the front and planned almost exactly like ours at home." On at least one occasion, Wallace proved that he knew a good deal about his new task of soldiering. He wrote that Grant had narrowly escaped disaster at Belmont when Union soldiers stopped to plunder the Rebel camp rather than pursue the enemy. "Such conduct proves," Wallace concluded, "that after all, our army is not yet an army." Wallace to Susan, November 9, 1861, October 5, October 15, 1861, *Wallace Collection.*

9. Wallace to Susan, September 22, 1861, *Wallace Collection.*

10. Grant to Paine, *OR*, 4:198; Frank Moore, ed., *The Rebellion Record: A Diary of American Events* (New York, 1862), 3:89; Simon, *Papers of Grant*, 4:189. In a fiery and highly imaginative report of the Newsham/Knefler encounter, one correspondent portrayed Wallace as a hero. The writer claimed that several onlookers cried out "kill him" and one "struck at him [Newsham] with a long knife, barely missing him." Wallace allegedly shoved Smith's staff officer out of harm's way and "only the presence of Gen. Wallace saved the Aid-de-Camp from being torn to pieces by the agitated bystanders." *Daily Wabash Express* (Terre Haute, Indiana) 8, no. 258 (December 7, 1861): 2.

11. Smith, General Orders No. 36, November 27, 1861; Moore, *The Rebellion Record, ibid.*, 3:418. Smith was a reserved man who generally kept things like this to himself. It is therefore unclear just how severely Wallace's role in the Woolfolk Affair damaged his relationship with Smith. When Wallace took issue with the content of an order issued by a superior officer, conflict and consternation of some sort generally ensued.

12. Evansville (Indiana) *Journal*, November 25, 1861, as reported in the *Philadelphia Inquirer*, December 5, 1861, 2; "Excitement in Paducah—Quarrel Among the Generals," St. Louis *Democrat*, November 28, 1861; reported as "Trouble at Paducah," *New York Times* 11, no. 3186 (December 8, 1861): 3.

13. Evansville *Journal*, November 25, 1861; Jeffrey L. Patrick, ed., *Three Years with Wallace's Zouaves: The Civil War Memoirs of Thomas Wise Durham* (Macon: Mercer Univ. Press, 2003), 60; St. Louis *Democrat*, November 28, 1861; The correspondent for the *Democrat* stated that Smith, through an aide, ordered Wallace to take down the Stars and Stripes. "Wallace refused to obey the order, and sent word to Smith that the flag should not be taken down while there was a live man in his brigade." *New York Times*, December 8, 1861.

14. Evansville *Journal*, November 25, 1861.

15. Wallace, *An Autobiography*, 1:344–45; also cited in Benjamin Franklin Cooling, "The Reliable First Team: Grant and Charles Ferguson Smith," in *Grant's Lieutenants: From Cairo to Vicksburg*, ed. Steven E. Woodworth (Lawrence: Univ. of Kansas Press, 2001), 55.

16. Wallace had two strong authority figures in his early life, his father and his father-in-law. His father kicked him out of the home, seemingly deserting him in a time of need. General Morris and General McClellan appeared to have done much the same thing in the days immediately after Romney. Wallace believed the renowned "old Maj.," Susan's father, never liked him or accepted him into the family. Smith and Grant at times appeared to Wallace to react the same way. At various times, they all felt the sting of Wallace's pen.

17. Wallace was having difficulties with military authority and others being critical of him and his actions as early as the Mexican War. John McDougal was the elected Captain of Company H, 1st Indiana Volunteers, and Wallace was its 2nd Lieutenant. In October 1846, "Brother Bill" wrote Lew that rumors were circulating accusing Wallace of conspiring to obtain McDougal's position. Lew brushed off these concerns, noting his "enemies back home" were spreading such untruths because they were jealous. In November, Wallace expressed his hope that McDougal would not make "any more charges against me. He was mean, perfidious and dastardly." Wallace to William Wallace, October 29, November 18, 1846, *Wallace Collection;* Oran Perry, *Indiana in the Mexican War* (Indianapolis: W. B. Burford, 1908), 360.

18. General Orders No. 36, Moore, *The Rebellion Record*, 3:418; Wallace, *An Autobiography*, 1:350–51. Wallace claimed to have written this order. Morsberger and Morsberger, *Wallace: Militant Romantic*, 64, agree. This is possible but suspect. In the final analysis, General Orders No. 36 appears to be a somber, theoretical discourse on the rule of law during wartime. Both Wallace and Smith were capable of being its author. Yet, while Wallace would probably have agreed with its tenets,

given the strong emotions of the moment, it is doubtful he would have thought that the Woolfolk Affair warranted such an intellectual analysis.

19. Simon, *Papers of Grant*, 4:189n; Wallace, *An Autobiography*, 1:343–45. The writer for the *Dispatch* chose to exploit the Woolfolk episode as propaganda against both Smith and Wallace. He declared that from a "strictly military view," Wallace's actions that day had been "highly reprehensible." He excused Wallace's conduct, however, noting that "the circumstances of the case are strongly palliative, if not exonerating." Obviously a staunch Southerner, he concluded that "the flaunting of a rebel flag in the faces of our soldiers would, in the opinion of a majority of loyal men, seem sufficiently aggravating to justify almost any excess." One need only substitute the words "Stars and Stripes" for "rebel flag" to appreciate the writer's propagandistic intent. Wallace would have been appalled if he had discovered his conduct had been twisted in such a manner as to support the Rebel cause. The *Richmond* (Virginia) *Dispatch* 20, no. 136 (December 11, 1861): 3.

20. Indianapolis *Daily Journal* 11, no. 129 (December 3, 1861): 2.

21. Wallace once described Smith as "not only the best soldier I ever knew, but the most loyal and true to the core of his heart." Smith epitomized "an ideal friend" while simultaneously personifying "my ideal soldier." Smith was "naturally kind, genial, communicative," and one "who seemed to know army regulations by heart." The irony is that from his first days in Paducah until Smith's accidental death several weeks after Shiloh, Wallace frequently gave the impression that he believed Smith to be less a mentor and more an obstacle to his career. Wallace, *Autobiographical Sketch*, 22; Wallace, *An Autobiography*, 1:446; Lew Wallace, "The Capture of Fort Donelson," *in* Robert Underwood Johnson and Clarence Clough Buel, eds., *From Fort Sumter to Shiloh: Battles and Leaders of the Civil War* (New York, 1887), 1:405.

22. George W. Cullum, *Biographical Register of the Officers and Graduates of the U.S. Military Academy at West Point, N.Y., from its Establishment, March 16, 1802*, 2nd ed. (New York, 1868), 1:588; Smith to Frémont, November 11, 1861, *OR*, 3:299–300; Smith to Paine, Special Orders, November 6, 1861, *OR*, 3:301; Smith, General Orders No. 32, November 11, 1861, *OR*, 3:300.

23. *St. Louis Democrat*, November 28, 1861.

24. Wallace to Newsham, January 1, 1862, *OR*, 7:66–68; Rawlins, Special Orders No. 24, January 28, 1862, Simon, *Papers of Grant*, 4:124n; Grant to Kelton, January 31, 1862, ibid., 123; Grant to Smith, January 31, 1862, ibid., 124 (also in *OR*, 7:575); Grant to Smith, February 1, 1862, *OR*, 7:578; Benjamin Franklin Cooling, *Forts Henry and Donelson: The Key to the Confederate Heartland* (Knoxville: University of Tennessee Press, 1987), 89.

4. *The Twin Rivers Campaign and Fort Henry*

1. Lew Wallace, *An Autobiography* (New York: Harper & Brothers, 1906), 1:340–41.

2. Whittlesey to Halleck, November 20, 1861, *The War of the Rebellion: A Compilation of the Official Records of the Union and Confederate Armies* (Washington, D.C.: Government Printing Office, 1899), 7:440, hereinafter cited *OR;* Charles Whittlesey, *War Memoranda: Cheat River to the Tennessee, 1861–1862* (Cleveland, Ohio: W. W.

Williams, 1884), 28; Buell to McClellan, November 27, 1861, *OR*, 7:451–52; Lloyd Lewis, *Sherman: Fighting Prophet* (New York: Harcourt, Brace and Company, 1932), 210; Stephen E. Ambrose, *Halleck: Lincoln's Chief of Staff* (Baton Rouge: Louisiana State Univ. Press, 1962), 19; John F. Marszalek, *Commander of All of Lincoln's Armies: A Life of General Henry W. Halleck* (Cambridge, Harvard Univ. Press, 2004), 114; William T. Sherman, *Memoirs of General William T. Sherman by Himself* (New York: D. Appleton and Company, 1875), 1:219–20. There never was only one author of the Twin Rivers campaign.

3. Thomas Lawrence Connelly, *Army of the Heartland: The Army of Tennessee, 1861–1862* (Baton Rouge: Louisiana State Univ. Press, 1967), 3–4; O. Edward Cunningham, *Shiloh and the Western Campaign of 1862*, ed. Gary D. Joiner and Timothy B. Smith (New York: Casemate Publishers, 2007), 1–3; Benjamin Franklin Cooling, *Forts Henry and Donelson: The Key to the Confederate Heartland* (Knoxville: The Univ. of Tennessee Press, 1987), xi–xii, 44–46; Spencer C. Tucker, *Unconditional Surrender: The Capture of Forts Henry and Donelson* (Abilene: McMurry Univ. Press, 2001), 14.

4. Cooling, *Forts*, 11–14; Stanley F. Horn, *The Army of Tennessee: A Military History* (Indianapolis: Bobbs-Merrill Company, 1941), 41; Edwin C. Bearss, *The Fall of Fort Henry* (Fort Donelson Military Park: Eastern National, 1999), 6. In 1861, both Washington and Richmond vigorously proclaimed Kentucky's neutrality but seldom gave more than lip service to the concept. By the time Grant destroyed the myth of Kentucky neutrality with the taking of Paducah, fort construction in northern Tennessee had advanced beyond the point of reversing course and relocating the forts elsewhere. Arndt Stickles, *Simon Bolivar Buckner: Borderland Knight* (Chapel Hill: Univ. of North Carolina Press, 1940), 70, 74–75, 88–125.

5. Robert R. Howison, "History of the War," *The Southern Literary Messenger* 38, no. 5 (Richmond, May 1864): 266.

6. Tilghman to Confederate Adj. Gen. Samuel Cooper, *OR*, 7:139; Jesse Taylor, "The Defense of Fort Henry," *From Fort Sumter to Shiloh: Battles and Leaders of the Civil War*, ed. Robert Underwood Johnson and Clarence Clough Buel (New York, 1887), 1:368–369. Horn, *Army of Tennessee*, 77–78.

7. Howison, "History of the War" 38, no. 5, 266; Henry Walke, "The Western Flotilla at Fort Donelson, Island Number Ten, Fort Pillow and Memphis," *From Fort Sumter to Shiloh*, 1:430–31.

8. George W. Beaman, "Narrative from Fort Donelson," *Missouri Democrat*, February 17, 1862, in Frank Moore, *The Rebellion Record: A Diary of American Events* (New York, 1861–1868), 4:178.

9. Lew Wallace, "The Capture of Fort Donelson," *From Fort Sumter to Shiloh*, 1:398; John Fiske, *The Mississippi Valley in the Civil War* (Boston and New York: Houghton, Mifflin and Company, 1900), 57–58. Wallace also wrote that at one point during an impromptu advance of Union forces against the fort on February 13, the only thing Union soldiers had to do to prevail was "descend a hill entangled for two hundred yard with underbrush, climb an opposite ascent partly shorn of timber; make way through an abatis of tree-tops; then, supposing all that successfully accomplished, they would be at last in face of an enemy whom it was possible to re-enforce with all the reserves of the garrison—with the whole garrison if need be." Wallace, "The Capture of Fort Donelson," 1:411.

10. Grant to Halleck, January 28, 1862, *OR*, 7:121, is but one example. Benjamin Franklin Cooling, "The First Nebraska Infantry Regiment and the Battle of Fort Donelson," *Nebraska History* 45, no. 2 (June 1964), 133–34; Flag Officer Andrew H. Foote to Halleck, January 28, 1862, *The Official Records of the Union and Confederate Navies in the War of Rebellion*, series 1 (Washington, D.C., 1904), 22:524, hereinafter cited as *ORN*, with all citations to series 1 unless otherwise noted. In this particular appeal, Foote went so far as to assure Halleck he had previously sought Grant's permission to make this request.

11. Halleck believed that before undertaking any offensive action, all the pieces on the chess board of war had to be aligned as perfectly as possible. Halleck's orders to his subordinates reflected this philosophy, as did his moniker of "Old Brains." Halleck had little tolerance for individual initiative. There was too much at stake to be anything other than abundantly cautious. He was convinced that he could exercise better tactical control of any battlefield scenario from his headquarters' desk than his subordinates could in the field. Thus, for example, in one of his earliest orders to Grant, Halleck instructed his brigadier to concentrate his command at Mayfield, Kentucky, and threaten Camp Beauregard, "letting it be understood that Dover [Tennessee] is the subject of your attack." Grant was to "make a great fuss." Halleck explicitly warned him, "do not advance far enough to expose your flank; and rear to an attack from Columbus, and by all means avoid a serious engagement." Once Grant had achieved his objective, limited to convincing the Rebels not to reinforce Bowling Green, he was "slowly [to] retire to your former positions, but, if possible keep up the idea of a general advance. Be very careful, however, to avoid a battle; we are not ready for that." Halleck to Grant, January 6, 1862, *OR*, 7:533–34. Insisting upon such caution was an overly familiar theme for Old Brains.

12. Grant to Halleck, January 29, 1862; John Y. Simon, ed., *The Papers of Ulysses S. Grant* (Carbondale: Southern Illinois Univ. Press, 1967–2000), 4:103.

13. Halleck to Grant, January 30, 1862, *OR*, 7:121–22; McClellan to Halleck, January 29, 1862, *OR*, 7:571.

14. Grant to Halleck, January 29, 1862, *OR*, 7:121; Halleck to Grant, January 30, 1862, *OR*, 7:122; Halleck to Grant, January 30, 1862, *OR*, 7:121.

15. Wallace, "The Capture of Fort Donelson," 1:399.

16. Grant to Washburne, March 22, 1862; Simon, *Papers of Grant*, 4:409. At this time, Grant was still being much too generous to and considerate of Halleck.

17. Grant, General Field Orders, No. 1, *OR*, 7:585–86; Foote, Special Orders No. 1, *ORN*, 22:535–36; Grant to Halleck, February 4, 1862, *OR*, 7:581; Roy P. Basler, ed., *The Collected Works of Abraham Lincoln* (New Brunswick: Rutgers Univ. Press, 1953), 4:147. At 10:00 A.M., on February 6, Confederate forces inside Fort Henry numbered some 2,610 men. At the last moment, Tilghman sent approximately 2,500 of them to Fort Donelson. They crossed unimpeded to that fort since McClernand was not scheduled to intersect the road until sometime after 11:00 that morning. This decision might well have prevented a greater disaster to Confederate arms than that at Fort Henry. Col. Adolphus Heiman to Col. W. W. Mackall, February 8, 1862, *OR*, 7:150.

18. *Cincinnati Gazette*, February 7, 1862; *Boston Journal*, undated; Moore, *Rebellion Record*, 4:70, 74.

19. Foote to Gideon Wells, Secretary of the Navy, February 6, 1862, *ORN*, 22:537. The surrender, Foote wrote, was "unconditional." Tilghman to Cooper, February 12, 1862, *OR*, 7:141.

20. Walke, "The Western Flotilla at Fort Donelson," *From Fort Sumter to Shiloh*, 1:362; Horn, *Army of Tennessee*, 80–82; Kendall Gott, *Where the South Lost the War: An Analysis of the Fort Henry-Fort Donelson Campaign* (Mechanicsburg, Pa.: Stackpole Books, 2003), 89; Herschel Gower and Jack Allen, eds., *Pen and Sword: The Life and Journals of Randal W. McGavock* (Jackson: Tennessee Historical Commission, 1960), 584; Roy B. Stonesifer Jr., "The Fort Henry-Heiman and Fort Donelson Campaign: A Study in Confederate Command" (unpublished Ph.D. dissertation, The Pennsylvania State University, 1965), 3–4.

21. Haynes to Cooper, March 22, 1862, *OR*, 7:145–48; Cooling, *Forts*, 103. Stephen D. Engle, *Struggle for the Heartland* (Lincoln: Univ. of Nebraska Press, 2001), 57.

22. Tilghman to Cooper, February 12, 1862, *OR*, 7:143; Haynes to Cooper, March 22, 1862, *OR*, 7:145; Taylor, "The Defense of Fort Henry," *From Fort Sumter to Shiloh*, 1:371.

23. Both correspondents, for the *St. Louis Democrat* and *Cincinnati Gazette*, dated their reports, February 7; Moore, *Rebellion Record*, 4:73, 79.

24. Grant to Halleck, February 6, 1862, *OR*, 7:124; Simon, *Papers of Grant*, 4:157, 163.

25. Wallace to Susan, February 5, 1862, *Wallace Collection* (Indianapolis: Indiana Historical Society).

26. Jeffrey L. Patrick, ed., *Three Years With Wallace's Zouaves: The Civil War Memoirs of Thomas Wise Durham* (Macon, Ga.: Mercer University Press, 2003), 64.

27. Wallace, *An Autobiography*, 1:371.

28. Ibid., 1:370.

5. Fort Donelson, February 13–14, 1862

1. Grant to Cullum, February 8, 1862, *The War of the Rebellion: A Compilation of the Official Records of the Union and Confederate Armies* (Washington, D.C.: Government Printing Office, 1899), 7:440, hereinafter cited *OR*, 7:596; John Y. Simon, ed., *The Papers of Ulysses S. Grant* (Carbondale: Southern Illinois Univ. Press, 1967–2000), 4:171–72.

2. Pillow to A. S. Johnston, February 18, 1862, *OR*, 7:278; Buckner to Cooper, August 11, 1862, *OR*, 7:328; Floyd to A. S. Johnston, February 27, 1862, *OR*, 7:269; Nathaniel Cheairs Hughes Jr., and Roy P. Stonesifer Jr., *The Life and Wars of Gideon J. Pillow* (Chapel Hill: Univ. of North Carolina Press, 1993), 213–17.

3. Frederick the Great, King of Prussia, is said to be the author of one of the more enduring military maxims of all times "l'audace, l'audace, toujours l'audace" ("audacity [or boldness], audacity, always audacity"). The maxim properly belongs to Georges Danton of French Revolutionary fame. In 1748, Frederick did write that "[i]t is better to make a bad decision and execute it on the spot than to make no decision." Later, he proclaimed, "[i]n all things there is a favorable or auspicious moment. If grasped when presented, it offers a hope of success, but if

it is allowed to pass by, it can scarcely be regained." Robert B. Asprey, *Frederick the Great: The Magnificent Enigma* (New York, 1986), 370–71, 383. Grant and Wallace were boldly audacious. This would be insufficient to sustain a long-term, working military relationship between the two.

4. Jean Edward Smith, *Grant (New York: Simon & Schuster, 2001)*, 131. In "Who Were the Top Ten Generals," *North and South* 6 (May 2003): 19, Keith Poulter characterizes Grant as "properly aggressive." The McPherson story is cited in Smith, *Grant*, 200; in James Lee McDonough, *Shiloh: In Hell before Night* (Knoxville: Univ. of Tennessee Press, 1977), 182; and in Bruce Catton, *Grant Moves South* (New York: Little, Brown and Company, 1960), 241. The Sherman story is cited in Smith, *Grant*, 201; in McDonough, *Shiloh*, 183; in Catton, *Grant Moves South*, p. 241; and in John F. Marszalek, "Sherman and Grant to the Fall of Vicksburg," *Grant's Lieutenants: From Cairo to Vicksburg, ed.* Steven E. Woodworth (Lawrence: Univ. of Kansas Press, 2001), 13. The best source for the Sherman incident is a personal interview Sherman granted to the *Washington Post* on December 30, 1893. See Albert Richardson, *A Personal History of Ulysses S. Grant* (Hartford, Conn.: American Publishing Company, 1868), 217. Whether Grant lore or fact, these incidents illustrate that as he fought, Grant had an abundance of "l'audace."

5. Grant to Julia Grant, February 24, 1862, Simon, *Papers of Grant*, 4:284. Mahan would certainly have endorsed this philosophy.

6. Ulysses S. Grant, *Personal Memoirs of Ulysses S. Grant* (New York: Charles L. Webster & Company, 1885), 1:250. At least three historians have accepted this story as Grant related it and agreed that for him the incident constituted a valuable lesson learned in the art of command. See Arthur L. Conger, *The Rise of U. S. Grant* (New York: Century Company, 1931), 5–7; Smith, *Grant*, 16; Catton, *Grant Moves South*, 12. There is no evidence to suggest that Wallace, until that fatal day at Shiloh, ever backed down from a fight or that he ever feared anyone or any situation, other than, perhaps, his wife Susan.

7. Kelton to Grant, August 8, 1861, *OR*, 3:430; Grant to Butler, August 23, 1861, *OR*, 3:452–53; Catton, *Grant Moves South*, 34. Wallace failed to entrench his division at both Donelson and Crump's Landing (Shiloh) without consequence. His failure to do so was probably born out of his inexperience as a civilian, amateur solider rather than as the result of any policy formed while fighting in the field. Like Grant, everything Wallace had ever read on waging war, including Mahan, advocated the practice of digging entrenchments and constructing fortifications at the appropriate time.

8. Kelton to Grant, August 8, 1861, *OR*, 3:430; Grant to Kelton, August 9, 1861, *OR*, 3:432. Conger, *Rise of Grant*, 11–15; General Sir James H. Marshall-Cornwall, *Grant as Military Commander* (New York: Barnes & Noble Books, 1995; originally published in London by B. T. Batsford, Ltd., 1970), 37.

9. Grant to McKeever, October 4, October 7, 1861, Simon, *Papers of Grant*, 3:17, 24; Benjamin Franklin Cooling, *Forts Henry and Donelson: The Key to the Confederate Heartland* (Knoxville: Univ. of Tennessee Press, 1987), 66. Wallace joined with Grant in his desire to seek out and destroy the enemy. There is no evidence he shared Grant's view that his enemy had an essentially passive nature and must be made to fight.

10. Ulysses S. Grant, *Personal Memoirs*, 1:298. Actually, the supposition that Polk or Hardee might withdraw from Columbus or Bowling Green to attack Grant

through Fort Henry was partially correct. On February 7, the day after Fort Henry surrendered, Confederate generals Johnston, Hardee, and Beauregard met at Covington House, Beauregard's Bowling Green headquarters, and fashioned an agreement known as the Covington House Memorandum. The generals acknowledged that Fort Henry had fallen and that defeat at Fort Donelson was inevitable. They agreed that Polk had to abandon Columbus and operate independently in the area of Humboldt, Tennessee, while Hardee must withdraw from Bowling Green, falling back on Nashville. The memorandum did not set forth any attack plans. Furthermore, it was agreed that the yet to be attacked Fort Donelson would not be given any support. Johnston was going to fight for Nashville at Fort Donelson but without giving it and the men inside any further aid or assistance. See *OR*, 7:861–62.

11. Wallace to Susan, February 11, 1862, *Wallace Collection (*Indianapolis: Indiana Historical Society).

12. Wallace to Susan, February 7, 1862; February 19, 1862, *Wallace Collection.*

13. Hillyer to Wallace, February 11, 1862, Simon, *Papers of Grant*, 3:193. Wallace would ultimately discover that opening himself up to a man like Hillyer was definitely an error. In the days after Donelson, he would begin to regret having had Hillyer, a man with significantly more ambition than character, as a "friend."

14. Grant to Cullum, February 16, 1862, *OR*, 7:159–60; Grant to Walke, February 13, 1862, Simon, Papers *of Grant*, 4:202; Walke to Foote, February 15, 1862, *The Official Records of the Union and Confederate Navies in the War of Rebellion*, series 1 (Washington, D.C., 1904), 22:585–86, hereinafter cited as *ORN*, 22:587–88. In his *Personal Memoirs*, Grant wrote that McClernand "had undertaken to capture a battery of the enemy which was annoying his men. Without orders or authority, he sent three regiments to make the assault. The battery was in the main line of the enemy, which was defended by his whole army present. Of course, the assault was a failure, and of course the loss on our side was great for the number of men engaged." Grant, *Personal Memoirs*, 1:300. A recent McClernand biographer, Richard Kiper, criticizes this action. He notes that McClernand assaulted an "entrenched" enemy position, defended by a number of Rebel soldiers armed with "rifled muskets" approximately equal in strength to his attacking force, without creating a "diversionary attack." Kiper concludes that this was at best "an amateurish" decision. Richard L. Kiper, *Major General John Alexander McClernand: Politician in Uniform* (Kent, Ohio: Kent State Univ. Press, 1999), 79.

15. Grant to Julia Grant, February 14, 1862; Simon, Papers *of Grant*, 4:211.

16. Foote to U.S. Secretary of the Navy Gideon Welles, February 15, 1862, *ORN*, 22:585–86; Cooling, *Forts*, 152; Roy B. Stonesifer, "The Forts Henry–Heiman and Fort Donelson Campaign: A Study of Confederate Command," unpublished Ph. D. dissertation, The Pennsylvania State University, 1965, 17, 24.

17. Cooling, *Forts*, 157–58; Stephen D. Engle, *Struggle for the Heartland* (Lincoln: Univ. of Nebraska Press, 2001), 71; Stonesifer, "The Forts Henry–Heiman," 249, 253.

18. Wallace to Susan, February 13, 1862, *Wallace Collection.* This letter also appears in Simon, *Papers of Grant*, 4:206 n.

19. Simon, *Papers of Grant*, 4:205. A "Butternut" is another name for a Confederate soldier. It was derived from the color of their uniforms, which in certain instances blended in with the woods and underbrush in which many battles were fought.

20. *Benjamin Franklin Cooling, "The First Nebraska Infantry Regiment and the Battle of Fort Donelson," Nebraska History* 45, no. 2 (June 1964): 127–28; Lew Wallace, *An Autobiography* (New York: Harper & Brothers, 1906), 1:390–92; M. F. Force, *Campaigns of the Civil War: From Fort Henry to Corinth* (New York: Charles Scribner's Sons, 1881), 44.

21. Foote to Wells, February 15, 17, 1862, *ORN, 22:586, 587.*

22. Floyd to Johnston, February 27, 1862, *OR, 7:268; Arndt Stickles, Simon Bolivar Buckner: Borderland Knight (Chapel Hill: Univ. of North Carolina Press, 1940), 133–63; Lew Wallace, "The Fall of Fort Donelson," in* Robert Underwood Johnson and Clarence Clough Buel, eds., *From Fort Sumter to Shiloh: Battles and Leaders of the Civil War* (New York: A. S. Barnes & Co., 1887), 1:401.

23. Nathaniel Cheairs Hughes Jr. and Roy P. Stonesifer Jr., *The Life and Wars of Gideon J. Pillow* (Chapel Hill: Univ. of North Carolina Press, 1993), 221–22; Buckner said the breakout scheduled for the 14th was called off in the early afternoon by Pillow, Floyd concurring. Buckner wrote that Pillow "thought it too late for the attempt." Buckner to Cooper, August 11, 1862, *OR,* 7:330; Col. William E. Baldwin, 14th Mississippi, to Maj. George B. Cosby, March 12, 1862, *OR,* 7:338; Maj. William N. Brown, 20th Mississippi, to Gen. George W. Randolph, Secretary of War, April 12, 1862, *OR,* 7:383. One theory as to why the breakout on the morning of the 14th was suddenly postponed is based upon the fact that just as Pillow's men were getting underway, a lucky shot from a Yankee sharpshooter struck and killed a Rebel infantryman from Mississippi.

24. Stanley F. Horn, *The Army of Tennessee: A Military History* (Indianapolis: Bobbs-Merrill Company, 1941), 91; Hughes and Stonesifer, *Pillow,* 221–22; Buckner to Cooper, August 11, 1862, *OR,* 7:330.

25. Grant to Cullum, February 14, 1862; Simon, *Papers of Grant,* 4:209.

26. Ibid.

27. Grant to McKeever, October 7, 1861, Simon, *Papers of Grant,* 3:17, 24.

28. Charles B. Kimbell, *History of Battery "A" First Illinois Light Artillery* (Chicago, Cushing Printing Company, 1899), 38.

29. Cooling, *Forts,* 163–65.

30. Foote to Welles, February 15, 1862, *ORN,* 22:586; Foote to Welles, February 17, 1862, *ORN,* 22:587; Foote to Grant, February 14, 1862, received at Grant's headquarters at approximately 4:00 A.M., February 15, Simon, *Papers of Grant,* 4:216 n. 2; Grant, *Personal Memoirs,* 1:305

31. Grant, *Personal Memoirs,* 1:305, 304; Force, *From Fort Henry to Corinth,* 48.

6. Fort Donelson, February 15, 1862, A.M.

1. Jean Edward Smith, *Grant* (New York: Simon & Schuster, 2001), 157; Charles Whittlesey, *War Memoranda: Cheat River to the Tennessee, 1861–1862* (Cleveland, Ohio: W.W. Williams, 1884), 31–32.

2. J. M. Roberts, "Experiences of a Private in the Civil War," *Journal of J. M. Roberts,* 1904, quoted in David R. Logsdon, ed., *Eyewitnesses at the Battle of Fort Donelson* (Nashville: Kettle Mills Press, 1998), 40; Benjamin Franklin Cooling, "The

Reliable First Team: Grant and Charles Ferguson Smith," in Steven E. Woodworth, ed., *Grant's Lieutenants: From Cairo to Vicksburg* (Lawrence: Univ. of Kansas Press, 2001), 53.

3. Lew Wallace, *An Autobiography* (New York: Harper & Brothers, 1906), 1:387–88. This undoubtedly was the substance of Wallace's initial orders from Grant. Given that one of the objectives Wallace always sought to prove was that his movements at Donelson on the morning of February 15 were directly in conflict with the orders given him by Grant, his written account of these orders seems a little too self-serving, although it is difficult to argue with the substance of what Wallace said were Grant's instructions.

4. Edward C. Bearss, *Troop Movement Maps: Ft. Donelson, February 12–16, 1862* (U.S. National Park Service), sheet 5 (of 11), 1959. Little is known of Wallace's thoughts on the afternoon of February 14. He did not explore such matters in his letters to Susan and his *Autobiography* is strangely silent on his thoughts during this important day in his life. In his article for *Battles and Leaders of the Civil War*, he discussed the gunboat attack and the Confederate council of war. He also mentioned how bitterly "cold," "dark," and "pitiless" it was the night of February 14. Lew Wallace, "The Capture of Fort Donelson," *From Fort Sumter to Shiloh: Battles and Leaders of the Civil War*, ed. Robert Underwood Johnson and Clarence Clough Buel (New York, A. S. Barnes & Company, 1887), 1:412–15.

5. Wallace, *An Autobiography*, 1:397–99.

6. W. H. L. Wallace to Ann Wallace, February 17, 1862, quoted in Victor Hinken, *Illinois in the Civil War* (Urbana: Univ. of Illinois Press, 2nd ed., 1991), 39.

7. U. S. Grant, *Personal Memoirs of Ulysses S. Grant* (New York: Charles L. Webster and Company, 1885), 1:304.

8. Wallace to Rawlins, February 20, 1862, *The War of the Rebellion: A Compilation of the Official Records of the Union and Confederate Armies* (Washington, D.C.: Government Printing Office, 1899), 7:236, hereinafter cited *OR;* "Testimony of General Lewis Wallace," July 9, 1862, *Report of the Joint Committee on the Conduct of the War* (Washington, D.C., Government Printing Office, 1863), 3:339. Stephen Woodworth has called Wallace's inclination to hold to the absolute letter of Grant's orders "patent nonsense" inasmuch as when Brayman first sought help, Pillow's breakout had been rolling back the Union right wing for over an hour. Steven E. Woodworth, *Nothing But Victory: The Army of the Tennessee 1861–1865* (New York: Knopf, 2005), 99. The criticism is overstated and unjustified. Wallace's initial hesitation was as intuitive and beneficial to Union arms as his decision to act would be two hours later. Had he acted too quickly, too impulsively, his totally inexperienced troops and officers would have been thrown headlong into the very maelstrom McClernand's men were fleeing. In this case, Wallace's haste and the results it would undoubtedly have produced would have made the situation worse rather than better.

9. On February 14, Wallace's 3rd Division numbered some 4,575 men. By the time the Wynn's Ferry Road action took place the next day, it had roughly 7,170. Kendall Gott, *Where the South Lost the War: An Analysis of the Fort Henry–Fort Donelson Campaign* (Mechanicsburg, Pa.: Stackpole Books, 2003), 284; Bearss, *Troop Movement Maps*, sheets 4 and 8. By February 14, Smith and McClernand had com-

manded, trained, and lived with their men for at least five months. Wallace and virtually all of his men were strangers, the men of the different regiments having known one another usually for less than a day. Other than Wallace, few had any battlefield experience. Understandably, Wallace knew nothing of the qualities or capabilities of his men or his officers.

10. McClernand to Grant, February 28, 1862, *OR*, 7:170–82; McArthur to Brayman, February 20, 1862, *OR*, 7:215–16; Oglesby to Brayman, February 20, 1862, *OR*, 7:183–87; W. H. L. Wallace to Brayman, February 17, 1862, *OR*, 7:192–98; Bearss, *Troop Movement Maps*, sheets 5 and 8. Pillow's men had pushed McClernand's forces back on Wynn's Ferry Road southwest at least three-quarters of a mile from their original positions.

11. Bruce Catton, *Grant Moves South* (New York: Little, Brown and Company, 1960), 165; Smith, *Grant*, 158; Whittlesey, *War Memoranda*, 34; Benjamin Franklin Cooling, *Forts Henry and Donelson: The Key to the Confederate Heartland* (Knoxville: Univ. of Tennessee Press, 1987), 168–69; Stacy D. Allen, "Lewis Wallace: If He Had Less Rank," in Woodworth, ed., *Grant's Lieutenants;* Bearss, *Troop Movement Maps*, sheets 8, 9, and 10.

12. McClernand to Grant, February 28, 1862, *OR*, 7:175; Cruft to Knefler, February 18, 1862, *OR*, 7:243; Bearss, *Troop Movement Maps*, sheets 7 and 8.

13. Gott, *Where the South Lost the War*, 211; Wallace to Susan, February 19, 1862, *Wallace Collection* (Indianapolis: Indiana Historical Society).

14. R. W. Burt, 76th Ohio, "Fort Donelson: Experiences of the 76th Ohio in the Siege," *National Tribune* 24, no. 1308 (September 13, 1906): 6.

15. Bearss, *Troop Movement Maps*, sheet 8.

16. Whittlesey, *War Memoranda*, 34; Wallace to Grant, February 20, 1862, *OR*, 7:237–38; Bearss, *Troop Movement Maps*, sheets 5 and 8; Charles B. Kimbell, *History of Battery "A": First Illinois Light Artillery* (Chicago: Cushing Printing Company, 1899), 38. Wallace had first laid eyes on Thayer the day before and had just met Whittlesey earlier that morning. As it turned out, both were precisely the right men to locate on his front line on Wynn's Ferry Road that morning.

17. Thayer to Knefler, February 18, 1862, *OR*, 7:252–53; Taylor to W. H. L. Wallace, February 18, 1862, *OR*, 7:210.

18. According to Thayer, "the enemy made an effort three times to push forward through our lines, but was as often driven back." Thayer to Knefler, February 18, 1862, *OR*, 7:252.

19. Burt, *National Tribune*, September 13, 1906, 6; Bearss, *Troop Movement Maps*, sheet 8; Kimbell, *Battery "A"*, 38. Several correspondents who reported on Wallace's stand on Wynn's Ferry Road mistakenly identified a Lieutenant Willard as being in command of Battery A. Kimbell stated that Lt. Peter P. Woods assumed command of Battery A from Willard on February 11, four days earlier. Kimbell, *Battery "A"*, 38. Correspondent for the *Missouri Democrat*, February 17, 1862, in Army Service School, *Donelson Campaign Sources Supplementing Volume 7 of the Official Records of the War of the Union and Confederate Armies in the War of the Rebellion* (Fort Leavenworth, Kan.: Army Service Schools Press, 1912), 93.

20. *Harper's Weekly* 6, no. 270 (March 1, 1862): 130. While the *Harper's* correspondent made a few errors reporting the battle, he accurately portrayed the

impact of the defensive line Wallace had established that morning. Unfortunately for Wallace and his quest for glory and honor, the correspondent neither mentioned his name nor associated his presence with this part of the action. In fact, Wallace was identified only as the general who had dispatched four regiments (Cruft's Brigade) to McClernand's aid when McClernand "suggested" this action. The Western press, other than *Frank Leslie's Illustrated Newspaper*, generally failed for some inexplicable reason to identify with Wallace to the extent its brethren in the East had done only seven months earlier.

21. Cooling believes Wallace saw "the flotsam" of a "destroyed" 1st Division and gave decisive orders that stopped the Confederate advance. Cooling, "The Reliable First Team: Grant and Smith," 53. Allen concludes that Wallace's quick action materially served to hasten the end of the Confederate thrust. Allen, "Wallace: If He Had Less Rank," 69. Stephens contends that Wallace grasped "the extent of the emergency" and disobeying Grant's orders, "moved forward." Gail Stephens, *Shadow of Shiloh: Major General Lew Wallace in the Civil War* (Indianapolis: Indiana Historical Society Press, 2010), 54. Although Wallace initially "hesitated," Gott applauds Wallace's initiative in detaching Cruft and sending him to McClernand, characterizing Wallace's decision to bring up additional wagons of ammunition as "foresight," and says his positioning of troops on Wynn's Ferry Road was "effective." Altogether, Gott concludes, "General Lew Wallace saved the day for the entire army" at Fort Donelson on Saturday, February 15. Gott, *Where the South Lost the War*, 217. Grant, *Personal Memoirs*, 1:304.

7. *Fort Donelson, February 15, 1862,* P.M.

1. Wallace to Rawlins, February 20, 1862, *The War of the Rebellion: A Compilation of the Official Records of the Union and Confederate Armies* (Washington, D.C.: Government Printing Office, 1899), 7:236, hereinafter cited *OR*. Grant's only other written statement concerning his instructions to Wallace appeared in his 1885 *Personal Memoirs*. Here, Grant wrote that he ordered his three division commanders early on the morning of February 15 to do nothing to instigate "an engagement" but to "hold their positions." Ulysses S. Grant, *Personal Memoirs of Ulysses S. Grant* (New York: Charles L. Webster & Company, 1885), 1:304. Grant gave no instructions concerning possible movements or dispositions by his division commanders in the event the Rebels broke out from the fort, initiating an attack. In his *Personal Memoirs*, Grant also indicated that on the afternoon of February 14 before Foote's bombardment began, he instructed Wallace to "hold the enemy within his lines" while the gunboats attacked (p. 302). Thus, Wallace had some basis for stating that Grant had ordered him to "repel any sally from the fort." By alleging that Grant had ordered him to be prepared to combat this very situation, Wallace perhaps succeeded in his intent to make Grant appear to be more in control of events on the morning of February 15 than he actually was. Wallace accomplished the same feat of literary legerdemain when he did not criticize Grant for his absence from the battlefield that morning. In fact, Wallace told Rawlins that Grant was "on board one of his gunboats, arranging, as was understood, an attack from the river." Wallace to Rawlins, February 20, 1862, *OR*, 7:237.

2. Wallace to Rawlins, February 20, 1862, *OR*, 7:237.

3. Ibid., 7:238. Cruft did not include this evaluation in his February 18 battlefield report. *OR, 7:243–46.* Whether Cruft ever made this statement or not is perhaps irrelevant. The essence of the statement appears to be not too far from the truth and, in Wallace's hands, it made for a descriptive embellishment. Interestingly, Wallace devoted only five of the eighteen paragraphs in his report to the action on Wynn's Ferry Road. Battlefield reports should be considered suspect. The winner of the engagement, focusing on his own self-importance, often tends to exaggerate his contribution to the outcome. The loser frequently looks for excuses and scapegoats. In this regard, Wallace's battlefield report was remarkably fair while the Confederate reports of the same event underscores the validity of this generalization.

4. Pillow to Derrick, February 18, 1862, *OR*, 7:282; Pillow to Mackall, March 14, 1862, *OR*, 7:290; Col. John C. Brown, brigade commander, to Buckner, *OR*, 7:346–49; Doss (14th Mississippi) to Brown, undated, *OR*, 7:344–45; Maj. Nathaniel F. Cheairs (3rd Tennessee) to Brown, March 10, 1862, *OR*, 7:349–51; Col. Joseph B. Palmer (18th Tennessee) to Brown, March 7, 1862, *OR*, 7:351–55; and Cook (32nd Tennessee) to Brown, February 16, 1862, *OR*, 7:355–57. Brown claimed the Rebels killed or wounded over 800 men of the 3rd Division. Like Cheairs, Brown reported that Confederate troops actually drove Wallace from the field. Palmer conceded that at the start of the Confederate charge, "the enemy opened a terrific fire upon us about the time or before we had fairly executed the deployment. The force here against us consisted of one battery, supported by six infantry regiments, all of which ultimately engaged in the fight." Palmer's 18th Tennesseans returned that fire "with unusual accuracy, which told desperately and rapidly upon the enemy, who under its terrific effect and force gave ground." Wallace's men "continued their retreat until they had gone beyond the reach of our guns," *OR*, 7:353.

5. Gower and Allen, eds., *Pen and Sword: The Life and Journals of Randal W. McGavock* (Jackson, Tenn.: Tennessee Historical Commission, 1960), 592.

6. Grant to Cullum, February 16, 1862, *OR*, 7:160; Grant, General Orders No. 2, *OR*, 7:629.

7. Grant, *Personal Memoirs,* 1:306.

8. McClernand to Grant, February 28, 1862, *OR*, 7:179; Grant to McLean, April 23, 1862, *OR*, 7:170; Benjamin Franklin Cooling, "The First Nebraska Infantry Regiment and the Battle of Fort Donelson," *Nebraska History* XLV, no. 2 (June 1964): 140–43; M. F. Force, *Campaigns of the Civil War: From Fort Henry to Corinth* (New York, 1881), 53; Grant to Halleck, April 25, 1862, *OR*, 10:174.

9. Wallace to Aaron Blair, April 3, 1862, *Wallace Collection* (Indianapolis: Indiana Historical Society); Wallace, "Testimony of General Lew Wallace," *Report of the Joint Committee on the Conduct of the War* (Washington, D.C., 1863), 3:339. Given his often expressed self-absorption, Wallace's response to the ceremonial sword was predictable. The gift had come from his friends and neighbors. Even so, he knew he deserved at least this much. He simply could not be gracious. Further, in his mind, a sword was an insignificant reward for the effort he had exerted and the decisive impact he knew he had produced.

10. Grant first came upon Wallace and McClernand sometime between 1:30 and 3:00 P.M., but definitely after Pillow had ordered the Confederate retreat. Cooling is

not sure of the exact time but states that it was after Thayer and the Chicago Board of Trade battery had reversed Brown's charge. Benjamin Franklin Cooling, *Forts Henry and Donelson: The Key to the Confederate Heartland* (Knoxville: Univ. of Tennessee Press, 1987), 183. Gott agrees. Kendall Gott, *Where the South Lost the War: An Analysis of the Fort Henry–Fort Donelson Campaign* (Mechanicsburg, Pa.: Stackpole Books, 2003), 222. In his *Personal Memoirs*, Grant recounted all these incidents in a perfunctory manner. It is not surprising that Grant's literary style was terse and unemotional. That was consistent with his basic personality. In this regard, Grant and Wallace were total opposites. On at least one occasion, however, Grant displayed a degree of excess emotion, judging that his decision to attack Fort Donelson that afternoon had "acted like a charm." Grant, *Personal Memoirs*, 1:307–8.

11. At this juncture, Grant had yet to inform Halleck of the failed naval bombardment. Foote did not telegraph his report to Wells until the afternoon of the 15th. At 1:00 P.M., on February 15, Halleck had no idea what had happened on the Cumberland the day before. Wallace alleged that when Grant first met with him and McClernand, Grant was carrying papers that, Wallace further implied, contained orders from Halleck to initiate a siege at Fort Donelson. Halleck was miles away in St. Louis. He was not privy to what had occurred earlier that day on Wynn's Ferry Road. As Grant announced his decision to attack, Wallace wrote, "with a sudden grip, he crushed those papers in his hand." This captivating portion of the story appears to be literary license as Wallace described the event more than two decades later. The drama of Grant "crushing" those unidentified papers in a "sudden grip" must have been irresistible to Wallace. It is doubtful that Wallace suggested to Grant that the road to Charlotte lay open for a possible Confederate retreat. As events later that afternoon strongly suggest, Wallace had little idea just how important that point on the extreme right of the Union line actually was. Lew Wallace, "Capture of Fort Donelson," in Robert Underwood Johnson and Clarence Clough Buel, eds., *From Fort Sumter to Shiloh: Battles and Leaders of the Civil War* (New York, 1887), 1:421–22; Wallace to the editor of the *Omaha Tribune and Republican*, August 30,1872, printed in the *New York Times*, September 11, 1872, 9; Lew Wallace, *An Autobiography* (New York: Harper & Brothers, 1906), 1:410–12; Cooling, *Forts*, 184; Jean Edward Smith, *Grant* (New York: *Simon & Schuster*, 2001), 157–58; William S. McFeely, *Grant: A Biography* (New York: W. W. Norton & Company, 1981), 99–101; Grant, *Personal Memoirs*, 1:307–8.

12. Wallace, "Capture of Fort Donelson," *From Fort Sumter to Shiloh*, 1:422; Wallace, *New York Times*, September 11, 1872, 9. Wallace's comments were written at a time when he was still seeking recognition from Grant that he had not erred at Shiloh. His exaggerated literary flourishes, cast before a backdrop of national crisis, notwithstanding, his picture of what actually drove Grant to success as a military figure seem remarkably accurate. These comments must, however, be viewed within the context of the fact that Wallace was still courting Grant's favor. Nevertheless, his evaluations of Grant and his character at this moment in time were insightful and quite accurate. The Corinth reference was a direct and unabashed criticism of Halleck's deficiencies as a tactical commander. Interestingly, Grant issued the order to retake the lost ground on the right to both Wallace and McClernand. The latter, alleging the men of the 1st Division were simply too

war-weary to participate further that day, declined and asked Wallace to lead the charge. Wallace did so on the right on Saturday afternoon.

13. Grant to Foote, February 15, 1862, *OR*, 7:618, John Y. Simon, ed., *The Papers of Ulysses S. Grant* (Carbondale: Southern Illinois Univ. Press, 1967–2000), 4:214; Roy B. Stonesifer, "The Forts Henry–Heiman and Fort Donelson Campaign: A Study of Confederate Command," unpublished Ph. D. dissertation, The Pennsylvania State University, 1965, 101–2, 112–13. At St. Louis, Halleck acted as if he had commanded the Navy at Fort Donelson as in fact he probably had. On the ground at Donelson, Grant dealt with Foote as an equal, not a subordinate. As both Henry and Donelson proved, it was an excellent working relationship. At 3:30 P.M., on February 15, 1862, however, Grant had little time to worry about such distinctions.

14. Col. James C. Veatch, 25th Indiana, to Col. Jacob G. Lauman, *OR*, 7:228; Col. James M. Tuttle, 2nd Iowa, to Lauman, *OR*, 7:229; Lt. Col. J. C. Parrott, 7th Iowa, to Lauman, *OR*, 7:231; Col. William T. Shaw, 14th Iowa, to Lauman, *OR*, 7:232. There is no official comment from Smith on this engagement. He was writing a report on Fort Donelson several months later when he unexpectedly died. Edwin C. Bearss, *Troop Movement Maps, Fort Donelson, February 12–16, 1862* (United States National Park Service: Fort Donelson National Military, 1959), sheet 10 shows the situation on the Union left at 5:00 P.M. on February 15. At this time, the Union regiment closest to the Fort was the 2nd Iowa, located some 500 feet away. Cooling, *Forts*, 185–88. Stonesifer, "Forts Henry–Heiman," 311–19, concludes that had it become necessary for Smith to renew the attack on the morning of February 16, Buckner's line, as it existed at 5:00 P.M., on February 15, would have been "difficult" to breach.

15. Dove to Foote, February 16, 1862, *The Official Records of the Union and Confederate Navies in the War of Rebellion*, series 1 (Washington, D.C., 1904), 22:588, hereinafter cited as *ORN*.

16. Wallace to Susan, September 22, 1861, February 13, 1862, *Wallace Collection*; General Field Orders No.14, February 14, 1862, Simon, *Papers of Grant*, 4:205.

17. Following a regional encampment in Louisville, Kentucky, in 1860, at which the Montgomery Guards played a prominent role, a correspondent for the Indianapolis *Daily Journal* wrote that the Montgomery Guards were "a little ahead of anything similar seen in these parts." Indianapolis *Daily Journal*, September 22, 1860, cited in Theodore G. Gronert, "The First National Pastime in the Middle West," *Indiana Magazine of History* 29 (September 1933): 180. The Montgomery Guards formed the nucleus of the 11th Indiana.

18. Bearss, *Troop Movement Maps*, sheet 10; Cooling, *Forts*, 188. In his battle report, Wallace described in more detail how the men of these two regiments fought that afternoon. He wrote that in response to the first Confederate volley, both colonels shouted to their commands to lie down. As the fury from the first Confederate volley dissipated, the men then "rose up and rushed on and in that way they at length closed upon the enemy, falling when the volleys grew hottest, dashing on when they slackened or ceased. Meanwhile their own fire was constant and deadly." Wallace to Rawlins, February 20, 1862, *OR*, 7:239. Private Durham, 11th Indiana, recalled in his *Memoirs* that as the attack commenced, he and his comrades initially charged the enemy line until they came within firing range, at which time

"we dropped flat on the ground (this was our Zouave tactics) and we crawled forward on our bellies, not firing a shot, letting the enemy shoot over us until they thought we had retreated and then slacked their fire; then we would spring to our feet, give them a volley and run at them with bayonet." Durham knew that success attended this maneuver because "the fact of us crawling toward them while they were firing surprised them, and when we gave them the volley and charged so close to them they did not understand our tactics." Jeffrey L. Patrick, ed., *Three Years With Wallace's Zouaves: The Civil War Memoirs of Thomas Wise Durham* (Macon, Ga.: Mercer University Press, 2003), 72–73.

19. Bearss, *Troop Movement Maps*, sheet 9; Gott, *Where the South Lost the War*, 286, 288.

20. Stonesifer, "Forts Henry–Heiman," 325, believes that if the fighting had continued the next day, February 16, Wallace would have had a "difficult time" breaching these substantial Confederate defenses.

21. Wallace to Rawlins, February 20, 1862, *OR*, 7:239.

22. Bearss, *Troop Movement Maps*, sheets 9, 10, and 11; Cooling, *Forts*, 190–95; Arn to Cruft, February 18, 1862, *OR*, 7:247; Smith to Knefler, February 18, 1862, *OR*, 7:233. The correspondent for the *Missouri Democrat* described the afternoon's activities: "with a cheer that resounded far and near, the irresistible Eighth Missouri and Eleventh Indiana, which occupied the front, advanced on the double-quick into the encounter they had so long been seeking. These two regiments, from their superiority in drill and fighting capacities, have been considered 'crack troops,' and most nobly did they uphold to the letter their enviable reputation." *Missouri Democrat*, February 17, 1862, in Frank Moore, ed., *The Rebellion Record: A Diary of American Events* (New York, 1861–1868), 4:182.

8. Breakfast at Fort Donelson

1. Herschel Gower and Jack Allen, eds., *Pen and Sword: The Life and Journals of Randal W. McGavock* (Jackson, Tenn.: Tennessee Historical Commission, 1960), 592; Stanley F. Horn, *The Army of Tennessee: A Military History* (Indianapolis: Bobbs-Merrill Company, 1941), 93–95; Benjamin Franklin Cooling, *Forts Henry and Donelson: The Key to the Confederate Heartland* (Knoxville: The University of Tennessee Press, 1987), 200–205.

2. Buckner to Cooper, August 11, 1862, *The War of the Rebellion: A Compilation of the Official Records of the Union and Confederate Armies* (Washington, D.C.: Government Printing Office, 1899), 7:333, hereinafter cited *OR;* sworn and notarized statement of Col. John Bunch to Pillow, March 15, 1862, *OR*, 7:293; sworn and notarized statement of Gus[tave] A. Henry to Pillow, March 13, 1862, *OR*, 7:296.

3. Bunch, *OR*, 7:293; Forrest sworn and notarized statement, March 15, 1862, *OR*, 7:295. Given its close proximity to the Charlotte road, Union failure to reoccupy Dudley's Hill the night of February 15 could have been significant. When Grant ordered Wallace to lead the counterattack on the right that afternoon, his only instruction was "Gentlemen, the ground on the right must be retaken." Wallace positioned Cruft on the right flank of the 3rd Division and told him to advance

toward the intersection of Wynn's Ferry Road and Forge Road. He did not specifically order Cruft to re-occupy the high ground of Dudley's Hill just to the east of that intersection. Wallace's command inexperience and ignorance of the terrain undoubtedly led him to make this mistake. Having been at Donelson for slightly more than a day, it is probable Wallace had yet to hear the name "Dudley's Hill" and had no idea what it meant. Both Grant and Wallace had a responsibility to be as informed on the subject of "reconnaissance" as possible. Dennis Hart Mahan, *An Elementary Treatise on Advanced-Guard, Out-Post, and Detachment Service of Troops and the Manner of Posting and Handling Them in the Presence of an Enemy* (New York: Wiley and Putnam, 1847), 111. True, they had no cavalry, but both failed that responsibility. Through their collective oversight, the road from Dover west across Lick Creek to Charlotte and Nashville was left open. Forrest's cavalry escaped down that road in the early morning hours of February 16. Had Floyd possessed the courage to order a similar attempt by his infantry, the outcome of the battle of Fort Donelson, as well as the continuation of both Wallace and Grant's military careers, might have developed quite differently.

4. Buckner told Cooper that both Floyd and Pillow had "correctly stated that I regarded the position of the army as desperate, and that an attempt to extricate it by another battle, in the suffering and exhausted condition of the troops was almost hopeless." That night, Buckner allowed his fears and concerns to trump his judgment. In Floyd and Pillow, he found a receptive and compliant audience for the conclusions he was forming in his increasingly agitated state of mind. Buckner to Cooper, August 11, 1862, *OR*, 7:333–34.

5. Arndt Stickles, *Simon Bolivar Buckner: Borderland Knight* (Chapel Hill: The Univ. of North Carolina Press, 1940), 155.

6. "Diary of John H. Beadle, Private, 31st Indiana," in John Thomas Smith, *A History of the Thirty-First Regiment of Indiana Volunteer Infantry in the War of the Rebellion* (Cincinnati, Ohio: Western Methodist Book Concern, 1900), 206, 142; Wilbur Fiske Crummer, *With Grant at Fort Donelson, Shiloh and Vicksburg and An Appreciation of General U. S. Grant* (Oak Park, Ill: E. C. Crummer and Company, 1915), 42–43.

7. One correspondent did praise Wallace, noting that he was quite popular with his troops: "Gen. Lewis Wallace commanded the successful charge on the right [Saturday afternoon]. He has always been a great favorite with the soldiers; his gallantry has strengthened the confidence previously felt in him, and victory is sure to follow where he leads." Substantial praise, indeed, but Wallace might have noted that it said nothing about his crucial and decisive stand on the Wynn's Ferry Road that morning. *Frank Leslie's Illustrated Weekly* 13, no. 330 (March 15, 1862): 288.

8. General Orders No. 2, February 17, 1862, *OR*, 7:629.

9. From Grant's perspective, the fall of Fort Donelson was indeed "the first major Union victory" of the war. Previously, however, on January 19, 1862, Union Brig. Gen. George Thomas had "sharply defeated" Confederates led by Maj. Gen. George B. Crittenden and Brig. Gen. Felix Zollicofer at the battle of Mill Springs, near Somerset, Kentucky. Zollicofer lost his life that day and the South began to lose its foothold in eastern Kentucky and eastern Tennessee. For Thomas and the Union, Mill Springs was a "tactically complete" victory. For the Confederacy, Mill Spring was not "strategically disastrous." For both sides, Mill Springs was a presage not a

precursor of the battles for forts Henry and Donelson. The successful conclusion of the Twin Rivers campaign had a greater impact on the course of the war in the West than did Mill Springs. Cooling, *Forts*, 73–82; Kendall Gott, *Where the South Lost the War: An Analysis of the Fort Henry-Fort Donelson Campaign* (Mechanicsburg, Pa.: Stackpole Books, 2003), 63–64; Herman Hattaway and Archer Jones, *How the North Won: A Military History of the Civil War* (Urbana: University of Illinois Press, 1983), 63. For a different perspective that equates the significance of Mills Springs to that of Fort Donelson as serious early challenges to Southern confidence on the battlefield, see Brian Steel Wills, *George Henry Thomas: As True as Steel* (Lawrence: University of Kansas Press, 2012), 140–41, 144.

10. While it is not known exactly what Wallace did after he reached his camp on the afternoon of February 14, it is difficult to believe he spent much time practicing the art of war. He neither entrenched his position nor, apparently, sent out the few scouts he had to discover more about where he was. Pillow's breakout the next morning surprised him every bit as much as it surprised Grant. In the Grant-inspired counterattack of February 15, Wallace failed to secure Dudley's Hill. Grant also made a number of mistakes at Donelson, including two of a quite serious nature. He erred badly, not in leaving the battlefield to meet with Foote, but in leaving his army on that battlefield literally at the mercy of whatever his enemy might choose to do in his absence. Grant failed to appoint a trusted subordinate as a temporary second-in-command for the time he was absent. Then, immediately prior to his departure, he burdened his division commanders with vague and unimaginative orders. Secondly, he underestimated the character and resolve of his enemy, believing them to lack the motivation and the raw gumption to take offensive action against him. It was fortunate for Grant that he had Wallace at hand and did not have to pay dearly for this second mistake.

11. Hillyer to Wallace, February 16, 1862, *Wallace Collection* (Indianapolis: Indiana Historical Society), reproduced in John Y. Simon, ed., *The Papers of Ulysses S. Grant* (Carbondale: Southern Illinois University Press, 1967–2000), 4:228n. This was a personal note from Hillyer. There is no evidence that it came from Grant. It is ironic that shortly thereafter, Hillyer turned on Wallace with a vengeance. A few days after Wallace filed his Donelson report, Hillyer asked him to amend it to mention Hillyer and another Grant aide in a favorable light. Wallace stated that he investigated the request but found it lacked merit. He therefore refused. Wallace wrote that several days later while at Grant's headquarters, "I was forced to take notice of a winter that had fallen upon the occupants there—a kind of interior winter peculiar in that it reserved its frost and ice for me." Lew Wallace, *An Autobiography* (New York: Harper & Brothers, 1906), 1:435–36. This was just the beginning of what Hillyer with his poetic and acerbic pen had in store for Wallace. Before it was over, Hillyer had effectively helped to close off almost all of the avenues leading to a mutually beneficial working relationship between Wallace and Grant and his aides. Hillyer might also have done more than any other individual, save Wallace himself, to poison Grant's mind toward Wallace. Gail Stephens, *Shadow of Shiloh: Major General Lew Wallace in the Civil War* (Indianapolis: Indiana Historical Society Press, 2010), 60–62, 150.

12. Wallace to Susan, February 19, 1862, *Wallace Collection.*

13. Thayer to Knefler, *OR*, 7:253; Pillow to Derrick, *OR*, 7:282; W. H. L. Wallace to Brayman, *OR*, 7:196. In making any assessment of this matter, it should be remembered that while Wallace was fighting on behalf of his country on the Union right that morning, Smith was whittling. Prior to successfully leading the counterattack Saturday afternoon on the left, Smith had presented Grant with neither time nor opportunity. In fact, he had presented him with nothing more than strict adherence to an incomplete and confusing order.

14. Lew Wallace, *The Official Records of the Union and Confederate Navies in the War of Rebellion*, series 1 (Washington, D.C., 1904), 22:588, hereinafter cited as *ORN*, 22:590; Wallace to Susan, February 17, 1862, *Wallace Collection;* Crummer, *With Grant*, 44. Wallace was extraordinarily pleased that Buckner was the man with whom he had breakfast. Even though he was a military enemy, Buckner was his friend. Before the war, the two had enjoyed many spirited military competitions with their own locally organized militia units, particularly at the Kentucky state guard encampments at Louisville in 1859 and 1860. Wallace would recall that when he first saw Buckner that morning he was "grave, dignified, silent; the grip he gave me, however, was an assurance of welcome quite as good as words." Wallace, *An Autobiography*, 1:426–33.

15. Wallace to Susan, February 17, 1862, *Wallace Collection.*

16. Wallace to Susan, February 24, 1862, *Wallace Collection.* The reference to "vine and fig tree" is interesting, particularly since Wallace quoted these words. Perhaps he was merely reflecting on Confederate Maj. Gen. and Episcopal bishop Leonidas Polk's proclamation of July 13, 1861, in which he stated, "All we desire is to be left alone, to repose in quietness under our own vine and our own fig tree." Polk, quoted in Thomas Lawrence Connelly, *Army of the Heartland: The Army of the Tennessee, 1861–1862* (Baton Rouge: Louisiana State Univ. Press, 1967), 55. It is doubtful that Wallace was being sarcastic here inasmuch as Polk was both quoting and paraphrasing from the Holy Bible, 1 Kings 4:26.

17. Wallace to Susan, February 24, 1862, *Wallace Collection;* Grant to Julia, February 24, 1862, Simon, *Papers of Grant*, 4:284; W. H. L. Wallace to Ann, February 20, 1862, in Isabel Wallace, *Life and Letters of General W. H. L. Wallace* (Chicago, 1909. Republished Carbondale: Southern Illinois University Press, Illinois, 2000), 167.

18. Special Field Orders, No. 10, February 16, 1862, *OR*, 7:626; Wallace to Rawlins, February 17, 1862, in Simon, *Papers of Grant*, 4:228–29fn.

19. Hillyer to Wallace, February 16, 1862, *Wallace Collection.*

20. Grant to Wallace, February 16, 1862, Simon, *Papers of Grant*, 4:228.

21. Wallace to Susan, February 19, 1862, *Wallace Collection.* Wallace's general condemnation of the Illinois regiments at Donelson is inconsistent with the warm feelings he expressed after the battle for Illinois Col. W. H. L. Wallace, the commander of McClernand's 3rd Brigade.

22. Wallace to Susan, February 27, 1862, *Wallace Collection.* Wallace implied in this letter that his men suffered because others wished to cause him pain. This was but another expression of his awareness that he was an outsider. He was not a West Pointer. Realistically, he had set out to do all he could to educate himself in the ways of the military. His formal education was nothing to brag about, but he had become an attorney and had been elected to the Indiana Legislature. He had

written not only legislation but poetry, plays, and a novel about Spanish Mexico in the days of Cortés and Montezuma. He had read Plutarch many times through while endlessly immersing himself in dozens of military manuals by Mahan, Hardee, Ellsworth, and others. True, through various channels of self-education, Wallace had gained the necessary credentials for acceptability by the clique. But rather than relying upon those credentials as a basis for working with the professionals, Wallace was always critical and dismissive of them. Rather than seeking to co-exist, then identify and possibly form alliances with them for the common good, Wallace preferred to stand aloof from such men. True, he probably would not have been successful in this adventure even had he tried. The point is, however, he never thought it necessary to try.

23. Wallace to Susan, February 27, 1862, *Wallace Collection.*

24. Lew Wallace, *Autobiographical Sketch. August 16, 1863. Wallace Collection* (Indianapolis: Indiana Historical Society), 30; Wallace, *An Autobiography,* 1:442–43. As one who yearned for adventure, his thirst was unquenchable.

25. Wallace to Susan, March 12, 1862, *Wallace Collection.*

9. *The Mind-Numbing Caveat*

1. Notwithstanding Grant's early achievements at Henry and Donelson, Halleck distrusted Grant and his command abilities. Suspicion and jealously surfaced as dominate elements of Halleck's response to Grant's achievements. His persistent attempts to control Grant from St. Louis had an overall negative impact on Grant as well as on the developing Shiloh campaign. For insights into Halleck's scheming, see: Halleck to McClellan, February 17, 1862 (10:00 A.M.), February 17, 1862 (1:30 P.M.), February 20, 1862, *The War of the Rebellion: A Compilation of the Official Records of the Union and Confederate Armies* (Washington, D.C.: Government Printing Office, 1899), 7:627, 628, 641, hereinafter cited *OR*.

2. Halleck to Grant, March 1, 1862, *OR*, 7:674. On March 5, Halleck changed Grant's tactical orders. While the primary objective of the campaign remained destruction of the railroad bridges at Eastport and the connecting railroad lines at Corinth, Halleck noted that Grant, "if successful, will not return to Paris, but will encamp at Savannah [east bank of the Tennessee River north of the Mississippi state line], unless threatened by superior numbers." Halleck to Grant, March 5, 1862, *OR*, 10:7, pt. 2. Jealous of Grant and desirous of remaining in control, Halleck had removed Grant from command of this expedition the day before.

3. Dennis Hart Mahan, *An Elementary Treatise on Advanced-Guard, Out-Post, and Detachment Service of Troops and the Manner of Posting and Handling Them in the Presence of an Enemy* (New York: Wiley and Putnam, 1847), 185–87.

4. Halleck to Grant, March 1, 1862, *OR*, 7:674.

5. Halleck to Grant, March 4, 1862, *OR*, 10:2, 3, pt. 2. Halleck allowed his distrust and jealousy of Grant as well as his personal ambition to overpower him. Further, he demonstrated an amusing lack of knowledge about his own command. Many of his orders were addressed to Major General Smith. At this time, Smith had not been confirmed as a major general. Technically, he was still a brigadier.

6. Grant to Smith, three telegrams all dated March 5, 1862, *OR*, 10:5–6. Note the uncertainty and reluctance exhibited by Grant in his use of the word "probably."

7. Grant to Halleck, March 7, March 9, March 13, 1862, *OR*, 10:15, 21, 30; John Y. Simon, ed., *The Papers of Ulysses S. Grant* (Carbondale: Southern Illinois Univ. Press, 1967–2000), 4:331, 334, 353.

8. Grant to Julia Grant, March 7, 1862, Simon, *Papers of Grant*, 4:326, 327.

9. Halleck to Grant, March 7, 1862, Simon, *Papers of Grant*, 4:332n. At Fort Henry, Grant now acted like a quartermaster and Halleck appeared to treat him as such.

10. Presidential War Order No. 3, March 11, 1862, *OR*, 10:28–29, pt. 2. On March 10, Halleck put the Corinth campaign into motion. Halleck to Maj. Gen. George B. McClellan, March 10, 1862, *OR*, 10:24–25, pt. 2. In this same communiqué, Halleck pointedly criticized McClellan for not supporting him in his relationship with Buell: "Believe me, general, you make a serious mistake in having three independent commands in the West." Halleck sought to school McClellan to the effect that "[t]here never will and never can be any co-operation at the critical moment; all military history proves it. You will regret your decision against me on this point. Your friendship for individuals has influenced your judgment." It is interesting that Halleck failed to apply this same logic to his own situation as he attempted to micromanage Grant and the Union Army of the Tennessee several hundreds of miles away from St. Louis on the banks of the Tennessee River. The next day, however, Lincoln promoted Halleck, expanding his command to territory previously delegated to Buell. Buell was now Halleck's subordinate, subject no longer to Halleck's entreaties but to his orders. Halleck soon discovered that having authority over Buell and having his orders to Buell obeyed in a timely fashion were two entirely different matters. Halleck also had the authority to order Grant to wait for Buell. As Buell procrastinated and disobeyed Halleck, Old Brains intensified the repetition of the caveat. A stalemate involving a war of words ensued. For the next three weeks, Johnston and Beauregard saw a Union army encamped at Pittsburg Landing going nowhere, doing nothing. The Union army's lack of movement and intensity presented the Rebels with an excellent opportunity to strike before Buell might arrive.

11. Maj. Charles S. Hayes to Wallace, March 14, 1862, *OR*, 10:10–11; Wallace to Smith, March 13, 1862, *OR*, 10:9–10.

12. Gen. Lorenzo Thomas to Halleck, March 10, 1862, *OR*, 7:683; Halleck to Thomas, March 15, 1862, *OR*, 7:683. On March 16, the day before Grant officially resumed command of the Army of the Tennessee, Halleck sent him a dispatch further reinforcing his stipulation that Grant avoid conflict until Buell joined him. "As the enemy is evidently in strong force, my instructions not to advance so as to bring on an engagement must be strictly obeyed," Halleck dictated, "We must strike no blow until we are strong enough to admit no doubt of the result." Halleck to Grant, March 16, 1862, *OR*, 10:41, pt. 2. Halleck had no intention of going quietly into the night.

13. Sherman to Smith, March 17, 1862, *OR*, 10:25; Sherman to Hurlbut, March 17, 1862, *OR*, 10:28; Grant to Sherman, March 17, 1862, *OR*, 10:43, pt. 2. Grant's decision to concentrate his army at Pittsburg Landing drew further inspiration from Sherman, who wrote that he was "strongly impressed with the importance of the

position for its land advantage and its strategic position. The ground itself admits of easy defense by a small command, and yet affords admirable camping ground for a hundred thousand men." Sherman to Grant, March 17, 1862, *OR*, 10:27.

14. Grant's decision to spend his nights at Savannah is puzzling. By doing so, he segregated overall field command of the army from the army itself. Every morning, he embarked upon a time-consuming ten-mile steamer trip upriver to Pittsburg Landing, returning downriver in the evening to Savannah. Depending on current strength, each trip took anywhere from twenty-five to fifty minutes. This was a relevant factor the first day of Shiloh but not a determinative one.

15. Grant to Halleck, March 19, 1862, *OR*, 10:48–49, pt. 2. Grant to Wallace and Grant to Smith, intended for Sherman, March 20, 1862, *OR*, 10:52–53. Grant and Halleck knew that the Confederate forces they faced were in Corinth. These dispatches, however, appear to be among the first, if not the first, that officially recognized Corinth as a strategic objective of the campaign. A similar scenario had played itself out when, after the fall of Fort Henry, the audacious Grant appeared unilaterally to inform Halleck that he would take Fort Donelson.

16. Halleck to Grant, March 20, 1862, *OR*, 10:50–51. It is unclear precisely what Halleck meant by "until you are properly fortified." Grant did not construe this as an order to entrench his army. If he did, he disregarded it. More likely, Grant interpreted the phrase as a reiteration of the caveat that he must "wait for Buell." There is no question that at this time Grant was contemplating an advance upon Corinth with or without Buell. He telegraphed Smith on March 23: "I am clearly of the opinion that the enemy are gathering strength at Corinth quite as rapidly as we are here, and the sooner we attack the easier will be the task of taking the place." Grant to Smith, March 23, 1862, *OR*, 10:62.

17. Grant to Halleck, March 20, 1862, *OR*, 10:51, pt. 2.

18. Grant to Halleck, March 21, 1862, *OR*, 10:55–56, pt. 2.

19. Grant to Sherman, April 4, 1862, *OR*, 10:91.

20. Grant to Julia, March 22, 23, 29, April 3, 1862, Simon, Papers *of Grant*, 4:406–7, 412–13, 443, 5:7.

21. Wallace to Susan, March 18, March 21, 1862, *Wallace Collection (Indianapolis: Indiana Historical Society)*.

22. Wallace to Susan, March 18, 1862, *Wallace Collection*. To understand fully the controversy surrounding Wallace at Shiloh, it is necessary, in the remainder of this chapter and the first half of the next, to leave Wallace at Crump's Landing guarding Grant's right flank, in order to focus on other facts and events leading up to the battle of Shiloh, facts and events likewise germane to the controversy.

23. Bruce Catton, *Grant Moves South* (New York: Little, Brown and Company, 1960), 222; Simon, Papers *of Grant*, 4:407n; Larry J. Daniel, *Shiloh: The Battle that Changed the Civil War* (New York: Simon and Schuster, 1997), 77. Grant did suggest that he chose to bivouac at Savannah because that was the location from which he could best direct to both landings the men and materials Halleck was daily sending him. It apparently never occurred to him that this was a function better suited for a quartermaster skilled in the art of logistics than for the commanding general. His conscious resolve to spend his nights at Savannah was similar to his decision to visit Flag Officer Foote on the morning of February 15. In this

instance, however, Grant at least designated Sherman as his temporary second-in-command on the battlefield during his absence.

24. Charles Morton, "A Boy at Shiloh." *Personal Recollections of the War of Rebellion. Addresses Delivered before the Commandery of the State of New York, Military Order of the Loyal Legion of the United States* (New York: G. P. Putnam's Sons, 1907), 3:52, 68, 57–58.

25. Warren Olney, "The Battle of Shiloh as Seen by a Private Soldier," *Paper Read before the California Commandery of the Military Order of the Loyal Legion of the United States, May 31, 1889* 17 (San Francisco, 1889), 6:9, 12. George Mason, who at war's end was a Brevet Major in the 9th Illinois, 2nd Division, fought at Shiloh. On May 5, 1880, he told the members of the Illinois Commandery that Pittsburg Landing was an aptly chosen site. "Nature," he said, "had done her share in the making of an almost impregnable position. The skill and labor of man, the erection of a few earthworks, was all that was needed." Mason lamented that "no special plan of defence [*sic*] seems to have been adopted, or even thought of, by our leaders. . . . It is easy to conjecture how much better able we would have been to meet them on that next Sunday morning, had even the ordinary precautions of war been taken." George Mason, "Shiloh," *Military Essays and Recollections. Papers read before the Illinois Commandery of the Military Order of the Loyal Legion of the United States* (Chicago: A. C. McClurg and Company, 1891), 1:95–96.

26. The day after Donelson surrendered, ambition and vanity consumed Halleck. He demanded that "in return for Forts Henry and Donelson," McClellan give him "command in the West." Halleck to McClellan, February 17, 1862, *OR*, 7:628. Two examples of Halleck's duplicity will suffice. In early February, Halleck had informed Buell that Grant and the navy would commence action against Donelson that very day. Nevertheless, Halleck asked, "why not come down and take the immediate command of the Cumberland column yourself." He told Buell he would effect this change in command, even on the eve of battle, merely by transferring "Sherman and Grant to the Tennessee column." Halleck to Buell, February 13, 1862, *OR*, 7:609. Halleck made two attempts at two levels to assert himself one step higher in the command structure in the West. On February 8, 1862, he sought to use Stanton and Brig. Gen. E. A. Hitchcock to accomplish this purpose. Halleck to Stanton, February 8, 1862, *OR*, 7:594. The same day, he stepped down one level, hoping to accomplish the same purpose. He told McClellan that he had "no desire for any larger command than I have now." He added, however, if he were to be the recipient of such a command, "this would avoid any clashing of interests or difference of plan and policy." Halleck to McClellan, February 8, 1862, *OR*, 7:595. McClellan was not fazed. Eight days later, Halleck was begging McClellan for just such an increase in command. Craig L. Symonds et al., "Who Were the Worst Ten Generals?" *North & South* 7, no. 3 (May 2004): 14, 17, 24.

27. Halleck to McClellan, March 4, 1862, *OR*, 7:682. The day before, Halleck criticized Grant in a telegraph to McClellan for "neglect and inefficiency" and opined that "satisfied with his victory, he [Grant] sits down and enjoys it without regard to the future." Halleck to McClellan, March 3, 1862, *OR*, 7:679–80. McClellan responded, sympathizing with Halleck, and, perhaps in an attempt to call his bluff, authorized him to arrest Grant "if the good of the service requires

it." Stanton approved McClellan's authorization. McClellan to Halleck, March 3, 1862, *OR*, 7:680. Halleck characteristically backed down even though he casually informed McClellan that "a rumor has just reached me that since the taking of Fort Donelson General Grant has resumed his former bad habits." Halleck to McClellan, March 4, 1862, *OR*, 7:682. Because of protest from both inside and outside the military and pressure from Washington, Halleck was compelled to restore Grant to command. Even so, he could still reaffirm his mind-numbing caveat.

28. Grant on one occasion did scout the terrain himself. On March 19, he informed Halleck that he had just returned from Pittsburg and Crump's Landing. These were, in his opinion, the only two places on the Tennessee River until one reached Eastport, Mississippi, "where a landing can be well effected on the west bank of the river." He immediately qualified his finding by noting "this, of course, only applies to the present stage of water." Grant to Halleck, *OR*, 10:48–49, pt. 2.

29. M. F. Force, *Campaigns of the Civil War: From Fort Henry to Corinth* (New York: Charles Scribner's Sons, 1881), 101. Force commanded the 20th Ohio, Whittlesey's 3rd Brigade, 3rd Division.

30. Perhaps Grant "consented" to the layout of the camp at Pittsburg Landing, particularly with two veteran divisions being located the greatest distance from the line closest to Corinth, precisely because he was concerned that should the Confederates launch an unexpected attack, it would likely fall upon Wallace's division at Crump's Landing. To that end, the Donelson veterans of the 1st and 2nd divisions should be where they were closest in proximity to Wallace. There is no evidence at all to suggest Grant even considered this possibility. It is merely suggested here in an attempt to discover as much as possible what truly constituted the "whys" and the "wherefores" leading up to Shiloh. In either instance, Union troops were poorly situated for any Rebel attack. The fact that Grant never addressed this concern was a mistake of some importance. Joseph W. Rich, *The Battle of Shiloh* (Iowa City: Iowa State Historical Society, 1911), 34. See also O. Edward Cunningham, *Shiloh and the Western Campaign of 1862*, ed. Gary D. Joiner and Timothy B. Smith (New York: Savas Beatie, 2007), map, 107. Grant never welded his army together at Shiloh. The Army of the Tennessee simply "grew by accretion." Rich, *Battle of Shiloh*, 47. On December 4, 1889, Captain C. L. Sumbardo, 12th Iowa, 2nd Division, addressed the Minnesota Commandery. As a non-commissioned officer, he and a quartermaster had selected a campsite for W.H.L. Wallace's division upon its arrival at Pittsburg Landing. Seeking high ground and proximity to fresh water, Sumbardo said, "[w]e paid no attention to the location of other troops." He bemoaned the fact that it would not be until "[l]ater in the war" [that] a private soldier, a non-commissioned officer, a captain, or even a general, would have instinctively camped his troops in order of battle, that the long roll, simultaneously sounding, should in five minutes, bring into line ready for action regiments, brigades, divisions, corps." C. L. Sumbardo, "Some Facts About the Battle of Shiloh," *Glimpses of the Nation's Struggle. Papers read before the Minnesota Commandery of the Military Order of the Loyal Legion of the United States*, 3rd series (New York, St. Paul: D. D. Merrill Company, 1893), 29–30. Sherman set up the 5th Division's campsite in battle-ready formation. See Orders, No. 15, March 19, 1862, *OR*, 10:50, pt. 2. However, even though he served Grant as the de-facto

commander at Pittsburg Landing, Sherman saw no reason even to suggest that similar preparedness formations be ordered for the rest of the camp.

31. Rich, *Battle of Shiloh*, 47. Justifying disobedience to Halleck's March 7 and March 16 orders to entrench, Grant wrote that for the reinforcements he was "almost daily" receiving, "drill and discipline were worth more . . . than fortifications." Later, Grant attempted to justify the absence of fortifications and entrenchments by noting that "the time of the pick and spade had been but little resorted to in the West." Ulysses S. Grant, *Personal Memoirs of Ulysses S. Grant* (New York: Charles L. Webster and Company, 1885), 1:357–58. The unhappy truth for many at Shiloh was that Grant gave little thought at this time in his career to defensive warfare.

32. Alfred T. Andreas, "The 'Ifs and Buts' of Shiloh," *Military Essays and Recollections. Papers Prepared for the Commandery of the State of Illinois. Military Order of the Loyal Legion of the United States* (Chicago: A. C. McClurg and Company, 1891), 1:108. Sumbardo made a similar observation. "There was a laxity of general discipline," he stated, "a freedom among the troops in those balmy April days, as they were scattered through that delightful Tennessee forest, which gave our army the appearance of a gigantic picnic." Sumbardo, "Some Facts About the Battle of Shiloh," 31–32.

33. Grant to Nelson, April 3, 1862, in W. B. Hazen, *A Narrative of Military Service* (Boston: Ticknor and Company, 1885), 24.

34. Grant to Jesse Grant, April 26, 1862, in Simon, *Papers of Grant*, 6:78–79.

35. Jacob Ammen, *Journal*, April 5, 1862, *OR*, 10:330–31; Rawlins to Nelson, April 6, 1862, *OR*, 10:95, pt. 2.

36. McClernand to Grant, March 29, 1862, in Simon, *Papers of Grant*, 4:430n; Richard L. Kiper, *Major General John A. McClernand: Politician in Uniform* (Kent, Ohio: Kent State Univ. Press, 1999), 101; Victor Hinken, *Illinois in the Civil War* (Urbana: Univ. of Illinois Press, 1991), 58. McClernand claimed credit easily and avoided blame adroitly. More than once, Grant reined in his subordinate. Grant to McLean, April 21, 1862, *OR*, 7:170. Although Grant could plausibly claim victory at Shiloh, he had good reason to be concerned that McClernand might go public with his comments. McClernand often talked to others outside the chain of command, particularly Lincoln. This might easily be a huge embarrassment for Grant. Originally, Grant had put Sherman in charge of all matters at Pittsburg Landing during his absence. There was nothing McClernand could do about this as both he and Sherman were brigadier generals commanding a division. Then, two or three days prior to McClernand's dispatch, Grant received a telegram stating that McClernand, among others, but not Sherman, had been promoted to the rank of major general. Grant understood that when this news became known, Sherman must step down to the role of a subordinate. McClernand would become the de facto commander at Pittsburg Landing. This was unacceptable. Grant first implied to Halleck that he had transferred the Pittsburg Landing command from Sherman to Smith, who had his major generalship confirmed the same day as McClernand. Grant acknowledged that because of the order of these promotions it was "necessary for me to move my headquarters from this place [Savannah] to Pittsburg." What Grant failed to tell Halleck was that putting Smith in command at Pittsburg Landing was nothing more than a temporary ruse. Smith was then confined to a

bed in the Cherry House with a leg wound that would soon result in his death. On March 31, the transfer of official headquarters to Pittsburg Landing was announced. No date was set for the transfer. Grant to Halleck, March 27, 1862, *OR*, 10:70, pt. 2; General Orders No. 30, March 31, 1862, *OR*, 10:84.

37. Andrew Hickenlooper, "The Battle of Shiloh," *Sketches of War History, 1861–1865. Paper Prepared for the Commandery of the State of Ohio. Military Order of the Loyal Legion of the United States* (Cincinnati, Ohio: The Robert Clarke Company, 1903), 5:426.

38. Lew Wallace, "Oration at the Dedication of the Indiana War Monuments at the Shiloh Battlefield, April 6, 1903," in John W. Coons, comp., *Indiana at Shiloh: Report of the Commission* (Indiana Shiloh National Park Commission, 1904), 274.

39. The objective of reconnaissance was "certainty," which then provided the basis for making sound command decisions. "It is in truth this feeling of certainty that constitutes all the difference; having it, the general makes his dispositions with confidence; without it, he acts hesitatingly; and thus communicates to others that want of confidence felt in his own mind," "Maxim #295," Mahan, *Out-Post*, 106. Even "more care" in the gathering of reconnaissance data was required, Mahan observed, if the army stopped "to take a position for some time, to wait or watch the enemy." In this instance, the reconnaissance that the commanding general must scrutinize had to include knowledge of "all the facilities either for an advance or a retrograde movement." Maxim no. 312, Mahan, *Out-Post*, 111–12. Not only was the quality of reconnaissance in the days before Shiloh suspect, haphazard, and incomplete, Grant did not seem to pay it much heed, either from an "advance" or a "retrograde" perspective. Grant paid no heed to Force's geographic truism that the road between Pittsburg Landing and Corinth ran both ways. Force, *From Fort Henry to Corinth*, 101.

40. Grant to Halleck, April 5, *OR*, 10:89, pt. 2.

41. Daniel, *Shiloh: The Battle*, 322. The numbers cited herein exclude the very minimal impact of Brig. Gen. Thomas J. Wood's 6th Division of Buell's Army of the Ohio. It is beyond the scope of this work to discuss in any further detail specific military events from those two days at Shiloh. Daniel has succeeded in putting the various troop movements, North and South, particularly during the first day of immense and nearly unprecedented confusion, together into a cohesive, readable, and highly informative narrative. He has described with detailed accuracy the failures of Confederate command decisions, beginning with Beauregard's confusing advance from Corinth and how his resulting line of battle on April 6 failed to address Johnston's tactical objective for the Confederate right. Daniel has captured the tenacity with which Grant held on that first day as well as the audacity of his decision not to retreat but to engage the enemy the next day. Add to Daniel, the depth of analysis found in O. Edward Cunningham, *Shiloh and the Western Campaign of 1862* and in Wiley Sword, *Shiloh: Bloody April* (New York: Morrow, 1974), and one has a very good idea of what occurred on April 6–7, 1862.

10. Shiloh, Surprise, Aftermath

1. Antoine Henri Jomini, *Summary of the Art of War*, trans. G. H. Mendell and W. P. Craighill. (Philadelphia: J. R. Lippincott & Co., 1862), 209. Jomini's defini-

tion of surprise is an appropriate description for the initial confrontation of the two armies at Shiloh as well as for the unfolding of events during most of the remainder of the first day. Grant had not formulated any plans for fighting his enemy at Pittsburg Landing. Thus, he spent most of the first day initiating "ad hoc" responses to Confederate advances.

2. D. W. Reed, "Review of 'Villard's Memoirs' and John Codman Ropes 'Story of the Civil War'," *Proceedings of the Society of the Army of the Tennessee at the Thirty-Sixth Meeting, November 8–9, 1906* (Cincinnati: Published by the Society and Chas. O. Ebel Printing Co., 1907), 216.

3. Sherman to Grant, April 5, 1862, *The War of the Rebellion: A Compilation of the Official Records of the Union and Confederate Armies* (Washington, D.C.: Government Printing Office, 1899), 10:93–94, pt. 2, hereinafter cited *OR;* John K. Duke, *History of the Fifty-third Regiment Ohio Volunteer Infantry During the War of the Rebellion 1861–1865* (Portsmouth, Ohio: The Blade Printing Company, 1909), 43. Private Duke participated in those moments, which he described some forty-seven years later. Larry J. Daniel, *Shiloh: The Battle That Changed the Civil War* (New York: Simon and Schuster, 1997), 158; and Lloyd Lewis, *Sherman: Fighting Prophet* (New York: Harcourt, Brace and Company, 1932), 220, have both accepted Duke's account as genuine, including Sherman's exclamation.

4. There were three reasons why Confederate forces failed that morning to roll the Union army right into the Tennessee River. First, during the initial stages of the attack, many Confederate troops stopped to raid a campsite as they overran it. In parts of the field, the attacking forces lost cohesion and slowed, allowing Union troops to regroup and counter. Second, Beauregard's attack plan was flawed in its inception. The Confederate line of attack stacked one corps upon another in successive waves, like a hammer directed against a specific point. Given the layout of the entire camp, Beauregard would have fared much better had he advanced in line rather than in column. The depth of Beauregard's attacking columns prevailed initially but ultimately failed to destroy the Union line because it lacked sufficient width. Not all Union troops were ensnared by Confederate surprise. Third, and most important, Johnston had gone into battle with one objective. He intended to strike a blow enveloping the extreme Union left (Stuart's Brigade of Sherman's Division) driving it back toward the landing and the Tennessee River before turning northwest to push the retreating Yankees into the soggy bottomland of Snake and Owl creeks. When Beauregard initiated the battle by concentrating his point of attack in column rather than in line, he frustrated Johnston's plan. The Rebel second-in-command failed to adopt, coordinate, and implement his field commander's plan of attack. Thus, there simply was insufficient Confederate manpower attacking on the Confederate right. Beauregard improperly deployed his forces. He failed to achieve the envelopment on the Confederate right that was the heart of Johnston's battle plan. Grant thus had the opportunity, virtually all day long, to pull troops on his flanks inward, reinforcing his line against what was at the moment the main thrust of the Confederate attack. Daniel, *Shiloh*, 163–64, 197–201, 116–21.

5. Charles Morton, "A Boy at Shiloh," *Personal Recollections of the War of Rebellion. Addresses Delivered before the Commandery of the State of New York. Military Order of the Loyal Legion of the United States* (MOLLUS), 3rd series (New York: G. P. Putnam's Sons, 1907), 68; George F. McGinnis, "Shiloh," *War Papers Read Before*

the Indiana Commandery. Military Order of the Loyal Legion of the United States (Indianapolis: Published by the Indiana Commandery, 1898), 3.

6. M. F. Force, *Campaigns of the Civil War: From Fort Henry to Corinth* (New York: Charles Scribner's Sons, 1881), 124.

7. D. Lloyd Jones, "The Battle of Shiloh," *War Papers Read Before the Commandery of the State of Wisconsin. Military Order of the Loyal Legion of the United States* (Milwaukee, Wis.: Burdick & Allen, 1914), 4:59–60; Andrew Hickenlooper, "The Battle of Shiloh," *Sketches of War History, 1861–1865. Paper Prepared for the Commandery of the State of Ohio. Military Order of the Loyal Legion of the United States (MOLLUS)* (Cincinnati, Ohio: The Robert Clarke Company, 1903), 5:426.

8. Mahan stated that "no pains should be spared to obstruct the approaches of the enemy." He also wrote that "[t]o do the greatest damage to our enemy with the least exposure to ourselves is a military axiom lost sight of by ignorance of the true ends of victory." Dennis Hart Mahan, *An Elementary Treatise on Advanced-Guard, Out-Post, and Detachment Service of Troops and the Manner of Posting and Handling Them in the Presence of an Enemy* (New York: Wiley and Putnam, 1847), 91, 31.

9. William T. Sherman, *Memoirs of General William T. Sherman* (2nd ed., New York: D. Appleton and Company, 1889), 1:257, 275; Ulysses S. Grant, *Personal Memoirs of Ulysses S. Grant* (New York: Charles L. Webster & Company, 1885), 1:357.

10. Hickenlooper, "The Battle of Shiloh," 447; J. E. Boos and Patrick H. White, "Civil War Diary of Patrick H. White," *Illinois State Historical Society Journal* 15, no. 3 (October 1922): 640, 15, no. 4 (January 1923): 655; Thomas M. Stevenson, *A History of the 78th Regiment of Ohio Infantry Volunteers from its 'Muster-In' to its 'Muster-Out'* (Zanesville, Ohio: Hugh Dunne, 1865), 151. Stevenson, Chaplain of the 78th Ohio, 3rd Division, accused "our generals" at Shiloh of "unpardonable neglect in having done nothing for the defense of the place and their camps, by establishing a line of fortifications."

11. Whitelaw Reid, "The Battle of Pittsburg Landing—Tennessee," *Cincinnati Gazette*, April 14, 1862, reproduced in James G. Smart, ed., *A Radical View: The Dispatches of Whitelaw Reid, 1861–1865* (Memphis, Tenn.: Memphis State Univ. Press, 1976), 129–30. Reid's observations concerning many "unloaded" guns and "accoutrements lying pell-mell" along with ammunition being "ill-supplied," if true, tend to support the applicability of Jomini's definition of "surprise" to the first day at Shiloh. Further, the more circulation such comments attained in the North, the more embarrassment Grant inevitably suffered.

12. H. S., letter to the Keokuk, Iowa, "Gate City," April 30, 1862, and Dr. A. Ady, letter to Muscatine, Iowa, "Journal," May 2, 1862, both quoted in "Letters from Shiloh," Mildred Thorne, ed., *Iowa Journal of History* 52, no. 3 (July 1954): 265–66, 238. After Donelson, Wallace wondered why the war correspondents who had so favored him during his tenure in the East knew little of his existence in the West. After Shiloh, he was usually dismissive of them. He amusingly described these battlefield scribes to Susan as "the Bohemian Brigade made up of valorous knights of the quill." He did not fear them but he had learned to respect them, telling Susan that each correspondent, including Reid, was "a fearful foe singly, but terrible when united." Wallace to Susan, May 23, 1862, *Wallace Collection* (Indianapolis: Indiana Historical Society).

13. Sherman did pursue the retreating Confederates at least to Fallen Timbers, a few miles southwest of the battlefield. Nathan Bedford Forrest and his Confederate cavalry quickly brought that effort to a fruitless conclusion.

14. Grant to George P. Irhie, April 25, 1862, John Y. Simon, *The Papers of Ulysses S. Grant* (Carbondale: Southern Illinois Univ. Press, 1967–2000), 5:73. Wallace said much the same thing in an April 17 letter to Susan. Grant followed his own advice and survived; Wallace repetitively explained himself and his actions. In large measure, he authored his own demise.

15. Halleck to Stanton, May 2, 1862, June 15, 1862, *OR*, 10:99. For more details on the battle of Shiloh, see: Daniel, *Shiloh;* Wiley Sword, *Shiloh, Bloody April* (New York: Morrow, 1974); James Lee McDonough, *Shiloh: In Hell before Night* (Knoxville: Univ. of Tennessee Press, 1977); and O. Edward Cunningham, *Shiloh and the Western Campaign of 1862*, ed. Gary D. Joiner and Timothy B. Smith (New York: Savas Beatie, 2007). The major mistakes at Shiloh, other than Grant's failure to entrench, his failure to review and then alter the disposition of his troops in camp, and his succumbing with such apparent ease to the mind-numbing impact of Halleck's caveat, should be assessed as the direct and proximate cause of Halleck's obsessions with Grant and his desire to micromanage events from St. Louis.

16. John W. Foster, *War Stories for My Grandchildren* (Washington, D.C.: The Riverside Press Cambridge, 1918), 61–62.

17. In 1838, Halleck entered his last year as a West Point cadet. At the time, he favored the army appropriations bill currently before Congress "provided the President [Van Buren] does not fill up the present vacancies with citizens. It is hard for us to be placed under citizens who have spent no time in preparation for their commissions, while we have spent four or five years here at hard toil fitting ourselves for the various duties of our station." Halleck to Theodore Miller, July 16, 1838, in John F. Marszalek, *Commander of all of Lincoln's Armies: A Life of General Henry W. Halleck* (Cambridge: Harvard Univ. Press, 2004), 21. Just before journeying up the Hudson River four years earlier to start his military training, however, Halleck had told this same friend that "the study of human nature is the main thing after all. Books may inform us what men of such and such dispositions and inclinations will do, but it is from observation alone that we learn what men possess these dispositions and inclinations." Halleck to Miller, September 13, 1834, Marszalek, *Commander of all of Lincoln's Armies*, 12–13. Apparently, during his four years at West Point, Halleck had learned that an inflexible predisposition to distrust and discount the intelligence, attitudes, and abilities of the civilian amateur soldier was a prerequisite to a successful military career.

18. Wallace to Susan, May 10, 1862, Wallace Collection. Years earlier, in 1846, while in Mexico, he had explained to his brother Bill that there were others in the 1st Indiana, along with some civilian politicians, who in active concert with others, sought his political/military demise. He refrained from naming names but stated unequivocally that he knew he was the victim of spurious claims "dictated by the malice of others." Wallace to William Wallace, October 29, 1846, *Wallace Collection.*

19. Wallace to Lane, March 18, 1862, *Wallace Collection.*

20. Halleck to Secretary of War, Edwin M. Stanton, May 3, 6, 13, 18, 1862, *OR*, 10:665–66.

21. Halleck to Stanton, May 22, 1862; Lincoln to Halleck, May 24, 1862, *OR*, 10:666–67.

22. Halleck to Stanton, May 30, 31, 1862, *OR*, 10:668.

23. "Testimony of General Lewis Wallace," *Report of the Joint Committee on the Conduct of the War* (Washington, D.C.: Government Printing Office, 1863), 3:343.

24. Wallace to Susan, June 1, 1862, *Wallace Collection.* "If the General commanding does not think my service of any value in this Department, I must perforce search for another in which work is yet to be done." At this time, Wallace was unsure just who his enemy was. Illustrative of his confusion, Wallace also began to complain about Morton: "Will Lane doubt any longer? I say Morton is a parasite and a double dealer." Wallace to Susan, November 13, 1862, *Wallace Collection.*

25. Wallace to Susan, June 14, 1862, *Wallace Collection.*

26. Grant to Halleck, April 28, 1862, *OR*, 10:135, pt. 2; Grant to Wallace, April 28, 1862, *OR*, in Simon, *Papers of Grant*, 5:92–93, 93n.

27. Wallace to Grant and Grant to Wallace, April 28, 1862, in Simon, *Papers of Grant*, 5:93, 93n.

28. Halleck to Grant, Grant to Halleck, June 29, 1862, and Halleck to Grant, July 3, 1862, *OR*, 17:46–47, 67–68, pt. 2. Wallace to C. T. Hotchkiss, acting assistant adjutant general to McClernand, June 18, 1862, *OR*, 17:14–15, pt. 2; Hotchkiss to Wallace, June 22, 1862, *OR*, 17:25, pt. 2. Hotchkiss reminded Wallace, "you will continue your efforts to prevent railroads within your reach from being injured." For his own reasons, Wallace chose to disregard this part of the order from his superior (McClernand).

29. Grant to Halleck, June 24, 1862, *OR*, 17:29–30, pt. 2.

11. Before the Committee

1. Proclamation, August 31, 1862, *The War of the Rebellion: A Compilation of the Official Records of the Union and Confederate Armies* (Washington, D.C.: Government Printing Office, 1899), 3:466–467, hereinafter cited *OR*. The committee issued its final report on the war in the West in April, 1863. Senator Benjamin Wade of Ohio, Senator Zachariah Chandler of New York, Representative George W. Julian of Indiana, and Representative John Covode of Pennsylvania, signed it. All were opponents of the Lincoln administration's policy of conciliation. However, Representative Daniel W. Gooch of Massachusetts and Representative Moses F. Odell of New York, the only Democrat, signed an appended minority statement claiming the report itself was "incomplete." The majority found that Frémont exhibited "no evidence of any tenderness toward treason." In the exercise of his duties, he never failed "to fully assert the dignity and power of the government of which he was a representative." *Report of the Joint Committee on the Conduct of the War*, 37th Congress, 3rd Session, 3 parts (Washington, D.C., Government Printing Office, 1863), pt. 3:3, 6; "Testimony of General Lewis Wallace," *Report of the Joint Committee*, ibid., 337–53; Bruce Tap, *Over Lincoln's Shoulder: The Committee on the Conduct of the War* (Lawrence: Univ. of Kansas Press, 1998), 11–37, 98; Mark Grimsley, *The Hard Hand of War: Union Military Policy toward Southern Civilians, 1861–1865* (Cambridge, Mass.: Cambridge Univ. Press, 1995) 123–26.

2. It is not known exactly "how" Wallace came to testify that day: whether he was asked by a member of the Joint Committee or subpoenaed, whether Lane or Colfax arranged his appearance, or whether Wallace simply volunteered. The "why" he testified is more readily discernible. He desperately wanted to tell his version of the Donelson story, to have his say on Halleck and Grant, and to voice his views on the mistaken impulses which underscored the policy of "conciliation." Once he was before the Committee, Covode and Julian were his principal interrogators; Chandler posed a question or two; but Wade and Odell failed to ask him anything. Wallace to Aaron Blair, April 3, 1862, *Wallace Collection* (Indianapolis: Indiana Historical Society).

3. Wallace testimony, *Joint Committee,* 3:343. Covode asked Wallace if at Donelson he had acted "on his own judgment," and, if in so doing, he had "saved the army." He quickly answered both questions affirmatively. To his chagrin, the amount of testimony devoted to Donelson encompassed little more than ten percent of the total printed testimony Wallace gave that day.

4. Ibid., 3:340.

5. Ibid., 3:340–42.

6. Ibid., 3:345.

7. Ibid., 3:340. With this question, Covode was attempting to elicit greater specificity from Wallace. Wallace had stated that immediately after the battle of Fort Donelson, Grant had ordered him to return to Fort Henry with the reserve. One statement later, Wallace jumped to the day more than three weeks later when he moved his division onto the steamers that would take them up the Tennessee River on the first leg of the Corinth campaign. Covode was seeking clarification whether Wallace meant he was going to Fort Henry or Savannah. Wallace answered Savannah, but then launched into an unsolicited explanation of the early phases of the Shiloh campaign mixed in with his comments about General Smith.

8. Ibid., 3:344, 345.

9. Ibid., 3:343. Tap, *Over Lincoln's Shoulder,* 27–28.

10. Lew Wallace, *Autobiographical Sketch, August 16, 1863, Wallace Collection* (Indianapolis: Indiana Historical Society), 36.

11. Proclamation, August 31, 1862, *OR,* 3:466–67; General Orders No. 3, November 20, 1861, *OR,* 8:370. The radical Republicans sought to wage a war that would make the South pay for starting it and lead to emancipation. Halleck, as one of several military-political front men for the administration, stood in their way. Most committee members only veiled their contempt for Halleck's military ineptness. Tap, *Over Lincoln's Shoulder,* 11–37; William Whatley Pierson Jr., "The Committee on the Conduct of the Civil War," *The American Historical Review* 23, no. 3 (April 1918): 552–58. See also: Mark Grimsley, *The Hard Hand of War.* Wallace shared the committee's anti-Halleck posture as well as its decided anti–West Point bias. The majority on the committee saw West Point as a bastion of incompetent, conservative elitism. The West Pointers who controlled the army were failing to use it as an agent of social change, specifically emancipation. Many members saw West Point as a useless and potentially destructive drain upon the country's resources. T. Harry Williams, "The Attack Upon West Point During the Civil War," *Mississippi Valley Historical Review* 25, no. 4 (March 1939): 491–504.

12. Wallace testimony, *Joint Committee,* 3:347.

13. Ibid., 3:348.

14. Ibid., 3:350.

15. Ibid., 3:350; Wallace to Susan, June 8, 1862, Wallace Collection.

16. Ibid., 3:351–52. Wallace surely enjoyed himself as he responded to Julian's questions. Julian asked, "You do not want our armies to go through the enemy's country like organized bible societies?" "No, sir, I do not," Wallace replied, "nor like knight-errants, each general travelling with his train following him in search of some enemy to fight him, and doing it upon the pure principles of the chivalry of olden times." Ibid., 3:352.

17. Ibid., 3:353.

18. The members of the committee had no intention of inquiring further into the actual military events that occurred in the West prior to July, 1862. They had launched a general probe, which they believed spoke eloquently to the inadequacies of Grant, and particularly Halleck, as military commanders. The committee members were certain that Wallace's testimony suited their purposes quite well. Throughout the day, they appeared more interested in using Wallace to get to Lincoln and Halleck as a means of discrediting soldiers and redressing the wrong done by Frémont's removal, repudiation, and disgrace. Wallace never lied to the committee, although at times it seems he spun a colorful web around the truth. Ibid., 3:341.

19. Unfortunately, this is a somewhat speculative conclusion. In late 1862, Grant informed Halleck he could work with Wallace, "if he only had less rank." This is the only written statement by Grant touching on his relationship with Wallace. Hillyer, Grant's aide and friend, had already turned on Wallace; Rowley and Rawlins now began the same process in earnest. As the trend intensified, Wallace suffered accordingly.

20. Wallace to Susan, May 10, 1862, *Wallace Collection* (Indianapolis: Indiana Historical Society).

21. Wallace testimony, *Joint Committee*, 3:343.

22. Lew Wallace, *An Autobiography* (New York: Harper & Brothers, 1906), 2:579–80.

12. Speechifying and One Last Adventure

1. J. T. M., "Letter from Washington," July 10, 1862, Indianapolis *Daily Journal* 12, no. 7 (July 14, 1862): 2. One correspondent thought "an unusually large concourse was present on the occasion." *The Goshen* (Indiana) *Times* 7, no. 29 (July 24, 1862): 1.

2. *Goshen Times*, ibid. Many Hoosiers still remembered "Buena Vista" and thanked Wallace accordingly. Liege Fletcher, son of Indianapolis merchant Calvin Fletcher and a boyhood friend, wrote Wallace that "to you we are in great measure indebted for the wiping out the Buena Vista stain." Fletcher fervently stated that "the slightest injustice toward you [in the aftermath of Shiloh] has stirred me to jealous madness." Wallace must have felt gratified many times over when Fletcher concluded his letter by observing, "[t]o me, you are not the Major General; but simply Lew Wallace. And while I feel myself honored by all your advancements, my greatest pleasure is that of the privilege of writing to you freely as a friend

whom I have known from boyhood upward." Liege Fletcher to Wallace, June 7, 1862, *Wallace Collection* (Indianapolis: Indiana Historical Society.

3. Fletcher to Wallace. June 7, 1862, Wallace Collection; *Vincennes* (Indiana) *Gazette* 31, no. 51 (July 19, 1862): 3; *Waukesha* (Wisconsin) *Freeman* 4, no. 18 (July 22, 1862): 1; *The Liberator* 32, no. 30 (July 25, 1862): 1. Wallace conceded that the Negro should and must be armed when, in the process of fulfilling his work duties for the Union army, he found himself in a position of imminent peril. This statement was greeted by "uproarous [*sic*] cheering [which] again drowned everything for some minutes." *Salem* (Indiana) *Union Advocate* 5, no. 16 (August 13, 1862): 1. Earlier that day before the Joint Committee, Wallace had refrained from any discussion of emancipation and freedom for the Negro. Now, as he broached the subject from the balcony of the National Hotel in Washington, quite possibly the first time he had done so before the public, he did so cautiously and with a fair degree of circumspection. Conversely, on the subject of utilizing the escaped slave as military labor and arming him under conditions of possible peril, Wallace's public discourse was direct, forceful, and without reservation, the same characteristics he demonstrated on the field of battle.

4. *Vincennes Gazette*, 31, no. 51 (July 19, 1862): 3; *The Liberator*, 32, no. 30 (July 25, 1862): 1. R. H. Holloway, Morton's private secretary, to the editor of the Evansville *Journal.* He exhorted the editor, "get him [Wallace] an audience worthy of so distinguished a general and soldier." Governor Oliver P. Morton, *Telegraph Books, 1861–1865*, no. 7, 32. See: http://www.in.gov/icpr/2566.htm

5. Indianapolis *Daily Journal* 12, no. 7 (July 14, 1862): 2.

6. Gail Stephens, *Shadow of Shiloh: Major General Lew Wallace in the Civil War* (Indianapolis: Indiana Historical Society Press, 2010), 122–23.

7. Indianapolis *Daily Journal* 12, no. 29 (August 8, 1862): 1.

8. Indianapolis *Daily Journal* 12, no. 35 (August 15, 1862): 3. The *Journal* believed "his efforts in increasing enlistments have been felt."

9. Evansville *Weekly Gazette* 2, no. 57 (August 9, 1862): 3. Wallace normally received more positive than negative press. "There is, perhaps," one commentator observed, "no man in the whole West who is dearer to the people than General Wallace. They delight to honor him for his gallant services in behalf of country, and wherever he may go, he will receive the homage of his fellow citizens." *Daily Wabash* (Terre Haute) *Express* 8, no. 457 (August 12, 1862): 2.

10. *Vincennes Gazette* 32, no. 2 (August 9, 1862), 2; *New York Times* 11, no. 3388 (August 3, 1862): 8, carried a lengthy telegraphic report of Wallace's Market Street Square speech supplied by the *Cincinnati Gazette.* Despite some misgivings, Wallace was still remembered in the East.

11. *New York Times*, op. cit.; *Vincennes Gazette*, op. cit.

12. *New York Times*, op. cit.; *Vincennes Gazette*, op. cit.

13. *New York Times*, op. cit.; *Vincennes Gazette*, op. cit.

14. *New York Times*, op. cit.; *Vincennes Gazette*, op. cit.

15. *New York Times*, op. cit.; *Vincennes Gazette*, op. cit.; *The Liberator* 32, no. 33 (August 15, 1862): 1.

16. *New York Times*, op. cit.; *Vincennes Gazette*, op. cit. In a patriotic recruiting speech given a few days later, Wallace denounced those who called the Union war effort an

abolitionist or Republican war and said that "traitors" who spoke in such a manner should be "crucified": "The secesh, of whom there were a number present, squirmed and shrugged; but it was of no use, they were compelled, for once, to hear the truth. . . . A few more such bold and manly appeals to patriotism, and open denunciation of treason, would have the effect to dry up even the whispers [the pro-secessionists in southern Indiana] except in secluded halls of the 'Golden Circle'." *The Stars and Stripes and Old Union Post* (Vincennes, Indiana) 1, no. 21 (August 9, 1862): 3.

17. The newspapers often got many of their facts wrong, but even when doing so, at least one exploited the idea of "news" to indulge in a bit of wit about Wallace. One Indiana paper noted that Wallace had just been assigned to Camp Chase for the purpose of guarding Rebel prisoners of war. That was correct only with respect to where Wallace went. "If the Government," the reporter concluded, "had as high an opinion of Wallace as W. has of himself, it would not be thus." *The Weekly Vincennes* (Indiana) *Western Sun* 7, no. 9 (September 27, 1862): 1.

18. Stephens, *Shadow of Shiloh,* 113–204, is based upon excellent research and has a good discussion of the events in Wallace's military career occurring between July 10, 1862 and late July, 1864. For the Sioux Indian uprising in Minnesota, see the *Philadelphia Inquirer,* September 22, 1862.

19. Special Orders No. 320, October 30, 1862, *The War of the Rebellion: A Compilation of the Official Records of the Union and Confederate Armies* (Washington, D.C.: Government Printing Office, 1899): 17, pt. 2, 308, hereinafter cited *OR;* Grant to Dodge, November 8, 1862, *OR,* 17, pt. 2, 327.

20. Lee Scott Theissen suggests Grant issued the new order because he rethought his position and decided that he, not Halleck, would choose the personnel for his army. Theissen, "The Public Career of General Lew Wallace, 1845–1905," unpublished Ph.D. dissertation, University of Arizona, 1973, 126. This is a distinct possibility. Further, if Grant were involved in changing Wallace's orders, he was probably signaling that he had thought through and finalized his personal views on Wallace. Grant would make these views known to Halleck in a December 14, 1862, letter. It seems more likely that Halleck issued the change in orders because he succumbed once more to his obsession that it was best for all concerned to keep Wallace off the battlefield. On the other hand, Grant's staff may have played a significant role in getting Wallace's orders changed.

21. Special Orders No. 356, November 20, 1862, *OR,* 16:7; Lew Wallace, *An Autobiography* (New York: Harper & Brothers, 1906), 2:641. Halleck probably made the final decision in the selection of the members of Buell's military tribunal as well as of the tribunal for the Lincoln conspirators and for Henry Wirz, commandant of Andersonville prison. Most of those Halleck selected were civilian, amateur officers. A good many of them were attorneys in civilian life. Undoubtedly, Halleck thought he had finally found a task worthy of their talents. Had Halleck ever convened a court-martial for Wallace, no doubt it would have been staffed entirely by professionally trained West Point general officers.

22. Grant to Halleck, December 14, 1862, *OR,* 52:313–14; Stacy D. Allen, "Lewis Wallace: If He Had Less Rank," in Steven E. Woodworth, ed., *Grant's Lieutenants: From Cairo to Vicksburg* (Lawrence: Univ. of Kansas Press, 2001), 86–89.

23. Grant to Halleck, *OR,* 52:314; Stacy D. Allen, "Lewis Wallace: If He Had Less Rank," 89.

24. The Indianapolis *Daily Journal* 12, no. 66 (September 20, 1862): 2. This editorial was reprinted verbatim in the *Vincennes Gazette* 32, no. 9 (September 27, 1862): 1. As near as can be ascertained, this was an unsolicited outpouring of support for Wallace; Purcell to Chase, October 7, 1862, *Wallace Collection.*

25. Lee Scott Theissen, "Forgotten Politician: The Public Career of Lew Wallace," in Robert G. Barrow, comp., *Their Infinite Variety: Essays on Indiana Politicians* (Indianapolis: Indiana Historical Bureau, 1981), 167–68; Stephens, *Shadow of Shiloh,* 148. Carl Sandburg related a delightful story of Lincoln, the politician, caught between Lane and Halleck. Lincoln reportedly told "a later caller" that "Halleck wants me to kick Wallace out, and Lane wants me to kick Halleck out." Lincoln's caller said, "Well, I'll tell you how to fix it to the satisfaction of both parties . . . kick 'em both out." Carl Sandburg, *Abraham Lincoln: The War Years* (New York, 1948), 4:48. Sandburg did not cite his source for this material.

26. George W. Julian, *Selected Speeches of Honorable George W. Julian of Indiana* (Cincinnati, Ohio: Gazette Steam Book and Job Printing, 1867), 16, 18.

27. *Harper's Weekly* 7 no. 327 (April 6, 1863): 224; see also *Harper's Weekly* 6, no. 310 (December 6, 1862): 784.

28. W. H. H. Terrell, *Indiana in the War of the Rebellion: Report of the Adjutant General* (Indianapolis: Indiana Historical Bureau, 1869), 225, 241–42. From the beginning of Morgan's raid, Morton was obsessed with the possibility that Confederate cavalry might appear on the streets of Indianapolis, Reluctantly, he turned to Wallace for help. He gave Wallace a newly formed regiment of Hoosier solders but since it was inappropriate for a major general to lead a regiment, Morton also gave Wallace the temporary rank of colonel. Lew did not hesitate; he would be back in the field in command. Morton took both the regiment and the rank away from Wallace as soon as the furor caused by the presence of Morgan in southern Indiana had died out. One historian has concluded that whereas for Morgan "the incident" was "a fiasco," for "the invaded," Morton, Wallace, and other political and military leaders in the state at that time, it was "complete confusion." Lorna Lutes Sylvester, "Oliver P. Morton and Hoosier Politics During the Civil War," unpublished Ph.D. dissertation, Indiana University, 1968, 225. See also: Margrette Boyer, "Morgan's Raid in Indiana," *Indiana Magazine of History* 8, no. 4 (December 1912): 152–53, 157, 163–64; William E. Wilson, "Thunderbolt of the Confederacy, or King of Horse Thieves," *Indiana Magazine of History* 54, no. 2 (June 1958): 127–30.

29. *Harper's Weekly* 7, no. 347 (August 22, 1863): 529–30. Today, Wallace's composition might be deemed merely a jingle but in its time it adorned the front page of a well-respected weekly journal. It was also adapted and arranged musically by R. Hastings for A. C. Peters & Bro. The sheet music was published in 1863 in Cincinnati. See: www.loc.gov/item/ihas.200000765; www.loc.gov/resource/ihas.200001329.

30. *New York Times,* 13, no. 3841 (January 15, 1864): 1. Halleck had given Stanton such a list the previous summer.

31. *The Weekly Vincennes Western Sun* (Vincennes, Indiana) 8, no. 27 (January 30, 1864), 1. The same "news from Washington" appeared in the *Daily Milwaukee News,* 16, no. 70 (January 21, 1864), 1, and the *Huntington Indiana Herald* 16, no. 18 (January 27, 1864): 2, under the heading of "Declines Doing It" which stated Lincoln "declined to issue the necessary orders" to approve the Secretary of War's "list of fifteen Major General, whom he [Stanton with Halleck's active support]

desired to discharge or muster out of the service in accordance with the 17th section of the act of July 17, 1862." The *Huntington Indiana Herald* news item can be found in the *Wallace Collection. New York Times* 13, no. 3890 (March 12, 1864): 6; Indianapolis *Daily Journal* 13, no. 215 (March 14, 1864): 4.

32. Halleck to Sherman, April 29, 1864, *OR*, 34:333, pt 3. It should come as no surprise that all the articles on this subject reported that all five of the names in Halleck's letter to Sherman were on the list Stanton gave to Lincoln.

33. Benjamin Franklin Cooling, *Jubal Early's Raid on Washington, 1864* (Baltimore, Md.: The Nautical and Aviation Publishing Company of America, 1989), 1–82. To Grant's credit, at the last minute, he dispatched Brig. Gen. James B. Ricketts and his 3rd Division, 6th Corps, from Petersburg to assist Wallace. Thus, Wallace did have some seasoned Union veterans under his command at Monocacy. There is no question that these battle-hardened veterans of the 1864 Richmond campaign contributed significantly to the fact that Wallace's defeat did not result in his annihilation. By the same token, Wallace had carefully chosen to fight in northwest Maryland because regardless of what happened there this location provided him the best opportunity to protect Washington, or Baltimore, or even to pursue Early into Pennsylvania if that was the Rebel general's destination.

34. Grant to Wallace, March 10, 1868, in Henry B. Carrington, "Major General Lew Wallace at Shiloh," *The Bay State Monthly* 2, no. 6 (March 1885): 2:340. After the battle, one correspondent wrote, "It will hardly be disputed that during the late incursion of Early's men into Maryland, Gen. Wallace showed a more thorough appreciation of what the emergency demanded, a more resolute purpose to discover and face the actual danger, whatever it might be, and did more practical service than any other military officer north of the Potomac." *New York Times* 13, no. 4002 (July 22, 1864): 4. As Grant and even Lincoln began to have a new appreciation of the significance of Wallace's accomplishments in western Maryland, both also came to realize that Halleck's attempts to protect the Capitol, perhaps like the rest of his career efforts, had been at best dithering and feeble as well as overloaded with ambition and jealousy. Time and again, however, Halleck had proven to be a very competent quartermaster.

13. The Genesis of the Shiloh Controversy

1. Hayes to Wallace, March 14, 1862, *The War of the Rebellion: A Compilation of the Official Records of the Union and Confederate Armies* (Washington, D.C.: Government Printing Office, 1899), 10:10, hereinafter cited *OR*. Hayes informed Wallace that he had "effectively crippled" further Confederate use of this bridge until "the whole structure is taken down and rebuilt." That same night, however, Confederate Maj. Gen. Braxton Bragg informed Maj. Gen. Leonidas Polk that the "damaged" bridge had been repaired and was operational. Bragg to Polk, *OR*, 10:11; Wallace to Smith, March 13, 1862, *OR*, 10:9–10. Wallace's bridge experiences had little impact on Confederate mobility. On the other hand, whether exaggerated or not, Wallace's report had specifically noted the presence of Confederate General Cheatham. This suggested that Polk, having retired from Columbus in the aftermath of Fort Henry,

might come even further south to conduct a joint Confederate operation against the Army of the Tennessee. This possibility had a major influence upon Smith's decision to keep Wallace at Crump's Landing, protecting his flank. Grant agreed.

2. Wallace to Smith, March 13, 1862, *OR*, 10:9–10; Thomas M. Stevenson, *History of the 78th Regiment of Ohio Infantry Volunteers from Its 'Muster-In' to its 'Muster-Out'* (Zanesville, Ohio: Hugh Dunne, 1865), 142.

3. *Atlas*, *OR*, plate 78, maps 3 and 6; Wallace to Halleck, March 14, 1863, *OR*, 10:174, map accompanying letter at 177; Lt. Col. James B. McPherson to Capt. John A. Rawlins, March 26, 1863, *OR*, 180, map accompanying report at 183; Larry J. Daniel, *Shiloh: The Battle That Changed the Civil War* (New York: Simon and Schuster, 1997), 107, 165; Gail Stephens, *Shadow of Shiloh: Major General Lew Wallace in the Civil War* (Indianapolis: Indiana Historical Society Press, 2010), 73; Wiley Sword, *Shiloh, Bloody April* (New York: Morrow, 1974), 93. On March 25, 1862, Grant sent a dispatch to Halleck accompanied by two maps. Map 6 showed the disposition of his five divisions at Pittsburg Landing. Map 3 included the locations of Crump's Landing, the Purdy Road, and three roads running south from the Purdy Road. Grant informed Halleck that "General Wallace is six miles below [at Crump's Landing], with a good road out, enabling them [3rd Division] to form a junction with the main column, when a move is made, six or seven miles before reaching Corinth." By this time, March 25, Grant was focused exclusively on Corinth. The words "Pittsburg Landing" are not found in the dispatch. Nothing contained therein indicates Grant knew anything about the "condition" of any of the roads Wallace might take. There is no evidence that Grant ever discussed with Wallace which would be the best road to take to merge with the army on its march to Corinth or, alternatively, to join the main army at Pittsburg Landing in the event of an emergency. In fact, this dearth of evidence strongly suggests that Grant knew little about a road named the Shunpike or even anticipated the role this road might play in any future decision by Wallace. Grant to Halleck, March 25, 1862, *OR*, 52:230.

4. The above is verifiable by examining map 3, "Sketch of Roads to Corinth, Miss.," dated March 25, 1862, found in *Atlas*, *OR*, plate 78; map accompanying Wallace's letter to Halleck on March 14, 1863, found in *OR*, 10:177; and map accompanying McPherson's letter to Rawlins, March 26, 1863, *OR*, 10:183. See Timothy B. Smith, "Why Lew Was Late," *Civil War Times* 46, no. 10 (January 2008): 32. It is unknown if Wallace had a copy of map 3 in his possession. However, Major Hayes and his 5th Ohio cavalry had engaged in a significant amount of reconnaissance of the roads in the Shunpike area and relayed this information to Wallace. Hence, it is reasonable to conclude that Wallace was well informed of the existence and condition of this alternative route to Pittsburg Landing whether he had ever seen map 3 or not. The Shunpike would take him to Corinth or to Sherman's right flank as orders and field conditions dictated at the time.

5. Wallace to Susan, March 18, 1862, *Wallace Collection* (Indianapolis: Indiana Historical Society).

6. Wallace to Smith, March 13, 1862, *OR*, 10:9.

7. Dennis Hart Mahan, *An Elementary Treatise on Advanced-Guard, Out-Post, and Detachment Service of Troops and the Manner of Posting and Handling Them in the Presence of an Enemy* (New York: Wiley and Putnam, 1847), 266.

8. Joseph W. Rich, *The Battle of Shiloh* (Iowa City: Iowa State Historical Society, 1918), 34, 47.

9. Wallace to Grant, April 4, 1862, *OR*, 10:90–91, pt. 2. The effective strength of the 3rd Division was at that time approximately 7,500 men.

10. Grant to W. H. L. Wallace, April 4, 1862, *OR*, 10:91.

11. Grant to Sherman, April 4, 1862, *OR*, 10:91.

12. Grant to Halleck, April 5, 1862, *OR*, 10:94.

13. Lew Wallace, *An Autobiography* (New York: Harper & Brothers, 1906), 1:448.

14. Ibid., 1:448–49.

15. Ibid., 1:457; Col. Bausenwein, *Report*, April 10, 1862, *OR*, 10:199; Ammen, *Journal*, *OR*, 331; Richard J. Fulfer, *A History of the Trials and Hardships of the Twenty-Fourth Indiana Volunteer Infantry* (Indianapolis: Indianapolis Printing Company, 1913), 35; George F. McGinnis, "Shiloh," in *War Papers Read Before the Indiana Commandery. Military Order of the Loyal Legion of the United States, (MOLLUS)* (Indianapolis, 1898), 15.

16. Wallace wrote Susan that Grant had ordered his command to be ready to march immediately on Corinth with ten days' rations. Halleck had quickly quashed that order since Buell was still en route from Nashville. The episode, however, might well have suggested to Wallace that when the Corinth campaign finally did begin, marching along the River, Road would be a longer, more tiring route than might otherwise exist. Wallace therefore had a second reason to send Hayes to find a possible alternative. Wallace to Susan, March 21, 1862, *Wallace Collection.*

17. Hayes to Capt. Fred Knefler, March 22, 1862, cited in Gail M. Stephens, "Lew Wallace's Fall From Grace," *North & South* 7, no. 3 (May, 2004): 45, 38, n. 21. Stephens makes the point that had Wallace traveled the Shunpike all the way to Sherman's camp during a Confederate attack, he would have marched along exterior lines, possibly exposing his men to an enemy flanking attack. The River Road, utilizing movement along only interior lines, was, if nothing else, a safer route.

18. Thomas Wise Durham, 11th Indiana, 1st Brigade, 3rd Division, recalled that one of the tasks to which he had been assigned in the week before April 6 was road improvement. Inasmuch as men of the 2nd Division were then busy working on the Wallace Bridge on the River Road, it is likely that Durham was referring to the improvements done to the Shunpike as well as the unnamed bridge on the Shunpike, which crossed Snake Creek northwest of the Wallace Bridge. Jeffrey L. Patrick, ed., *Three Years With Wallace's Zouaves: The Civil War Memoirs of Thomas Wise Durham* (Macon, Ga.: Mercer Univ. Press, 2003), 82–83.

19. Lew Wallace to W. H. L. Wallace, April 5, 1862, in Ulysses S. Grant, *Personal Memoirs of Ulysses S. Grant* (New York: Charles L. Webster and Company, 1885), 1:351. This is the letter that was found in W. H. L. Wallace's pocket as he was taken dying from the Shiloh battlefield. It was given to his widow, Ann, who sent it to Grant in 1885.

20. Grant, *Personal Memoirs*, 1:352. Grant also stated in the most backhanded fashion possible that given "no more experience than he had at the time in the profession of arms," Wallace's decision to come to Pittsburg Landing by way of the Shunpike was "natural."

21. Grant to Wallace, March 19, 1862; March 21, 1862 in John Y. Simon, ed., *The Papers of Ulysses S. Grant* (Carbondale: Southern Illinois Univ. Press, 1967–2000),

4:401; Wallace to Rawlins, March 21, 1862, in Simon, *Papers of Grant*, 4:402fn; Wallace to Susan, March 21, 1862, *Wallace Collection*.

22. Wallace to Grant, April 12, 1862, *OR*, 10:169–74.

23. Grant to Halleck, April 7, 1862, *OR*, 10:108; April 8, *OR*, 10:108; April 9, *OR*, 10:108–9. Initially, the Confederates massed against the Union right and center. The heavy fighting on the left of Grant's line took place later that afternoon. Either Grant erred when he filed this report or he remained confused.

24. Grant to Halleck, April 9, 1862, *OR*, 10:109–10. Strangely, Grant never mentioned the death of W. H. L. Wallace or, for that matter, the death of the Confederate leader, Albert Sydney Johnston.

25. Rowley to Rawlins, April 4, 1863, *OR*, 10:179, hereinafter "Rowley"; McPherson to Rawlins, March 26, 1863, *OR*, 10:181, hereinafter "McPherson"; and Rawlins to Grant, *OR*, 10:185, hereinafter "Rawlins." These statements constitute the cover-up that will later become a part of the controversy. The five reports Grant sent to Halleck concerning the battle were dated April 7, 8, 9, 25, 1862, and April 13, 1863, and are found in *OR*, 10:108, 109, 174, 178. After the war, Rawlins spoke frequently about Shiloh. He invariably talked about Wallace's casual march to the battlefield, which remained casual, according to Rawlins, even after Rowley had directed him to the River Road. Coming from a man of Rawlins's presumed stature, these statements gained a certain aura of "fact." After all, by war's end, Rawlins was a brevet major general in the regular army and chief of staff of general headquarters. He soon became the first president of a very large collection of veterans known as The Society of the Army of the Tennessee.

26. Grant, *Personal Memoirs*, 1:337.

27. The five division commanders at Pittsburg Landing had a much easier time than Wallace communicating with Grant. Grant spent most of each day at his headquarters at the Landing even though he journeyed up and down the Tennessee River to Savannah each morning and evening, passing Wallace's camp at Crump's Landing. This is not to suggest that Grant intentionally and purposefully never communicated with Wallace in the days leading up to the battle. The evidence, however, strongly suggests an amazing dearth of communication between the two men at this time.

28. Wallace to Susan, March 18, 1862, *Wallace Collection*.

29. George Washington Cable, in James Lee McDonough, *Shiloh: In Hell before Night* (Knoxville: Univ. of Tennessee Press, 1977), 225; Sword, *Shiloh, Bloody April*.

14. The Controversy Begins

1. Wallace to Halleck, March 14, 1863, *The War of the Rebellion: A Compilation of the Official Records of the Union and Confederate Armies* (Washington, D.C.: Government Printing Office, 1899), 10:174, hereinafter cited *OR*.

2. Ibid.

3. Grant to McLean, April 9, 1862, *OR*, 10:109; Grant to Halleck, April 25, 1862, *OR*, 10:174.

4. Halleck played a decisive, albeit indirect, role in the controversy. He refused to correspond directly with Wallace to answer his questions. He further muddled

the matter when he sent all of Wallace's correspondence to Grant but then intentionally failed to forward any response from Grant to Wallace. In so doing, he prolonged and even possibly escalated the controversy. Halleck knew he could not afford to take the chance that Wallace might prevail in some way in this matter. Old Brains continued to insist in his own mind that the civilian amateur soldier deserved no leadership role in the war effort. Interestingly, Halleck did not restrict his belief to military men and matters. On an earlier occasion, he dismissively suggested to Missouri Congressman Francis P. Blair Jr that he, better than a politician, could handle a political problem originating within the district he commanded. "All I ask," he wrote, "of my Washington friends is to keep cool and let me work out my plans. I understand the problem and will solve it in time." A few weeks later, when several politically powerful German-Americans expressed dissatisfaction with the administration's removal of Frémont, Halleck brusquely told Lincoln to get out of the way and let him handle the matter. "Any yielding on the part of the Government will only create new difficulties and give rise to new demands. Being a German myself by descent, I know something of the German character, and I am confident that in a few weeks, if the Government does not interfere, I can reduce these disaffected elements to order and discipline." In a similar manner, Halleck would eliminate the likes of a Wallace from his world. Although it often seemed that Halleck was waging a vendetta, there was little personal anger associated with his agenda—it was merely a matter of exclusivity. Halleck to Blair, January 6, 1862, *OR*, 8:490; Halleck to Lincoln, January 21, 1862, *OR*, 10:827.

5. Wallace to Halleck, March 14, 1863, *OR*, 10:174. One charge against Wallace was that he refused to march anywhere without a signed order. Wallace denied this. When Wallace was "found" later that day he was not at Crump's Landing but was marching down the Shunpike. Apparently, he had never ascribed much significance to whether or not the order was signed. As he told Halleck, he had "resolved to march toward the cannonading at 12 o'clock without orders." Therefore, to have an order, even if unsigned, was preferable to having no orders. *OR*, 10:175. This issue of a "signed" order, like the dispute over the time when the order was received, was likewise inconsequential. Both parties agreed it was a "written" order.

6. Wallace to Halleck, March 14, 1863, *OR*, 10:175; Wallace to Rawlins, April 12, 1862, *OR*, 10:170. The description Wallace gave in March, 1863, to describe Grant's order was not an exact repetition of the description of that order he gave in his battlefield report. The meaning in both instances was virtually identical. Wallace's version of the order had varied only slightly in the first eleven months following the battle; Grant had suggested three different versions of his order in the first three weeks. Fully aware of the unintended consequences of the "lost" order, Wallace undoubtedly vowed never to let that happen again. He was constantly perfecting his craft. For example, around 11:00 on the morning of July 9, 1864, he was preparing his men to counter Confederate Lt. Gen. Jubal A. Early's advance from Frederick, Maryland, southeast against either Washington or Baltimore. As the Battle of Monocacy began, Wallace became aware that a number of Confederate skirmishers had broken away from the main body of Early's army and were advancing toward a cornfield. He realized that Brig. Gen. James B. Ricketts's 3rd Division, part of the VI Corps that Grant had dispatched from around Richmond

to aid him, must be directed against these skirmishers. Wallace wrote in his *Autobiography* that he called an orderly to him and had two of his aides on horseback flank the messenger. Each aide wrote out the order for Ricketts as Wallace dictated it: "'Make haste,' I said to the orderly, giving him one of the duplicates and retaining the other." Lew Wallace, *An Autobiography* (New York: Harper and Brothers, 1906), 2:766.

7. Grant to Halleck, *OR*, 10:108–9, 174. By self-imposed silence, Grant efficiently and effectively isolated himself from any of the controversy's effects. Grant to Halleck, April 13, 1863, *OR*, 10:178.

8. Wallace to Halleck, March 14, 1863, *OR*, 10:175.

9. Ibid. Wallace's use of the phrase, "close to Pittsburg Landing," seemed to indicate that he believed that when Grant employed the words Pittsburg Landing, he meant the landing's actual physical location. Wallace told Halleck that Sherman's camp of April 5 was over two-and-a-half miles from the landing.

10. Ibid., 10:176.

11. Ibid.

12. Grant to Kelton, April 13, 1863, *OR*, 10:178.

13. Ibid; Grant to McLean, April 9, 1862, *OR*, 10:108; Rawlins, *OR*, 10:185. Presumably, when Grant wrote 10:00, he meant 1:00. Obviously, it would have been impossible for Smith to have arrived on the field of battle by "10:00" when Grant had earlier insisted that his order to Wallace was delivered at "11:00." Mistake or not, Grant's letter to Halleck displays a state of mind that suggests a serious character flaw—an inability to take responsibility for one's actions. Morgan Smith was a competent soldier, although Halleck would never have agreed, since Smith, like Wallace, was a civilian amateur. Grant lacked a specific recollection of what his order had said. It is thus impossible to know exactly how Smith would have reacted to this order or to anything else had he been in command. Thus, while it is acceptable for Grant to engage in wishful thinking, the conclusion concerning Smith that he drew from this exercise was simply absurd. The situation had all the trappings of a Fort Donelson redo. Even a year after Shiloh, Grant still seemed confused about some of the events of the day.

14. Halleck's role in the controversy was limited but nefarious nonetheless. His primary reason for refusing Wallace's request for a court of inquiry had nothing to do with saving Wallace from any further embarrassment. He turned his back on Wallace and the problem because he wanted to keep as much information as possible about Grant's and Wallace's role during that first day at Shiloh from the prying eyes of the newspaper correspondents, various members of Congress, and the public in general. He appeared to have been indifferent to any rights Wallace might otherwise possess to confront witnesses assembled against him.

15. Wallace to Grant, June 27, 1863, *Wallace Collection* (Indianapolis: Indiana Historical Society), 1–2.

16. Ibid., 2–3.

17. Ibid., 8, 4, 6, 7.

18. Ibid., 2, 4.

19. Ibid., 7. This was the only occasion when Wallace sought to identify a scapegoat for the events of April 6. The speed with which he subsequently departed from

this line of defense does him some credit. After the June letter to Grant, Wallace never again blamed any individual by name for the problems associated with the march. In fact, by the time the second and last round of the controversy came into being in 1868, Wallace simply referred to the contents of an order delivered that morning by "a messenger." It is not suggested, however, that Wallace remained at any time above embellishment for the sake of a good story. In his Joint Committee testimony, for example, he had colored several "facts." He maintained that neither Rowley, who found him on the Shunpike, nor Rawlins, who came upon him later as he approached the River Road, had "orders or directions for me." Wallace claimed he stopped his march upon the Shunpike and returned to the River Road "for reasons satisfactory to myself." He also suggested that all things considered, "I think I would have been justified in going back to Crumps Landing with my command for the purpose of saving it." Wallace even went so far as to assert that upon his arrival on the battlefield on Sunday night he had asked Grant for "a diagram showing me the enemy's lines and our lines." He said that "it was promised me, but I never got it." Wallace knew what his audience in Washington wanted to hear. Unabashedly, he gave it to them. "Testimony of General Lewis Wallace," *Report of the Joint Committee on the Conduct of the War* (Washington, D.C., 1863), 3:341.

20. Wallace seldom disguised his feelings. He seldom evidenced a talent for the bluff. His forte was unequivocal directness, often preceded with a dose of fawning or sycophancy as he thought the circumstances dictated. Grant had neither the time nor the enthusiasm for such posturing from his subordinates.

21. Strickland to Wallace, June 24, 1863, *Wallace Collection;* Ross to Wallace, June 26, 1863, *Wallace Collection;* Ware to Wallace, undated, in Henry B. Carrington, "Major General Lew Wallace at Shiloh," *Bay State Monthly* 2, no. 6 (March 1885): 339. Strickland also made the only comment at that time concerning the condition of the River Road. He observed that upon reaching the River Road following the countermarch, the 3rd Division had to deal with "a small stream where the mud was very deep."

22. Knefler to Wallace, June 23, 1863; Simson to Wallace, June 24, 1863, *Wallace Collection.*

23. Strickland to Wallace, June 24, 1863; Ross to Wallace, June 26, 1863; Knefler to Wallace, June 23, 1863; and Simson to Wallace, June 24, 1863, *Wallace Collection;* Ware to Wallace, undated, in Carrington, "Major General Lew Wallace at Shiloh," 339.

24. Sherman told Grant that he believed Albert Sydney Johnston had sent a Confederate detachment to guard and defend the Owl Creek bridge but was unsure of its size and strength.

25. Gail Stephens, *Shadow of Shiloh: Major General Lew Wallace in the Civil War* (Indianapolis: Indiana Historical Society Press, 2010), 152. The original of this memorandum is to be found in the National Archives, General's Papers and Books, Halleck RG 94, Entry 159.

26. Wallace to Stanton, July 18, 1863, *OR,* 10:188–89. Wallace asked that a court be convened. It was apparent, however, from the distant and official tone of his letter that Wallace believed the time had long since come to "demand" this court.

27. Wallace to Stanton, *OR,* 10:189.

28. Ibid. In his letter to Grant several weeks earlier, Wallace had suggested that if Grant's interpretation correctly defined his actions that day, he would have had "but two motives in disobeying it: one a wish to see you defeated and ruined, the other cowardice." Wallace categorically denied that either was true. Grant did not rise to the bait. Wallace to Grant, June 27, 1863, *Wallace Collection*, 8–9.

29. Halleck endorsement, July 24, 1863, appended to the War Department's summary of Wallace's letter, *Wallace Collection.*

30. Wallace to Sherman, August 16, 1863, *Wallace Collection;* Sherman to Rawlins, August 27, 1863, *Wallace Collection.*

31. Sherman to Wallace, August 27, 1863, *Wallace Collection.* Whether Sherman at this time was a friend or a foe is strictly a matter of interpretation of where Sherman believed himself to be. Stacy D. Allen, "Lewis Wallace: If He Had Less Rank," in Steven E. Woodworth, ed., *Grant's Lieutenants: From Cairo to Vicksburg* (Lawrence: Univ. of Kansas Press, 2001), 88; Stephens, *Shadow of Shiloh*, 153; and Lloyd Lewis, *Sherman: Fighting Prophet* (New York: Harcourt, Brace and Company, 1932), 301, all believe Sherman's motives toward Wallace were sincere. This is suspect. The advice Sherman gratuitously offered Wallace is altogether consistent with the duplicity he manifested in his "confidential" telegram to Rawlins. Much like his early mentor Halleck, Sherman sought only to silence the Hoosier general. It is very difficult to apply such words as "honest" and "unselfish" to Sherman's actions toward Wallace at this time.

32. Sherman to Wallace, August 27, 1863, *Wallace Collection.* As another example, Sherman was also corresponding with Buell at this time. Sitting on the shelf like Wallace, Buell had solicited Sherman's advice about writing a history of the early years of the war. Sherman thought such a venture "look[ed] childish, foolish, yes, criminal." It would appear imprudent "for sensible men to be away at the rear, sitting in security, torturing their brains and writing on reams of foolscap to fill a gap future historians will dispose of by a very short and maybe unimportant chapter or even paragraph." Sherman undoubtedly criticized Buell's proposal because he did not want him writing anything that might reflect badly upon him. Buell had been Sherman's commanding officer in Kentucky during those "early" years when quite a few, somewhat reasonably, judged Sherman to be insane. Lewis, *Sherman*, 301–2.

33. Wallace to Stanton, September 16, 1863, *OR*, 10:189–90. Sherman wrote Wallace one more time. He had spoken to Grant but Grant had told him he had too many general officers and insufficient manpower for all of them to have a command. He declined to write a letter to the War Department on Wallace's behalf. Wallace should find some command somewhere and "trust to events." No further assistance was offered. Sherman to Wallace, October 9, 1863, *Wallace Collection.*

34. Lossing to Wallace, March 17, 1863, *Wallace Collection.*

35. A. K. McClure, *Abraham Lincoln and Men of War-Times. Some Personal Recollections of War and Politics during the Lincoln Administration*, 2nd ed. (Philadelphia, 1892), 177–80; idem, *Lincoln's Yarns and Stories: A Complete Collection of the Funny and Witty Anecdotes that Made Abraham Lincoln Famous as America's Greatest Story Teller* (Chicago, 1901), 295.

36. Wallace to Susan, August 8, 1864, *Wallace Collection.* Following a "warm" and "cordial" meeting at which the events of April 6 were not discussed, Wallace

told Susan he was hopeful Grant might offer him the position of chief of staff. Wallace to Susan, September 12, 1864, *Wallace Collection.* Wallace was engaging in a monumental flight of fancy. There was no way that Grant would sacrifice Rawlins for Wallace. John Y. Simon, ed., *The Papers of Ulysses S. Grant* (Carbondale: Southern Illinois Univ. Press, 1967–2000), 11:376fn.

15. The Cover-Up

1. Grant to Halleck, April 25, 1862, *The War of the Rebellion: A Compilation of the Official Records of the Union and Confederate Armies* (Washington, D.C.: Government Printing Office, 1899), 10:174, hereinafter cited *OR;* Wallace to Halleck, March 14, 1863, *OR.*

2. Grant to Baxter, March 30, 1863, in John Y. Simon, ed., *The Papers of Ulysses S. Grant* (Carbondale: Southern Illinois Univ. Press, 1967–2000), 8:62fn; Baxter interview, New York *Mail and Express,* November 4, 1886, in "The March of Lew Wallace's Division to Shiloh," in Robert Underwood Johnson and Clarence Clough Buel, eds., *From Fort Sumter to Shiloh: Battles and Leaders of the Civil War* (New York, 1887), 1:607. Baxter was not a major player in either the controversy or the cover-up. What he did say, however, was significantly more pro-Wallace than pro-Grant.

3. Rowley to Rawlins, April 4, 1863, *OR,* 10:178–80; McPherson to Rawlins, March 26, 1863, *OR,* 10:180–83; Rawlins to Grant, April 1, 1863, *OR,* 10:183–88. The respective dates of each report suggest that Rawlins wrote his report several days before Rowley. That is very suspect. There was undoubtedly much discussion among the participants before each recounted his version of events. Rawlins read and certainly analyzed the reports of McPherson and Rowley before he wrote his own. Rawlins's report should have been dated after Rowley's. Even so, the dating of all these reports is yet another reason to be suspicious of their overall integrity.

4. Two Wallace aides, Ross and Knefler, told Wallace in 1863 and again in 1868 that when Baxter arrived at Crump's with orders from Grant, he volunteered that Union arms were then prevailing in the battle. Ross was certain that Baxter had told Wallace that "Grant was driving the enemy at all points." Knefler recalled that Baxter "brought the very cheering intelligence that our army was successful." As late as the summer of 1863, Wallace had not acted upon this information. In February, 1868, however, Wallace would write to Grant that when Rowley found him on the Shunpike, he conveyed "a very different story from the one brought me by Captain Baxter." Baxter steadfastly denied having made such categorical assertions. There are several reasons why Baxter, as opposed to Wallace and his men, was telling the truth. Baxter, by his own admission, never left the landing area, where he acted as a quartermaster prior to Rawlins finding him and sending him downriver to find Wallace. Hence, Baxter had no way of assessing battlefield conditions and whether or not the statements he allegedly made were true. The fact that Wallace never claimed in his 1862 report, his 1863 letter to Halleck, or his 1863 letter to Grant that Baxter ever spoke to him further suggests that Baxter never said these things. Last, Wallace's first act after receiving Grant's orders was to pause briefly to allow his men to have a last-minute repast before battle. Had

Wallace perceived that success in battle was slipping beyond his reach, taking the time to eat first would have been quite secondary to the adventure of battle and the acquisition of glory and honor. Wallace feared being "left behind."

5. The Wallace supporter who succumbed the most readily to this type of speculative argument was Brig. Gen. George F. McGinnis. As late as 1898, he claimed that when Baxter arrived, Wallace specifically asked him "how is the battle going?" Baxter replied, according to McGinnis, "We are driving them all along the line." George F. McGinnis, "Shiloh," in *War Papers Read Before the Indiana Commandery. Military Order of the Loyal Legion of the United States, (MOLLUS)* (Indianapolis, 1898), 9–10; in Henry B. Carrington, "Major General Lew Wallace at Shiloh," *Bay State Monthly* 2, no. 6 (March 1885): 335, 337, 367. It is quite possible that the Wallace faction, particularly McGinnis, imagined they heard Baxter's comments on early-morning Union successes in order to amplify the wisdom of Wallace's decision to march down the Shunpike.

6. Hillyer was not part of the official cover-up. After Donelson, however, his anger with Wallace was well known among Grant's aides. As the author of "Lampoon of General Lew Wallace," he played a significant role in widening the gap between Wallace and Grant. Gail Stephens, *Shadow of Shiloh: Major General Lew Wallace in the Civil War* (Indianapolis: Indiana Historical Society Press, 2010), 61–62. Yet, on April 11, 1862, he seemed much more in agreement with McPherson than with either Rowley or Rawlins. For instance, he stated that "about eleven o'clock," Wallace was ordered "to move up to Pittsburg." Hillyer does not mention the River Road. He only became critical of Wallace when he observed that Wallace "should have been there by noon." W. S. Hillyer to his wife, April 11, 1862, in *The Confederate Veteran Magazine 1893* (Nashville: Tennessee, 1893), 1:298, 299.

7. Sylvanus Cadwallader, ed. Benjamin P. Thomas, *Three Years with Grant as Recalled by War Correspondent Sylvanus Cadwallader* (Lincoln: Univ. of Nebraska Press, 1966), 228–29. The first two names and middle initials are set forth in brackets in the original text. Cadwallader, a war correspondent for the Chicago *Times*, joined Grant in October, 1862. From then until April, 1865, he was privy to much of what went on in Grant's camp. Cadwallader expressed surprise in his book that Grant in his 1885 *Memoirs* had praised Wallace for his performance at Monocacy. Cadwallader was under the distinct impression that few in Grant's circle had anything good to say about Wallace, *Three Years with Grant*, viii–ix, xv. Add Wallace's testimony before the Joint Committee into the mix of Hillyer's anger, the horrors of Shiloh, and the desire to protect Grant, and it is easy to see that Wallace did not fare well with other members of Grant's official military family. Perhaps each member of Grant's family perceived his report to be just retribution for the volumes of innuendo and slander Wallace allegedly uttered against him and Grant.

8. Rowley, *OR*, 10:178.

9. Rawlins, *OR*, 10:185.

10. Rawlins, *OR*, 10:183; Grant to Nelson, April 6, 1862, and Grant to Buell, April 6, 1862, *OR*, 10:95, pt. 2; Col. Jacob Ammen's Diary, *OR*, 10:330. In 1900, historian John Fiske raised this issue of Grant's failure to communicate with Wallace with a precise written order. "Serious peril" would have been avoided at Shiloh had Grant initially sent "a businesslike written order" to Wallace specifically designating the route

to the battlefield Wallace was to take. "Napoleon . . . ín his best days left but little room open for contingencies and misunderstandings." John Fiske, *The Mississippi Valley in the Civil War* (Boston and New York: Houghton, Mifflin and Company, 1900), 80–81.

11. McPherson, *OR*, 10:181; Rowley, *OR*, 10:180; Rawlins, *OR*, 10:188; Grant to Kelton, April 13, 1862, *OR*, 10:178; Wallace to Rawlins, April 12, 1862, *OR*, 10:170. Col. Valentine Bausenwein, 58th Ohio, 2nd Brigade, 3rd Division, stated that on April 6 that "we marched all the afternoon in quick-time through ravines and swamps until we arrived." Bausenwein to Strickland, April 16, 1862, *OR*, 10:199. Col. Alvin P. Hovey, 24th Indiana, 1st Brigade, 3rd Division, wrote that his brigade "bivouacked for the night [April 6], sleeping on their arms, under one of the most severe rains of the season," *OR*, 10:191. In 1912, Pvt. Samuel H. Fletcher, Company A, 2nd Illinois Cavalry, wrote that "the roads were very muddy, and after crossing Snake Creek, were almost impassable. The horses constantly floundered in mud and water which was often up to the saddle-skirts." He concluded that "the condition of Wallace's men upon reaching the front [having traveled along the River Road] was pitiable—especially that of the infantry. They floundered and wallowed in the mud and water in which they frequently sank to their hips; but, with all this, nothing but eagerness was shown by officers and men to get to the front." Samuel H. Fletcher, *History of Company A, Second Illinois Cavalry* (Chicago: D. H. Fletcher, 1892), 50–51. Pvt. Richard J. Fulfer, Company A, 24th Indiana, wrote in 1913 that at Crump's Landing around 11:00 P.M. on April 5, "the rain was falling as fast as I ever saw rain fall. The water was from shoe-top deep to knee deep, all over the road." Richard J. Fulfer, *A History of the Trials and Hardships of the Twenty-fourth Indiana Volunteer Infantry* (Indianapolis, 1913), 35.

12. Rowley, *OR*, 10:180; McPherson, *OR*, 10:182; Rawlins, *OR*, 10:188; Wallace to Halleck, March 14, 1863, *OR*, 10:175; Ulysses S. Grant, *Personal Memoirs of Ulysses S. Grant* (New York: Charles L. Webster & Company, 1885), 1:336.

13. Rowley, *OR*, 10:179–80; McPherson, *OR*, 10:182; Rawlins, *OR*, 10:185–86, 187–88. Before he had finished his report, McPherson had tempered his criticism. McPherson acknowledged he had allowed his own impatience to move the 3rd Division onto the field of battle long before nightfall to color his anxiety over Wallace's alleged slowness. McPherson's concession dampened to a degree what had appeared to be a consensus among the three reports. In summary, McPherson's only consistent complaint of Wallace's actions that day was that he had initially taken the wrong road and as a result gotten lost.

16. The Cover-Up Continues—"Oh! The Lies"

1. Wallace to Grant, April 12, 1862, *The War of the Rebellion: A Compilation of the Official Records of the Union and Confederate Armies* (Washington, D.C.: Government Printing Office, 1899), 10:170, hereinafter cited *OR*. Later, for example when he wrote and talked personally to Halleck, Wallace acknowledged that Grant's order as received was written, just not signed. Wallace to Halleck, March 14, 1862, *OR*, 10:175. There had been no written order sending him to Romney and no written order Saturday morning at Donelson sending him onto the Wynn's Ferry Road.

2. Rowley, *OR*, 10:179. This is the first reference in the cover-up to the River Road.

3. Ibid. Rowley believed this episode gave him the opportunity, as Rawlins had twice done, to portray Wallace as a military prima donna, a strutting popinjay. Thus, Rowley alleged that he told Wallace that Grant knew Wallace would not march without a "written" order. Wallace called that a "damn lie." He then further proclaimed his innocence on that point by cavalierly observing, "Here you find me on the road." This alleged conversation underscores a problem the pro-Wallace faction always had when addressing the elements of the controversy on an official level. Until Rowley's report became public knowledge in the mid-1880s, there is nothing to indicate that Wallace was ever aware of Rowley's unfounded, exaggerated statement. Similarly, many of the allegations by the pro-Grant faction made directly to Halleck never saw the light of day, as Halleck refused to release them to Wallace. This explains why, during the immediate postwar harangues centering on the controversy, Wallace and his supporters often appeared to be tilting at windmills. They simply had no idea where to begin their rebuttal. Not only did McPherson fail to mention this straw man, Wallace never acknowledged his existence. The two orderlies who rode with Rowley at Grant's instruction never entered the history books in any fashion other than as Rowley had created them.

4. Rawlins, *OR*, 10:185–86. This was not the only occasion when Rawlins made a statement in his report that contradicted an earlier assertion.

5. Ibid. There is reason to believe that Rawlins's "cavalry officer" did exist although the mission Grant might have sent him on was substantively different than what both Rawlins and Rowley described. Samuel Fletcher wrote in 1912 that he was present when Grant ordered a Lieutenant Bennett to take Fletcher's Company A, 2nd Illinois Cavalry, to Crump's Landing "with as much dispatch as possible," find Wallace, and "tell him to come immediately, *you being the escort* [emphasis added]." Fletcher wrote that Bennett found Wallace and spoke to him whereupon "the order was at once given to fall in line." Fletcher said nothing about "written orders." Fletcher further stated that the 2nd Illinois stayed with Wallace the entire march and came to the battlefield after nightfall, presumably with Bennett still in command of the 2nd Illinois contingent. Both Rawlins and Rowley had their straw man, possibly Bennett, reporting on the field to Grant that afternoon. Fletcher does not suggest that Bennett returned to talk to Grant that afternoon as both Rowley and Rawlins represented. If he had, his act would have been in direct disobedience to his orders to be "the escort." Samuel H. Fletcher, *History of Company A, Second Illinois Cavalry* (Chicago: D. H. Fletcher, 1892), 50–53. Bennett presumably existed and presumably Grant sent him and Company A to speed Wallace along. If so, Rowley and Rawlins are not guilty of inventing a straw man but certainly are liable for exploiting the lieutenant solely for their own invented needs and purposes.

6. Wallace to Halleck, *OR*, 10:175.

7. General Orders No. 30, March 31, 1862, *OR*, 10:84, pt. 2; Rawlins, *OR*, 10:184. Apparently for Rawlins, "steam continually kept up" equated to preparedness, regardless of the costs and inconvenience.

8. Lt. Putnam, a paymaster, contradicted Rawlins's point about "steam." In 1888, Putnam told the members of the Ohio Commandery that on April 6 he volunteered to join Grant on the *Tigress*, which "started up the river as soon as steam was raised."

It required the better part of a half hour to "raise the steam." Douglas Putnam Jr, "Reminiscences of the Battle of Shiloh," *Sketches of War History, 1861–1865. Papers Prepared for the Ohio Commandery of the Military Order of the Loyal Legions of the United States, 1888–1890* (Cincinnati: Robert Clarke & Co., 1890), 198.

9. Rawlins, *OR*, 10:184.

10. Buell to Grant, *OR*, 10:92–93, pt. 2; Grant to Buell, April 5, 1862, *OR*, 10:93.

11. Charles A. Dana, *Recollections of the Civil War with the Leaders at Washington and in the Field of the Sixties* (New York: D. Appleton and Company, 1902), 61; Albert O. Marshall, *Army Life From a Soldier's Journal* (Joliet, Ill.: Chicago Legal News Company, 1883), 274; *New York World*, February 20, 1863, and *New York Times*, June 21, 1863, both cited in Jean Edward Smith, *Grant* (New York: Simon & Schuster, 2001), 232–33, and in Bruce Catton, *Grant Moves South* (New York: Little, Brown and Company, 1960), 390–91.

12. Putnam, "Reminiscences of the Battle of Shiloh," 200. Putnam quite likely had an agenda undergirding his observations, but, if so, it essentially remained a hidden one. There is little evidence Putnam and Rawlins did not get along. There does not seem to exist a photograph of Grant on the battlefield of Shiloh dressed in full military regalia.

13. Rawlins, *OR*, 10:187–88, 186. Rawlins attributed certain flowery and grandiose statements to Wallace that afternoon, but he might have better served his general had he first addressed a certain question concerning human nature, to wit: in an emotional and stress-filled setting, permeated by the guns of battle, does a soldier tend to wax eloquent like a poet or resort to the more basic speech pattern of a seasoned trooper? Not only was Wallace an unrestrained product of the American frontier of the time, one of his colleagues, W. H. L. Wallace, once observed that he liked Wallace well enough except for his proclivity for profanity. W. H. L. Wallace to Ann Wallace, February 17, 1862, quoted in Victor Hinken, *Illinois in the Civil War* (Urbana: Univ. of Illinois Press, 2nd ed., 1991), 39.

14. Rawlins, *OR*, 10:187–88, 186. Another problem with this argument was Rawlins's ignorance of geography. Assuming the first incident occurred where Rawlins said, at the "main Pittsburg Landing road," then the second incident, concerning checking the status of the bridge over Snake Creek, would have occurred within no more than a mile of the first. Wallace knew the men of the 3rd Division were in sufficient physical shape and thus quite competent to march more than a mile before they required a second period of rest.

15. In his report, Rawlins reproduced "substantially" what he said he had dictated to Baxter. He must have been gifted with an extraordinary memory. Rawlins described the location of the road Grant allegedly ordered Wallace to take, but he failed to identify it specifically as the "River Road." In the context of making the cover-up as above reproach as possible, that failure is problematical. Rawlins, *OR*, 10:185.

16. Ibid., 10:188.

17. Ibid.

18. Rowley, *OR*, 10:179. Rowley stated that when he caught up to Wallace, the 3rd Division had already traveled five or six miles on the Shunpike. Rowley calculated Wallace had covered that distance in less than two hours, approximately twice the speed and with twice the sense of urgency Rawlins ascribed to the man.

19. Rawlins, *OR*, 10:188. Altogether, McPherson's report was quite unlike Rowley's and Rawlins' narratives. McPherson chose to emphasize what he deemed to be an even greater mistake made that day. Union forces had been effectively surprised. To McPherson, this mistake was all the more glaring and incredible because "it was well known the enemy was approaching our lines, and there had been more or less skirmishing for three days preceding the battle." McPherson, *OR*, 10:181. Unlike the other two reports, McPherson's narrative was free of internal contradictions and intentional distortions. Were it not for the fact that it, too, was written pursuant to Grant's request, it would not merit much consideration as part of the controversy or the cover-up.

20. Wallace to Grant, September 16, 1884, in Robert Underwood Johnson and Clarence Clough Buel, eds., *From Fort Sumter to Shiloh: Battles and Leaders of the Civil War* (New York: A. S. Barnes & Co., 1887), 1:610.

21. "General Rawlins' Address," November 14, 1866, *Report of the Proceedings of the Society of the Army of the Tennessee at the First Annual Meeting, November 14 and 15, 1866* (Cincinnati, 1877), 37–39.

22. Grant to Halleck, April 13, 1863, *OR* 10:178. Following his lament about not replacing Wallace with Morgan Smith, Grant personally adopted a posture of stony silence to all things Wallace and the march to Shiloh. His continued silence strongly suggests he willingly acquiesced in the controversy and thus the cover-up, thereby extending the lives of both. For Grant, it all boiled down to one consideration—from the very first, Wallace had been a lightning rod. With Wallace, there had always been a multiplicity of problems and issues to resolve, the majority of which had little to do with fighting a battle. Grant viewed the storm brewing over the events of April 6 as yet another such Wallace-inspired crisis. By this time, he had grown quite tired of his altogether too independent-minded, too argumentative, too self-centered, too self-righteous, and too loquacious subordinate. He must be freed, or so he believed, from the burden of this Shiloh problem as well as the man who had created it for him. More likely than not, he was blissfully unaware that he had just endorsed the Rawlins-inspired cover-Up. For Grant, it was the only thing to do.

23. Grenville M. Dodge, "Personal Recollections of General Grant, and his Campaigns in the West," *Personal Recollections of the War of Rebellion. Addresses Delivered Before the Commandery of the State of New York, Military Order of the Loyal Legion of the United States* (New York, 1907), 3:372.

24. Lew Wallace, "Dedication," in John Thomas Smith, *A History of the Thirty-first Regiment of Indiana Volunteer Infantry in the War of the Rebellion* (Cincinnati, Ohio: Western Methodist Book Concern, 1900), 197.

17. "Except in Sympathy and to Defend"

1. Grant to Wallace, March 10, 1868, in Henry B. Carrington, "Major General Lew Wallace at Shiloh," *Bay State Monthly* 2, no. 6 (March 1885): 340.

2. Adam Badeau, *Military History of Ulysses S. Grant. From April, 1861, to April, 1865* (New York: D. Appleton and Company, 1868), 1:81. Wallace observed that if

this statement were true and if in fact he and his men had marched "but five miles in seven [six] hours," then Grant would be more than justified in criticizing the slowness of the march. "I must confess," Wallace wrote, "that your moderation was greater than mine would likely have been, had our positions been reversed." Wallace to Grant, February 29, 1868, cited in Carrington, "Major General Lew Wallace at Shiloh," 334. Thus, Badeau introduced a new element into the controversy in 1868; specifically, how far Wallace had actually marched on April 6. Ross, in 1868, would contend that the march had been not less than sixteen or seventeen miles. Ross to Wallace, January 25, 1868, in Carrington, "Major General Lew Wallace at Shiloh," 338. Whittlesey, in 1875, thought it was at least twelve miles. Charles Whittlesey, "General Wallace's Division—Battle of Shiloh—Was it Tardy?" *Wallace Collection* (Indianapolis: Indiana Historical Society).

3. Wallace to Grant, February 29, 1868, cited in Carrington, "Major General Lew Wallace at Shiloh," 335–36.

4. Badeau, *Grant*, 1:89.

5. Badeau, *Grant*, 1:77, 78, 80. Badeau was not a historian but a political campaign biographer. His bias was obvious. Badeau did not join Grant's staff until mid-1864, two years after Shiloh and a year after round one of the controversy had died an ignominious death. Perhaps, as Cadwallader suggested, Badeau got his information and developed his version of the facts by listening to those rehearsals of the events of the controversy that took place around Grant's campfire. His book is important, however, for it compelled Wallace to write to Grant once more, thereby initiating round two of the controversy.

6. Lew Wallace to W. H. L. Wallace, April 5, 1862, in Isabel Wallace, *Life and Letters of General W. H. L. Wallace* (Chicago, 1909. Republished Carbondale: Southern Illinois University Press, 2000), following p. 114; quoted verbatim in George F. McGinnis, "Shiloh," in *War Papers Read Before the Indiana Commandery. Military Order of the Loyal Legion of the United States, (MOLLUS)* (Indianapolis, 1898), 38.

7. Ulysses S. Grant, *Personal Memoirs of Ulysses S. Grant* (New York: Charles L. Webster & Company, 1885), 1:352. It was a rather equivocal compliment. To Wallace, however, it must have sounded far better than all those years of silence. Speaking to the Indiana Commandery in 1898, McGinnis told his colleagues that these words, written and dated by Grant on June 21, 1885, might very well have been among the last ever written by the general. He died on July 23, 1885. When the various articles which had first been published in "The Century Magazine" appeared in hardback form in the *Battles and Leaders of the Civil War* series, the note that Grant had appended to his *Personal Memoirs* was also published in volume 1 as part of his article on Shiloh. All Wallace had asked for in 1863 and then again in 1868 was a note from Grant.

8. Ralph B. Buckland, "Description of the Battle of Shiloh," *Report of the Proceedings of the Society of the Army of the Tennessee at the Fourteenth Annual Meeting, April 6 and 7, 1881* (Cincinnati, Ohio: F. W. Freeman Press, 1885), 87–88; Wallace to Smith, undated letter, in John Thomas Smith, *A History of the Thirty-first Regiment of Indiana Volunteer Infantry in the War of the Rebellion* (Cincinnati, Ohio: Western Methodist Book Concern, 1900), 98.

9. Historian Edward Cunningham pointed to the irony of Rowley stopping Wallace where he did on the Shunpike and, in a move that undoubtedly would have

gained Grant's approval, "suggesting" that Wallace reverse his course. Cunningham writes that had this not occurred, Wallace would have struck the Rebels on their exposed left flank. Thus, the act of reversing Wallace's line of march did a "major disservice" to the Union that day. Cunningham further argued that had Wallace continued on, then the least that would have occurred would have been that Confederate leader Albert Sydney Johnston would have been compelled to divert Breckinridge's command back toward Shiloh Church to confront Wallace's 3rd Division, thus weakening the Rebel advance against the Union right. Cunningham concluded that had Wallace continued on down the Shunpike, the Confederate army might have been "routed." O. Edward Cunningham, *Shiloh and the Western Campaign of 1862*, ed. Gary D. Joiner and Timothy B. Smith (New York: Savas Beatie, 2007), 338–39. One interesting thing about Buckland's 1881 presentation was his conclusion. He maintained he was neither attempting to assess fault nor to defend Halleck, Grant, or Sherman. He desired merely "to state facts within my own knowledge and observation, and such as I believe to be true . . . and leave the reader to determine in his own mind, from the facts, where the blame or credit should be awarded."

10. Isabel Wallace, *Life and Letters of General W. H. L. Wallace*, 192; Douglas Putnam Jr, "Reminiscences of the Battle of Shiloh," in *Sketches of War History, 1861–1865. Papers Prepared for the Ohio Commandery of the Military Order of the Loyal Legions of the United States, (MOLLUS), 1888–1890* (Cincinnati, Ohio: Robert Clarke & Co., 1890),199; Warren Olney, "Shiloh as Seen by a Private Soldier," *Paper Read before the California Commandery of the Military Order of the Loyal Legion of the United States (MOLLUS), May 31, 1889* 6, no. 17 (1889): 19; William Hemstreet, "Little Things About Big Generals," in *Personal Recollections of the War of Rebellion. Addresses Delivered Before the Commandery of the State of New York, Military Order of the Loyal Legion of the United States* (New York: G. P. Putnam's Sons, 1907), 3:159. This was not a personal observation, since Hemstreet was a member of the 6th Division commanded by Prentiss and certainly could not have seen Wallace sitting anywhere that day. It illustrated the extent to which some were willing to go to fan the flames of the controversy.

11. On January 25, 1883, Maj. Gen. Alvin P. Hovey spoke to a veterans' group in Evansville, Indiana. Having command the 24th Indiana at Shiloh, Hovey declared there were many debatable questions about that battle but he wished to consider only two—(1) Was the Union army "surprised" that morning, and (2) Was Wallace's march to Shiloh "in any regard censurable or objectionable?" Persuasively critical of Sherman's lack of preparedness which made "surprise" both possible and all too real, Hovey then noted that he and Wallace had "never been what the world would call close or bosom friends. Our natures, as the Spanish would say, are not *simpatice;* but I know and respect him as a true, brave soldier and a patriot, and can only feel indignation at the attempt to make him the scapegoat for other men's mistakes and blunders and deem it but justice to tell the truth in vindication of history and the right." After a lengthy examination of the second question, Hovey's answer was both succinct and passionate. "To say that Wallace missed his road to Shiloh, or Pittsburg Landing, is more than absurd. It is cruel; criminal!" Alvin P. Hovey, "Pittsburg Landing," *National Tribune*, 2, no. 77 (February 1, 1883): 1.

12. "Speech by Lew Wallace," April 6, 1903, in John W. Coons, *Indiana at Shiloh: Report of the Commission* (Indiana Shiloh National Park Commission, 1904), 278.

Conclusion

1. Benjamin Marshall Mills to Caleb Mills, July 1, 1864, "Letters of Caleb Mills to his son, Lieutenant Benjamin Marshall, 1864–1865, and Letters from Lieutenant Benjamin Marshall Mills to his father, 1864–1865, from photocopies of originals in the possession of Helen Condit," Robert T. Ramsey, Jr., Archival Center, Lilly Library, Wabash College, Crawfordsville, Indiana. Mills was only nineteen years old at the time he wrote this letter. He had been on active duty for about seven weeks, having been mustered into service on April 14, 1864. He learned his lessons quickly. The author of this work is a direct descendant of Caleb Mills, the father of this young, wise, and apparently quite perceptive lieutenant.

2. Wallace Testimony, *Report of the Joint Committee on the Conduct of the War, 37th Congress, 3rd Session, 3 parts* (Washington, D.C., 1863), 3:343.

3. Not surprisingly, Wallace expected unquestioned obedience from his junior officers and his men. A long-time associate observed that Wallace always was a good comrade to his subordinate officers, but "as their superior officer, he was an inflexible disciplinarian." Mary Hanna Krout, "Personal Reminiscences of Lew Wallace," *Harper's Weekly* 49 (February 1905): 406. A correspondent for *Harper's Weekly*, commenting on this same theme, described an incident he found "amusing." Wallace strictly enforced existing army regulations forbidding looting and pillaging innocent citizens. Shortly after Shiloh, four of Wallace's soldiers returned to camp carrying half a domesticated, and altogether dead, ox. They obviously were guilty of pillaging. Wallace first ordered each of the perpetrators to carry the carcass on his shoulders for an hour, walking around a tree "with the performance to last a whole day under the boiling sun." On the second day, the four spent the entire day fanning the dead ox "so as to keep off the flies." On the third and final day of this unusual and extended tour of punishment, Wallace ordered the four to bury the rotting carcass with "appropriate ceremonies." *Harper's Weekly* 289, no. 6 (July 12, 1862): 439. Wallace, not at all amused by this incident, would never have admitted the possibility that the punishment far exceed the severity of the crime.

4. Lew Wallace, *An Autobiography* (New York: Harper & Brothers, 1906), 2:577–78.

5. Wallace's vanity was presumably stung by the fact that he was not accepted by the members of this club and could never hope to join in any circumstances. For example, he once complained to Lane that he daily confronted "a clique" of West Pointers "that has given me nothing but opposition and ridicule, simply because I was not a West Pointer." Subject to their intense scrutiny simply because he was not like them militarily, Wallace concluded he was aware "so far as I am personally concerned, that it is harder to maintain a reputation once gained than it is to gain it originally." Wallace to Lane, March 18, 1862, *Wallace Collection* (Indianapolis: Indiana Historical Society).

6. Knefler to Wallace, August 28, 1862, *Wallace Collection*. See Edward M. Coffman, "The Duality of the American Military Tradition: A Commentary," *Journal of Military History* 64 (Oct. 2000), 968–69.

7. Albert Richardson, the war correspondent who had known Grant since before Donelson, also wrote a campaign biography in 1868. He described Grant as "unimaginative—when he has nothing to say, he says nothing." Richardson also

found him to be "utterly undramatic—he acts his convictions instead of talking them." Albert Richardson, *A Personal History of Ulysses S. Grant* (Hartford, Conn.: American Publishing Company, 1868), vii–vii. It is little wonder that Grant soon grew tired of Wallace.

8. If the cover-up had been engineered in the twenty-first century of 24/7 news demand and coverage, the results would undoubtedly have been quite different. An examination and analysis of the arguments of the cover-up, focusing particularly upon what Rawlins wrote, would have resulted in the undoing of the "Grant men" and of Grant himself. It is doubtful, however, that it would have simultaneously made Wallace into any kind of national hero, acceptable over the long term to the military and political elite. Wallace was the kind of man who others already in power could easily tire of, and quickly.

9. Hemstreet's 1899 speech to the New York Commandery is a perfect example of this. With much descriptive fervor, Hemstreet stated he had personally seen Wallace during the march, sitting on a log, with a cigar in his mouth, wasting the day. The "sitting on a log" scenario came directly out of Rawlins's cover-up report. Rawlins, *OR*, 10:188. Rawlins himself voiced this thought in his1866 speech before the Society of the Army of the Tennessee. Hemstreet did not bother to explain how he observed Wallace in mid-afternoon while simultaneously being miles away on the battlefield with Prentiss's ill-fated 6th Division. In this instance, clearly the story victimized the truth.

10. Wallace to Gen. James Grant Wilson, November 6, 1896, *Wallace Collection* (copy; original in William P. Palmer Collection, Western Reserve Historical Society); Wallace, in James Grant Wilson, *General Grant* (New York: D. Appleton and Company, 1897), 141. Historian Gail Stephens wrote that in October, 2005, she and several historians from Shiloh National Military Park retraced Wallace's famous march. Armed with GPS indicators rather than heavy muskets and the like, the group found that the 3rd Division covered 16.75 miles. The distance and time of the march were substantially similar to what the 3rd Division experienced in 1862. Whereas Wallace's troops, laden down with the accoutrements carried into battle, required less than eight hours to make that march, the Stephens group spent seven and three-quarter hours covering essentially the same distance. Gail Stephens, *Shadow of Shiloh: Major General Lew Wallace in the Civil War* (Indianapolis: Indiana Historical Society Press, 2010), 91–92. Sixteen and three-quarters miles traveled in seven and three quarter hours computes to an average of 2.16 miles per hour. This was a significantly faster speed than attributed to Wallace by the Grant supporters, who, with Badeau's statement firmly in mind, had calculated the average speed of the Wallace march at 0.75 miles per hour. The fact that all the Grant men knew in 1868 that Wallace had marched many more than six miles made Badeau's conclusion all the more galling for Wallace. After all, Rowley had found him on the Shunpike and Rawlins had discovered him before he got to the River Road. Yet, neither said anything about the actual distance that Wallace marched that day.

11. Grant to Wallace, March 10, 1868, in Henry B. Carrington, "Major General Lew Wallace at Shiloh," *Bay State Monthly* 2, no. 6 (March 1885): 340.

12. Wallace to Rawlins, April 12, 1862, *OR*, 10:170; Wallace to Halleck, March 14, 1863, *OR*, 10:175–76.

13. Wallace to Grant, September 16, 1884, in "The March of Lew Wallace to Shiloh," in Robert Underwood Johnson and Clarence Clough Buel, eds., *From Fort Sumter to Shiloh: Battles and Leaders of the Civil War* (New York: A. S. Barnes & Co., 1887), 1:610.

14. Wallace to Wilson, November 6, 1896, *Wallace Collection.*

15. Ibid. Wallace finally went public with this series of comments in 1900. He sent a letter to William T. Smith intimating his understanding that whatever thoughts he expressed would find their way into a book Smith was then preparing on the Thirty-first Indiana Volunteers. Thus, he wrote to Smith, "I still think, if my march to the battlefield as I begun it, had not been countermanded, we would have done more than win a victory that first day, we would have captured a great part of the Confederate army. The surprise would have been to them, not our people." Wallace to Smith, undated letter, in John Thomas Smith, *A History of the Thirty-first Regiment of Indiana Volunteer Infantry in the War of the Rebellion* (Cincinnati, Ohio: Western Methodist Book Concern, 1900), 197.

16. In 1898, Wallace was seventy-one years old. Although he had not been on active duty for thirty-three years, he still held the rank of Major General of Volunteers. He had never surrendered his commission and it had never been taken from him. Several times that year, he applied for reinstatement to active duty so that he might fight for his country in the Spanish-American War. Each time he was refused. His foe, yet good friend from Donelson days, Simon Bolivar Buckner, likewise applied and was not accepted. Had Wallace been successful in that quest, it certainly would have been an adventure worth living.

SELECTED BIBLIOGRAPHY

Primary Sources

Andreas, Alfred T. "The 'Ifs and Buts' of Shiloh." In *Military Essays and Recollections. Papers Prepared for the Commandery of the State of Illinois. Military Order of the Loyal Legion of the United States,* 1. Chicago: A. C. McClurg and Company, 1891, 107–24.

Army Service School. *Donelson Campaign Sources Supplementing Volume 7 of the Official Records of the War of the Union and Confederate Armies in the War of the Rebellion.* Fort Leavenworth: Kan.: Army Service Schools Press, 1912.

Badeau, Adam. *Military History of Ulysses S. Grant. From April, 1861, to April, 1865.* 2 vols. New York: D. Appleton and Company, 1868.

Barber, Lucius W. *Army Memoirs of Lucius W. Barber, Company "D," 15th Illinois Volunteer Infantry, May 24, 1861, to September 30, 1865.* Chicago: The J. M. Jones Stationery and Printing Co., 1894.

Buckland, Ralph B. "Description of the Battle of Shiloh." In *Report of the Proceedings of the Society of the Army of the Tennessee at the Fourteenth Annual Meeting, April 6th and 7th, 1881.* Cincinnati, Ohio: F. W. Freeman Press, 1885.

Buell, Don Carlos. "Shiloh Reviewed." In *From Fort Sumter to Shiloh: Battles and Leaders of the Civil War,* vol. 1. Edited by Robert Underwood Johnson and Clarence Clough Buel. New York: A. S. Barnes & Co., 1887, 487–536.

Burt, R. W. "Fort Donelson: Experiences of the 76th Ohio in the Siege." *National Tribune* 24, no. 1308 (September 13, 1906): 6.

Cadwallader, Sylvanus. *Three Years with Grant.* Edited by Benjamin P. Thomas. New York, 1955 (reprt. Lincoln: University of Nebraska Press, 1966).

Carrington, Henry B. "Major General Lew Wallace at Shiloh." *Bay State Monthly* 2, no. 6 (March 1885): 330–40, 367.

Clausewitz, Carl von. *On War.* 3 vols. Trans. by J. J. Graham. London: Kegan Paul, Trench, Trübner & Co., 1908.

Cockrill, John A. "A Boy at Shiloh." In *Sketches of War History, 1861–1865. Papers Prepared for the Commandery of the State of Ohio. Military Order of the Loyal Legion of the United States,* 6. Cincinnati, Ohio: Montfort & Company, 1908, 1–35.

Coons, John W., comp. *Indiana at Shiloh: Report of the Commission.* Issued by Indiana Shiloh Park Commission, 1904.

Crummer, Wilbur Fiske. *With Grant at Fort Donelson, Shiloh and Vicksburg, and an Appreciation of General U. S. Grant.* Oak Park, Ill: E. C. Crummer & Co., 1915.

Cullum, George W. *Biographical Register of the Officers and Graduates of the U.S. Military Academy at West Point, N.Y., from its Establishment, March 16, 1802.* New York: D. Van Norstand, 2nd ed., 1868.

Dana, Charles A. *Recollections of the Civil War: With the Leaders at Washington and in the Field in the Sixties.* New York: D. Appleton and Company, 1892.

Dodge, Grenville M. "Personal Recollections of General Grant, and His Campaigns in the West." In *Personal Recollections of the War of Rebellion. Addresses Delivered Before the Commandery of the State of New York. Military Order of the Loyal Legion of the United States,* 3. New York: G. P. Putnam's Sons, 1907, 347–72.

Duke, John K., *History of the Fifty-third Regiment Ohio Volunteer Infantry During the War of the Rebellion, 1861–1865.* Portsmouth, Ohio: The Blade Printing Company, 1909.

Durham, Thomas Wise. *Three Years With Wallace's Zouaves: The Civil War Memoirs of Thomas Wise Durham.* Edited by Jeffrey L. Patrick. Macon, Ga.: Mercer University Press, 2003.

Eyewitnesses at the Battle of Fort Donelson. Edited by David R. Logsdon. Nashville, Tenn.: Kettle Mills Press, 1998.

Eyewitnesses at the Battle of Shiloh. Edited by David R. Logsdon. Nashville, Tenn.: Kettle Mills Press, 1994.

Fletcher, Calvin. *The Dairy of Calvin Fletcher, including Letters to and from Calvin Fletcher.* Edited by Gayle Thornbrough, Dorothy L. Riker, and Paula Corpuz, 9 vols. Indianapolis: Indiana Historical Society, 1972–1983.

Fletcher, Samuel H. *History of Company A, Second Illinois Cavalry.* Chicago: D. H. Fletcher, 1892.

Force, M. F. *Campaigns of the Civil War: From Fort Henry to Corinth.* New York: Charles Scribner's Sons, 1881.

Foster, Major John W. *War Stories for My Grandchildren.* Washington, D.C.: The Riverside Press Cambridge, 1918.

Fulfer, Richard J. *A History of the Trials and Hardships of the Twenty-fourth Indiana Volunteer Infantry.* Indianapolis: Indianapolis Printing Company, 1913.

Grant, Ulysses S. "The Battle of Shiloh." In *From Fort Sumter to Shiloh,* vol. 1, 465–86.

Hazen, W. B. *A Narrative of Military Service.* Boston: Ticknor and Company, 1885.

Hemstreet, William. "Little Things About Big Generals." In *Personal Recollections of the War of Rebellion. Addresses Delivered Before the Commandery of the State of New York. Military Order of the Loyal Legion of the United States,* 3rd series. New York: G. P. Putnam's Sons, 1907, 148–66.

Hickenlooper, Andrew. "The Battle of Shiloh." In *Sketches of War History, 1861–1865. Paper Prepared for the Commandery of the State of Ohio. Military Order of the Loyal Legion of the United States,* 5. Cincinnati, Ohio: The Robert Clarke Company, 1903, 402–38, 439–83.

Hillyer, William S. "Letter." *The Confederate Veteran Magazine, 1893.* Nashville, Tenn.: S. A. Cunningham, 1893.

Hovey, Alvin P. "Pittsburg Landing," *National Tribune* 2, no. 77 (February 1, 1883): 1.

Howison, Robert R. "History of the War." *The Southern Literary Messenger* 38, nos. 4–6 (April–June 1864): 193–205, 263–69, 321–33.

Jomini, Antoine Henri. *Summary of the Art of War.* Trans. by G. H. Mendell and W. P. Craighill. Philadelphia: J. P. Lippincott & Co., 1862.

Jones, D. Lloyd. "The Battle of Shiloh." In *War Papers Read Before the Commandery of the State of Wisconsin. Military Order of the Loyal Legion of the United States*, 4. Milwaukee, Wis.: Burdick & Allen, 1914, 51–60.

Julian, George W. *Selected Speeches of Honorable George W. Julian of Indiana.* Cincinnati, Ohio: Gazette Steam Book and Job Printing Establishment, 1867.

Kimbell, Charles B. *History of Battery "A": First Illinois Light Artillery.* Chicago: Cushing Printing Company, 1899.

Krout, Mary Hannah. "Personal Reminiscences of Lew Wallace." *Harper's Weekly* 49 (February 1905): 405–8.

"Letters of Caleb Mills to His Son, Lieutenant Benjamin Marshall Mills, 1864–1865, and Letters from Lieutenant Benjamin Marshall Mills to His Father, Caleb Mills, 1864–1865, from Photocopies of Originals in the Possession of Helen Condit." Robert T. Ramsey Jr., Archival Center, Lilly Library, Wabash College, Crawfordsville, Ind.

"Letters from Shiloh." Edited by Mildred Thorne. *Iowa Journal of History* 52, no. 3 (July 1954): 238–66.

Lincoln, Abraham. *The Collected Works of Abraham Lincoln.* Edited by Roy P. Basler. 9 vols. New Brunswick, N.J.: Rutgers University Press, 1953–1955.

McClure, A. K., *Abraham Lincoln and Men of War-Times: Some Personal Recollections of War and Politics during the Lincoln Administration.* 2nd ed. Philadelphia: Times Publishing Co., 1892.

——— *Lincoln's Yarns and Stories: A Complete Collection of the Funny and Witty Anecdotes that made Abraham Lincoln Famous as America's Greatest Story Teller.* Chicago: copyright by Henry Neil, 1901.

McCook, Alexander McDowell. "Six Weeks in the Mud." *Overland Monthly and Out West Magazine* 2, no. 3 (March 1869): 215–21.

McGavock, Randal W. *Pen and Sword: The Life and Journals of Randal W. McGavock.* Edited by Herschel Gower and Jack Allen. Jackson, Tenn.: Tennessee Historical Commission, 1960.

McGinnis, George F. "Shiloh." In *War Papers Read Before the Indiana Commandery. Military Order of the Loyal Legion of the United States*, 1. Indianapolis: Published by the Commandery, 1898, 1–41.

Mahan, Dennis Hart. *An Elementary Treatise on Advanced-Guard, Out-Post, and Detachment Service of Troops and the Manner of Posting and Handling Them in the Presence of an Enemy.* New York: Wiley and Putnam, 1847.

Marshall, Albert O. *Army Life: From a Soldier's Journal, 1861–1864.* Joliet, Ill.: Chicago Legal News Company, 1883.

Mason, George. "Shiloh." In *Military Essays and Recollections. Papers read before the Illinois Commandery of the Military Order of the Loyal Legion of the United States*, 1. Chicago: A. C. McClurg and Company, 1891, 93–104.

Morton, Charles. "A Boy at Shiloh." In *Personal Recollections of the War of Rebellion.*

Addresses Delivered before the Commandery of the State of New York. Military Order of the Loyal Legion of the United States, 3rd series. New York: G. P. Putnam's Sons, 1907, 452–69.

Morton, Governor Oliver P. *Telegraph Books, 1861–1865*. www.in.gov/ipcr/2566.htm.

Olney, Warren. "The Battle of Shiloh as Seen by a Private Soldier." *Paper Read before the California Commandery of the Military Order of the Loyal Legion of the United States*, 5. San Francisco: Published by the Commandery, 1889, 3–26.

Personal Memoirs of Ulysses S. Grant. 2 vols. New York: Charles L. Webster & Company, 1885.

Perry, Oran, comp. *Indiana in the Mexican War*. Indianapolis: W. B. Burford, 1908.

Putnam, Douglas, Jr. "Reminiscences of the Battle of Shiloh." In *Sketches of War History, 1861–1865. Papers Prepared for the Ohio Commandery of the Military Order of the Loyal Legions of the United States*, 3. Cincinnati, Ohio: Robert Clarke & Co., 1890, 197–211.

Rawlins, John A. "General Rawlins' Address." In *Report of the Proceedings of the Society of the Army of the Tennessee at the First Annual Meeting*. Cincinnati, Ohio: Published by the Society, F. W. Freeman, 1877, 24–59.

Reed, D. W. "Review of 'Villard's Memoirs' and John Codman Ropes 'Story of the Civil War'." In *Proceedings of the Society of the Army of the Tennessee at the Thirty-sixth Meeting, November 8–9, 1906*. Cincinnati, Ohio: Published by the Society, Chas. O. Ebel Printing Co., 1907, 203–27.

Reid, Whitelaw. "The Battle of Pittsburg Landing—Tennessee." *Cincinnati Gazette*, April 14, 1862. Reproduced in James G. Smart, ed. *A Radical View: The Dispatches of Whitelaw Reid, 1861–1865*. Memphis, Tenn.: Memphis State University Press, 1976, 129–30.

Report of the Joint Committee on the Conduct of the War. 37th Congress, 3rd Session, 3 parts, Washington, D.C.: Government Printing Office, 1863.

Rich, Joseph W. *The Battle of Shiloh*. Iowa City: Iowa State Historical Society, 1918.

Richardson, Albert. *A Personal History of Ulysses S. Grant*. Hartford, Conn.: American Publishing Company, 1868.

Sherman, William T. *Memoirs of General William T. Sherman*. 2 vols. 2nd ed. New York: D. Appleton and Company, 1889.

Smith, John Thomas. *A History of the Thirty-first Regiment of Indiana Volunteer Infantry in the War of the Rebellion*. Cincinnati, Ohio: Western Methodist Book Concern, 1900.

Stevenson, Thomas M. *History of the 78th Regiment of Ohio Infantry Volunteers from Its 'Muster-In' to Its 'Muster-Out'*. Zanesville, Ohio: Hugh Dunne, 1865.

Sumbardo, C. L. "Some Facts About the Battle of Shiloh." In *Glimpses of the Nation's Struggle. Papers read before the Minnesota Commandery of the Military Order of the Loyal Legion of the United States*, 3rd series. New York, St. Paul: D. D. Merrill Company, 1893, 26–41.

Taylor, Jesse. "The Defense of Fort Henry." In *From Fort Sumter to Shiloh*, vol. 1, 368–72.

Terrell, W. H. H. *Indiana in the War of the Rebellion: Report of the Adjutant General*. 8 vols. Indianapolis: Indiana Historical Bureau, 1869.

"The March of Lew Wallace's Division to Shiloh." In *From Fort Sumter to Shiloh*, vol. 1, 607–10.

The Official Records of the Union and Confederate Navies in the War of the Rebellion. 30 vols. Washington, D.C.: Government Printing Office, 1894–1922.

The Papers of Ulysses S. Grant. Edited by John Y. Simon. 24 vols. Carbondale: Southern Illinois University Press, 1967–2000.

The Rebellion Record: A Diary of American Events. Edited by Frank Moore. 12 vols. New York: Arno Press, 1861–1868.

The War of the Rebellion: A Compilation of the Official Records of the Union and Confederate Armies, 1861–1865. 128 vols. Washington, D.C.: Government Printing Office, 1880–1891.

Walke, Henry. "The Western Flotilla at Fort Donelson, Island Number Ten, Fort Pillow and Memphis." In *From Fort Sumter to Shiloh*, vol. 1, 430–52.

Wallace, Isabel. *Life and Letters of General W. H. L. Wallace.* Chicago, 1909. Republished Carbondale: Southern Illinois University Press, 2000.

Wallace, Lew. *An Autobiography.* 2 vols. New York: Harper & Brothers, 1906.

———. *Autobiographical Sketch. August 16, 1863. Wallace Collection.* Indianapolis: Indiana Historical Society.

———. "The Capture of Fort Donelson." In *From Fort Sumter to Shiloh*, vol. 1, 398–428.

———. "Letters." *Wallace Collection.* Indianapolis: Indiana Historical Society.

———. "Oration at the Dedication of the Indiana War Monuments at the Shiloh Battlefield, April 6, 1903." In *Indiana at Shiloh: Report of the Commission.* Comp. by John W. Coons. Indiana Shiloh National Park Commission, 1904.

———. "Testimony of General Lewis Wallace." In *Report of the Joint Committee on the Conduct of the War.* 3 vols. Washington, D.C.: Government Printing Office, 1863.

White, Patrick. In "Civil War Diary of Patrick H. White." By J. E. Booe. *Journal of the Illinois State Historical Society* 15, nos. 3–4 (October 1922–January 1923): 640–63.

Whittlesey, Charles. *War Memoranda: Cheat River to the Tennessee, 1861–1862.* Cleveland, Ohio: W.W. Williams, 1884.

Wilson, James Grant. *General Grant.* New York: D. Appleton and Company, 1897.

Wilson, James Harrison. *The Life of John A. Rawlins: Lawyer, Assistant Adjutant General, Chief of Staff, Major General of Volunteers, and Secretary of War.* New York: The Neale Publishing Company, 1916.

NEWSPAPERS

The Atlantic Monthly
Boston Journal
Chicago Tribune
Cincinnati Gazette
Daily Wabash (Terre Haute, Indiana) *Express*
Evansville (Indiana) *Journal*
Evansville (Indiana) *Weekly Gazette*

Frank Leslie's Illustrated Newspaper
Harper's Weekly
The Goshen (Indiana) *Times*
Huntington Indiana Herald
Indianapolis *Daily Journal*
The Liberator
Memphis Daily Appeal
Milwaukee Daily News
Missouri Democrat (St. Louis)
New-York Daily Tribune
New York Herald
New York Times
The National Tribune
Philadelphia Inquirer
The Richmond (Virginia) *Dispatch*
St. Louis Democrat
Salem (Indiana) *Union Advocate*
The Stars and Stripes and Old Union Post (Vincennes, Indiana)
The Vincennes (Indiana) *Gazette*
The Waukesha (Wisconsin) *Freeman*
The Weekly Vincennes (Indiana) *Western Sun*
Wisconsin Patriot

Secondary Sources

Allen, Stacy D. "Lewis Wallace: If He Had Less Rank." In *Grant's Lieutenants: From Cairo to Vicksburg.* Edited by Steven E. Woodworth. Lawrence: University of Kansas Press, 2001, 63–89.

Ambrose, Stephen E. *Halleck: Lincoln's Chief of Staff.* Baton Rouge: Louisiana State University Press, 1962.

——— The Union Command System and the Donelson Campaign." *Military Affairs* 24, no. 2 (Summer 1960): 78–86.

Anders, Curt. *Henry Halleck's War: A Fresh Look at Lincoln's Controversial General-in-Chief.* Carmel: Guild Press of Indiana, 1999.

Aspey, Robert B. *Frederick The Great: The Magnificent Enigma.* New York: Ticknor & Fields, 1986.

Bearss, Edwin C. *The Fall of Fort Henry. West Tennessee Historical Society Journal 17 (1963).* Repr. Dover, Tenn.:, Eastern National, Fort Donelson National Military Park, 1999.

———. *Troop Movement Maps, Fort Donelson, February 12–16, 1862.* 11 sheets. Dover, Tenn.: Department of the Interior, National Park Service: Fort Donelson National Military Park, 1959. Drawing No. NMP-DON, 3012.

Boyer, Margrette. "Morgan's Raid in Indiana." *Indiana Magazine of History* 8, no. 4 (December 1912): 149–65.

Burley, R. C. "Indiana in the Mexican War: The Indiana Volunteers." *Indiana Magazine of History* 15, no. 3 (September 1919): 260–92.

———. "Indiana In the Mexican War: The Buena Vista Campaign." *Indiana Magazine of History* 15, no. 4 (December 1919): 293–326.

———. "Indiana in the Mexican War: The Buena Vista Controversy." *Indiana Magazine of History* 16, no. 1 (March 1920): 46–48.

Catton, Bruce. *Grant Moves South.* New York: Little, Brown and Company, 1960.

Clary, David A. *Eagles and Empire: The United States, Mexico, and the Struggle for a Continent.* New York: Bantam Books, 2009.

Coffman, Edward M. "The Duality of the American Military Tradition." *The Journal of Military History* 64, no. 4 (October 2000): 967–80.

Conger, Arthur L. *The Rise of U .S. Grant.* New York: Century Company, 1931.

Connelly, Thomas Lawrence. *Army of the Heartland: The Army of the Tennessee, 1861–1862.* Baton Rouge: Louisiana State University Press, 1967.

Cooling, Benjamin Franklin. *Forts Henry and Donelson: The Key to the Confederate Heartland.* Knoxville: The University of Tennessee Press, 1987.

———. "The Reliable First Team: Grant and Charles Ferguson Smith." In *Grant's Lieutenants: From Cairo to Vicksburg.* Edited by Steven E. Woodworth. Lawrence: University of Kansas Press, 2001, 43–61.

———. *Jubal Early's Raid on Washington, 1864.* Baltimore, Md.: The Nautical & Aviation Publishing Company of America, 1989.

———. "The First Nebraska Infantry Regiment and the Battle of Fort Donelson." *Nebraska History* 45, no. 2 (June 1964): 131–45.

Cottman, George S. "The Whitewater Valley." *Indiana Magazine of History* 1 (December 1905): 204–8.

Cunningham, O. Edward. *Shiloh and the Western Campaign of 1862.* Edited by Gary D. Joiner and Timothy B. Smith. New York: Savas Beatie, 2007.

Daniel, Larry J. *Shiloh: The Battle That Changed the Civil War.* New York: Simon and Schuster, 1997.

Dupuy, R. Ernest, and Trevor N. DuPuy. *Military Heritage of America.* New York: McGraw-Hill, 1956.

Engle, Stephen D. *Struggle for the Heartland.* Lincoln: University of Nebraska Press, 2001.

Ferraro, William M. "A Struggle for Respect: Lew Wallace's Relationship with Ulysses S. Grant and William T. Sherman After Shiloh." *Indiana Magazine of History* 104, no. 2 (June 2008): 125–52.

Fiske, John. *The Mississippi Valley in the Civil War.* Boston and New York: Houghton, Mifflin and Company, 1900.

Foote, Shelby. *The Civil War: A Narrative.* 3 vols. New York: Vintage Books, 1958.

Forbes, John D. "Lew Wallace, Romantic." *Indiana Magazine of History* 44, no. 4 (December 1948): 385–92.

Gott, Kendall. *Where the South Lost the War: An Analysis of the Fort Henry-Fort Donelson Campaign.* Mechanicsburg, Pa.: Stackpole Books, 2003.

Grimsley, Mark. *The Hard Hand of War: Union Military Policy Toward Southern Civilians, 1861–1865.* Cambridge, Mass.: Cambridge University Press, 1995.

Gronert, Theodore G. "The First National Pastime in the Middle West." *Indiana Magazine of History* 29 (September 1933): 171–86.

Hanson, Victor Davis. "Lew Wallace and the Ghosts of the Shunpike." In *What Ifs? Of American History*. Edited by Robert Cowley. New York: G. P. Putnam's Sons, 2003.

Harsh, Joseph L. "Battlesword and Rapier: Clausewitz, Jomini, and the American Civil War." *Military Affairs* 38 (December 1974): 133–38.

Hattaway, Herman, and Archer Jones. *How the North Won: A Military History of the Civil War*. Urbana: University of Illinois Press, 1983.

Hess, Earl J. *The Civil War in the West: Victory and Defeat from the Appalachians to the Mississippi*. Chapel Hill: University of North Carolina Press, 2012.

Hinken, Victor. *Illinois in the Civil War*. 2nd ed. Urbana: University of Illinois Press, 1991.

Horn, Stanley F. *The Army of Tennessee: A Military History*. Indianapolis: Bobbs-Merrill Company, 1941.

Hughes, Nathaniel Cheairs, Jr., and Roy P. Stonesifer Jr. *The Life and Wars of Gideon J. Pillow*. Chapel Hill: The University of North Carolina Press, 1993.

Keegan, John. *The American Civil War: A Military History*. New York: Alfred J. Knopf, 2009.

Kiper, Richard L. *Major General John A. McClernand: Politician in Uniform*. Kent, Ohio: Kent State University Press, 1999.

Lawlis, Chelsea L. "Migration to the Whitewater Valley, 1820–1830." *Indiana Magazine of History* 43, no. 3 (September 1947): 225–39.

Leech, Margaret. *Reveille in Washington, 1860–1865*. New York: Time Incorporated, 1962.

Lewis, Lloyd. *Captain Sam Grant*. Boston: Little, Brown and Company, 1950.

———. *Sherman: Fighting Prophet*. New York: Harcourt, Brace and Company, 1932.

McDonough, James Lee. *Shiloh: In Hell before Night*. Knoxville: University of Tennessee Press, 1977.

McFeely, William S. *Grant: A Biography*. New York: W. W. Norton & Company, 1981.

McKee, Irving. *"Ben-Hur" Wallace: The Life of General Lew Wallace*. Berkeley: University of California Press, 1947.

———. "The Early Life of Lew Wallace." *Indiana Magazine of History* 37 (September 1941), 205–16.

McPherson, James M. *Battle Cry of Freedom: The Civil War Era*. New York: Oxford University Press, 1988.

Marshall-Cornwall, General Sir James H. *Grant as Military Commander*. New York: Van Nostrand Reinhold Company, repub. New York: Barnes & Noble Book, 1995, 1970.

Marszalek, John F. *Commander of all of Lincoln's Armies: A Life of General Henry W. Halleck*. Cambridge, Mass.: Harvard University Press, 2004.

———. "Sherman and Grant to the Fall of Vicksburg." *Grant's Lieutenants. From Cairo to Vicksburg*. Edited by Steven E. Woodworth. Lawrence: University of Kansas Press, 2001.

Morsberger, Robert E., and Katharine M. Morsberger. *Lew Wallace: Militant Romantic*. New York: McGraw-Hill, 1980.

Nevins, Allan. *Ordeal of the Union.* 2 vols. New York: Charles Scribner's Sons, 1947.

———. *The Emergence of Lincoln.* 2 vols. New York: Charles Scribner's Sons, 1950.

———. *The War for the Union.* 2 vols. New York: Charles Scribner's Sons, 1959–1960.

Parsons, Joseph A., Jr. "Indiana and the Call for Volunteers." *Indiana Magazine of History* 54, no. 1 (March 1958): 1–23.

Pierson, William Whatley, Jr. "The Committee on the Conduct of the Civil War." *The American Historical Review* 23, no. 3 (April 1918): 550–76.

Poulter, Keith, et al. "Who Were the Top Ten Generals?" *North & South* 6, no. 4 (May 2003)" 14–22.

Reardon, Carol. *With a Sword in One Hand and Jomini in the Other.* Chapel Hill: University of North Carolina Press, 2012.

Ridgley, Ronald H., "Henry Smith Lane: Republican Progenitor." In *Their Infinite Variety: Essays on Indiana Politicians.* Edited by Robert G. Barrows. Indianapolis: Indiana Historical Bureau, 1981, 49–75.

Riker, Dorothy, ed. *Messages and Papers relating to the Administration of David Wallace, Governor of Indiana, 1837–1840.* Indianapolis: Indiana Historical Bureau,1963.

Sandburg, Carl. *Abraham Lincoln: The War Years,* vol. 2. New York: Harcourt, Brace and Company, 1948.

Smith, Jean Edward. *Grant.* New York: Simon & Schuster, 2001.

Smith, Timothy B. "Why Lew Was Late." *Civil War Times* 46, no. 10 (January 2008): 30–37.

Stephens, Gail. *Shadow of Shiloh: Major General Lew Wallace in the Civil War.* Indianapolis: Indiana Historical Society Press, 2010.

———. "Lew Wallace's Fall From Grace." *North & South* 7, no. 3 (May 2004): 32–46.

Stephenson, Margaret. "Reminiscences of Logansport Civil War Veterans." *Indiana Magazine of History* 28, no. 4 (December 1932): 269–81.

Stickles, Arndt. *Simon Bolivar Buckner: Borderland Knight.* Chapel Hill: The University of North Carolina Press, 1940.

Stonesifer, Roy B., Jr. "The Forts Henry–Heiman and Fort Donelson Campaign: A Study of Confederate Command." Unpublished Ph. D. dissertation, The Pennsylvania State University, 1965.

Sword, Wiley. *Shiloh, Bloody April.* New York: Morrow, 1974.

Sylvester, Lorna Lutes, "Oliver P. Morton and Hoosier Politics During the Civil War." Unpublished Ph.D. dissertation, Indiana University, 1968.

Symonds, Craig L., et al. "Who Were the Worst Ten Generals?" *North & South* 7, no. 3 (May 2004): 12–26.

Tap, Bruce. *Over Lincoln's Shoulder: The Committee on the Conduct of the War.* Lawrence: University of Kansas Press, 1998.

Theissen, Lee Scott. "The Public Career of General Lew Wallace, 1845–1905." Unpublished Ph.D. dissertation, University of Arizona, 1973.

———. "Forgotten Politician: The Public Career of Lew Wallace." In *Their Infinite Variety,* 155–94.

Thornbrough, Emma Lou. *Indiana in the Civil War Era, 1850–1880.* Indianapolis: Indiana Historical Bureau & Indiana Historical Society, 1965.

Treichel, James A. "Lew Wallace at Fort Donelson." *Indiana Magazine of History* 49, no. 1 (March 1963): 3–18.

Tucker, Spencer. *Unconditional Surrender: The Capture of Forts Henry and Donelson.* Abilene, Tex.: McMurray University Press, 2001.

Wallace, Harold Lew. "Lew Wallace's March to Shiloh Revisited." *Indiana Magazine of History* 49, no. 1 (March 1963): 19–30.

Walsh, George. *"Whip the Rebellion": Ulysses S. Grant's Rise to Command.* New York: A Tom Doherty Associates Book, 2005.

Wernle, Robert F. *Henry Smith Lane: The Old War Horse.* Crawfordsville, Ind: Montgomery County Historical Society, 1983.

Williams, T. Harry. "The Attack Upon West Point During the Civil War." *Mississippi Valley Historical Review* 25, no. 4 (March 1939): 491–504.

———. *McClellan, Grant and Sherman.* Chicago: Ivan R. Dee, 1962.

Williams, Kenneth P. *Lincoln Finds a General: A Military Study of the Civil War.* 5 vols. New York: The Macmillan Company, 1949–1959.

Wills, Brian Steel. *George Henry Thomas: True As Steel.* Lawrence: University of Kansas Press, 2012.

Wilson, William E. "Thunderbolt of the Confederacy, or King of Horse Thieves." *Indiana Magazine of History* 54, no. 2 (June 1958), 119–30.

Woodworth, Steven E. *Manifest Destinies: American Expansion and the Road to the Civil War.* New York: Knopf, 2010.

———. *Nothing But Victory: The Army of the Tennessee 1861–1865.* New York: Knopf, 2005.

INDEX